The Complete Book of
BABY NAMES

foulsham
LONDON • NEW YORK • TORONTO • SYDNEY

foulsham

The Publishing House, Bennetts Close, Cippenham,
Berkshire, SL1 5AP, England

ISBN 978-0-572-02667-7

Printed in Great Britain by CPD Wales, Ebbw Vale

Choosing a name for your new baby is a big decision. Only a very small number of people ever change their given names — and those usually for very specific reasons most often associated with show business! — so you are choosing a name which your child will carry with him throughout his life, and which will come to define him as an individual. Daunting? Yes! Exciting? Certainly! And with this book you will have all the help you need to make the right choice.

Clearly organised in two main sections for girls and boys, this is the most comprehensive selection of names you will find—about 12,000, in fact—all fully cross-referenced so that even if you have only overheard a name you like as you were standing next to someone in the supermarket queue, you should be able to locate it in this selection! With that scope of choice, you will be sure to find the perfect name for your child.

To make your selection easier, go through the book and highlight your favourites, so that you can carry on thinking about your decision and reducing your short-list until you make that final and all-important choice.

Things to think about when choosing a name

Not many years ago, our choices of name tended to be fairly traditional, but now the scope is much broader and parents choose names from all kinds of sources, create spelling variations and combine names together to make something new. Be adventurous, by all means, but do remember that a child might not enjoy too weird a name while she is growing up—if it is likely to cause her to be constantly teased, it is not the best idea.

Look for a name which has positive associations and a meaning or history which matches what you want for your child in life. Think about the characteristics associated with the name, and any religious associations if appropriate.

Think first about your surname and remember that the two will be used together. Say them together to make sure they sound right. Ada Friend or Honey Combe could be misleading.

If the name you choose begins with the same letter as your surname, make sure the combination has the effect you want. Sometimes it works, sometimes it doesn't. George Graham works, but Holly Hobson sounds like a rag doll.

Make sure the first name and surname do not rhyme; the effect of a name like Mary Clary is best avoided.

If you have a long surname, it can be best

complemented with a simpler first name, or vice versa, to create a pleasing rhythm; Tom Wilkinson rather than Templeton Wilkinson.

Similarly, if you have a common surname, try to choose a more unusual first name so that your child does not encounter too many people with the same name. Jacinta Smith will have fewer problems on that score than Ann Smith.

Look at the initials of the chosen names together and remember that many people use their initials for their website addresses and at other times. Beatrice Ursula Mills would not be the best combination.

If you have more than one child, it can be confusing if they have the same initials, or if they have the same initials as you, especially if they are the same sex. If a personal letter arrives for Mr J. Smith and there are three men of that name in the house, it could be confusing. If you do choose a first name starting with the same letter, make sure the second names are different.

Similarly, contractions of the first name which make an inappropriate combination with your surname are best avoided. Christopher Mass might not be the best choice.

You do not have to give your child more than one name, but it can be a good idea to give them a second name in case they come across other people with the same name. This is particularly true if you have a common surname, or if you choose a popular first name.

Traditionally, you should register the full name, even if you plan to use the contraction, although this practice is not pursued to the same extent as it used to be.

It is almost inevitable that the name you choose will be shortened by friends. Make sure you like the familiar forms and contractions of the name, even if you intend to use the full name yourself.

Nicknames are often associated with the child's name, so spare a thought for any obvious nicknames and make sure you are happy with them.

The more popular the name you select, the greater the number of other children who will share the name.

The more unusual the name you select, the more potential there is for mispronunciation or misspelling. Think about this when making your choice.

Some names can be given both to girls and boys and you might prefer a name which is gender-specific.

It is generally a good idea to avoid names with bad connotations or names which are associated with stereotypes, such as Cain, Judas or Adolph.

Spellings of most names vary considerably. Choose a spelling you are happy with and one which is least likely to be confusing to others. If you select an unusual spelling of a more common name, you can expect it to be spelt wrongly most of the time.

Names from countries or cultures other than your own are increasingly common and offer some excellent choices. Make sure the pronunciation does not cause problems in your native language.

The old tradition of naming a child after its parents is now fairly uncommon as it can lead to a child having a name which sounds old-fashioned and out of date, as well as creating confusion between two people in the house.

Most people make selections for a boy and a girl. Unless you are 100 per cent sure, don't be caught out by having only names for one or the other.

Registering your child's birth

All babies born in England and Wales should be registered within 42 days of birth, 21 days in Scotland.

Babies should be registered at the local register office, the address of which is in the telephone book. Most hospitals are also visited by a registrar on a regular basis so that you can register the child's name at the hospital.

The child's parents must register the birth; a relative or friend cannot do this.

The baby does not need to be taken to the register office.

If the child's parents are married, either one can register the birth.

If the child's parents are not married, the mother must register the birth. The father should collect a form in advance from the register office so that his name can be included on the birth certificate. If the father's name is left blank, it can be filled in later, and the registrar will provide full information on how to do this.

The following information will be required:

the parents' names;

the child's place and date of birth (and time if the child is one of a multiple birth, or always in Scotland);

the child's sex;

the child's names;

the mother's full name, maiden name, place and date of birth, occupation, current address, date of marriage, if appropriate, and number of other children;

the father's full name, date and place of birth, and occupation.

You will be given a free short certificate and can purchase a full certificate if you wish. Charges are made for additional copies.

If you have not chosen a name by the time the limit for registration has expired, you must still register the baby, leaving the name blank. You have a year to fill in a name, although this might create an additional charge. You will need to take a baptism certificate or ask for a certificate of naming from the registrar.

Scottish registrars have the right to refuse to register a name they feel might be potentially offensive. In England and Wales, registrars can recommend that you reconsider, but have no power to refuse the names you choose.

You will find the address of your local register office in your telephone book, or contact:

The General Register Office, Smedley Hydro, Trafalgar Road, Birkdale, Southport PR8 2HH (0704 69824) for England and Wales;

or The Registrar General's Office for Scotland, New Register House, Edinburgh (031 334 0380) for Scotland.

Aasta *(Teutonic)* 'Love'

Abagael *see* Abigail

Abbe *see* Abigail

Abbey *see* Abigail

Abbie *see* Abigai

Abby *see* Abigail

Abeer *(Arabic)* 'Fragrance'

Aberah *see* Avera

Abia *(Arabic)* 'Great'

Abigael *see* Abigail

Abigail *(Hebrew)* 'A
father's joy'
Abagael, Abbe, Abbey,
Abbie, Abby, Abigael,
Gael, Gail, Gale, Gayla,
Gayle, Gayleen,
Gaylene

Abijah *(Hebrew)* 'God is
my father'
Abisha

Abisha *see* Abijah

Abnaki *(Native American)*
'Land of the morning'

Abra *(Hebrew)* 'Mother of
multitudes'

Abrona *(Latin)* 'Goddess of
beginning journeys'

Acacia *(Greek)* 'Innocent'.
The symbol of
immortality

Acantha *(Greek)* 'Thorny'

Accalia *(Latin)* Foster
mother of Romulus and
Remus, founders of
Rome

Achala *(Sanskrit)*
'Constant'

Acima *(Hebrew)* 'The
Lord's judgement'

Acola *(Teutonic)* 'Cool'

Actia *(Greek)* 'Ray of
sunlight'

Ada *(Teutonic)* 'Prosperous
and joyful'. A popular
name in Victorian
times.
Adda, Addia, Aida

Adabel *see* Adabelle

Adabela *see* Adabelle

Adabella *see* Adabelle

Adabelle *(Latin)* 'Joyous, happy and beautiful' Adabel, Adabela, Adabella

Adah *(Hebrew)* 'The crown's adornment'. One who gives lustre to the most eminent position

Adalia *(Teutonic)* An early Saxon tribal name, the origin of which is not known

Adaline *see* Adelaide

Adamina *(Latin)* 'From the red earth, mortal'. Also feminine of Adam Addie, Addy, Mina

Adar *(Hebrew)* 'Fire'. A name sometimes given to Jewish daughters born in the sixth month of the Jewish year, which is known by the same name

Adara *(Greek)* 'Beauty'

Adda *see* Ada

Addi *see* Adelaide

Addia *see* Ada

Addie *see* Adamina

Addula *(Teutonic)* 'Noble cheer'

Addy *see* Adamina

Adela *see* Adelaide

Adelaida *see* Adelaide

Adelaide *(Teutonic)* 'Noble and kind'. A gracious lady of noble birth. A name popular in 19th-century Britain as a compliment to the Queen Consort Adaline, Addi, Adela, Adelaida, Adele, Adelia, Adelina, Adelind, Adeline, Adelle, Dela, Della, Edelina, Edeline

Adele *see* Adelaide

Adelfia *see* Adelphia

Adelia *see* Adelaide

Adelicia (Teutonic) 'Noble happiness'

Adelina *see* Adelaide

Adelind *see* Adelaide

Adelinda *(French)* 'Noble and sweet'

Adeline *see* Adelaide

Adelle *see* Adelaide

Adelpha *see* Adelphia

Adelphia *(Greek)* 'Sisterly'. The eternal friend and sister to mankind Adelfia, Adelpha

Adena *(Greek)* 'Accepted'

Aderyn *(Welsh)* 'Bird'

Adiba (Arabic) 'Cultured'

Adicia *(Greek)* 'Unjust'

Adiel *(Hebrew)* 'Ornament of the Lord'

Adila *(Arabic)* 'Equal, like'

Adilah *(Arabic)* 'Honest'

Adima *(Teutonic)* 'Noble, famous'

Adina *(Hebrew)* 'Voluptuous'. One of mature charm *see also* Dena

Adione *(Latin)* Goddess of travellers

Adnette *(French from Old German)* 'Noble'

Adolfa *see* Adolpha

Adolfina *see* Adolpha

Adolpha *(Teutonic)* 'The noble she-wolf'. Feminine of Adolf. The noble matriarch who will sacrifice everything, including life, for her young Adolfa, Adolfina, Adolphina

Adolphina *see* Adolpha

Adoncia *(Spanish)* 'Sweet'

Adonia *(Greek)* 'Beautiful goddess of the resurrection'

Adora *(Latin)* 'Adored and beloved gift' Adorée

Adorabella *(Combination Adora/Bella)* 'Beautiful gift'

Adorée *see* Adora

Adorna *(Latin)* 'Adorned with jewels'

Adraima *(Arabic/Hebrew)* 'Fruitful'

Adria *see* Adrienne

Adriana *see* Adrienne

Adriane *see* Adrienne

Adrianna *see* Adrienne

Adrianne *see* Adrienne

Adrienne *(Latin)* 'Dark lady from the sea'. Feminine of Adrian. A dark, mysterious lady Adria, Adriana, Adriane, Adrianna, Adrianne, Hadria

Aelda *see* Aldora

Aeldra *see* Aldora

Aeldrida *see* Eldrida

Aelfreda *see* Elfreda

Aelwen *(Welsh)* 'Beautiful brow'

Aenea *(Hebrew)* 'Worthy of praise'

Aerona *(Welsh)* 'Like a berry'

Aeronwen *(Welsh)* 'Fair berry'

Affrica *see* Africa

Afra *(Teutonic)* 'Peaceful leader' *(Hebrew)* 'Dust' *see also* Aphra

Africa *(Celtic)* 'Pleasant'. 12th-century queen of the Isle of Man Affrica, Africah, Afrika, Afrikah

Africah *see* Africa

Afrika *see* Africa

Afrikah *see* Africa

Afton *(Old English)* 'One from Afton'

Agace *see* Agatha

Agalia *(Greek)* 'Brightness'

Agata *see* Agatha

Agatha *(Greek)* 'Of impeccable virtue' Agace, Agata, Agathe, Agathy, Aggie, Aggy, Agueda

Agathe *see* Agatha

Agathy *see* Agatha

Agave *(Greek)* 'Illustrious and noble'

Agee *(Hebrew)* 'One who runs away'

Aggie *see* Agatha

Aggy *see* Agatha

Aglaia *(Greek)* 'Splendour'

Agna *see* Agnes

Agnella *(Greek)* 'Pure'

Agnes *(Latin)* 'Lamb'. Gentle and pure Agna, Aigneis, Agneta, Agnola, Annis, Ina, Ines, Inessa, Inez, Nessa, Nessi, Nessie, Nesta, Neysa, Ynes, Ynez

Agneta *see Agnes*

Agnola *(Latin)* 'Angel' *see* Agnes

Agrippa *(Latin)* 'Born feet first' Agrippina

Agrippina *see* Agrippa

Agueda *see* Agatha

Ahuda *(Hebrew)* 'Praise' or 'sympathetic'

Aida *see* Ada

Aidan *(Gaelic)* 'Little fire'.
A girl with bright red
hair *see also* Edana

Aiden *see* Edana

Aigneis *see* Agnes

Aiko *(Japanese)* 'Little
love, beloved'

Aila *see* Aileen

Ailee *see* Aileen

Aileen *(Greek)* 'Light'. Also
an Irish form of Helen
Aila, Ailee, Ailey, Aili,
Aleen, Alene, Eileen,
Elene, Ileana, Ilene,
Iline, Illeana, Illene,
Illona, Ilona, Isleen

Ailey *see* Aileen

Aili *see* Aileen

Aillsa *see* Ailsa

Ailsa *(Old German)* 'Girl of
good cheer'
Aillsa, Ailssa, Ilsa

Ailssa *see* Ailsa

Aimee *see* Amy

Aindrea *see* Andrea

Ainslee *see* Ainsley

Ainsley *(Gaelic)* 'From
one's own meadow'
Ainslee, Ainslie

Ainslie *see* Ainsley

Aisha *(African)* 'Life'
Ashia

Aisha *(Arabic)* 'Living'

Aisleen *(Gaelic)* 'The
vision'
Helen

Aisling *(Old Irish)* 'Dream'
or 'vision'

Akasuki *(Japanese)* 'Bright
helper'

Akela *see* Akili

Akeyla *see* Akili

Akeylah *see* Akili

Akili *(Tanzanian)* 'Wisdom'
Akela, Akeyla, Akeylah

Alain *see* Alana

Alaine *see* Alana

Alame *(Spanish)* 'Stately
poplar tree'

Alameda *(Spanish)* 'Poplar
tree' or 'poplar grove'

Alana *(Celtic)* 'Bright, fair
one'. A term of
endearment used by
the Irish
Alain, Alaine, Alanah,
Alanna, Alayne, Alina,
Allene, Allyn, Lana,
Lanetta, Lanette

Alanah *see* Alana

Alanna *see* Alana

Alarica *see* Alarice

Alarice *(Teutonic)* 'Ruler of all'. Feminine of Alaric
Alarica, Alarise

Alarise *see* Alarice

Alayne *see* Alana

Alba *(Latin)* 'White'

Alberta *(Teutonic)* 'Noble and brilliant'. Feminine of Albert. A nobly born and highly intelligent girl. Popular name in Victorian times in compliment to the Prince Consort
Albertina, Albertine, Alverta, Auberta, Berta, Berte, Bertie, Elberta, Elbertine

Albertina *(Anglo-Saxon)* 'Illustrious' *see also* Alberta

Albertine *see* Alberta

Albina *(Latin)* 'White lady'. One whose hair and colouring is of the fairest
Albinia, Alvina, Aubina, Aubine

Albinia *see* Albina or Elvira

Alciana *see* Alcina

Alcina *(Greek)* 'Strong-minded one'. The legendary Grecian lady who could produce gold from stardust. One who knows her own mind
Alciana, Alcinette

Alcinette *see* Alcina

Alda *(Teutonic)* 'Wise and rich'
Eada, Elda

Aldara *(Greek)* 'Winged gift'

Aldis *(Old English)* 'From the old house'

Aldora *(Anglo-Saxon)* 'Of noble rank'
Aelda, Aeldra

Alecia *see* Alice

Aleda *see* Alida

Aleece *see* Alice

Aleen *see* Aileen or Alena

Aleena *see* Alena

Aleesha *see* Alisha

Aleeza *see* Aliza

Alegria *(Spanish)* 'Happiness' *see also* Allegra

Alejandra *see* Alexandra

Alena *(Russian)* Form of Helen
Aleen, Aleena, Alenah, Alene, Alenka, Allene, Alyna

Alenah *see* Alena

Alene *see* Aileen or Alena

Alenka *see* Alena

Aleria *(Latin)* 'Eagle-like'

Alesha *see* Alice or Alisha

Alessandra *see* Alexandra

Aleta *see* Alida

Aletha *see* Alice or Althea

Alethea *see* Alice, Althea or Okethea

Aletta *(Latin)* 'Little wing, bird-like'

Alex *see* Alexandra

Alexa *see* Alexandra

Alexandra *(Greek)* 'The helper of mankind'. Popular in the early 20th century in Britain as a compliment to Queen Alexandra
Alejandra, Alessandra, Alex, Alexa, Alexandrina, Alexia, Alexina, Alexine, Alexis, Alix, Lexie, Lexine, Sandy, Sandra, Sasha, Sashenka, Saskia, Zandra

Alexandrina *see* Alexandra

Alexia *see* Alexandra

Alexina *see* Alexandra

Alexine *see* Alexandra

Alexis *see* Alexandra

Alfie *see* Alfreda

Alfonsine *see* Alphonsine

Alfreda *(Teutonic)* 'Wise counsellor'. Feminine of Alfred. A name popular in Britain in Anglo-Saxon times, but one which died out after the Norman conquest
Aelfreda, Alfie, Allie, Elfreda, Elfreida, Elfrieda, Elfrida, Elfride, Elva, Elga, Freda

Alice *(Greek)* 'Truth'
Alecia, Aleece, Alesha, Aletha, Alethea, Alicea, Alicia, Alika, Alisa, Aliss, Alissa, Alithia, Alla, Allie, Allis, Ally, Allyce, Allys, Alyce, Alys, Alysia, Alyssa, Elisa, Elissa, Elke

Alicea *see* Alice

Alicia *see* Alice

Alida *(Latin)* 'Little winged
  one'. One who is as
  small and lithe as the
  woodlark
  Aleda, Aleta, Alita,
  Leda, Lissie, Lita

Alieza *see* Aliza

Aliezah *see* Aliza

Alika *see* Alice

Alima *(Arabic)* 'Learned in
  music and dancing'

Alina *see* Alana

Alinia *see* Elvira

Alisa *see* Alice

Alisha *(Sanskrit)*
  'Protected by god'

Alisha *(Greek)* 'Truthful'
  Aleesha, Alesha

Alison *(Greek)* 'Alyssum
  flower' *(Teutonic)*
  'Truthful warrior maid'
  Allie, Allison, Allyson
  see also Louise

Aliss *see* Alice

Alissa *see* Alice

Alita *see* Alida

Alithia *see* Alice

Alitza *see* Aliza

Alix *see* Alexandra

Aliya *(Hebrew)* 'Ascend'
  (Arabic) 'Sublime,
  exalted'
  Aliyah

Aliyah *see* Aliya

Aliza *(Hebrew)* 'Joyful'
  Aleeza, Alieza, Aliezah,
  Alitza, Alizah

Alizah *see* Aliza

Alla *see* Alice

Alleen *see* Helen

Allegra *(Latin)* 'Cheerful'.
  As blithe as a bird *see*
  also Alegria

Allene *see* Alena

Allie *see* Alfreda, Alice or
  Alison

Allis *see* Alice

Allison *see* Alison or
  Louise

Alloula *see* Alula

Allula *see* Alula

Ally *see* Alice

Allyce *see* Alice

Allyn *see* Alana

Allys *see* Alice

Allyson *see* Alison

Alma *(Latin)* 'Cherishing spirit'. Popular in Britain after the Battle of Alma in the Crimean War

Almeda *(Latin)* 'Ambitious' Almeta

Almeira *see* Almira

Almeria *see* Almira

Almeta *see* Almeda

Almira *(Arabic)* 'Truth without question' or 'princess' Almeira, Almeria, Elmira

Alodia *see* Alodie

Alodie *(Anglo-Saxon)* 'Wealthy, prosperous' Alodia

Aloha *(Hawaiian)* 'Greetings'. A romantic name from the Hawaiian islands

Aloisa *(Teutonic)* 'Feminine' Aloysia *see also* Louise

Alonza *see* Alphonsine

Aloula *see* Alula

Aloysia *see* Aloisa or Louise

Alpha *(Greek)* 'First one'. A suitable name for a first daughter

Alphonica *see* Alphonsine

Alphonsina *see* Alphonsine

Alphonsine *(Teutonic)* 'Noble and eager for battle' Alfonsine, Alonza, Alphonica, Alphonsina

Alta *(Latin)* 'Tall in spirit'

Althea *(Greek)* 'The healer' Aletha, Alethea, Althee, Altheta, Thea

Altheda *(Greek)* 'Flower-like'

Althee *see* Althea

Altheta *see* Althea

Aludra *(Greek)* 'Virgin'

Alula *(Arabic)* 'The first' *(Latin)* 'Winged one' Alloula, Allula, Aloula

Aluma *(Hebrew)* 'Girl'

Alura *(Anglo-Saxon)* 'Divine counsellor'

Alva *(Latin)* 'White lady'

Alverta *see* Alberta

Alvina *(Teutonic)* 'Beloved and noble friend'
Alvine, Alvinia, Vina
see also Albina

Alvine *see* Alvina or Alviona

Alvinia *see* Alvina

Alviona *(Teutonic)* 'Beloved and noble friend'
Alvine, Vina

Alvira *(Teutonic)* 'Elfin arrow'

Alvita *(Latin)* 'Vivacious'

Alyce *see* Alice

Alyna *see* Alena

Alys *see* Alice

Alysia *(Greek)* 'Unbroken chain' *see also* Alice

Alyssa *(Greek)* 'Sane one'. White flower *see also* Alice

Alzena *(Arabic)* 'Woman'. The embodiment of feminine charm and virtue

Am-ee *see* Amy

Ama *(African)* 'Born on Saturday'

Amabel *(Latin)* 'Sweet, lovable one'. A tender, loving, loyal daughter
Amabella, Amabelle

Amabella *see* Amabel

Amabelle *see* Amabel

Amadea *(Latin)* 'The beloved of God'

Amadora *see* Amadore

Amadore *(Italian)* 'Gift of love'
Amadora

Amala *(Sanskrit)* 'Pure one' *(Arabic)* 'Hope'
Amla

Amalee *see* Amelia

Amalia *see* Amelia

Amalie *see* Amelia

Amalinda *see* Amelinda

Amana *(Hebrew)* 'Faithful'

Amanda *(Latin)* 'Worthy of being loved'
Manda, Mandie, Mandy

Amanta *(Latin)* 'Loving one'

Amany *(Arabic)* 'Aspiration'

Amapola *(Arabic)* 'Flower'

Amara *(Greek)* 'Of eternal beauty'
Amargo

Amarantha *(Greek)* 'Unfading'

Amarette *see* Amorette

Amargo *see* Amara

Amarillis *see* Amaryllis

Amaris *(Latin)* 'Child of the moon'

Amaris *(Hebrew)* 'Promised by God'

Amaryllis *(Greek)* 'Fresh, new, sparkling'. The name of a flower
Amarillis, Marilla

Amata *(Latin)* 'Beloved'

Amber *(Sanskrit)* 'The sky' *(Arabic)* 'Jewel'
Amberly, Ambur

Amberly *see* Amber

Ambrin *(Arabic)* 'Fragrant'

Ambrosia *see* Ambrosine

Ambrosina *see* Ambrosine

Ambrosine *(Greek)* 'Divine, immortal one'. Feminine of Ambrose
Ambrosia, Ambrosina

Ambur *see* Amber

Amealia *see* Amelia

Ameerah *(Arabic)* 'Princess'

Amelea *see* Amelia

Amelia *(Teutonic)* 'Industrious and hard-working'
Amalee, Amalia, Amalie, Amealia, Amelea, Amelie, Ameline, Amelita, Emelda, Emelina, Emeline, Emily, Emmalee, Emmalynn, Mell, Mellie, Milicia, Mill, Millie

Amelie *see* Amelia

Amelinda *(Spanish)* 'Beloved and pretty'
Amalinda, Amelinde

Amelinde *see* Amelinda

Ameline *see* Amelia

Amelita *see* Amelia

Amena *(Celtic)* 'Honest'. One of incorruptible truth
Amina

Amethyst *(Greek)* Semi-precious stone which is said to be able to ward off intoxication

Ami *see* Amy

Amie *see* Amy

Amilia *(Latin)* 'Affable'

Amina *see* Amena or
Amine

Amine *(Arabic)* 'Faithful'
Amina

Aminta *(Greek)* 'Protector'.
The name of a
shepherdess in Greek
mythology
Amintha, Aminthe

Amintha *see* Aminta

Aminthe *see* Aminta

Amira *(Arabic)* 'Princess,
cultivated' *(Hebrew)*
'Speech'

Amity *(Old French)*
'Friendship'

Amla *(Sanskrit) see* Amala

Amma *(Hindi)* 'God-like'.
Another name for the
goddess Shakti

Amoret *see* Amorette

Amorette *(Latin)* 'Darling'
Amarette, Amoret,
Amorita, Morette

Amorita *see* Amorette

Amrit *(Sanskrit)*
'Ambrosia'

Amy *(French)* 'Beloved
friend'
Aimee, Am-ee, Ami, Amie

Amyntas *(Greek)* 'Helper'

Ana *see* Anastasia or Anne

Anabel *see* Annabelle

Anaïs *(French)* 'Faithful'
(Hebrew) 'Gracious'

Anal *(Sanskrit)* 'Fiery'
Anala

Anala *see* Anal

Anamari *(Basque)*
Derivation of Anna
Maria

Anastasia *(Greek)* 'She
who will rise again'
Ana, Anstice, Stacey,
Stacia, Stacie, Stacy

Anatholia *see* Anatola

Anatola *(Greek)* 'Woman of
the east', 'sunrise'.
Feminine of Anatole
Anatholia, Anatolia

Anatolia *see* Anatola

Ancelin *(Latin)* 'Fairest
handmaid'
Celine

Anchoret *(Welsh)* 'Much
loved'

Ancita *(Hebrew)* 'Grace'

Andeana *(Spanish)*
'Traveller on foot'

Andre *see* **Andrea**

Andrea *(Latin)* 'Womanly'. The epitome of feminine charm and beauty
Aindrea, Andre, Andreana, Andree, Andria, Andriana *see also* Edrea

Andreana *see* Andrea

Andree *see* Andrea

Andria *see* Andrea

Andriana *see* Andrea

Andromeda *(Greek)* 'Ruler of men'. The princess rescued by Perseus in Greek mythology

Aneira *(Welsh)* 'Honourable' or 'golden'

Anemone *(Greek)* 'Windflower'. The nymph of Greek mythology who, when pursued by the wind, turned into the anemone flower

Angel *see* Angela

Angela *(Greek)* 'Heavenly messenger'. The bringer of good news
Angel, Angelina, Angeline, Angelita, Angie

Angelica *(Latin)* 'Angelic one'. A name often used by medieval writers in Britain to typify the perfect woman
Angelique

Angelina *see* Angela

Angeline *see* Angela

Angelique *see* Angelica

Angelita *see* Angela

Angharad *(Welsh)* 'Free from shame'

Angie *see* Angela

Angwen *(Welsh)* 'Very beautiful'

Ani *(Hawaiian)* 'Beautiful'

Ania *see* Anya

Aniela *(Italian)* 'Angel'

Anika *(Czech)* 'Gracious'. A form of Anne
Anneka, Annika

Anila *(Sanskrit)* 'Wind'

Anita *see* Anne

Anitra *see* Anne

Ann *see* Anne

Anna *see* Anne

Annabel *see* Annabelle

Annabella *see* Annabelle

Annabelle *(Combination Anne/Belle)*
Anabel, Annabel, Annabella, Annie, Bella, Belle

Anne *(Hebrew)* 'Full of grace'. One of the most popular feminine names in the UK and the name of a British queen and several queens consort
Ana, Anita, Anitra, Ann, Anna, Annette, Annie, Nan, Nana, Nancy, Nanetta, Nanette, Nanice, Nanine, Nanna, Nanon, Nina, Ninette, Ninon, Nita

Anneka *see* Anika

Annetta *see* Annette

Annette *(French)* 'Grace'. A familiar form of Anne
Annetta

Annia *see* Anya

Annie *see* Anne or Annabelle

Annika *see* Anika

Annis *see* Agnes or Anaïs

Annissa *(Arabic)* 'Charming, gracious'

Annona *(Latin)* 'Fruitful' or 'annual crops'. The Roman goddess of crops
Annora, Anona, Nona, Nonnie

Annora *see* Annona

Annunciata *(Latin)* 'Bearer of news'. A suitable name for a girl born in March, particularly 24th March, as it derives from the 'Annunciation' – the announcement of the Virgin's conception *see also* Nunciata

Anona *see* Annona

Anora *(English)* 'Light and graceful'

Anselma *(Norse)* 'Divinely protected'
Anselme, Selma, Zelma

Anselme *see* Anselma

Anstice *see* Anastasia

Anthea *(Greek)* 'Flower-like'. One of delicate, fragile beauty
Anthia, Bluma, Thea, Thia

Anthelia *(Greek)* 'Facing the sun'

Anthia *see* Anthea

Anthonia *see* Antonia

Antoinette *see* Antonia

Antoinietta *see* Antonia

Antoni *see* Antonia

Antonia *(Latin)* 'Beyond
   price, excellent'.
   Feminine of Anthony.
   A jewel beyond
   compare
   Anthonia, Antoinette,
   Antoinietta, Antoni,
   Antonina, Netta, Nettie,
   Netty, Toinette, Toni,
   Tonia

Antonina *see* Antonia

Anusha *(Hindi)* 'A star'

Anwyl *(Welsh)* 'Precious'

Anya *(Hebrew)* 'Grace',
   'mercy'
   Ania, Annia

Anysia *(Greek)* 'Whole'

Anzonetta *(Teutonic)*
   'Little holy one'

Aphra *(Hebrew)* 'Female
   deer'
   Afra

Apollene *see* Appoline

Appoline *(Greek)* 'Sun'
   Apollene

April *(Greek)* 'The
   beginning of spring'.
   The name of the first
   month of the Roman
   calendar and the fourth
   month of the Julian
   calendar

Aquilina *(Latin)* 'Little
   eagle'

Ara *(Greek)* 'Spirit of
   revenge'. The Greek
   gdddess of vengeance
   and destruction

Arabela *see* Arabella

Arabella *(Latin)* 'Beautiful
   altar'
   Arabela, Arabelle,
   Aralia, Arbel, Arbele,
   Arbelia, Arbelle, Bel,
   Bella, Belle

Arabelle *see* Arabella

Arabinda *(Sanskrit) see*
   Arvinda

Aradhana *(Sanskrit)*
   'Worship'

Aralia *see* Arabella

Aramanta *(Hebrew)*
   'Elegant lady'
   Aramenta

Aramenta *see* Aramanta

Araminta *(Greek)*
'Beautiful, sweet-
smelling flower'

Arbel *see* Arabella

Arbelia *see* Arabella

Arbelie *see* Arabella

Arbelle *see* Arabella

Arcadia *(Greek)* 'Perfect
place'

Arda *see* Ardelle

Ardana *(Sanskrit)* 'Restless
one'

Ardath *(Hebrew)* 'Field of
flowers'
Ardatha, Aridatha

Ardatha *see* Ardath

Ardeen *see* Arden

Ardelis *see* Ardelle

Ardella *see* Ardelle

Ardelle *(Latin)*
'Enthusiasm, warmth'
Arda, Arden, Ardelis,
Ardella, Ardere

Arden *(Old English)* 'Eagle
valley'
Ardeen, Ardene

Ardene *see* Arden

Ardere *see* Ardelle

Ardine *(Greek)* 'One who
quenches the thirst'

Ardis *(Latin)* 'One who
gratifies'

Ardra *(Latin)* 'Ardent'

Ardun *(Welsh)* 'Sublime'

Areta *(Greek)* 'Of excellent
virtue'
Arete, Aretha, Aretta,
Arette, Retha

Arete *see* Areta

Aretha *see* Areta

Arethusa *(Greek)*
'Virtuous'. A nymph
who was turned into a
fountain to escape her
pursuers

Aretta *see* Areta

Arette *see* Areta

Arezou *(Persian)* 'Wishful'

Argenta *(Latin)* 'Silvery
one'. Argente, Argentia

Argente *see* Argenta

Argentia *see* Argenta

Aria *(Latin)* 'Beautiful
melody'

Ariadna *see* Ariadne

Ariadne *(Greek)* 'Holy one'. The mythological maiden who told Theseus how he could escape from the labyrinth after he had killed the minotaur
Ariadna, Ariane

Ariane *see* Ariadne

Arianwen *(Welsh)* 'Silvery one'

Aric *(Scandinavian) see* Erica

Aridatha *see* Ardath

Ariel *see* Ariella

Ariella *(Hebrew)* 'God's lioness'
Ariel, Arielle

Arielle *see* Ariella

Arilda *(German)* 'Hearth, home'

Ariminta *(Hebrew)* 'Lofty'

Arista *(Greek)* 'The best'

Arlana *see* Arlene

Arleas *see* Arlene

Arleen *see* Arlene

Arlen *see* Arlene

Arlena *see* Arlene

Arlene *(Celtic)* 'A pledge'
Arlana, Arleas, Arleen, Arlen, Arlena, Arletta, Arlette, Arlina, Arline, Arlyne, Herleva

Arletta *see* Arlene

Arlette *see* Arlene

Arlina *see* Arlene

Arline *see* Arlene

Arlyne *see* Arlene

Armelle *(French from Celtic)* 'Princess'

Armida *(Latin)* 'Small warrior'

Armilla *(Latin)* 'Bracelet'
Armillette

Armillette *see* Armilla

Armina *(Teutonic)* 'Warrior maid'
Armine, Arminia, Erminia, Erminie

Armine *see* Armina

Arminia *see* Armina

Armorel *(Irish)* 'Sea-dweller'

Arnalda *(Teutonic)* 'Eagle-like ruler'. Feminine of Arnold

Arnhilda *(Teutonic)* 'Maiden ready for battle'

Arnoldine *(Teutonic)* 'The eagle's mate'

Arpita *(Sanskrit)* 'Dedicated'

Arselma *(Norse)* 'Divine protective helmet'

Artemia *(Greek)* The goddess of the moon

Artemisia *(Greek/Spanish)* 'Perfect'

Artis *(Gaelic)* 'Noble' or 'lofty hill'

Aruna *(Sanskrit)* 'Sunrise' or 'reddish-brown'
Aruni, Arunima

Aruni *see* Aruna

Arunima *see* Aruna

Arva *(Latin)* 'Pastureland, seashore'

Arvinda *(Sanskrit)* 'Lotus blossom'
Arabinda

Aseema *see* Ashima

Asha *(Sanskrit)* 'Hope, desire'

Ashanti *(Swahili)* From the West African tribe

Ashia *see* Aisha

Ashima *(Sanskrit)* 'Without limit'
Aseema

Ashira *(Hebrew)* 'Wealthy'

Ashley *(Old English)* 'From the ash tree meadow'

Ashlyn *(English)* 'Pool by the ash tree'

Ashna *(Sanskrit)* 'Friend'

Asia *(Greek)* 'Resurrection'

Asisa *(Hebrew)* 'Ripe'

Asma *(Arabic)* 'More eminent' or 'more prestigious'

Aspasia *(Greek)* 'Welcome' or 'radiant'

Aspen *(English)* 'Aspen tree'

Asphodel *(Greek)* 'The wild lily of Greece'

Assumpta *see* Assunta

Assunta *(Italian)* From the Assumption of Mary
Assumpta

Asta *(Greek)* 'Star-like'
Astera, Astra, Astrea

Astera *see* Asta

Astra *see* Asta

Astrea *see* Asta

Astred *see* Astrid

Astrid *(Norse)* 'Divine strength'
Astred

Atalanta *(Greek)* 'Might bearer'. The legendary Greek huntress
Atalante, Atlanta

Atalante *see* Atalanta

Atalia *see* Athalia

Atalya *(Spanish)* 'Guardian'. One who protects hearth and home

Atara *(Hebrew)* 'Crown'

Athalea *see* Athalia

Athalia *(Hebrew)* 'God is exalted'
Atalia, Athalea, Athalie, Athie, Attie

Athalie *see* Athalia

Athena *(Greek)* The Greek goddess
Athene, Athenee

Athene *see* Athena

Athenee *see* Athena

Athie *see* Athalia

Atiya *(Arabic)* 'Gift'

Atlanta *see* Atalanta

Attie *see* Athalia

Aubary *see* Aubrey

Auberi *see* Aubrey

Auberta *see* Alberta

Aubery *see* Aubrey

Aubina *see* Albina

Aubine *see* Albina

Aubre *see* Aubrey

Aubrea *see* Aubrey

Aubreah *see* Aubrey

Aubree *see* Aubrey

Aubrei *see* Aubrey

Aubreigh *see* Aubrey

Aubrette *see* Aubrey

Aubrey *(French)* 'Blonde ruler' *(Teutonic)* 'Noble'
Aubary, Auberi, Aubery, Aubre, Aubrea, Aubreah, Aubree, Aubrei, Aubreigh, Aubrette

Audie *see* Audrey

Audrey *(Anglo-Saxon)* 'Strong and noble'. Derives from the Anglo-Saxon name Aethelthryth
Audie, Audrie, Audry, Dee

Audrie *see* Audrey

Audry *see* Audrey

Augusta *(Latin)* 'Sacred
and majestic'. Popular
name in royal and
noble families in the
18th and early 19th
century
Auguste, Augustina,
Augustine, Austine,
Gussie, Gusta

Auguste *see* Augusta

Augustina *see* Augusta

Augustine *see* Augusta

Aura *(Latin)* 'Gentle
breeze'. A name said to
endow its owner with
gentility
Aure, Auria, Ora *see
also* Aurelia

Aure *see* Aura

Aurea *see* Aurelia

Aurel *see* Aurelia

Aurelia *(Latin)* 'Golden'.
The girl of the dawn
Aurea, Aurel, Aurelie,
Aurie, Auristela,
Aurora, Aurore, Ora,
Oralia, Oralie, Oriel,
Oriole *see also* Aura

Aurelie *see* Aurelia

Auria *see* Aura

Aurie *see* Aurelia

Auristela *see* Aurelia

Aurora *see* Aurelia

Aurore *see* Aurora

Austine *see* Augustine

Autumn *(Latin)* Season

Ava *see* Avis

Avel *(Hebrew)* 'Breath'

Aveline *(Hebrew)*
'Pleasant' *see also* Hazel

Avena *(Latin)* 'Oatfield'. A
girl with rich, golden
hair
Avene

Avene *see* Avena

Avenida *(Chilean)* 'An
avenue'

Avera *(Hebrew)*
'Transgressor'
Aberah

Averi *see* Avery

Averil *(Old English)* 'Slayer
of the Boar'
Averyl, Avril, Avyril

Avery *(Old French)* 'To
confirm'
Averi

Averyl *see* Averil

Avi *see* Avis

Avice *(French)* 'War-like'
Avisa, Hadwisa *see also*
Avis

Avicia *(German)* 'Refuge in war'

Avis *(Latin)* 'A bird'
Ava, Avi, Avisa, Avissa
see also Avice

Avisa *see* Avice or Avis

Avishag *(Hebrew)* 'Father's delight'

Avissa *see* Avis

Avital *(Hebrew)* 'God protects'

Aviva *(Hebrew)* 'Springtime'
Avivah, Avrit

Avivah *see* Aviva

Avonwy *(Welsh)* 'Someone who lives by the river'

Avril *see* Averil

Avrit *see* Aviva

Avyril *see* Averil

Awel *(Welsh)* 'Gentle breeze'

Awena *(Welsh)* 'Poetry', 'prophecy'

Aya *(Hebrew)* 'Swift flyer'

Ayala *(Hebrew)* 'Deer'

Ayanna *(Hindi)* 'Innocent one'

Ayesha *(Persian)* 'Happy one'

Ayla *(Hebrew)* 'Oak tree'

Aylwen *(Welsh)* 'Fair brow'

Azalea *(Latin)* 'Dry earth'. From the flower of the same name
Azalee, Azalia, Azaliea

Azalee *see* Azalea

Azalia *see* Azalea

Azaliea *see* Azalea

Azaria *(Hebrew)* 'Blessed by God'
Azeria, Zaria

Azeria *see* Azaria

Azura *(French)* 'The blue sky'. One whose eyes are blue

Bab *(Arabic)* 'From the gateway' *see also* Barbara

Babb *see* Barbara

Babe *see* Barbara

Babette *see* Barbara

Babita *see* Barbara

Babs *see* Barbara

Badriyah *(Arabic)* 'Full moon'

Bailey *(French)* 'Steward'

Bala *(Sanskrit)* 'Girl'

Balbina *(Latin)* 'She who hesitates'
Balbine, Balbinia

Balbine *see* Balbina

Balbinia *see* Balbina

Bambi *(Latin)* 'The child'. Suitable name for anyone of tiny stature

Baptista *(Latin)* 'Baptised'. A name symbolic of man's freedom from sin through baptism
Baptiste, Batista, Battista

Baptiste *see* Baptista

Bara *see* Barra

Barb *see* Barbara

Barbara *(Latin)* 'Beautiful stranger'. The lovely but unknown visitor
Bab, Babb, Babe, Babette, Babs, Babita, Barb, Barbetta, Barbie, Barbra, Bas

Barbetta *see* Barbara

Barbie *see* Barbara

Barbra *see* Barbara

Barra *(Hebrew)* 'To choose'. Bara

Barrie *(Gaelic)* 'Markswoman'

Bas *see* Barbara

Basia *(Hebrew)* 'Daughter of God'

Basile 'Feminine of Basil'

Basilia *(Greek)* 'Queenly, regal'. Feminine of Basil

Basima *(Arabic)* 'Smiling'

Bathilda *(Teutonic)* 'Battle commander'. Traditionally one who fought for honour and truth
Bathilde, Batilda, Batilde

Bathilde *see* Bathilda

Bathsheba *(Hebrew)* 'Seventh daughter'. Bathsheba was the wife of King David in Biblical times
Batsheva

Batilda *see* Bathilda

Batilde *see* Bathilda

Batista *see* Baptista

Batsheva *see* Bathsheba

Battista *see* Baptista

Bea *see* Beata or Beatrice

Beata *(Latin)* 'Blessed, divine one'. Blessed and beloved of God
Bea

Beathag *see* Sophia

Beatrice *(Latin)* 'She who brings joy'
Bea, Beatrix, Bee, Beitris, Trix, Trixie, Trixy

Beatrix *see* Beatrice

Bebba *(Swiss from Hebrew)* 'God's oath'

Bebhinn *see* Bevin

Becca *see* Rebecca

Beckie *see* Rebecca

Becky *see* Rebecca

Beda *(Anglo-Saxon)* 'Warrior maiden'

Bedelia *(Celtic)* 'Mighty'
Delia

Bee *see* Beatrice

Beertilda *see* Berthilda

Behira *(Hebrew)* 'Brilliant'

Beitris *see* Beatrice

Beka *(Hebrew)* 'Half-sister'

Bekky *see* Rebecca

Bel *see* Arabella or Isabel

Bela *(Slavonic)* 'White'

Belda *(French)* 'Beautiful lady'

Belicia *(Spanish)* 'Dedicated to God'

Belinda *(Italian)* 'Wise and immortal beauty'
Bella, Belle, Linda, Lindie, Lindy *see also* Linda

Beline *(French/Old German)* 'Goddess'

Belisama *(Latin)* Roman divinity like Minerva, goddess of wisdom

Belita *(Spanish from Latin)* 'Beautiful'

Bell *see* Belle

Bella *see* Annabelle, Arabella, Belinda, Clarabella or Isabel

Bellanca *see* Blanche

Bellance *(Italian)* 'Blonde beauty'
Blanca

Belle *(French)* 'Beautiful woman'. Can also be used as diminutive of Belinda and Isabel
Bell, Bella, Bellina, Belva, Belvia *see also* Annabelle, Arabella, Belinda or Isabel

Bellina *see* Belle

Bellona *(Latin)* 'War goddess'

Belva *see* Belle

Belvia *see* Belle

Belvina *(Latin)* 'Fair girl'

Bema *(Greek)* 'Fair speech'

Bena *(Hebrew)* 'The wise one'. A woman whose charm is enhanced by wisdom

Benecia *see* Benedicta

Benedetta *see* Benedicta

Benedicta *(Latin)* 'Blessed one'. Feminine of Benedict
Benedetta, Benecia, Benedikta, Benita, Bennie, Benoite, Binnie, Dixie

Benedikta *see* Benedicta

Benigna *(Latin)* 'Gentle, kind and gracious'. A great lady

Benilda *(Latin)* 'Well-intentioned'

Benita *(Spanish)* 'Blessed'. Benitia *see also* Benedicta

Benitia *see* Benita

Bennie *see* Benedicta

Benoite *see* Benedicta

Berdine *(Teutonic)* 'Glorious one'

Berengaria *(Teutonic)* 'Spearer of bears'. A warrior huntress of renown

Berenice *see* Bernice

Beril *see* Beryl

Berit *(Teutonic)* 'Glorious'

Berlin *see* Berlynn

Berlyn *see* Berlynn

Berlynn *(English)*
Combination of Bertha
and Lynn
Berlin, Berlyn

Berna *see* Bernadette

Bernadette *(French)* 'Brave
as a bear'
Berna, Bernadene,
Bernadina, Bernadine,
Bernardina, Berneta,
Berney, Bernie, Bernita

Bernadina *see* Bernadette

Bernadine *see* Bernadette

Berneen *(Celtic)* 'Little
one, brave as a bear'

Bernessa *(Teutonic)* 'With
the heart of a bear'

Berneta *see* Bernadette

Berney *see* Bernadette

Bernia *(Latin)* 'Angel in
armour'
Bernie

Bernice *(Greek)* 'Herald of
victory'
Berenice, Berny,
Bunny, Burnice,
Veronica

Bernie *see* Bernadette or
Bernia

Bernita *see* Bernadette

Berny *see* Bernice

Berri *see* Beryl

Berrie *see* Beryl

Berry *see* Beryl or
Beverley

Berta *see* Alberta or Bertha

Berte *see* Alberta

Bertha *(Teutonic)* 'Bright
and shining'. The
Teutonic goddess of
fertility
Berta, Berthe, Bertie,
Bertina, Berty

Berthe *see* Bertha

Berthelda *(Teutonic)* 'Girl
who goes into battle'

Berthilda (Anglo-Saxon)
'Shining warrior maid'
Beertilda, Berthilde,
Bertilde

Berthilde *see* Berthilda

Bertie *see* Alberta, Bertha
or Roberta

Bertilde *see* Berthilda

Bertina *see* Bertha

Bertrada *see* Bertrade

Bertrade *(Anglo-Saxon)*
'Shining adviser'
Bertrada

Berty *see* Bertha

Berura *(Hebrew)* 'Pure'

Beryl *(Greek)* 'Precious jewel'. This stone, and therefore the name, is said to bring good luck
Beril, Berri, Berrie, Berry, Beryle

Beryle *see* Beryl

Bess *see* Elizabeth

Bessie *see* Elizabeth

Bessy *see* Elizabeth

Beth *see* Bethel or Elizabeth

Bethany *(Aramaic)* 'House of poverty'
Bethena, Bethina

Bethel *(Hebrew)* 'House of God'
Beth

Bethena *see* Bethany

Bethesda *see* Bethseda

Bethia *(Hebrew)* 'Daughter of God'

Bethina *see* Bethany

Bethinn *see* Bevin

Bethseda *(Hebrew)* 'House of Mercy'
Bethesda

Betina *see* Elizabeth

Betsy *see* Elizabeth

Betta *see* Elizabeth

Bette *see* Elizabeth

Betty *see* Elizabeth

Beula *see* Beulah

Beulah *(Hebrew)* 'The married one'. The traditional wife
Beula

Bev *see* Beverley

Beverley (Anglo-Saxon) 'Ambitious one'
Berry, Bev, Beverlie, Beverly

Beverlie *see* Beverley

Beverly *see* Beverley

Bevin *(Gaelic)* 'Melodious lady'. One whose voice is so beautiful that even the birds will cease singing to listen to her
Bebhinn, Bethinn

Bianca *(Italian)* 'White'

Bibi *(Arabic)* 'Lady'

Bibiana *(Spanish) see* Vivian

Biddie *see* Bridget

Biddy *see* Bridget

Bienvenida *(Spanish)* 'Welcome'

Bijou *(Old French)* 'Jewel'

Bik *(Chinese)* 'Jade'

Billie *(Teutonic)* 'Wise, resolute ruler'
Billy, Billye, Willa *see also* Wilhelmina

Billy *see* Billie or Wilhelmina

Billye *see* Billie

Bina *(African)* 'To dance'
Binah *see also* Sabina

Binah *see* Bina

Binga *(Teutonic)* 'From the hollow'

Binnie *see* Benedicta or Sabina

Birdie *(Mod. English)* 'Sweet little bird'

Birjis *(Arabic)* 'Planet Jupiter'

Birkita *see* Bridget

Blaine *(Gaelic)* 'Thin'
Blane, Blayne

Blair *(Gaelic)* 'Dweller on the plain'
Blaire

Blaire *see* Blair

Blaise *see* Blasia

Blake *(Old English)* 'Fair haired'
Blakelee, Blakeley

Blakelee *see* Blake

Blakeley *see* Blake

Blanca *see* Bellance or Blanche

Blanch *see* Blanche

Blanche *(French)* 'Fair and white'. A very popular name in medieval times when it was supposed to endow its user with all feminine virtues
Bellanca, Blanca, Blanch, Blanka, Blinne, Blinnie, Bluinse, Branca

Blanda *(Latin)* 'Seductive, flattering, caressing'
Blandina, Blandine

Blandina *see* Blanda

Blandine *see* Blanda

Blane *see* Blaine

Blanka *see* Blanche

Blasia *(Latin)* 'She who stammers'
Blaise

Blayne *see* Blaine

Blenda *(German)* 'Glorious, dazzling'

Blessin *(Old English)* 'Consecrated'
Blessing

Blessing *see* Blessin

Blinne *see* Blanche

Blinnie *see* Blanche

Bliss *(Old English)*
'Gladness, joy'
Blita, Blitha

Blita *see* Bliss

Blith *see* Blyth

Blitha *see* Bliss

Blithe *see* Blyth

Blodwen *see* Blodwyn

Blodwyn *(Welsh)* 'White
flower'
Blodwen

Blondelle *(French)* 'Little
fair one'
Blondie

Blondie *see* Blondelle

Blossom *(Old English)*
'Fragrant as a flower'

Bluinse *see* Blanche

Bluma *see* Anthea

Blyth *(Anglo-Saxon)* 'Joyful
and happy'
Blith, Blithe, Blythe

Blythe *see* Blyth

Bo *(Chinese)* 'Precious'

Bobbie *see* Roberta

Bobby *see* Roberta

Bobette *see* Roberta

Bobina *see* Roberta

Bodgana *(Polish)* 'God's
gift'

Bona *see* Bonita

Bonfilia *(Italian)* 'Good
daughter'

Bonita *(Latin)* 'Sweet and
good'
Bona, Bonne,
Bonnibelle, Bonnie,
Nita

Bonne *see* Bonita

Bonnibelle *see* Bonita

Bonnie *see* Bonita

Bradlee *see* Bradley

Bradleigh *see* Bradley

Bradley *(Old English)*
'From the broad
meadow'
Bradlee, Bradleigh

Branca *see* Blanche

Brandais *see* Brandy

Brandea *see* Brandy

Brandice *see* Brandy

Brandy *(Dutch)* 'Brandy'
Brandais, Brandea,
Brandice

Branwen *(Welsh)* 'Beautiful
raven'

Breana *see* Breanna

Breann *see* Breanna

Breanna *(Irish)* 'Strong and honourable'
Breana, Breann, Breanne, Breighann

Breena *(Irish)* 'Fairy palace'
Breina, Brena, Brina

Breighann *see* Breanna

Breina *see* Breena

Breita *see* Bridget

Bren *see* Brenda

Brena *see* Breena

Brenda *(Teutonic)* 'Fiery' or *(Irish)* 'raven'
Bren

Brenna *(Irish)* 'Raven-haired beauty'

Breona *see* Briana

Brett *see* Brittany

Bria *see* Briana

Briallen *(Welsh)* 'Primrose'

Briana *(Celtic)* 'Strength, virtue, honour'
Breona, Bria, Brianna, Brienne, Briona, Bryana *see also* Bryna

Brianna *see* Briana

Briar *(French)* 'Heather'
Bryar

Bridey *see* Bridget

Bridget *(Irish/Celtic)* 'Strong and mighty'
Biddie, Biddy, Birkita, Breita, Bridey, Bridie, Brie, Brieta, Brietta, Brigette, Brigid, Brigida, Brigitte, Brita, Brydie

Bridie *see* Bridget

Brie *see* Bridget

Brienne *see* Briana

Brier *(French)* 'Heather'

Brieta *see* Bridget

Brietta *see* Bridget

Brigette *see* Bridget

Brigid *see* Bridget

Brigida *see* Bridget

Brigitte *see* Bridget

Brina *see* Breena or Sabrina

Briona *see* Briana

Briony *see* Bryony

Brisa *see* Bryssa

Brissa *see* Bryssa

Brita *see* Bridget

Britannia *see* Brittany

Britney *see* Brittany

Britta *see* Brittany

Brittany *(Latin)* 'Britain'
Britannia, Britney, Britta

Brittney *see* Brittany

Brittny *see* Brittany

Bronhilde *see* Brunhilda

Bronwen *(Welsh/Celtic)* 'White bosomed' Bronwyn

Bronwyn *see* Bronwen

Bronya *(Russian)* 'Armour'

Brook *(Old English)* 'Living near the brook' Brooke

Brooke *see* Brook

Brooklyn *(American)* Place name

Brucie *(French)* 'From the thicket'. Feminine of Bruce

Bruella *see* Brunella

Bruelle *see* Brunella

Brunella *(Italian)* 'One with brown hair.' The true brunette Bruella, Bruelle, Brunelle

Brunelle *see* Brunella

Brunetta *(French)* 'Dark-haired maiden'

Brunhild *see* Brunhilda

Brunhilda *(Teutonic)* 'Warrior heroine' Bronhilde, Brunhild, Brunhilde

Brunhilde *see* Brunhilda

Bryana *see* Briana

Bryar *see* Briar

Brydie *see* Bridget

Bryna *(Irish)* 'Strength with virtue'. Feminine of Brian Brina *see also* Briana

Bryony *(Old English)* 'A twining vine' Briony

Bryssa *(Spanish)* 'Beloved' Brisa, Brissa

Buena *(Spanish)* 'The good one' Buona

Buffee *see* Buffy

Buffey *see* Buffy

Buffie *see* Buffy

Buffy *(American)* 'From the plains', 'buffalo' Buffee, Buffey, Buffie, Buffye Buffye

Bunny *(English)* 'Little rabbit' *see also* Bernice

Buona *see* Buena

Burgundy *(French)* French wine

Burnetta *(French)* 'Little brown one'

Burnice *see* Bernice

Cachée *see* Cachet

Cachet *(French)* 'Desirous'
Cachée

Cacy *see* Casey

Cadena *see* Cadence

Cadence *(Latin)*
'Rhythmic'. One who is
graceful and charming
Cadena, Cadenza

Cadenza *see* Cadencc

Cae *see* Cai

Caera *(Gaelic)* 'Spear,
ruddy'

Cai *(Vietnamese)* 'Feminine'
Cae, Cay, Caye

Cailey *see* Cayla

Cailin *see* Colleen

Caireen *see* Catherine

Cairistiona *see* Christine

Cairstine *see* Christine

Caitlin *(Gaelic)* 'Pure girl'.
Form of Catherine

Caitrin *see* Catherine

Cal *see* Calandra or
Calantha

Cala *(Arabic)* 'Castle'

Calandra *(Greek)* 'Lark'.
One who is as light and
gay as a lark
Cal, Calandre,
Calandria, Callie, Cally

Calandre *see* Calandra

Calandria *see* Calandra

Calantha *(Greek)* 'Beautiful
blossom'. A woman of
child-like beauty and
innocence
Cal, Calanthe, Callie,
Cally, Kalantha,
Kalanthe

Calanthe *see* Calantha

Caldora *(Greek)* 'Beautiful
present'

Caledonia *(Latin)* 'Scottish
lassie'. One who comes
from the part of Scotland
formerly known as
Caledonia
Caledonie

Caledonie *see* Caledonia

Calida *(Spanish)* 'Ardently loving'. A woman capable of great affection

Calista *(Greek)* 'Most beautiful of women'. A name for a girl thought to be beautiful beyond the ordinary
Callista, Calisto, Kallista, Kallisto

Calisto *see* Calista

Calla *(Greek)* 'Beautiful'
Calli

Callena *(Teutonic)* 'One who talks a lot'

Calli *see* Calla

Callidora *(Greek)* 'Gift of beauty'

Callie *see* Calandra or Calantha

Calligenia *(Greek)* 'Daughter of beauty'

Calliope *(Greek)* 'The music of poetry

Callista *see* Calista

Callula *(Latin)* 'Little beautiful one'

Cally *see* Calandra or Calantha

Calosa *(Greek)* 'Beautiful to look at'

Caltha *(Latin)* 'Yellow flower

Calvina *(Latin)* 'Bald'. Feminine of Calvin. A name sometimes used in strongly Calvinistic families

Calypso *(Greek)* 'Concealer'. The legendary sea nymph who held Odysseus captive
Kalypso

Cam *(Vietnamese)* 'Sweet citrus fruit'
Kam *see also* Camilla

Camala *see* Camilla

Camelia *see* Camilla

Camella *see* Camilla

Camellia *see* Camilla

Cameo *(Italian)* 'Sculptured jewel'

Cameran *see* Cameron

Cameren *see* Cameron

Cameron *(Scottish)* 'Crooked nose' Cameran, Cameren, Cam

Camesha *see* Cameron

Camile *see* Camilla

Camilla *(Latin)* 'Noble and righteous'. The name given to the young and beautiful handmaiden in pagan ceremonies Cam, Camala, Camelia, Camella, Camellia, Camile, Camille, Cammi

Camille *see* Camilla

Cammi *see* Camilla

Canace *(Latin)* 'The daughter of the wind' Kanaka, Kanake

Candace *(Latin)* 'Pure, glittering, brilliant white'. One whose purity and virtue is beyond suspicion Candice, Candida, Candie, Candy

Candice *see* Candace

Candida *see* Candace

Candie *see* Candace

Candra *(Latin)* 'Luminescent' *see also* Chandra

Candre *see* Chandra

Candy *see* Candace

Cantara *(Arabic)* 'Small bridge'

Capriccia *see* Caprice

Caprice *(Italian)* 'Fanciful' Capriccia

Capucine *(French)* 'Cape'

Cara *(Celtic)* 'Friend' *(Italian)* 'Dearest one'. A term of endearment Caralie, Cariad, Carina, Carine, Kara, Karine, Karina

Caragh *(Irish)* 'Love'

Caralie *see* Cara

Caressa *see* Carissa

Caresse *see* Carissa

Carey *see* Caroline

Cari *(Turkish)* 'Flows likc water'

Cariad *see* Cara

Carilla *see* Caroline

Carina *(Latin)* 'Keel' Karina *see also* Cara

Carine *see* Cara or Catherine

Carissa *(Latin)* 'Most dear one' Caressa, Caresse, Carisse

Carisse *see* Carissa

Carita *(Latin)* 'Beloved little one' Karita

Carla *see* Charlotte

Carlie *see* Charlotte

Carlin *see* Caroline

Carline *see* Caroline

Carliss *see* Corliss

Carlissa *see* Corliss

Carlotta *see* Charlotte

Carly *see* Caroline or Charlotte

Carma *(Sanskrit)* 'Destiny'. From the Buddhist 'Karma' meaning 'fate' *see also* Carmel or Carme

Carmacita *see* Carmen

Carmel *(Hebrew)* 'God's fruitful vineyard' Carma, Carmela, Carmelina, Carmeline, Carmelita, Carmella, Carmie, Melina

Carmela *see* Carmel

Carmelina *see* Carmel

Carmeline *see* Carmel

Carmelita *see* Carmel or Carmen

Carmella *see* Carmel

Carmen *(Latin)* 'Songstress'. One who has a beautiful voice Carma, Carmacita, Carmelita, Carmencita, Carmia, Carmina, Carmine, Carmita, Charmaine

Carmencita *see* Carmen

Carmia *see* Carmen

Carmie *see* Carmel

Carmina *see* Carmen

Carmine *see* Carmen

Carmita *see* Carmen

Carnation *(French)* 'Fresh colour'. One with perfect features and colouring

Caro *see* Caroline

Carol *see* Caroline

Carola *see* Caroline

Carole *see* Caroline

Carolina *see* Caroline

Caroline *(Teutonic)* 'Little woman, born to command'. The power behind the throne; the hand which rocks the cradle and rules the world. One who is all that is feminine but who rules and controls. Also used as the feminine of Charles Carey, Carilla, Carly, Carlin, Carline, Caro, Carol, Carola, Carole,

Carolina, Caryn,
Charleen, Charlene,
Charline, Lena, Lina,
Line, Sharleen,
Sharlene, Sharline *see
also* Charlotte

Caron *see* Cheron

Caronwen *(Welsh)* 'Little
fair love'

Carrie *see* Caroline

Carryl *see* Caryl

Caryl *(Welsh)* 'Beloved'
Carryl, Carys

Caryn *see* Catherine

Carys *see* Caryl

Casey *(Irish)* 'Brave'
Cacy, Casie

Casia *see* Cassia

Casie *see* Casey

Casilda *(Spanish)* 'The
solitary one'
Casilde

Casilde *see* Casilda

Casimira *(Latin)* 'Bringer
of peace'

Casmira *see* Kasmira

Cass *see* Cassandra

Cassandra *(Greek)*
Prophetess ignored by
men
Cass, Cassandre, Cassie,
Kassandra

Cassandre *see* Cassandra

Cassia *(Greek)* 'Spicy
cinnamon'

Cassidy *(Irish)* 'Clever'

Cassie *see* Cassandra

Cassiopeia *(Greek)* 'Scent
of flowers'

Casta *(Latin)* 'Of pure
upbringing'
Caste

Caste *see* Casta

Catalina *see* Catherine

Caterina *see* Catherine

Catharina *see* Catherine

Catharine *see* Catherine

Cathelle *see* Catherine

Catherine *(Greek)* 'Pure
maiden'. The saint who
was martyred on a
spiked wheel
Caireen, Caitlin,
Caitrin, Carine, Caryn,
Catalina, Caterina,
Catharina, Catharine,
Cathelle, Cathie,
Cathleen, Cathy,
Catriona, Kaitlyn, Kate,
Katerine, Kateryn,
Katie, Katharina,
Katharine, Katherina,
Katherine, Kathryn,
Kathy, Katrina, Katrine,
Katy, Kit, Kitty

Cathie see Catherine

Cathleen see Catherine

Cathlin (Celtic) 'One with beautiful eyes'

Cathy see Catherine

Catriona (Scottish) 'Pure maiden'. Scottish variation of Catherine

Cattima (Latin) 'Delicate reed'

Cay see Cai

Caye see Cai

Cayla (Hebrew) 'Crown of laurel leaves'
Kayla, Caily

Ceara (Irish) 'Spear'. A warrior who fought with a spear

Cecelia see Cecilia

Cecil see Cecilia

Cecile see Cecilia

Cecilia (Latin) The patron saint of music
Cecelia, Cecil, Cecile, Cecily, Cele, Celia, Cicely, Ciel, Cissie, Sileas, Sisile, Sisle, Sisley, Sissie

Cecily see Cecilia

Cedrella (Latin) 'Silver fir tree'

Cein (Celtic) 'Jewel'

Ceinlys (Welsh) 'Sweet gems'

Ceinwen (Welsh) 'Beautiful gems'

Ceiridwen (Welsh) The goddess of bardism
Ceri, Kerridwen

Celandine (Greek) 'Swallow' or 'yellow water flower'
Celandon

Celandon see Celandine

Cele see Cecilia or Celeste

Celene see Selena

Celesta see Celeste

Celeste (Latin) 'Heavenly'. A woman of divine beauty
Cele, Celesta, Celestina, Celestine, Celestyna, Celia, Celina, Celinda, Celinka

Celestina see Celeste

Celestine see Celeste

Celestyna see Celeste

Celia see Cecilia or Celeste

Celie see Selena

Celina see Celeste or Selena

Celinda *see* Celeste or Selena

Celine *see* Ancelin

Celinka *see* Celeste

Celo *(Greek)* 'Flame-like'

Celosia *(Greek)* 'Burning flame'
Kelosia

Cerelia *(Latin)* 'Spring-like'. A woman of spring-blossom beauty
Cerealia, Cerelie, Cerellia

Cerelie *see* Cerelia

Cerella *(Latin)* 'Springtime'

Cerellia *see* Cerelia

Ceri *see* Ceiridwen or Ceridwen

Cerian *(Welsh)* 'Loved one'

Ceridwen *(Welsh)* 'Fair poetry'
Ceri

Cerrita *(Spanish)* 'Closed, silent'

Cerys *(Welsh)* 'Love'

Chakara *see* Chakra

Chakra *(Sanskrit)* 'Circle of energy'
Chakara, Shakra

Champa *(Sanskrit)* 'Flower'
Champak

Champak *see* Champa

Chan *(Cambodian)* 'Sweet-smelling tree'

Chandni *(Sanskrit)* 'Moonlight'

Chandra *(Sanskrit)* 'The moon who outshines the stars'
Candra, Candre, Chandre

Chandre *see* Chandra

Chanel *(Old French)* 'Wine jar'

Chantal *see* Chantelle

Chantel *see* Chantelle

Chantelle *(French)* 'Little singer'
Chantal, Chantel

Chantesuta *(Native American)* 'Resolute'

Chantrea *(Cambodian)* 'Moonbeam'
Chantria

Chantria *see* Chantrea

Chantrice *(French)* 'Singer'

Charis *(Greek)* 'Grace'

Charissa *see* Charity

Charita *see* Charity

Charity *(Latin)*
'Benevolent and loving'.
One who gives with
generosity and
affection
Charissa, Charita,
Charry, Cherry

Charleen *see* Caroline

Charlene *see* Caroline

Charlie *see* Charlotte

Charline *see* Caroline

Charlotta *see* Charlotte

Charlotte *(Teutonic)* A
form of Caroline
Carla, Carlie, Carly,
Carlotta, Charlie,
Charlotta, Charmian,
Charo, Charyl, Cheryl,
Sharleen, Sherry,
Sheryl and all the
variations of Caroline

Charma *(Greek)* 'Delight'

Charmain *see* Charmaine

Charmaine *(Latin)* 'Little
song'
Carmen, Charmain,
Charmian *see also*
Carmen

Charmian *see* Charlotte or
Charmaine

Charmian *(Greek)* 'Little
joy'

Charo *see* Charlotte

Charry *see* Charity

Charyl *see* Charlotte

Chastity *(Latin)* 'Purity'

Chatura *(Sanskrit)* 'Clever
one'

Chaya *(Hebrew)* 'Life-
giving'
Chayra

Chayra *see* Chaya

Chelsea *(Old English)* 'A
port of ships'
Chelsey, Chelsy,
Cheslie, Kelsie

Chelsey *see* Chelsea

Chelsy *see* Chelsea

Chenoa *(Native American)*
'White bird'

Cher *(French)* 'Beloved',
'dearest'
Chere, Sher

Chere *see* Cher

Cheri *see* Cherie

Cherida *see* Cherie or
Querida

Cherie *(French)* 'Dear,
beloved one'. A term of
endearment
Cheri, Cherida, Cherry,
Cheryl, Sherrie, Sherry,
Sheryl

Cherise *(Old French)* 'Cherry-like'

Cherish *(English)* 'Precious'

Cheron *(French)* 'Beloved'
Caron

Cherry *see* Charity or Cherie

Cheryl *see* Charlotte or Cherie

Cheslie *see* Chelsea

Chesna *(Slavic)* 'Peaceful'

Cheyenne *(American)* Tribal name

Chiara *(Italian)* 'Famous, light'

Chika *(Japanese)* 'Near, thousand rejoicings'

Chilali *(Native American)* 'Snow bird'

Chimalis *(Native American)* 'Blue bird'

Chinika *(Swahili)* 'God receives'

Chiquita *(Spanish)* 'Little one'. A term of endearment for a small girl

Chispa *(Spanish)* 'Spark from a fire'

Chitsa *(Native American)* 'Beautiful one'

Chlarimonda *see* Clarimond

Chlarimonde *see* Clarimond

Chlarinda *see* Claramae

Chlaris *see* Clarice

Chloe *(Greek)* 'Fresh young blossom'. The Greek goddess of unripened grain
Chlöe, Cloe, Kloe

Chlora *(Greek)* 'Spring freshness'

Chloras *see* Chloris

Chlores *see* Chloris

Chlori *see* Chloris

Chlorinda *see* Claramae

Chlorinde *see* Clorinda

Chloris *(Greek)* 'Goddess of the flowers'
Chloras, Chlores, Chlori, Loris *see also* Clarice

Cho *(Korean)* 'Beautiful' *(Japanese)* 'Butterfly'

Cholena *(Native American)* 'Bird'

Chris *see* Christine

Chrissie *see* Christine

Chrissy *see* Christine

Christabel *(Latin)*
'Beautiful bright-faced
Christian'
Christabella,
Christabelle, Kristabel,
Kristabella, Kristabelle

Christabella *see* Christabel

Christabelle *see* Christabel

Christalle *see* Crystal

Christan *see* Christine

Christanta *(Colombian)* 'A
chrysanthemum'

Christian *see* Christine

Christiana *see* Christine

Christiane *see* Christine

Christina *see* Christine

Christine *(French)*
'Christian one'
Cairistiona, Cairstine,
Chris, Chrissie, Chrissy,
Christan, Christian,
Christiana, Christiane,
Christina, Christye,
Christyna, Chrystal,
Cristina, Cristine,
Crissie, Crissy, Cristen,
Cristiona, Crystal,
Kristen, Krystina, Tina

Christye *see* Christine

Christyna *see* Christine

Chryseis *(Latin)* 'Golden
daughter'

Chrysilla *(Greek)* 'One with
golden hair'

Chrystal *see* Christine or
Crystal

Chun *(Chinese)*
'Springtime'

Cicely *see* Cecilia

Ciel *see* Cecilia

Cilla *(French)* 'The cilla
flower' *see also* Priscilla

Cinderella *(French)* 'Girl of
the ashes'. From the
French fairy tale
Cindie, Cindy, Ella

Cindie *see* Cinderella

Cindy *see* Cinderella or
Cynthia

Cipressa *see* Cypris

Cirila *see* Cyrilla

Cirilla *see* Cyrilla

Cissie *see* Cecilia

Claire *see* Clara

Clairine *(Latin)* 'Bright
maiden'

Clanenda *(Latin)*
'Becoming brighter'

Clara *(Latin)* 'Bright, shining girl'. One of clear, outstanding beauty
Claire, Clare, Clareta, Clarette, Clarine, Klara *see also* Clarabella

Clarabella *(Latin/French)* 'Bright, shining beauty'
Bella, Clara, Clarabelle

Clarabelle *see* Clarabella

Claramae *(English)* 'Brilliant beauty'
Chlarinda, Chlorinda, Clarinda, Clorinda

Clare *see* Clara

Claresta *(English)* 'The most shining one'. A woman to outshine all others
Clarista

Clareta *see* Clara

Clarette *see* Clara

Claribel *(Latin)* 'Fair and bright'

Clarice *(French)* 'Little, shining one'. French form of Clara
Chlaris, Clariss, Clarissa, Clarisse *see also* Chloris

Clarimond *(Teutonic)* 'Brilliant protector'
Chlarimonda, Chlarimonde, Clarimonda, Clarimonde

Clarimonda *see* Clarimond

Clarimonde *see* Clarimond

Clarinda *see* Claramae or Clorinda

Clarinde *see* Clorinda

Clarine *see* Clara

Clariss *see* Clarice

Clarissa *see* Clarice

Clarisse *see* Clarice

Clarista *see* Claresta

Claude *see* Claudia

Claudell *see* Claudia

Claudette *see* Claudia

Claudia *(Latin)* 'The lame one'. Feminine of Claud
Claude, Claudell, Claudette, Claudie, Claudina, Claudine, Gladys

Claudie *see* Claudia

Claudina *see* Claudia

Claudine *see* Claudia

Clea *(Literary)* A name perhaps coined by Lawrence Durrell in *The Alexandria Quartet*

Cleantha *see* Cliantha

Cleanthe *see* Cliantha

Clearests *(Greek)* 'Pinnacle of achievement'

Clematis *(Greek)* 'Sweet wine'

Clemence *(Latin)* 'Merciful and kind'. One who tempers justice with mercy
Clemency, Clementia, Clementina, Clementine

Clemency *see* Clemence

Clementia *see* Clemence

Clementina *see* Clemence

Clementine *see* Clemence

Cleo *see* Cleopatra

Cleopatra *(Greek)* 'Her father's glory'. A girl who will add lustre to her father's name
Cleo

Cleophila *(Greek)* 'Lover of glory'

Cleosa *(Greek)* 'Famous'

Cleva *(Old English)* 'Cliff dweller'. Feminine of Clive

Cliantha *(Greek)* 'Flower of glory'
Cleantha, Cleanthe, Clianthe

Clianthe *see* Cliantha

Clio *(Greek)* 'She who proclaims'. The Greek muse of history

Clodagh *(Irish)* A river in Ireland

Cloe *see* Chloe

Clorinda *(Latin)* 'Famed for her beauty'
Chlorinda, Chlorinde, Clarinda, Clarinde, Clorinde *see also* Claramae

Clorinde *see* Clorinda

Clothilda *see* Clotilda

Clothilde *see* Clotilda

Clotilda *(Teutonic)* 'Famous battle maiden'. A warrior who fought alongside her father and brothers
Clothilda, Clothilde, Clotilde

Clotilde *see* Clotilda

Clover *(English)* 'Meadow blossom'. From the flower
Clovie

Clovie *see* Clover

Clydia *(Greek)* 'Glorious'
Clydina

Clymene *(Greek)* 'Fame and renown'

Clytie *(Greek)* 'Splendid daughter'. The mythical nymph who was turned into a heliotrope, so that she could worship the sun

Cocheta *(Native American)* 'Unknown one'

Cody *(Old English)* 'A cushion'

Coleen *see* Colleen

Colene *see* Colleen

Colette *(Latin)* 'Victorious'. A form of Nicolette
Collete, Collette

Coline *see* Colleen or Columba

Colinette *(Latin)* 'Tiny dove'

Colleen *(Gaelic)* 'Girl'. The name given to a young girl in Ireland
Cailin, Coleen, Colene, Coline, Colline, Collete
see Colette

Collete *see* Colette

Colline *see* Colleen

Colly *see* Columba

Colombe *see* Columba

Columba *(Latin)* 'The dove'. One of a peaceful disposition
Coline, Colly, Colombe, Columbia, Columbine

Columbia *see* Columba

Columbine *see* Columba

Comfort *(French)* 'One who gives comfort'. One of the virtue names popular with English and American Puritan families

Con *see* Constance

Concepcion *see* Conception

Conceptia *see* Conception

Conception *(Latin)* 'Beginning'
Concepcion, Conceptia, Concha, Conchita

Concessa *(Latin)* 'One who grants a favour'

Concetta *(Italian)* 'An ingenious thought'

Concha *see* Conception

Conchita *see* Conception

Concordia *(Latin)* 'Harmony and peace'
Concordie, Concordina, Concordy

Concordie *see* Concordia

Concordina *see* Concordia

Concordy *see* Concordia

Connal *(Latin)* 'Faithful one'

Connie *see* Conradine, Constance or Consuela

Conrada *see* Conradine

Conradina *see* Conradine

Conradine *(Teutonic)* 'Bold and wise'. Feminine of Conrad
Connie, Conrada, Conradina

Consolata *(Latin)* 'One who consoles'
Consolation

Consolation *see* Consolata

Constance *(Latin)* 'Constant'. One who is firm and unchanging
Con, Connie, Constancy, Constanta, Constantia, Constantina, Constantine, Constanze

Constancy *see* Constance

Constanta *see* Constance

Constantia *see* Constance

Constantina *see* Constance

Constantine *see* Constance

Constanze *see* Constance

Consuela *(Spanish)* 'Consolation'. A friend in need
Connie, Consuelo

Consuelo *see* Consuela

Cora *(Greek)* 'The maiden'. From Kore, the daugher of the Greek goddess Demeter
Corella, Corett, Coretta, Corette, Corin, Corina, Corinna, Corinne, Correna, Coretta, Corie, Corin, Corina, Corrie, Corrina, Corrine

Corabella *(Combination Cora/Bella)* 'Beautiful maiden'
Corabelle

Corabelle *see* Corabella

Coral *(Latin)* 'Sincere' or 'from the sea'
Corale, Coralie, Coraline

Coralie *see* Coral

Coraline *see* Coral

Corazon *(Spanish)* 'Heart'

Cordana *(Teutonic)* 'Harmony'

Cordelia *(Welsh)* 'Jewel of the sea'. The daughter of Lear, the sea king
Cordelie, Cordie, Cordula, Delia

Cordelie *see* Cordelia

Cordie *see* Cordelia

Cordula *see* Cordelia

Corella *see* Cora

Corett *see* Cora

Coretta *see* Cora

Corette *see* Cora

Corey *(Gaelic)* 'From the hollow'

Corie *see* Cora

Corin *see* Cora

Corina *see* Cora

Corinna *see* Cora

Corinne *see* Cora

Corissa *(Latin/Greek)* 'Most modest maiden'
Corisse

Corisse *see* Corissa

Corla *(Old English)* 'Curlew'

Corliss *(English)* 'Cheerful and kind-hearted'
Carliss, Carlissa, Corlissa

Corlissa *see* Corliss

Cornela *see* Cornelia

Cornelia *(Latin)* 'Womanly virtue'
Cornela, Cornelie, Cornelle, Cornie, Nela, Nelie, Nelli

Cornelie *see* Cornelia

Cornelle *see* Cornelia

Cornie *see* Cornelia

Corolla *(Latin)* 'Tiny crown'

Corona *(Spanish)* 'Crowned maiden'
Coronie

Coronie *see* Corona

Correna *see* Cora

Corrie *see* Cora

Corrina *see* Cora

Cosetta *see* Cosette

Cosette *(French)* 'Victorious army'
Cosetta

Cosima *see* Cosina

Cosina *(Greek)* 'World harmony'
Cosima

Cottins *(Greek)* 'Crown of wild flowers'

Coulava *(Celtic)* 'One with soft hands'

Courtenay *see* Courtney

Courtney *(Old English)* 'From the court'
Courtenay

Coyetta *(Teutonic)* 'Caged'

Coyne *(French)* 'Modest'

Crescent *(French)* 'The creative one'
Crescenta, Crescentia

Crescenta *see* Crescent

Crescentia *see* Crescent

Cresseide *see* Cressida

Cressida *(Greek)* 'The golden one'
Cresseide

Crisiant *(Welsh)* 'Crystal'

Crispina *(Latin)* 'Curly haired'. Feminine of Crispin
Crispine

Crispine *see* Crispina

Crissie *see* Christine

Crissy *see* Christine

Cristal *see* Crystal

Cristen *see* Christine

Cristina *see* Christine

Cristine *see* Christine

Cristiona *see* Christine

Crystal *(Latin)* 'Clear'
Christalle, Cristal, Chrystal, Krystal *see also* Christine

Cybil *see* Sybil

Cyn *see* Cynthia

Cynara *(Greek)* 'Artichoke'. A beautiful maiden, protected by thorns

Cynth *see* Cynthia

Cynthia *(Greek)* 'Moon goddess'. Another name for Diana, Goddess of the Moon, born on Cynthos
Cindy, Cyn, Cynth, Cynthie

Cynthie *see* Cynthia or Hyacinth

Cynthis *see* Hyacinth

Cypress *see* Cypris

Cypressa *see* Cypris

Cypris *(Greek)* 'Born in Cyprus'
Cipressa, Cypress, Cypressa

Cyra *(Persian)* 'The Sun God'

Cyrena *(Greek)* 'From Cyrene'. A water nymph loved by Apollo, the Sun God
Cyrenia, Kyrena, Kyrenia

Cyrene *(Greek)* 'River nymph'

Cyrenia *see* Cyrena

Cyrilla *(Latin)* 'Lordly one'. Feminine of Cyril
Cirila, Cirilla

Cytherea *(Greek)* 'From Cythera'. Another name for Aphrodite
Cytherere, Cytheria, Cytherine

Cytherere *see* Cytherea

Cytheria *see* Cytherea

Cytherine *see* Cytherea

GIRLS

D'Arcie *see* Darcie

Dacey *(Gaelic)* 'Southerner'

Dacia *(Greek)* 'From Dacia'

Dael *see* Dale

Daffodil *(Greek)* 'Golden spring flower'

Dagania *(Hebrew)* 'Ceremonial grain' Daganya

Daganya *see* Dagania

Dagmar *(Norse)* 'Glory of the Danes'

Dahlia *(Greek)* 'Of the valley'. From the flower of the same name

Dai *(Japanese)* 'Great'

Daile *see* Dale

Daina *(Teutonic)* 'Disdainful'

Daisy *(Anglo-Saxon)* 'The day's eye'. Also a nickname for Margaret (Marguerite), French for daisy

Dakapaki *(Native American)* 'Blossom'

Dakota *(American)* 'Friend, partner'. Tribal name

Dale *(Teutonic)* 'From the valley'. An earlier form of Dahlia Dael, Daile

Dalila *see* Delilah

Dallas *(Gaelic)* 'Wise'

Dalta *(Gaelic)* 'Favourite child'

Damara *(Greek)* 'Gentle girl' Damaris, Mara, Maris

Damaris *see* Damara

Damasa *(French)* 'Maiden'

Damia *(Greek)* 'Goddess of forces of nature'

Damiana *(Greek)* 'Soothing one'. Feminine of Damian Damiann, Damianna, Damianne

Damiann *see* Daniana

Damianna *see* Damiana

Damianne *see* Damiana

Damica *(French)* 'Friendly'
Damika

Damika *see* Damica

Damita *(Spanish)* 'Little
noble lady'

Dana *(Scandinavian)* 'From
Denmark'
Dayna

Danae *(Greek)* Mother of
Perseus

Danella *see* Danielle

Danelle *see* Danielle

Danica *(Norse)* 'The
morning star'
Danika

Danice *see* Danielle

Daniela *see* Danielle

Danielea *see* Danielle

Danielle *(Hebrew)* 'God is
my judge'. Feminine of
Daniel
Danella, Danelle,
Danice, Daniela,
Danielea, Danila,
Danita, Danya,
Danyelle

Danika *see* Danica

Danila *see* Danielle

Danita *see* Danielle

Danuta *(Polish)* 'Young deer'

Danya *see* Danielle

Danyelle *see* Danielle

Daphne *(Greek)* 'Bay tree'.
Symbol of victory. The
nymph who was turned
into a laurel bush to
escape the attentions of
Apollo

Dara *(Hebrew)* 'Charity,
compassion and
wisdom'
Darya

Daraka *(Sanskrit)* 'Gentle
and shy'

Daralis *(Old English)*
'Beloved'

Darcia *see* Darcy

Darcie *(French)* 'From the
fortress'. Feminine of
D'Arcy
D'Arcie

Darcy *(Celtic)* 'Girl with
dark hair'
Darcia, Dercia, Dercy

Darea *see* Darlene

Dareece *see* Darice

Dareen *see* Darlene

Darees *see* Darice

Darel *(Anglo-Saxon)* 'Little
dear one'. Another form
of Darlene
Darelle, Darrelle,
Darry, Daryl

Darelle *see* Darel

Daria *(Persian)* 'Wealthy queen'. Feminine of Darius

Darice *(Persian)* 'Queenly' Dareece, Darees

Darleen *see* Darlene

Darlene *(Anglo-Saxon)* 'Little darling' Darea, Dareen, Darleen, Darline, Daryl

Darline *see* Darlene

Daron *(Gaelic)* 'Great'

Darrelle *see* Darel

Darry *see* Darel

Darya *see* Dara

Daryl *see* Darel or Darlene

Dasha *(Russian)* 'Gift of God'

Daveen *see* Davina

Davida *see* Davina

Davina *(Hebrew)* 'Beloved'. Feminine of David Daveen, Davida, Davita

Davita *see* Davina

Dawn *(Anglo-Saxon)* 'The break of day'. One who lightens the darkness

Dayna *see* Dana

Dea *(Latin)* 'Goddess'

Deana *see* Dena

Deane *see* Dena

Deanna *see* Diana

Debbie *see* Deborah

Debby *see* Deborah

Debor *see* Deborah

Debora *see* Deborah

Deborah *(Hebrew)* 'The bee'. An industrious woman who looks only for what is sweet in life Debbie, Debby, Debor, Debora, Debra, Devora

Debra *see* Deborah

Decima *(Latin)* 'Tenth daughter' or 'dark beauty' *see also* Diana

Dee *(Welsh)* 'Black, dark' Dee Ann *see also* Audrey or Diana

Dee Ann *see* Dee

Deel *see* Dorothy

Deerdre *see* Deirdre

Deidre *see* Deirdre

Deiphila *(Greek)* 'Divine love'

Deirdre *(Gaelic)* 'Sorrow'. A legendary Irish beauty Deerdre, Deidre

Deja *(French)* 'Before'

Dela *see* Adelaide

Delcine *see* Dulcie

Delfina *see* Delfine

Delfine *(Greek)* 'The larkspur or delphinium flower'
Delfina, Delphina, Delphine, Delveen

Delia *(Greek)* 'Visible'. Another name for the Moon goddess *see also* Bedelia or Cordelia

Delicia *(Latin)* 'Delightful maiden' or 'spirit of delight'

Delie *(French)* 'Slim and delicate'

Delight *(French)* 'Pleasure'. One who brings happiness to her family

Delila *see* Delilah

Delilah *(Hebrew)* 'The gentle temptress'. The woman who betrayed the Biblical Samson
Dalila, Delila, Lila

Delinda *(Teutonic)* 'Gentle'

Delizea *(Latin)* 'Delight'

Della *see* Adelaide

Dellora *see* Delora

Delma *(Spanish)* 'Of the sea'
Delmar, Delmare

Delmar *see* Delma

Delmare *see* Delma

Delora *(Latin)* 'From the seashore'
Dellora *see also* Dolores

Delores *see* Dolores

Deloris *see* Dolores

Delorita *see* Dolores

Delphina *see* Delfine

Delphine *(Greek)* 'Calmness and serenity' *see also* Delfine

Delta *(Greek)* 'Fourth daughter'. The fourth letter of the Greek alphabet

Delveen *see* Delfine

Delwen *(Welsh)* 'Neat, fair'

Delyth *(Welsh)* 'Neat, pretty'

Demelza *(English)* 'Hill-fort'

Demeter *see* Demetria

Demetria *(Greek)* 'Fertility'. The Greek goddess of fertility
Demi, Demeter

Demetris *see* Demetria

Demi *see* Demeter

Dena *(Anglo-Saxon)* 'From the valley'
Deana, Deane *see also* Adina

Denaneer *(Arabic)* 'Piece of gold'

Denice *see* Denise

Denise *(French)* 'Wine goddess'. Feminine of Dionysus, God of wine
Denice, Denny, Denys

Denni *see* Denise

Denys *see* Denise

Dercia *see* Darcy

Dercy *see* Darcy

Derede *(Greek)* 'Gift of God'

Derika *(Teutonic)* 'Ruler of the people'

Derora *(Hebrew)* 'Brook'

Derry *(Irish)* 'Red-haired girl'

Derryth *(Welsh)* 'Of the oak'

Dervia *(Old Irish)* 'Daughter of the poet'

Desdemona *(Greek)* 'One born under an unlucky star'. After the heroine of Shakespeare's *Othello*
Desmona

Desiree *(French)* 'Desired one'

Desma *(Greek)* 'A pledge'

Desmona *see* Desdemona

Desta *see* Modesty

Destinee *(Old French)* 'Destiny'

Destiny *(French)* 'Fate'

Deva *(Sanskrit)* 'Divine'. The Moon Goddess

Devi *(Hindu)* Name of a Hindu goddess

Devin *(Gaelic)* 'Poet'

Devnet *(Celtic)* 'White wave'

Devona *(Teutonic)* 'Brave girl'

Devona *(English)* 'From Devon'. Someone born in the English country of Devon, the name of which means 'people of the deep valley'
Devondra

Devondra *see* Devona

Devora *see* Deborah

Dextra *(Latin)* 'Skilful, adept'

Di *see* Diana

Diadema *(Greek)* 'Jewel'

Diahann *see* Diana

Diamanta *(French)* 'Diamond-like'. One who is as precious as the rarest jewel

Diamond *(Latin)* 'Precious jewel'

Dian *see* Diana

Diana *(Latin)* 'Divine Moon goddess'. Roman goddess of the Moon and of hunting
Deanna, Dee, Decima, Di, Diahann, Dian, Diandra, Diane, Dianna, Dianne, Dyana, Dyane, Dyanna

Diandra *see* Diana

Diane *see* Diana

Dianna *see* Diana

Dianne *see* Diana

Diantha *(Greek)* 'Divine flower of Zeus'
Dianthe, Dianthia

Dianthe *see* Diantha

Dianthia *see* Diantha

Diaphenia *(Greek)* 'Shedding light'

Dicentra *(Greek)* 'Flower'. Flower commonly known as bleeding heart

Dickie *see* Ricarda

Dicky *see* Ricarda

Didi *(Hebrew)* 'Beloved'

Didiane *(French)* Feminine of Didier
Didière

Didière *see* Didiane

Dido *(Greek)* 'Teacher'

Diella *(Latin)* 'One who worships God'

Dilys *(Welsh)* 'Perfect'

Dimphia *see* Dymphia

Dinah *(Hebrew)* 'Judgement'. One whose understanding is complete

Dione *(Greek)* 'The daughter of heaven and earth'
Dionia, Dionne

Dionia *see* Dione

Dionne *see* Dione

Dior *(French)* 'Golden'

Disa *(Greek)* 'Double'
(Norse) 'Lively spirit'

Divia *see* Divya

Divya *(Hindi)* 'Divine,
heavenly'
Divia

Dixey *see* Dixie

Dixie *(French)* 'The tenth'
Dixey, Dixil, Dixy *see
also* Benedicta

Dixil *see* Dixie

Dixy *see* Dixie

Doanna *(Combination of
Dorothy/Anna)*

Docie *see* Endocia

Docila *(Latin)* 'Gentle
teacher'

Dodi *see* Doris

Dodie *(Hebrew)* 'Beloved'

Dolley *see* Dorothy

Dollie *see* Dorothy

Dolly *see* Dolores or
Dorothy

Dolores *(Spanish)* 'Lady of
sorrow'
Delora, Delores,
Deloris, Delorita, Dolly,
Doloritas, Lola, Lolita

Doloritas *see* Dolores

Domenica *see* Dominica

Domeniga *see* Dominica

Domina *(Latin)* 'The lady'.
One of noble birth

Dominga *see* Dominica

Domini *see* Dominica

Dominica *(Latin)* 'Child
born on a Sunday'

Dominica *(Latin)*
'Belonging to the Lord'.
Feminine of Dominic
Domenica, Domeniga,
Dominga, Domini,
Dominique

Dominique *see* Dominica

Dona *see* Donna

Donabella *(Spanish)*
'Beautiful woman'

Donalda *(Gaelic)* 'Ruler of
the world'. Feminine of
Donald

Donata *(Latin)* 'The gift'

Donella *(Spanish)* 'Little
girl'

Donna *(Italian)* 'Noble
lady'
Dona

Dora *see* Doreen, Doris,
Dorothy, Eudora,
Isadora or Theodora

Dorcas *(Greek)* 'Graceful'. One with the grace of a gazelle

Dore *(French)* 'Golden maiden' *see also* Dorothy

Dorea *(Greek)* 'Gift'

Doreen *(Gaelic)* 'Golden girl' or 'the sullen one' Dora, Dorene, Dori, Dorie, Dori, Dorie, Dorine, Dory

Dorene *see* Doreen

Doretta *see* Dorothy

Dorhissa *(Hebrew)* 'Gift of the promise'

Dori *see* Doreen or Isadora

Dorianne *(Greek)* 'From Doria'

Dorice *see* Doris

Dorie *see* Doreen

Dorinda *(Greek/Spanish)* 'Beautiful golden gift'

Dorine *see* Doreen

Doris *(Greek)* 'From the sea'. The daughter of Oceanus Dodi, Dora, Dorice, Dorise, Dorita, Dorris

Dorise *see* Doris

Dorita *see* Doris

Dorleta *(Basque)* Name for the Virgin Mary

Dorothea *see* Dorothy

Dorothi *see* Dorothy

Dorothoe *see* Dorothy

Dorothy *(Greek)* 'Gift of God' Deel, Dolley, Dollie, Dolly, Dora, Dore, Doretta, Dorothea, Dorothi, Dorothoe, Dorthea, Dot, Theodora *see also* Theodora

Dorris *see* Doris

Dorthea *see* Dorothy

Dorthy *see* Dorothy

Dory *see* Doreen or Isadora

Dorymene *(Greek)* 'Brave, courageous'

Dot *see* Dorothy

Dotty *see* Dorothy

Douce *(French)* 'Sweet'

Douna *(Slavic)* 'Valley'

Dove *(English)* 'Bird of peace'

Doxie *see* Endocia

Doxy *see* Endocia

Drew *(Greek)* 'Courageous'

Dromicia *(Greek)* 'Fast'

Druella *(Teutonic)* 'Elfin vision'
Druilla

Druilla *see* Druella

Drusilla *(Latin)* 'The strong one'. One with patience and fortitude

Duana *(Gaelic)* 'Little dark maiden'
Duna, Dwana

Duena *(Spanish)* 'Chaperone'. Women of good birth who were responsible for the manners of young girls in their charge
Duenna

Duenna *see* Duena

Dulce *see* Dulcie

Dulcea *see* Dulcie

Dulciana *see* Dulcie

Dulcibella *see* Dulcie

Dulcibelle *see* Dulcie

Dulcie *(Latin)* 'Sweet and charming'. One who believes hat love is the sweetest thing
Delcine, Dulce, Dulcea, Dulciana, Dulcibella, Dulcibelle, Dulcine, Dulcinea

Dulcine *see* Dulcie

Dulcinea *see* Dulcie

Duna *see* Duana

Durene *(Latin)* 'The enduring one'

Duretta *(Spanish)* 'Little reliable one'

Durga *(Hindi)* 'Mythological figure, wife of Siva'

Duscha *(Russian)* 'Soul'

Dwana *see* Duana

Dyana *see* Diana

Dyane *see* Diana

Dyani *(Native American)* 'Deer'

Dyanna *see* Diana

Dympha *see* Dymphia

Dymphia *(Latin)* 'Nurse'
Dimphia, Dympha

Dymphna *see* Dympna

Dympna *(Irish)* 'Eligible'
Dymphna

Dyna *(Greek)* 'Powerful'

Dyota *(Sanskrit)* 'Sunshine'

Dysis *(Greek)* 'Sunset'

GIRLS

Eada *see* Alda or Eda

Eadie *see* Edith

Eadith *see* Edith

Eadrea *see* Edrea

Eadwina *see* Edwina

Eadwine *see* Edwina

Eady *see* Edith

Eaidie *see* Edith

Earlene *(Anglo-Saxon)* 'Noble woman'. Feminine of Earl Earley, Earlie, Earline, Erlene, Erline

Earley *see* Earlene

Earlie *see* Earlene

Earline *see* Earlene

Eartha *(Old English)* 'Of the earth' Erda, Ertha, Herta, Hertha

Easter *(Old English)* 'Born at Easter'. Derivation of Eostre, the pre-Christian goddess of spring

Eastre *see* Eostre

Ebba *(Anglo-Saxon)* Form of Eve

Eberta *(Teutonic)* 'Brilliant'

Ebony *(Greek)* 'A hard, dark wood'

Echo *(Greek)* 'Repeating sound'. A Greek nymph who pined away for love

Ed *see* Edwina

Eda *(Anglo-Saxon)* 'Poetry' *(Greek)* 'Loving mother of many' or 'prosperous' Eada, Edda *see also* Edith

Edana *(Gaelic)* 'Little fiery one'. A warmly loving child whose ardent nature is said to have been given by God Aidan, Aiden, Eidann

Edda *see* Eda

Eddie *see* Edwina

Ede *see* Edith

Edelina *see* Adelaide

Edeline *see* Adelaide

Eden *(Hebrew)*
'Enchanting'. The epitome of all female charm

Edia *(Teutonic)* 'Rich friend'

Edie *see* Edith

Edina *(Scottish)* Another form of Edwina

Edith *(Teutonic)* 'Rich gift'
Eadie, Eadith, Eaidie, Eady, Eda, Edythe, Ede, Edie, Editha, Edithe, Ediva, Edythe

Editha *see* Edith

Edithe *see* Edith

Ediva *see* Edith

Edla *(Teutonic)* 'Woman of noble birth'

Edlyn *(Anglo-Saxon)* 'Noble maiden'

Edmee *(Anglo-Saxon)* 'Fortunate protector'

Edmonda *(Anglo-Saxon)* 'Rich protector'. Feminine of Edmund
Edmunda

Edmunda *see* Edmonda

Edna *(Hebrew)*
'Rejuvenation'. One who knows the secret of eternal youth
Ed, Eddie, Edny

Edny *see* Edna

Edra *(Hebrew)* 'Mighty'

Edrea *(Anglo-Saxon)*
'Powerful and prosperous'. Feminine of Edric
Eadrea *see also* Andrea

Edwardina *(Anglo-Saxon)*
'Rich guardian'. Feminine of Edward

Edwina *(Anglo-Saxon)* 'Rich friend'
Eadwina, Eadwine, Edina, Edwine, Win, Wina, Winnie

Edwine *see* Edwina

Edythe *see* Edith

Effie *(Greek)* 'Famous beauty'
Effy *see also* Euphemia

Effy *see* Euphemia

Efrat *(Hebrew)* 'Honoured'
Efrata

Efrata *see* Efrat

Egberta *(Anglo-Saxon)*
'Bright, shining sword'.
Feminine of Egbert
Egberte, Egbertha,
Egberthe, Egbertina,
Egbertine

Egberte *see* Egberta

Egberthe *see* Egberta

Egbertina *see* Egberta

Egbertine *see* Egberta

Eglantina *see* Eglantine

Eglantine *(French)* 'The
wild rose'
Eglantina, Eglintyne,
Eglyntine

Egllintyne *see* Eglantine

Eglyntine *see* Eglantine

Eiblin *(Gaelic)* 'Pleasant'.
Eveleen

Eidann *see* Edana

Eileen *see* Aileen or Helen

Eilien *(Greek)* 'Light'

Eilwen *(Welsh)* 'Fair brow'

Eir *(Norse)* 'Peace and mercy'.
The goddess of healing

Eirena *see* Irene

Eirene *see* Irene

Eirian *(Welsh)* 'Silver'

Eiric *see* Henrietta

Eirlys *(Welsh)* 'Snowdrop'

Eirwen *(Welsh)* 'Snow-
white'

Eister *see* Esther

Ekata *(Sanskrit)* 'Unity'

Ekaterina *see* Catherine

Elaine *(French)* French
form of Helen. Lainey
see Helen

Elama *(Greek)* 'From the
mountains'

Elana *(Hebrew)* 'Oak tree'

Elane *see* Helen

Elata *(Latin)* 'Lofty, noble'.
A woman of high birth
and beauy

Elberta *(Teutonic)* 'Brilliant'
see also Alberta

Elbertine *see* Alberta

Elda *(Anglo-Saxon)*
'Princess' *see also* Alda

Eldora *(Spanish)* 'Gilded
one'. From El Dorado,
the land of gold

Eldreda *(Anglo-Saxon)*
'Wise companion'
Eldrida

Eldrida *(Teutonic)* 'Old and
wise adviser'. Feminine
of Eldred
Aeldrida *see also*
Eldreda

Eleanor *(French)* A medieval form of Helen Eleanora, Eleanore, Elinor, Elinora, Elinore, Eleonor, Eleonora, Eleonore, Ellie, Lenora, Leonora, Nora

Eleanora *see* Eleanor

Eleanore *see* Eleanor or Helen

Electra *(Greek)* 'Brilliant one'

Elefteria *(Greek)* 'Freedom'

Elena *see* Helen

Elene *see* Aileen

Elenora *see* Helen

Elenore *see* Helen

Eleonor *see* Eleanor

Eleonora *see* Eleanor

Eleonore *see* Eleanor

Eleora *see* Eliora

Eleta *(Spanish)* 'Astonished'

Eleuneria *(Greek)* Daughter of Jupiter and Juno

Elfie *see* Elva

Elfreda *see* Alfreda

Elfride *see* Alfreda

Elfrida *see* Alfreda

Elfrieda *see* Alfreda

Elga *(Slav)* 'Consecrated' Olga *see also* Alfreda

Elicia *see* Elysia

Elinel *(Celtic)* 'Shapely'

Elinor *see* Eleanor or Helen

Elinora *see* Eleanor or Helen

Elinore *see* Eleanor or Helen

Eliora *(Hebrew)* 'God is my light' Eleora

Elisa *see* Alice or Elizabeth

Elisabeth *see* Elizabeth

Elise *see* Elizabeth or Elysia

Elissa *see* Alice or Elizabeth

Elita *(Old French)* 'Chosen' *see also* Melita

Eliza *see* Elizabeth

Elizabeth *(Hebrew)* 'Consecrated to God' Bess, Bessie, Bessy, Beth, Betina, Betsy, Betta, Bette, Betty, Elisa, Elisabeth, Elise, Elissa, Eliza, Ellissa, Elsbeth, Else, Elsie, Elspeth, Elysa, Elyse, Helsa, Ilse, Libb, Libby,

Lisa, Lisbeth, Liza,
Lizabeta, Lizbeth, Lizzy
see also Elsa or Isabel

Elkana *(Hebrew)* 'God has
acquired'

Elke *see* Alice

Ella *(Teutonic)* 'Beautiful
fairy maiden'. Beauty
bestowed by fairies as a
birth gift *see also*
Cinderella and Helen

Ellen *see* Helen

Ellene *see* Helen

Ellenis *(Greek)* 'Priestess'

Ellice *(Greek)* 'Jehovah is
God'. Feminine of Elias
Ellis

Ellie *see* Eleanor

Ellis *see* Ellice

Ellissa *see* Elizabeth

Ellora *(Greek)* 'Happy one'

Ellyn *see* Helen

Elma *(Greek)* 'Pleasant and
amiable'

Elmina *(Old German)* 'Awe-
inspiring fame'

Elmira *see* Almira

Elna *see* Helen

Elnore *see* Eleanor

Elodie *(Greek)* 'Fragile
flower'

Eloine *(Latin)* 'Worthy to
be chosen'

Eloisa *see* Louise

Eloise *(French)* 'Noble one'
see also Louise or
Elizabeth

Elora *(Greek)* 'Light'

Elrica *see* Ulrica

Elsa *(Old German)* 'Noble'
see also Elizabeth

Elsbeth *see* Elizabeth

Else *see* Elizabeth

Elsie *see* Elizabeth

Elspeth *see* Elizabeth

Elswyth *(Old English)*
'Noble strength'

Eluned *(Welsh)* 'Idol'

Elva *(Anglo-Saxon)* Friend
of the elves'
Elfie, Elvia, Elvie, Ivina
see also Alfreda

Elvera *see* Elvira

Elvia *see* Elva

Elvie *see* Elva

Elvina *(Teutonic)* 'Wise and
friendly'

Elvira *(Latin)* 'White woman'
Albinia, Alinia, Elvera, Elvire, Elwira

Elvire *see* Elvira

Elvita *(Latin)* 'Life'

Elwira *see* Elvira

Elwy *(Welsh)* 'Benefit'

Elwyn *(Welsh)* 'One with brown hair'

Elysa *see* Elizabeth

Elyse *see* Elizabeth

Elysia *(Latin)* 'Blissful sweetness'. From Elysium
Elicia, Elise

Ema *see* Emma

Emanuela *(Hebrew)* 'God is with you'

Embla *(Scandinavian)* The first woman in Norse mythology

Emelda *see* Amelia

Emelina *see* Amelia or Emma

Emeline *see* Amelia or Emma

Emer *(Irish)* 'Gifted'

Emerald *(French)* 'The bright green jewel'
Emerande, Emerant, Eneraude, Esme, Esmeralda, Esmeralde

Emerande *see* Emerald

Emerant *see* Emerald

Emily *(Teutonic)* 'Hard-working'

Emina *(Latin)* 'Highly born maiden'. Daughter of a noble house

Emma *(Teutonic)* 'One who heals the universe'. A woman of command
Ema, Emelina, Emeline, Emmeline

Emmalee *see* Amelia

Emmalynn *see* Amelia

Emmanuela *(Hebrew)* 'God with us'

Emmeline *see* Emma

Emmeranne *(French/Old German)* 'Raven'

Emogene *see* Imogen

Emrys *(Celtic)* 'Immortal'
Emryss

Emryss *see* Emrys

Ena *(Gaelic)* 'Little ardent one' *see also* Eugenia

Enda *(Sanskrit)* 'The last one'

Endocia *(Greek)* 'Of spotless reputation' Docie, Doxie, Doxy, Eudosia, Eudoxia *see also* Eudosia

Endora *(French/Old German)* 'Noble'

Eneraude *see* Emerald

Enfys *(Welsh)* 'Rainbow'

Engacia *see* Grace

Engacie *see* Grace

Engelberga *see* Engelberta

Engelbert *see* Engelberta

Engelberta *(Teutonic)* 'Bright angel'. One of the bright defenders of legend Engelberga, Engelbert, Engelbertha, Engelberthe

Engelbertha *see* Engelberta

Engelberthe *see* Engelberta

Engracia *(Spanish)* 'Graceful' *see also* Grace

Enid *(Celtic)* 'Purity of the soul'

Ennata *(French/Greek)* 'Goddess'

Enona *(Greek)* Nymph of Mount Ida, who married Paris

Enone *(Greek)* 'Flower in the hedgerow'

Enora *(French/Greek)* 'Light'

Enrica *(Italian)* Italian form of Henrietta *see also* Henrietta

Enya *(Irish)* 'Kernel'

Eolande *see* Iolanthe or Violet

Eostre *(Old English)* The pre-Christian Goddess of Spring Eastra

Ephratah *(Hebrew)* 'Fruitful'

Eranthe *(Greek)* 'Flower of spring'

Erda *see* Eartha

Erena *see* Irene

Erica *(Norse)* 'Powerful ruler'. Symbol of royalty. Feminine of Eric Aric, Erika

Erika *see* Erica

Erin *(Gaelic)* 'From Ireland'. One born in the Emerald Isle *see also* Erina

Erina *(Gaelic)* 'Girl from Ireland' *see also* Erin

Erlene *see* Earlene

Erlina *(Old English)* 'Little elf'

Erline *see* Earlene

Erma *(Teutonic)* 'Army maid'
Ermina, Erminia, Erminie, Hermia, Hermina, Hermione *see also* Irma

Erme *see* Irma

Ermina *see* Erma

Erminia *see* Armina or Erma

Erminie *see* Armina or Erma

Erna *(Anglo-Saxon)* 'Eagle' Ernaline *see also* Ernestine

Ernaline *see* Erna

Ernesta *see* Ernestine

Ernestine *(Anglo-Saxon)* 'Purposeful one'. Erna, Ernesta

Ertha *see* Eartha

Erwina *(Anglo-Saxon)* 'Friend from the sea'

Esha *(Sanskrit)* 'One who desires' Eshita

Eshita *see* Esha

Esme *see* Emerald

Esmeralda *see* Emerald

Esmeralde *see* Emerald

Essa *see* Esther

Essylt *(Welsh)* 'Beautiful to behold'

Esta *(Italian)* 'From the East'

Estaphania *(Greek)* 'Crown'

Estella *see* Estelle

Estelle *(French)* 'Bright star' Estella, Estrelita, Estrella, Stella, Stelle

Esther *(Hebrew)* 'The star' Eister, Essa, Etty, Hessy, Hester, Hesther, Hetty

Estra *(Anglo-Saxon)* Goddess of Spring

Estrelita *see* Estelle

Estrella *see* Estelle

Eswen *(Welsh)* 'Strong one'

Esyllt *see* Isolde

Etain *(Irish)* 'Shining'

Ethel *(Teutonic)* 'Noble maiden'. The daughter of a princely house
Ethelda, Etheline, Ethyl, Ethylyn *see also* Ethelinda

Ethelda *see* Ethel

Ethelinda *(Teutonic)* 'Noble serpent'. The symbol of immortality *see also* Ethel

Etheline *see* Ethel

Ethyl *see* Ethel

Ethylyn *see* Ethel

Etoile *(French)* 'Star'

Etsu *(Japanese)* 'Delight'

Etta *see* Henrietta

Etty *see* Esther

Euclea *(Greek)* 'Glory'

Eudine *(French/Old German)* 'Noble'

Eudocia *see* Eudosia

Eudora *(Greek)* 'Generous gift'
Dora, Eudore

Eudore *see* Eudora

Eudosia *(Greek)* 'Esteemed'
Eudocia *see also* Endocia

Eudoxia *see* Endocia

Eugenia *(Greek)* 'Well born'. A woman of noble family
Ena, Eugenie, Gena, Gene, Genie, Gina

Eugenie *see* Eugenia

Eula *see* Eulalia

Eulalia *(Greek)* 'Fair spoken one'
Eula, Eulalie, Lallie

Eulalie *see* Eulalia

Eunice *(Greek)* 'Happy and victorious'

Euphemia *(Greek)* 'Of good reputation'
Effie, Effy, Euphemie, Phemie

Euphemie *see* Euphemia

Euphrasia *(Greek)* 'Delight'

Eurielle *(Celtic/French)* 'Angel'

Eurwen *(Welsh)* 'Gold-fair'

Eurydice *(Greek)* 'Broad'

Eustacia *(Latin)* 'Tranquil maiden' or 'fruitful'
Eustacie, Stacey, Stacie, Stacy

Eustacie *see* Eustacia

Eva *see* Eve

Evadne *(Greek)* 'Fortunate'

Evangelina *see* Evangeline

Evangeline *(Greek)* 'Bearer
of glad tidings'
Eva, Evangelina, Vancy,
Vangie

Evania *(Greek)* 'Tranquil,
untroubled'
Evanne

Evanne *see* Evania

Evanthe *(Greek)* 'Lovely
flower'

Eve *(Hebrew)* 'Life-giver'
Eva, Eveleen, Evelina,
Eveline, Evelyn, Evie,
Evita, Evonne

Eveleen *see* Eiblin or Eve

Evelina *see* Eve

Eveline *see* Eve

Evelyn *see* Eve

Everilde *(French from Old
German)* 'Honour in
battle'

Evette *see* Yvonne

Evie *see* Eve

Evita *see* Eve or Vita

Evodie *(Greek)* 'One who
follows the right path'

Evonne *see* Eve or Yvonne

Ezara *(Hebrew)* 'Little
treasure'

GIRLS

Fabia *(Latin)* 'Bean-grower'
Fabiana Fabianna,
Fabienne

Fabiana *see* Fabia

Fabianna *see* Fabia

Fabienne *see* Fabia

Fabiola *(Latin)* 'Woman
who does good works'

Fabriana *see* Fabrianna

Fabrianna *see* Fabrianne

Fabrianne *(Latin)* 'Girl of
resourcefulness'
Fabrianna, Fabrienne,
Frabriane

Fabrienne *see* Fabrianne

Fadilla *see* Frances

Fae *see* Faith or Fay

Faida *(Arabic)* 'Abundant'

Faine *(Old English)* 'Joyful'

Faith *(Teutonic)* 'Trust in
God'. One who is loyal
and true
Fae, Fay, Faye

Faline *(Latin)* 'Cat-like'

Fallon *(Gaelic)* 'Grandchild
of the ruler'

Fan *see* Frances

Fanchon *(French)* 'Free
being'

Fania *(Teutonic)* 'Free'

Fanny *see* Frances

Fanshom *(Teutonic)* 'Free'

Farah *see* Farrah

Farha *(Sanskrit)*
'Happiness'
Farhad, Farhat

Farhad *see* Farha

Farhanna *(Arabic)* 'Joyful'

Farhat *see* Farha

Farica *(Teutonic)* 'Peaceful
rule' *see also* Frederica

Farida *(Arabic)* 'Unique,
precious gem'

Farideh *(Persian)* 'Glorious'

Fariha *(Arabic)* 'Happy'

Farrah *(Middle English)*
'Beautiful'
Farah

Faten *(Arabic)* 'Fascinating, charming'

Fathia *(Arabic)* 'My conquest'

Fatima *(Arabic)* 'Unknown'

Faun *see* Fawn

Faunia *see* Fawn

Fausta *(Italian/Spanish)* 'Fortunate' *see also* Faustine

Faustina *see* Faustine

Faustine *(Latin)* 'Lucky omen'
Fausta, Faustina

Favor *(French)* 'The helpful one'
Favora

Favora *see* Favor

Fawn *(French)* 'Young deer'. A lithe, swift-footed girl
Faun, Faunia, Fawnia

Fawnia *see* Fawn

Fay *(Irish)* 'A raven' *(French)* 'A fairy'. A fairy-like person
Fae, Faye, Fayette, Fayina *see also* Faith

Faye *see* Faith or Fay

Fayette *see* Fay

Fayina *see* Fay

Fayme *(French)* 'Of high reputation'. Beyond reproach

Fayola *(Nigerian)* 'Lucky'

Fayre *(Old English)* 'Beautiful'

Fe *(Spanish)* 'Faith'

Feadora *see* Theodora

Feadore *see* Theodora

Fealty *(French)* 'Faithful one'. One who is loyal to God, sovereign, country and friend

Fedora *see* Theodora

Fedore *see* Theodora

Felda *(Teutonic)* 'From the field'. For one born at harvest time

Felice *see* Felicia

Felicia *(Latin)* 'Joyous one'. Feminine of Felix
Felice, Felicidad, Felicie, Felicity, Felis, Felise, Feliza

Felicidad *see* Felicia

Felicie *see* Felicia

Felicity *see* Felicia

Felipa *(Greek)* 'One who loves horses'

Felis *see* Felicia

Felise *see* Felicia

Felita *(Latin)* 'Happy little one'

Feliza *see* Felicia

Fenella *(Gaelic)* 'White-shouldered'
Finella, Fionnula

Fenix *see* Phoenix

Feodora *see* Theodora

Feodore *see* Theodora

Ferdinanda *see* Fernanda

Feride *(Turkish)* 'Unique'

Feriga *(Italian/Teutonic)* 'Peaceful ruler'

Fern *(Anglo-Saxon)* 'Fern-like'

Fernanda *(Teutonic)* 'Adventurous'. One who is daring and courageous
Ferdinanda, Fernandina

Fernandina *see* Fernanda

Feronia *(Latin)* A goddess of the forests

Ffion *(Welsh)* 'Foxglove flower'

Fidela *(Latin)* 'Faithful one'
Fidele, Fidelia, Fidelity

Fidele *see* Fidela

Fidelia *see* Fidela

Fidelity *see* Fidela

Fifi *see* Josephine

Filana *see* Philana

Filantha *see* Philantha

Filberta *see* Philberta

Filberte *see* Philberta

Filbertha *see* Philberta

Filberthe *see* Philberta

Filida *see* Phyllis

Filipa *see* Philippa

Filippa *see* Philippa

Filis *see* Phyllis

Fillida *see* Phyllis

Fillis *see* Phyllis

Filma *(Anglo-Saxon)* 'Misty veil'. An ethereal type of beauty
Philmen, Pholma

Finella *see* Fenella

Finette *(Hebrew)* 'Little addition'

Fingal *(Celtic)* 'Beautiful stranger'

Finley *(Gaelic)* 'Sunbeam'

Finna *(Celtic)* 'White'

Fiona *(Gaelic)* 'Fair one'
Fionn, Fionna

Fionn *see* Fiona

Fionna *see* Fiona

Fionnula *see* Fenella

Fiore *see* Florence

Firoenza *see* Florence

Flanna *(Gaelic)* 'Red-haired'

Flavia *(Latin)* 'Yellow-haired'

Fleda *see* Fleta

Fleta *(Anglo-Saxon)* 'The swift one'
Fleda

Fleur *(French)* 'A flower'. The French version of Florence
Fleurette *see also* Florence

Fleurdelice *(French)* 'Iris', 'lily'

Fleurette *see* Fleur

Flo *see* Florence

Flor *see* Florence

Flora *see* Florence

Florance *see* Florence

Flore *see* Florence

Florella *see* Florence

Florence *(Latin)* 'A flower'
Fiora, Firoenza, Fleur, Flo, Flor, Flora, Florance, Flore, Florella, Florencia, Florentia, Florenza, Floria, Florinda,

Florine, Floris, Florrie, Florry, Flossie, Flower

Florencia *see* Florence

Florentia *see* Florence

Florenza *see* Florence

Floretta *see* Florette

Florette *(French)* 'Little flower'
Floretta

Floria *see* Florence

Florida *(Latin)* 'Flowery'

Florimel *(Greek)* 'Flower honey'

Florinda *see* Florence

Florine *see* Florence

Floris *see* Florence

Florrie *see* Florence

Florry *see* Florence

Flossie *see* Florence

Flower *(English)* The English version of Florence

Fonda *(English)* 'Affectionate'

Fontanna *(French)* 'Fountain'

Fortuna *see* Fortune

Fortune *(Latin)* 'Fate'. The woman of destiny
Fortuna

Fossetta *(French)* 'Dimpled'

Frabriane *see* Fabrianne

Fran *see* Frances

Frances *(Latin)* 'Free' or 'girl from France'
Fadilla, Fan, Fanchon, Fanny, Fran, Francesca, Francine, Francisca, Franciska, Francoise, Frankie, Frannie, Franny

Francesca *see* Frances

Francine *see* Frances

Franciska *see* Frances

Françoise *see* Frances

Francy *see* Frances

Frankie *see* Frances

Frannie *see* Frances

Freda *(Teutonic)* 'Peace'. One who is calm and unflurried
Freddie, Freida, Frida, Frieda, Friedie *see also* Alfreda or Wilfreda

Freddie *see* Freda, Frederica or Wilfreda

Freddy *see* Frederica

Frederica *(Teutonic)* 'Peaceful ruler'
Farica, Freddie, Freddy, Fredericka, Frederika, Frederique, Frerika, Frerike, Friederik

Frederika *see* Frederica

Frederique *see* Frederica

Fredicia *(Teutonic)* 'Peaceful leader'

Freida *see* Freda or Halfrida

Frenka *see* Frederica

Frerika *see* Frederica

Frerike *see* Frederica

Fresa *(Teutonic)* 'One with curly hair'

Freya *(Norse)* 'Noble goddess of love'. The Norse Goddess of Love

Frida *see* Freda or Halfrida

Frieda *see* Freda or Halfrida

Friederik *see* Frederica

Friedie *see* Freda

Fritzi *see* Frederica

Frodine *(Teutonic)* 'Wise
companion'

Frodis *see* Fronde

Froma *(Teutonic)* 'Holy
one'

Frond *see* Fronde

Fronde *(Latin)* 'Leaf of the
fern'
Frodis, Frond

Fulca *(Latin)*
'Accomplished'

Fulvia *(Latin)* 'Golden girl'.
The daughter born at
high summer

Gabbie *see* Gabrielle

Gabinia *(Latin)* Famous Roman family. City in central Italy

Gabriel *see* Gabrielle

Gabriela *see* Gabrielle

Gabriele *see* Gabrielle

Gabriella *see* Gabrielle

Gabrielle *(Hebrew)* 'Woman of God'. The bringer of good news Gabbie, Gabriel, Gabriela, Gabriele, Gabriella, Gabrila, Gaby, Gavrielle

Gabrila *see* Gabrielle

Gaby *see* Gabrielle

Gaea *(Greek)* 'The earth'. The Goddess of the Earth Gaia

Gael *see* Abigail

Gaerwen *(Welsh)* 'White castle'

Gai *see* Gay

Gaia *see* Gaea

Gail *see* Abigail

Galane *(French)* 'Flower name' Galliane

Galatea *(Greek)* 'Milky white'

Gale *see* Abigail

Galia *(Hebrew)* 'God has redeemed'

Galiana *see* Galiena

Galiena *(Teutonic)* 'Lofty maiden'. A tall, statuesque girl Galiana

Galilah *(Hebrew)* Place name in Galiliee

Galina *see* Helen

Galliane *see* Galane

Garda *see* Gerda

Gardenia *(Latin)* 'White, fragrant flower'

Garland *(French)* 'Crown of blossoms'

Garlanda *(Latin)* 'Decorated with flowers'

Garnet *(English)* 'Deep-red-haired beauty'
Garnette

Garnette *see* Garnet

Gartred *see* Gertrude

Gaviota *(Spanish)* 'Seagull'

Gavra *(Hebrew)* 'God is my rock'

Gavrielle *see* Gabrielle

Gavrila *(Hebrew)* 'Heroine'

Gay *(French)* 'Lively'
Gai, Gaye

Gaye *see* Gay

Gayla *see* Abigail

Gayle *see* Abigail

Gayleen *see* Abigail

Gaylene *see* Abigail

Gaynor *see* Genevieve or Guinevere

Gazella *(Latin)* 'The antelope'. One who is graceful and modest

Gedalia *(Hebrew)* 'God is great'

Geena *(Sanskrit)* 'Silvery'

Geeta *(Sanskrit)* The holy book of advice from Lord Krishna to Arjuna

Gelasia *(Greek)* 'Laughing water'. One who is like a fresh and gurgling stream
Gelasie

Gelasie *see* Gelasia

Gemini *(Greek)* 'Twin'

Gemma *(Latin)* 'Precious stone'
Gemmel

Gemmel *see* Gemma

Gena *see* Eugenia

Gene *see* Eugenia

Genesa *see* Genesia

Genesia *(Latin)* 'Newcomer'
Genesa, Genisia, Jenesia

Geneva *(French)* 'Juniper tree'
Genevre, Genvra, Ginerva *see also* Genevieve and Guinevere

Genevieve *(French)* 'Pure white wave'
Gaynor, Geneva, Genevra, Genevre, Genovera, Ginette, Ginevra, Guenevere, Guinevere, Jennifer, Jenny, Vanora

Genevra *see* Geneva or Genevieve

Genevre *see* Genevieve

Genie *see* Eugenia

Genisia *see* Genesia

Genna *see* Jena

Genovera *see* Genevieve

Genvra *see* Geneva

Georgana *see* Georgina

Georganne *see* Georgina

Georgene *see* Georgina

Georgette *see* Georgina

Georgia *(Greek)* 'Farm girl' *see also* Georgina

Georgiana *see* Georgina

Georgianna *see* Georgina

Georgie *see* Georgina

Georgina *(Greek)* 'Girl from the farm'. Feminine of George
Georgana, Georganne, Georgene, Georgette, Georgia, Georgiana, Georgianna, Georgie, Georgine, Georgy, Girogia

Georgine *see* Georgina

Georgy *see* Georgina

Geralda *see* Geraldine

Geraldina *see* Geraldine

Geraldine *(Teutonic)* 'Noble spear-carrier'
Geralda, Geraldina, Gerhardine, Geri, Gerianna, Gerrilee, Gerry, Giralda, Jeraldine, Jeri, Jerri, Jerry

Geranium *(Greek)* 'Bright red flower'

Gerda *(Norse)* 'Protected one'. One who has been brought up strictly
Garda *see also* Gertrude

Gerhardine *see* Geraldine

Geri *see* Geraldine

Gerianna *see* Geraldine

Germain *see* Germaine

Germaine *(French)* 'From Germany'
Germain

Gerrilee *see* Geraldine

Gerry *see* Geraldine

Gert *see* Gertrude

Gertie *see* Gertrude

Gertrud *see* Gertrude

Gertruda *see* Gertrude

Gertrude *(Teutonic)* 'Spear maiden'. One of the Valkyrie
Gartred, Gerda, Gert, Gertie, Gertrud, Gertruda, Gertrudis, Gerty, Trudie, Trudy

Gertrudis *see* Gertrude

Gerty *see* Gertrude

Gervaise *(French from Teutonic)* 'Eager for battle'

Giacinta *see* Hyacinth

Gianina *(Hebrew)* 'The Lord's grace'

Gigi *see* Gilberta

Gilah *(Hebrew)* 'Joy'

Gilberta *(Teutonic)* 'Bright pledge'. Feminine of Gilbert
Gigi, Gilberte, Gilbertha, Gilberthe, Gilbertina, Gilbertine, Gillie, Gilly

Gilberte *see* Gilberta

Gilbertha *see* Gilberta

Gilberthe *see* Gilberta

Gilbertina *see* Gilberta

Gilbertine *see* Gilberta

Gilda *(Celtic)* 'God's servant'

Gill *see* Gillian

Gillian *(Latin)* 'Young nestling'
Gill, Gillie, Jill, Jillian, Jillie *see also* Juliana

Gillie *see* Gilberta or Gillian

Gilly *see* Gilberta

Gina *see* Eugenia or Regina

Ginerva *see* Guinevere or Geneva

Ginette *see* Genevieve

Ginger *see* Virginia

Ginnie *see* Virginia

Ginny *see* Virginia

Giorsal *see* Grace

Giralda *see* Geraldine

Girogia *see* Georgina

Gisela *see* Giselle

Gisele *see* Giselle

Gisella *see* Giselle

Giselle *(Teutonic)* 'A promise'. One who stands as a pledge for her family
Gisela, Gisele, Gisella, Gizela

Gita *(Hindi)* 'Song'

Gitana *(Spanish)* 'The gypsy' *see also* Tizane

Githa *see* Gytha

Gittle *(Hebrew)* 'Innocent flatterer'
Gytle

Gizela *see* Giselle

Glad *see* Gladys

Gladdie *see* Gladys

Gladine *see* Gladys

Gladis *see* Gladys

Gladys *(Celtic)* 'Frail, delicate flower'
Glad, Gladdie, Gladine, Gladis, Gleda, Gwladys, Gwyladys *see also* Claudia

Gleda *(Anglo-Saxon)* Old English version of Gladys *see also* Gladys

Glenda *see* Glenna

Glenine *see* Glenna

Glenn *see* Glenna

Glenna *(Celtic)* 'From the valley'. One of the oldest names on record
Glenda, Glenine, Glenn, Glennis, Glynis

Glennis *see* Glenna

Glenys *(Welsh)* 'Holy'

Glinys *(Welsh)* 'Little valley'

Gloire *see* Gloria

Glori *see* Gloria

Gloria *(Latin)* 'Glorious one'. An illustrious person. This name was often used of Queen Elizabeth I of Britain by her sycophantic courtiers
Gloire, Glori, Gloriana, Gloriane, Glorianna, Glorianne, Glory

Gloriana *see* Gloria

Gloriane *see* Gloria

Glorianna *see* Gloria

Glorianne *see* Gloria

Glory *see* Gloria

Glynis *see* Glenna

Goda *see* Guda

Godgifu *see* Godiva

Godine *(Teutonic)* 'Friend of God'

Godiva *(Anglo-Saxon)* 'Gift of God'
Godgifu

Golda *see* Goldie

Goldie *(Anglo-Saxon)* 'Pure gold'
Golda, Goldina

Goldina *see* Goldie

Gondoline *(Teutonic)* 'Brave and wise'

Goneril *(Latin)* 'Honoured'

Gorvena *(Teutonic)* 'One who lives in the forest'

Grace *(Latin)* 'The graceful one'
Engacia, Engracia, Giorsal, Gracia, Gracie, Gratiana, Grayce, Grazia

Gracia *see* Grace

Gracie *see* Grace

Gracienne *(Latin)* 'Small one'

Graciosa *(Spanish)* 'Graceful and beautiful'

Graine *(Celtic)* 'Love'

Grainne *(Irish)* 'Love'
Grania

Grania *see* Grainne

Gratiana *see* Grace

Grayce *see* Grace

Grazia *see* Grace

Grazina *(Italian)* 'Grace, charm'

Gredel *(Teutonic)* 'Pearl'

Greer *(Greek)* 'The watchful mother'. The eternal matriarch
Gregoria

Gregoria *see* Greer

Greta *see* Margaret

Gretchen *see* Margaret

Grete *see* Margaret

Grethe *see* Margaret

Grimonia *(Latin)* 'Wise old woman'

Griselda *(Teutonic)* 'Grey heroine'
Griselde, Grishelda, Grishelde, Grishilda, Grishilde, Grizelda, Selda, Zelda

Griselde *see* Griselda

Grishelda *see* Griselda

Grishelde *see* Griselda

Grishilda *see* Griselda

Grishilde *see* Griselda

Grizelda *see* Griselda

Guadalupe *(Arabic)* 'River of black stones'

Guda *(Anglo-Saxon)* 'The good one'
Goda

Gudila *(Teutonic)* 'God is my help'

Gudrid *(Teutonic)* 'Divine impluse'

Gudrun (German) 'War' or rune'

Guenevere *see* Guinevere

Guenna *see* Guinevere or Gwendoline

Guida *(Latin)* 'The guide'

Guilla *see* Wilhelmina

Guinevere *(Celtic)* 'White phantom'
Gaynor, Ginerva, Guenna, Guinivere, Guenevere, Gwenhwyvar, Jennifer
see also Genevieve

Guinivere *see* Guinevere

Gundred *(Teutonic)* 'Courageous and wise'

Gunhilda *(Norse)* 'Warrior maid'
Gunhilde

Gunhilde *see* Gunhilda

Gussie *see* Augusta or Gustava

Gussy *see* Gustava

Gusta *see* Augusta

Gustava *(Scandinavian)* 'Staff of the Goths'
Gussie, Gussy, Gustave

Gustave *see* Gustava

Gwen *see* Gwendoline

Gwenda *see* Gwendoline

Gwendolen *see* Gwendoline

Gwendolene *see* Gwendoline

Gwendoline *(Celtic)* 'White-browed maid'
Guenna, Gwenda, Gwendolen, Gwendolene, Gwendolyn, Gwendolyne, Gwen, Gwennie, Gwyn, Wendy

Gwendolyn *see* Gwendoline

Gwendolyne *see* Gwendoline

Gwendydd *(Welsh)* 'Morning star'

Gweneal *(Celtic)* 'White angel'

Gweneira *(Welsh)* 'White snow'

Gwenhwyvar *see* Guinevere

Gwenllian *(Welsh)* 'Fair, flaxen'

Gwennie *see* Gwendoline

Gwennol *(Welsh)* 'Swallow'

Gwenog *(Welsh)* 'Smiling one'

Gwenonwyn *(Welsh)* 'Lily of the valley'

Gwladys *see* Gladys

Gwyladys *see* Gladys

Gwylfai *(Welsh)* May festival

Gwyn *see* Gwendoline

Gwyneth *(Welsh)* 'Blessed'

Gwynne (Old Welsh) 'White or fair one'

Gyda *(Teutonic)* 'Gift'

Gypsy *(Anglo-Saxon)* 'The wanderer'
Gipsy *see also* Gitana

Gytha *(Anglo-Saxon)* 'Warlike'
Githa

Gytle *see* Gittle

GIRLS

Habiba *(Sanskrit)* 'Beloved'

Hadria *see* Adrienne

Hadwisa *see* Avice

Hafwen *(Welsh)* 'Summer-beautiful'

Hagar *(Hebrew)* 'Forsaken'

Haidee *(Greek)* 'Modest, honoured'. A girl well-known for her natural modesty

Hailey *see* Hayley

Halcyon *see* Halcyone

Halcyone *(Greek)* 'The kingfisher'. The mythological Greek who was turned into a bird when she drowned herself
Halcyon

Haldana *(Norse)* 'Half Danish'

Haldis *(Teutonic)* 'Resolute'

Haleigh *see* Haley

Halette *see* Hallie

Haley *(Scandinavian)* 'Hero'
Haleigh

Halfreida *see* Halfrida

Halfrida *(Teutonic)* 'Peaceful heroine'. A diplomat not a warrior
Halfreida, Halfrieda, Hallie, Halliee, Freida, Frida, Frieda *see also* Freda

Halfrieda *see* Halfrida

Hali *see* Hallie

Halima *(Arabic)* 'Kind, humane'

Halimeda *(Greek)* 'Sea thoughts'. One who is drawn to the sea
Hallie, Meda

Halla *(African)* 'Unexpected gift'

Halley *see* Hallie

Hallie *(Greek)* 'Thinking of the sea'
Halette, Hali, Halley *see also* Halfrida or Halimeda

Halliee *see* Halfrida

Halona *(Native American)* 'Fortunate'

Hameline *(Teutonic)* 'Homely'

Hana *(Japanese)* 'Flower' Hanako

Hanako *see* Hana

Hannah *(Hebrew)* 'Full of grace'

Hanusia *(Hebrew)* 'Grace of the Lord

Happy *(English)* 'Happy'

Haracia *see* Horatia

Haralda *(Norse)* 'Army ruler'. Feminine of Harold Haraldina, Harolda, Haroldina

Haraldina *see* Haralda

Harika *(Turkish)* 'Most beautiful'

Harlene *see* Harley

Harley *(Old English)* 'From the long field' Harlene, Harlie

Harlie *see* Harley

Harmonia *see* Harmony

Harmonie *see* Harmony

Harmony *(Latin)* 'Concord and harmony' Harmonia, Harmonie

Harolda *see* Haralda

Haroldina *see* Haralda

Harriet *see* Henrietta

Harriette *see* Henriette

Harriot *see* Henriette

Harriotte *see* Henriette

Harshada *(Sanskrit)* 'Joy-bringer'

Harshini *see* Harshita

Harshita *(Sanskrit)* 'Happy' Harshini

Haru *(Japanese)* 'Springtime'

Hasina *(Sanskrit)* 'Beautiful one'

Hasita *(Sanskrit)* 'Laughing one'

Hasna *(Arabic)* 'Beautiful'

Hatsu *(Japanese)* 'First-born'

Hattie *see* Henrietta

Hatty *see* Henriette

Hayfa *(Arabic)* 'Slender'

Hayley *(English)* From the surname Hailey, Haylie *see also* Haley

Haylie *see* Hayley

Hazar *(Arabic)* 'Nightingale'

Hazel *(English)* 'The hazel tree'
Aveline

Heather *(Anglo-Saxon)* 'Flower of the moors'

Hebe *(Greek)* Goddess of Youth

Hedda *(Teutonic)* 'War'. A born fighter
Heddi, Heddy, Hedy

Heddi *see* Hedda

Heddy *see* Hedda

Hedia *(Greek)* 'Pleasing'

Hedva *(Greek)* 'Industrious worker'

Hedwig *(Teutonic)* 'Safe place in time of trouble'

Hedy *see* Hedda

Heera *(Sanskrit)* 'Diamond'

Heidi *see* Hilda

Heidy *see* Hilde

Helbona *(Hebrew)* 'Fruitful'

Helen *(Greek)* 'Light'. According to tradition, the most beautiful woman, Helen of Troy. There are so many variations of this name that it is not possible to list them all, but we have included a representative selection
Aileen, Aisleen, Alena, Alleen, Eileen, Elaine, Elane, Eleanor, Eleanore, Elena, Elenora, Elenore, Elinor, Elinora, Elinore, Ella, Ellen, Ellene, Ellyn, Galina, Helena, Helene, Ileane, Ilena, Illonna, Illone, Ilona, Isleen, Lana, Lena, Lenora, Leona, Leonora, Leonore, Leora, Lina, Lora, Nell, Nora, Norah *see also* Aileen

Helena *see* Helen

Helene *see* Helen

Helga *(Teutonic)* 'Pious, religious and holy' *see also* Olga

Helia *(Greek)* 'Sun'

Helianthe *(Greek)* 'Bright flower, sunflower'

Helice *(Greek)* 'Spiral'
Helixa

Helixa *see* Helice

Helma *(Teutonic)* 'A helmet'
Hilma *see also* Wilhelmina

Heloise *see* Louise

Helonia *(Greek)* 'Marsh lily'

Helsa *(Danish) see* Elizabeth

Helvitia *(Latin)* 'Home on the hill'

Hendrika *see* Henrietta

Henrietta *(Teutonic)* 'Ruler of home and estate'. Feminine of Henry Eiric, Enrica, Etta, Harriet, Harriette, Harriot, Harriotte, Hattie, Hatty, Henriette, Hendrika, Henrika, Hettie, Hetty, Minette, Netie, Netta, Yetta

Henriette *see* Henrietta

Henrika *see* Henrietta

Hephzibah *(Hebrew)* 'My delight'

Hera *(Latin)* 'Queen of the heaven'. The wife of the Greek ruler of heaven, Zeus

Herleva *see* Arlene

Hermia *see* Erma or Hermione

Hermina *see* Erma or Hermione

Herminia *see* Hermione

Hermione *(Greek)* 'Of the earth'. Daughter of Helen of Troy Hermia, Hermina, Hermine, Herminia *see also* Erma

Hermosa *(Spanish)* 'Beautiful'

Hernanda *(Spanish)* 'Adventuring life'

Hero *(Greek)* Mythological lover of Leander

Herta *see* Eartha

Hertha *see* Eartha

Hesper *(Greek)* 'The evening star' Hespera, Hesperia

Hespera *see* Hesper

Hesperia *see* Hesper

Hessy *see* Esther

Hester *see* Esther

Hesther *see* Esther

Hestia *(Greek)* 'A star'

Hettie *see* Henrietta

Hetty *see* Esther, Henrietta or Mehitabel

Heulwen *(Welsh)* 'Sunshine'

Heutte *(Old English)*
'Brilliant'
Huetta, Hugette,
Hughette

Hiberna *(Latin)* 'Girl from
Ireland'
Hibernia

Hibernia *see* Hiberna

Hibiscus *(Latin)* 'The
marshmallow plant'

Hidé *(Japanese)* 'Excellent,
fruitful, superior'

Hidie *see* Hilde

Hilaire *see* Hilary

Hilaria *see* Hilary

Hilary *(Latin)* 'Cheerful
one'. One who is always
happy
Hilaire, Hilaria

Hild *see* Hilda

Hilda *(Teutonic)* 'Battle
maid'. A handmaiden of
the warriors of Valhalla
Heidi, Heidy, Hidie,
Hild, Hilde, Hildie, Hildy

Hildagard *see* Hildegarde

Hilde *see* Hilda

Hildegaard *see* Hildegarde

Hildegarde *(Teutonic)*
'Battle stronghold'
Hildagard, Hildegarde

Hildemar *(Teutonic)* 'Battle
celebrated'

Hildie *see* Hilda

Hildreth *(Teutonic)* 'Battle
adviser'
Hildretha

Hildretha *see* Hildreth

Hildy *see* Hilda

Hilma *see* Helma

Hina *(Hebrew)* 'Female
deer'

Hippolyta *(Greek)* 'Horse
destruction'

Hitty *see* Mehitabel

Holda *(Norse)* 'Muffled'
Holde, Holle, Hulda

Holde *see* Holda

Holle *see* Holda

Hollie *see* Holly

Holly *(Anglo-Saxon)*
'Bringer of good luck'. A
child born during the
Christmas season
Hollie

Honesta *(Latin)*
'Honourable'

Honey *(English)* 'Sweet
one'. A term of
endearment, especially
in the USA *see also*
Honora

Honi *(Hebrew)* 'Gracious'

Honor *see* Honora

Honora *(Latin)* 'Honour'
Honey, Honor,
Honoria, Honour, Nora,
Norah, Noreen, Norine,
Norrey, Norrie, Norry

Honoria *see* Honora

Honour *see* Honora

Hope *(Anglo-Saxon)*
'Cheerful optimism'

Horacia *see* Horatia

Horatia *(Latin)* 'Keeper of
the hours'. Feminine of
Horace
Haracia, Horacia

Hortense *(Latin)* 'Of the
garden'. One with green
fingers
Hortensia

Hortensia *see* Hortense

Hoshi *(Japanese)* 'Star'

Howin (Chinese) 'Loyal
swallow'

Huberta *(Teutonic)*
'Brilliant girl'
Hubertha, Huberthe

Hubertha *see* Huberta

Huberthe *see* Huberta

Huda *(Arabic)* 'Guidance'

Huetta *see* Heutte

Huette *(Anglo-Saxon)*
'Brilliant thinker'.
Feminine of Hugh
Huetta, Hugette

Hugette *see* Heutte or
Huette

Hughette *see* Heutte

Huguette *(Teutonic)*
'Intellectual'

Hulda *see* Holda

Huriyah *(Arabic)* 'Virgin of
paradise'

Hyacinth *(Greek)*
'Hyacinth flower'
Cynthie, Cynthis,
Giacinta, Hyacintha,
Hyacinthia, Jacinth,
Jacintha, Jacinthia,
Jackie, Jakinda

Hyacintha *see* Hyacinth

Hyacinthia *see* Hyacinth

Hypatia *(Greek)* 'Highest'

GIRLS

Ianira *(Greek)* 'Enchantress'

Iantha *see* Ianthe

Ianthe *(Greek)* 'Violet-coloured flower'
Iantha, Ianthina, Janthina, Janthine

Ianthina *see* Ianthe

Icasia *(Greek)* 'Happy'

Ida *(Teutonic)* 'Happy'. The name comes from Mount Ida in Crete, where Jupiter is supposed to have been hidden
Idalina, Idaline, Idalle, Idelea, Idella, Idelle *see also* Idalia or Idelia

Idalia *(Spanish)* 'Sunny' *see also* Ida

Idalina *see* Ida

Idaline *see* Ida

Idalle *see* Ida

Idelea *see* Ida

Idelia *(Teutonic)* 'Noble' *see also* Ida

Idella *see* Ida

Idelle *see* Ida

Idmonia *(Greek)* 'Skilful'

Idonia *see* Iduna

Idonie *see* Iduna

Iduna *(Norse)* 'Lover'. The keeper of the golden apples of youth
Idonia, Idonie

Ierne *(Latin)* 'From Ireland'

Ignacia *see* Ignatia

Ignatia *(Latin)* 'Fiery ardour'. Feminine of Ignatius
Ignacia *see also* Iniga

Ignes *(Latin)* 'Pure'

Ila *(French)* 'From the island'
Ilde

Ilana *(Hebrew)* 'Tree

Ilde *see* Ila

Ileana *(Greek)* 'Of Ilion (Troy)' *see also* Aileen

Ileane *see* Helen

Ilena *see* Helen

Ilene *see* Aileen

Iline *see* Aileen

Ilka (Slavic) 'Flattering'

Illeana *see* Aileen

Illene *see* Aileen

Illona *see* Aileen or Helen

Illone *see* Helen

Ilona *see* Aileen or Helen

Ilsa *see* Ailsa

Ilse *see* Elizabeth

Iluminada (*Spanish*) 'Illuminated'

Ilythia (*Greek*) Goddess of Childbirth

Imalda *see* Imelda

Imani (*Arabic*) 'Believer'

Imelda (*Latin*) 'Wishful' Imalda, Melda

Immaculada (*Spanish*) 'Immaculate conception'

Imogen *see* Imogene

Imogene (*Latin*) 'Image of her mother' Imogen

Imperia *see* Imperial

Imperial (*Latin*) 'Imperial one' Imperia

Ina *see* Agnes

India (*Hindi*) 'From India'

Indira (*Hindi*) 'Beauty' or 'splendid'

Ines *see* Agnes

Inessa *see* Agnes

Inez *see* Agnes

Inga *see* Ingrid

Ingaberg *see* Ingrid

Ingebiorg *see* Ingrid

Ingeborg *see* Ingrid

Inger *see* Ingrid

Ingibiorg *see* Ingrid

Ingrid (*Norse*) 'Hero's daughter'. Child of a warrior Inga, Ingaberg, Ingeborg, Ingebiorg, Inger, Ingibiorg, Ingunna

Ingunna *see* Ingrid

Iniga (*Latin*) 'Fiery ardour' Ignatia

Inocencia (*Spanish*) 'Innocence'

Intisar (*Arabic*) 'Triumph'

Iola (*Greek*) 'Colour of the dawn cloud' Iole

Iolana *(Hawaiian)* 'Soaring like a hawk'

Iolanthe *(Greek)* 'Violet flower'
Eolande, Yolanda, Yolande *see also* Violet

Iole *see* Iola

Iona *see* Ione

Ione *(Greek)* 'Violet-coloured stone'
Iona

Iorwen *(Welsh)* 'Beautiful'

Iphigenia *(Greek)* 'Sacrifice'. In mythology the daughter of the Greek leader Agamemnon. In one myth she was sacrificed to a goddess; in another she was saved

Irena *see* Irene

Irene *(Greek)* 'Peace'. The goddess of peace
Eirena, Eirene, Erena, Irena, Irenna, Irina, Rena, Renata, Rene, Reini, Rennie, Renny

Irenna *see* Irene

Ireta *(Latin)* 'Enraged one'
Irete, Iretta, Irette

Irete *see* Ireta

Irette *see* Ireta

Irina *see* Irene

Iris *(Greek)* 'The rainbow'. The messenger of the gods
Irisa

Irisa *see* Iris

Irma *(Latin)* 'Noble person'
Erma, Erme, Irme, Irmina, Irmine

Irma *(Teutonic)* 'Strong'
Erma, Erme, Irmina, Irmine, Irme

Irme *see* Irma

Irmina *see* Irma

Irmine *see* Irma

Irvetta *see* Irvette

Irvette *(English)* 'Sea friend'
Irvetta

Isa *(Teutonic)* 'Lady of the iron will'. A determined girl

Isabeau *see* Isabel

Isabel *(Hebrew)* Spanish form of Elizabeth
Bel, Bella, Belle, Isabeau, Isabella, Isabelle, Isbel, Ishbel, Isobel, Ysabeau, Ysabel, Ysabella, Ysabelle, Ysobel, Ysobella, Ysobelle *see also* Elizabeth

Isabella *see* Isabel

Isabelle *see* Isabel

Isadora *(Greek)* 'The gift of Isis'
Dora, Dori, Dory, Isadore, Isidora, Isidore, Issie, Issy, Izzy

Isadore *see* Isadora

Isbel *see* Isabel

Iseult *see* Isolde

Ishbel *see* Isabel

Isidora *see* Isadora

Isidore *see* Isabora

Isis *(Egyptian)* 'Supreme goddess'. The Goddess of Fertility

Isla *(Latin/French)* 'Island'

Islamey *(Arabic)* 'Obedient to Allah'

Isleen *see* Aileen or Helen

Ismena *(Greek)* 'Learned'

Isobel *see* Isabel

Isoda *see* Isolde

Isola *(Latin)* 'The isolated one'. A loner

Isolabella *(Combination Isola/Bella)* 'Beautiful lonely one'
Isolabelle

Isolabelle *see* Isolabella

Isolde *(Celtic)* 'The fair one'
Esyllt, Iseult, Isoda, Yseult, Ysolda, Ysolde

Issie *see* Isadora

Issy *see* Isadora

Ita *(Gaelic)* 'Desire for truth'
Ite

Ite *see* Ita

Iva *(French)* 'The yew tree'
Ivanna, Ivanne

Ivanna *see* Iva

Ivanne *see* Iva

Iverna *(Latin)* An old name for Ireland

Ivina *see* Elva

Ivonne *see* Yvonne

Ivory *(Welsh)* 'High-born lady'

Ivy *(English)* 'A vine'. The sacred plant of the ancient religions

Ixia *(Greek)* 'Mistletoe'

Izora *(Arab)* 'Dawn'

Izzy *see* Isadora

GIRLS

Jacenta *see* Jacinda

Jacinda *(Greek)* 'Beautiful and comely'
Jacenta *see also* Hyacinth

Jacinth *see* Hyacinth

Jacintha *see* Hyacinth

Jacinthia *see* Hyacinth

Jackeline *see* Jacqueline

Jackelyn *see* Jacqueline

Jacketta *see* Jacqueline

Jackie *see* Hyacinth or Jacqueline

Jacklyn *see* Jacqueline

Jacky *see* Jacqueline

Jacoba *(Latin)* 'The supplanter'. The understudy who is better than the star
Jacobina, Jacobine

Jacobina *see* Jacoba or Jacqueline

Jacobine *see* Jacoba

Jacqueleine *see* Jacqueline

Jacqueline *(Hebrew)* 'The supplanter'
Jackeline, Jackelyn, Jacketta, Jackie, Jacklyn, Jacky, Jacobina, Jacqueleine, Jacquelyn, Jacquetta, Jacqui, Jamesina, Jaquith

Jacquelyn *see* Jacqueline

Jacquetta *see* Jacqueline

Jacqui *see* Jacqueline

Jada *see* Jade

Jade *(Spanish)* 'Daughter'. A mother's most precious jewel
Jada

Jaea *see* Jaya

Jaffa *(Hebrew)* 'Beautiful'

Jagoda *(Slavonic)* 'Strawberry'

Jahanara *(Sanskrit)* 'Queen of the world'

Jahola *(Hebrew)* 'Dove'

Jaia *see* Jaya

Jaime *(French)* 'I love'
Jaimee, Jaimey,
Jamey, Jamie, Jaymee

Jaimee *see* Jaime

Jaimey *see* Jaime

Jakinda *see* Hyacinth

Jala *(Arabic)* 'Clarity'

Jalaya *(Sanskrit)* 'Lotus
blossom'

Jalila *(Arabic)* 'Great'

Jamesina *see* Jacqueline

Jamey *see* Jaime

Jamie *see* Jaime

Jamila *(Muslim)* 'Beautiful'

Jamuna *(Sanskrit)* 'Holy
river'

Jan *see* Jane

Jana *see* Jane

Jane *(Hebrew)* 'God's gift of
grace'. With Mary, one
of the most
consistently popular
girl's names, with a
huge range of
variations
Jan, Jana, Janet,
Janette, Janetta, Janice,
Janina, Janna, Jayne,
Jaynell, Jean, Jeanette,
Jeanne, Jenda, Jenete,
Jeniece, Joan, Joana,
Joanna, Joanne,
Johanna, Johanne,
Joni, Juana, Juanita,
Nita, Sean, Seon,
Seonaid, Sheena,
Shena, Si,n, Sine,
Sinead, Siobhan,
Yoanna, Zaneta

Janet *see* Jane

Janetta *see* Jane

Janette *see* Jane

Janice *see* Jane

Janina *see* Jane

Janna *see* Jane

Janthina *see* Ianthe

Janthine *see* Ianthe

Jaquith *see* Jacqueline

Jarita *(Hindi)* 'Legendary
bird'

Jarmila *(Slavic)* 'Spring'

Jarvia *(Teutonic)* 'Keen as a
spear'

Jasmin *see* Jasmine

Jasmina *see* Jasmin

Jasmine *(Persian)*
'Fragrant flower'
Jasmin, Jasmina,
Jessamie, Jessamine,
Jessamy, Jessamyn,
Yasmin, Yasmina,
Yasmie

Jaspreet *(Punjabi)* 'Virtuous'
Jasprit

Jasprit *see* Jaspreet

Jawahir *(Arabic)* 'Jewels'

Jaya *(Hindi)* 'Victory'
Jaea, Jaia, Jayla

Jayata *see* Jayati

Jayati *(Sanskrit)*
'Victorious'
Jayata

Jayla *see* Jaya

Jaymee *see* Jaime

Jayne *(Sanskrit)* 'God's
victorious smile' *see
also* Jane

Jaynell *see* Jane

Jean *see* Jane

Jeanette *see* Jane

Jeanne *see* Jane

Jeannette *see* Jane

Jelena *(Greek)* 'Light'

Jemie *see* Jemina

Jemina *(Hebrew)* 'The
dove'. Symbol of peace
Jemie, Jemmie, Mina

Jemmie *see* Jemina

Jena *(Arabic)* 'A small bird'
Genna, Jenna

Jenda *see* Jane

Jenesia *see* Genesia

Jenette *see* Jane

Jeniece *see* Jane

Jenna *see* Jena

Jennifer *see* Genevieve or
Guinevere

Jenny *see* Jennifer

Jeraldine *see* Geraldine

Jeremia *(Hebrew)* 'The
Lord's exalted'.
Feminine of Jeremiah
Jeri, Jerrie, Jerry

Jeri *see* Geraldine or
Jeremia

Jeroldine *see* Geraldine

Jerri *see* Geraldinc

Jerrie *see* Jeremia

Jerry *see* Geraldine or
Jeremia

Jerusha *(Hebrew)* 'The
married one'. The
perfect wife
Yerusha

Jessalyn *see* Jessica

Jessamie *see* Jasmin

Jessamine *see* Jasmin

Jessamy *see* Jasmin

Jessamyn *see* Jasmin

Jessica *(Hebrew)* 'The rich
one'
Jessalyn

103

Jessie *(Hebrew)* 'God's grace'

Jevera *(Hebrew)* 'Life'

Jewel *(Latin)* 'Most precious one'. The ornament of the home

Jill *see* Julia or Gillian

Jillian *see* Gillian

Jillie *see* Gillian

Jinny *see* Virginia

Jinx *(Latin)* 'Charming spell'. A girl who can enchant others with her beauty and grace Jynx

Jo *see* Josephine

Joakima *(Hebrew)* 'The Lord's judge' Joachima

Joan *see* Jane

Joana *see* Jane

Joanna *see* Jane

Joanne *see* Jane

Jobina *(Hebrew)* 'The afflicted'. 'Persecuted'. Feminine of Job Joby, Jobyna

Jobyna *see* Jobina

Jocasta *(Greek)* 'Shining moon'

Joccoaa *(Latin)* 'The humorous one'. Girl with a lively wit

Jocelin *see* Jocelyn

Joceline *see* Jocelyn

Jocelyn *(Latin)* 'Fair and just'. Feminine of Justin Jocelin, Joceline, Jocelyne, Joscelin, Josceline, Joscelyn, Joscelyne, Joselen, Joselene, Joselin, Joseline, Joselyn, Joselyne, Josilen, Josilene, Josilin, Josiline, Josilyn, Josilyne, Joslin, Josline, Justina, Justine, Lyn, Lynne

Jocelyne *see* Jocelyn

Jocunda *(Latin)* 'Full of happiness'

Jodette *(Latin)* 'Active and sporty'

Jodie *see* Judith

Jody *see* Judith

Joelle *(Hebrew)* 'The Lord is willing'

Joette *see* Josephine

Jofrid *(Teutonic)* 'Lover of horses'

Johanna *see* Jane

Johanne *see* Jane

Joice *see* Joyce

Joicelin *see* Joyce

Joicelyn *see* Joyce

Jolee *see* Jolie

Joleen *see* Jolene

Jolene *(Middle English)* 'He will increase'
Joleen, Jolyn

Joletta *see* Joliette

Jolie *(French)* 'Pretty'
Jolee, Joly

Joliette *(French)* 'Violet'
Joletta

Joly *see* Jolie

Jolyn *see* Jolene

Joni *see* Jane

Jonquil *(Latin)* From the name of the flower

Jordan *see* Jordana

Jordana *(Hebrew)* 'The descending'
Jordan

Joscelin *see* Jocelyn

Josceline *see* Jocelyn

Joscelyn *see* Jocelyn

Joscelyne *see* Jocelyn

Joselen *see* Jocelyn

Joselin *see* Jocelyn

Joseline *see* Jocelyn

Joselyn *see* Jocelyn

Joselyne *see* Jocelyn

Josepha *see* Josephine

Josephina *see* Josephine

Josephine *(Hebrew)* 'She shall add'. Feminine of Joseph
Fifi, Jo, Joette, Josepha, Josephina, Josetta, Josette, Josie, Pepita, Yosepha, Yusepha

Josetta *see* Josephine

Josette *see* Josephine

Josie *see* Josephine

Josilen *see* Jocelyn

Josilene *see* Jocelyn

Josilin *see* Jocelyn

Josiline *see* Jocelyn

Josilyn *see* Jocelyn

Josilyne *see* Jocelyn

Joslin *see* Jocelyn

Josline *see* Jocelyn

Jovanna *(Latin)* 'Majestic'

Jovita *(Latin)* 'The joyful one'. The feminine of Jove. Bringer of jollity

Joy *see* Joyce

Joyce *(Latin)* 'Gay and joyful'
Joice, Joicelin,
Joicelyn, Joy, Joycelin,
Joycelyn, Joyous

Joycelin *see* Joyce

Joycelyn *see* Joyce

Joyous *see* Joyce

Juana *see* Jane or June

Juanita *see* Jane

Judie *see* Judith

Judith *(Hebrew)* 'Admired,
praised'. One whose
praises cannot be over
emphasised
Jodie, Jody, Judie,
Juditha, Judy, Siobhan,
Siuban

Juditha *see* Judith

Judy *see* Judith

Julia *(Greek)* 'Youthful'.
Young in heart and mind
Jill, Juli, Juliana,
Juliane, Julianna,
Julianne, Julie, Juliet,
Julietta, Julina, Juline,
Sile, Sileas

Juliana *see* Julia

Juliane *see* Julia

Julianna *see* Julia

Julianne *see* Julia

Julie *see* Julia

Juliet *see* Julia

Julietta *see* Julia

Julina *see* Julia

Juline *see* Julia

Jumanah *(Arabic)* 'Pearl'

Jun *(Chinese)* 'Truthful'

Juna *see* June

June *(Latin)* 'Summer's
child'. One born in the
early summer
Juana, Juna, Junia,
Juniata, Junette,
Junine

Junette *see* June

Junia *see* June

Juniata *see* June

Junine *see* June

Junko *(Japanese)*
'Obedient'

Juno *(Latin)* 'Heavenly
being'. The wife of
Jupiter, Greek ruler of
the heavens

Jurisa *(Slavonic)* 'Storm'

Justina *see* Jocelyn

Justine *see* Jocelyn

Jutta *(Latin)* 'Near'

Jyoti *(Hindi)* 'Light'

Jyotsna *(Sanskrit)*
'Moonlight'

Kabira *(Arabic)* 'Powerful'

Kachina *(Native American)* 'Sacred dance'

Kaela *(Hebrew)* 'Sweetheart'
Kaelah, Kayla, Kaylah, Keyla, Keylah

Kaelah *see* Kaela

Kagami *(Japanese)* 'Mirror'

Kahuna *see* Kaulana

Kai *(Hawaiian)* 'Sea'

Kairos *(Greek)* 'Goddess born last to Jupiter'

Kaitlyn *see* Catherine

Kaja *see* Kaya

Kala *(Hindi)* 'Black' or 'time'

Kalama *(Native American)* 'Wild goose'

Kalamit *(Hebrew)* 'Flower'

Kalantha *see* Calantha

Kalanthe *see* Calantha

Kaldora *(Greek)* 'Lovely gift'

Kaleena *see* Kalinda

Kali *(Sanskrit)* 'Energy'

Kalika *(Sanskrit)* 'A bud'

Kalila *(Arabic)* 'Beloved'
Kally, Kaylee, Kylila

Kalinda *(Sanskrit)* 'Sun'
Kaleena, Kalindi

Kalindi *see* Kalinda

Kallista *see* Calista

Kallisto *see* Calista

Kally *see* Kalila

Kalma *(Teutonic)* 'Calm'

Kalonice *(Greek)* 'Beauty's victory'

Kalwa *(Finnish)* 'Heroic'

Kalya *(Sanskrit)* 'Healthy'

Kalyana *(Sanskrit)* 'Virtuous one'

Kalyca *(Greek)* 'Rosebud'

Kalypso *see* Calypso

Kam *see* Cam

Kama *(Sanskrit)* 'Love'. The Hindu god of love, like Cupid

Kamakshi *(Sanskrit) see* Kamalakshi

Kamalakshi *(Sanskrit)* 'Girl whose eyes are as beautiful as the lotus flower'
Kamakshi

Kamama *(Native American)* 'Butterfly'

Kamana *(Sanskrit)* 'Desire'

Kameko *(Japanese)* 'Child of the tortoise'. The tortoise is a symbol of long life

Kamila *see* Kamilah

Kamilah *(Arabic)* 'The perfect one'
Kamila

Kamra *(Arabic)* 'Moon'

Kanaka *see* Canace

Kanakabati *(Sanskrit)* 'Fairy-tale princess'

Kanake *see* Canace

Kanda *(Native American)* 'Magical power'

Kane *(Japanese)* 'Ambidextrous'

Kanya *(Thai)* 'Young lady'

Kara *see* Cara or Katherine

Karabel *(Spanish)* 'Lovely face'

Karen *see* Katherine

Karena *see* Katherine

Karima *(Arabic)* 'Generous'

Karin *see* Katherine

Karina *see* Cara or Carina

Karita *see* Carita

Karma *(Sanskrit)* 'Destiny'

Karyn *see* Katherine

Kasia *(Greek)* 'Pure'

Kasmira *(Slavic)* 'Commands peace'
Casmira

Kassandra *see* Cassandra

Kate *see* Catherine or Katherine

Katerine *see* Catherine

Kateryn *see* Catherine

Katharina *see* Catherine or Katherine

Katharine *see* Catherine or Katherine

Katherina *see* Catherine or Katherine

Katherine *(Greek)* 'Pure maiden'
Kara, Karen, Karena, Karin, Karyn, Kate, Katharina, Katharine, Katherina, Katheryn, Kathie, Kathleen,

Kathlene, Kathryn,
Kathy, Katie, Katrin,
Katrina, Katrine,
Katryn, Kay, Ketti,
Kitty *see also* Catherine

Katheryn *see* Katherine

Kathie *see* Katherine

Kathleen *see* Katherine

Kathlene *see* Katherine

Kathryn *see* Catherine or
Kathcrinc

Kathy *see* Katherine

Katie *see* Catherine or
Katherine

Katrin *see* Katherine

Katrina *see* Catherine or
Katherine

Katrine *see* Catherine or
Katherine

Katryn *see* Katherine

Katy *see* Catherine

Kaula *see* Kaulana

Kaulana *(Hawaiian)*
'Famous'
Kaula, Kauna, Kahuna

Kaumudi *(Sanskrit)*
'Moonlight'

Kauna *see* Kaulana

Kavita *(Sanskrit)* 'A poem'

Kay *see* Katherine

Kaya *(Japanese)* 'Resting
place'
Kaja, Kayia

Kayia *see* Kaya

Kayla *(Hebrew)* 'Crown'

Kayla *see* Cayla

Kayla *see* Kaela

Kaylah *see* Kaela

Kaylee *see* Kalila

Kayleigh *(Modern from
Arabic)* 'Beloved'.
Modern name derived
from Kalila

Kazia *see* Keziah

Keara *(Irish)* 'Dark'
Kiara

Keely *(Gaelic)* 'The
beautiful one'

Keena *(Irish)* 'Brave'
Kccnya, Kina

Keenya *see* Keena

Kei *(Japanese)* 'Reverent'
Keiana, Keikann,
Keikanna, Keionna

Keiana *see* Kei

Keikann *see* Kei

Keikann *see* Kei

Keikanna *see* Kei

Keiko *(Japanese)* 'Happy
child'

Keile *(Hawaiian)* 'Gardenia blossom'
Kiela, Kieli

Keionna *see* Kei

Kelci *see* Kelsey

Kelda *(Norse)* 'Bubbling spring'
Kelly

Kelila *(Hebrew)* 'Crown, laurel'
Kelula

Kellina *see* Kelly

Kelly *(Irish Gaelic)* 'Warrior maid'
Kellina *see also* Kelda

Kelosia *see* Celosia

Kelsey *(Scandinavian)* 'From the island of the ships'
Kelci, Kelsi, Kesley

Kelsi *see* Kelsey

Kelsie *(Scottish)* Scottish form of Chelsea
Kelula Kelila

Kendall *(English)* 'Ruler of the valley'
Kendell, Kendyll

Kendell *see* Kendall

Kendra *(Old English)* 'Knowledgeable'
Kenna

Kendyll *see* Kendall

Kenna *see* Kendra

Kenzie *(Scottish)* 'Light-skinned'

Keren *(Hebrew)* 'Horn of antimony'

Kerri *see* Kerry

Kerrianne *see* Kerry

Kerridwen *see* Ceiridwen

Kerry *(Gaelic)* 'Dark one'
Kerri, Kerrianne

Keshena *(Native American)* 'Swift in flight'

Keshina *(Sanskrit)* 'Girl with beautiful hair'

Kesi *(Swahili)* 'Born during difficult times'

Kesia *(African)* 'Favourite'

Kesley *see* Kelsey

Kessie *(Ashanti)* 'Chubby baby'

Ketti *see* Katherine

Ketura *(Hebrew)* 'Incense'

Kevin *(Gaelic)* 'Gentle and lovable'
Kelvina, Kevyn

Kevina *see* Kevin

Kevyn *see* Kevin

Keyla *see* Kaela

Keylah *see* Kaela

Keyne *(Celtic)* 'Jewel'

Kezia *see* Keziah

Keziah *(Hebrew)* 'Like cinnamon'
Kezia

Khalida *(Arabic)* 'Immortal, everlasting'

Khalipha *(Arabic)* 'Successor'

Ki *(Korean)* 'Arisen'

Kia *(African)* 'The beginning of the season'

Kiah *(African)* 'Season's beginning'

Kiara *see* Keara

Kiela *see* Kiele

Kieli *see* Kiele

Kiku *(Japanese)* 'Chrysanthemum'

Kilah *see* Kyla

Kim *(Origin not known)* 'Noble chief'

Kimberley *(English)* 'From the royal meadow'
Kimberlyn, Kimbra

Kimberlyn *see* Kimberley

Kimbra *see* Kimberley

Kimi *(Japanese)* 'Righteous'
Kimia, Kimiko

Kimia *see* Kimi

Kimiko *see* Kimi

Kina *see* Keena

Kina *(Greek)* 'Christian'

Kineta *(Greek)* 'Active and elusive'

Kinnereth *(Hebrew)* 'From the Sea of Galilee'

Kinsey *(English)* 'Relative'

Kiona *(Native American)* 'Brown hills'

Kira *(Persian)* 'Sun'

Kirbee *see* Kirby

Kirbie *see* Kirby

Kirby *(Old English)* 'From the church town'
Kirbee, Kirbie

Kirima *(Eskimo)* 'A hill'

Kirsten *see* Kirstin

Kirstie *see* Kirstin

Kirstin *(Norse)* 'The annointed one'
Kirsten, Kirstie, Kirstina, Kirsty, Kirstyn

Kirstina *see* Kirstin

Kirsty *see* Kirstin

Kirstyn *see* Kirstin

Kishi *(Japanese)* 'Long and happy life'

Kit *see* Catherine

Kita *(Japanese)* 'North'

Kitty *see* Catherine or Katherine

Kloe *see* Chloe

Kohana *(Japanese)* 'Little flower'

Kolfinna *(Celtic)* 'Cool, white lady'

Kolina *(Greek)* 'Pure'

Kolotosa *(Native American)* 'Star'

Komal *see* Komala

Komala *(Sanskrit)* 'Charming', 'tender' Komal

Kora *(Greek)* 'Young girl, maiden' Korella, Koressa

Korella *see* Kora

Koren *(Greek)* 'Beautiful maiden'

Koressa *see* Kora

Koto *(Japanese)* 'Harp'

Kotsasi *(Native American)* 'White flower'

Krishna *(Sanskrit)* Hindu god

Kristabel *see* Christabel

Kristabella *see* Christabel

Kristabelle *see* Christabel

Kristen *see* Christine

Krystal *see* Crystal

Krystina *see* Christine

Kuki *(Japanese)* 'Snow'

Kundanika *(Sanskrit)* 'Flower'

Kuni *(Japanese)* 'Born in the countryside'

Kuntal *see* Kuntala

Kuntala *(Sanskrit)* 'Girl with beautiful hair' Kuntal

Kurva *(Japanese)* 'Mulberry tree'

Kwai *(Chinese)* 'Rose-scented'

Kyla *(Gaelic)* 'Pretty one' Kilah, Kylah, Kylie

Kylah *see* Kyla

Kylie *see* Kyla

Kylila *see* Kalila

Kylynn *see* Kyle

Kyna *(Gaelic)* 'Great wisdom'

Kyoko *(Japanese)* 'Mirror'

Kyrenia *see* Cyrena

La Roux *(French)* 'The red-haired one'
Larousse, Roux

Labhaoise *see* Louise

Labiba *(Arabic)* 'Wise'

Lacee *see* Larissa

Lacey *see* Larissa

Lacinia *see* Lucy

Lada *(Russian)*
'Mythological goddess of beauty'

Ladonna *(French)* 'The lady'

Laetitia *see* Letitia

Laila *see* Layla

Laina *see* Lane

Lainey *see* Elaine

Lakia *(Arabic)* 'Discovered treasure'

Lala *(Slavic)* 'The tulip flower'

Lalage *(Greek)* 'Gentle laughter'

Lalan *(Sanskrit) see* Lalana

Lalana *(Sanskrit)* 'Beautiful one'
Lalan

Laleh *(Persian)* 'Tulip'

Lalit *see* Lalita

Lalita *(Sanskrit)* 'Beautiful', 'without guile'
Lalit

Lallie *see* Eulalia

Lalota *(Sanskrit)* 'Pleasing'

Lamya *(Arabic)* 'Dark lips'

Lana *see* Alana or Helen

Lane *(Middle English)*
'From the narrow road'

Lanelle *(Old French)* 'From the little lane'

Lanetta *see* Alana

Lanette *(French) see* Alana

Lani *(Hawaiian)* 'The sky'

Lara *(Latin)* 'Famous'

Laraine *see* Lorraine

Larayne *see* Lorraine

Lareena *see* Larine

Larene *see* Larine

Larentia *(Latin)* 'Foster mother'
Laurentia

Larianna *see* Larine

Larina *see* Lorraine

Larine *(Latin)* 'Girl of the sea'
Lareena, Larene, Larianna *see also* Lorraine

Laris *see* Larissa

Larissa *(Greek)* 'Cheerful maiden'. One who is as happy as a lark
Lacee, Lacey, Laris

Lark *(English)* 'Singing bird'

Larousse *see* La Roux

Larraine *see* Lorraine

Lasca *(Latin)* 'Weary one'

Lassie *(Scottish)* 'Little girl'

Latona *see* Latonia

Latonia *(Latin)* 'Belonging to Latona'. The mother of the Greek goddess Diana
Latona, Latoya

Latoya *see* Latonia

Laura *(Latin)* 'Laurel wreath'. The victor's crown of laurels
Laure, Laureen, Laurel, Lauren, Laurena, Laurene, Lauretta, Laurette, Laurie, Lora, Loralie, Loree, Lorelie, Loren, Lorena, Lorene, Lorenza, Loretta, Lorette, Lori, Lorie, Lorinda, Lorine, Lorita, Lorna, Lorne, Lorrie

Laure *see* Laura

Laureen *see* Laura

Laurel *see* Laura

Lauren *(Latin)* 'Laurel wreath'. Familiar form of Laura

Laurena *see* Laura

Laurene *see* Laura

Laurentia *see* Larentia

Lauretta *see* Laura

Laurette *see* Laura

Laurie *see* Laura

Laveda *(Latin)* 'One who is purified'
Lavetta, Lavette

Lavelle *(Latin)* 'Cleansing'

Lavena *(Celtic)* 'Joy'

Lavender *(English)* 'Sweet-smelling flower'
Lavvie

Laverna *see* Laverne

Laverne *(French)* 'Spring-like' or 'alder tree'
Laverna, Vern, Verna, Verne

Lavetta *see* Laveda

Lavette *see* Laveda

Lavina *see* Lavinia

Lavinia *(Latin)* 'Lady of Rome'
Lavina, Vina, Vinia

Lavvie *see* Lavender

Layla *(Arabic)* 'Night'
Laila *see also* Leila

Layne *see* Lane

Lea *see* Leah

Leah *(Hebrew)* 'The weary one'
Lea, Lee, Leigh

Leala *(French)* 'The true one'. One who is true to home, family and friends

Leana *see* Liana

Leandra *(Latin)* 'Like a lioness'
Leodora, Leoline, Leonelle

Leane *see* Liana

Leanna *see* Lee or Liana

Leanor *see* Eleanor

Leatrice *(Hebrew)* 'Tired but joyful'. Combination of Leah and Beatrice
Leatrix

Leatrix *see* Leatrice

Lechsinska *(Polish)* 'Woodland spirit'

Leda *(Greek)* 'Mother of beauty'. The mother of Helen of Troy *see also* Alida, Letha or Letitia

Lee *(English)* 'From the fields'. Also a variation of Leah
Leanna, Leeann *see also* Leah or Leila

Leeann *see* Lee

Leela *see* Leila

Leena *(Sanskrit)* 'Devoted one'

Lefa *(Teutonic)* 'The heart of the tree'

Leigh *(Old English)* 'From the meadow' *see also* Leah

Leila *(Arabic)* 'Black as the night'
Layla, Lee, Leela, Leilah, Leilia, Lela, Lila, Lilah, Lilia *see also* Lilian

Leilah *see* Leila

Leilani *(Hawaiian)*
'Heavenly blossom'.
The tropical flower of
the islands
Lillani, Lullani

Leilia *see* Leila

Leithia *see* Letha

Lela *see* Leila or Lilian

Lelah *see* Lilian

Lelia *see* Lilian

Lemma *(Ethiopian)*
'Developed'

Lemuela *(Hebrew)*
'Dedicated to God'. A
daughter dedicated to
the service of God
Lemuella

Lemuella *see* Lemuela

Lena *(Latin)* 'Enchanting
one'
Lenette, Lina *see also*
Caroline, Helen,
Madeleine or Selena

Lene *see* Lenis

Leneta *see* Lenis

Lenette *see* Lena

Lenis *(Latin)* 'Smooth and
white as the lily'
Lene, Leneta, Lenita,
Lenta, Lenos

Lenita *see* Lenis

Lennie *see* Leona

Lenny *see* Leona

Lenora *see* Eleanor or
Helen

Lenore *see* Eleanor

Lenos *see* Lenis

Lenta *see* Lenis

Lentula *(Celtic)* 'Gentle one

Leocadia *(Spanish from
Greek)* 'Lion-like'

Leoda *(Teutonic)* 'Woman of
the people'
Leola, Leota

Leodora *see* Leandra

Leola *see* Leoda or Leona

Leoline *see* Leandra

Leoma *(Anglo-Saxon)*
'Bright light'. One who
casts radiance around
her

Leona *(Latin)* 'The lioness'
Lennie, Lenny, Leola,
Leone, Leonelle, Leoni,
Leonie *see also* Helen

Leonarda *(French)* 'Like a
lion'
Leonarde, Leonardina,
Leonardine

Leonarde *see* Leonarda

Leonardina *see* Leonarda

Leonardine *see* Leonarda

Leone *see* Leona

Leonelle *see* Leandra or Leona

Leoni *see* Leona

Leonie *see* Leona

Leonora *see* Eleanor or Helen

Leonore *see* Eleanor or Helen

Leontina *see* Leontine

Leontine *(Latin)* 'Like a lion'
Leontina, Leontyne

Leontyne *see* Leontine

Leopolda *see* Leopoldina

Leopoldina *(Teutonic)* 'The people's champion'. Feminine of Leopold
Leopolda, Leopoldine

Leopoldine *see* Leopoldina

Leor *(Hebrew)* 'I have light'

Leora *(Greek)* 'Light' *see also* Helen

Leota *see* Leoda

Les *see* Lesley

Lesham *(Hebrew)* 'Precious stone'

Leshia *see* Letitia

Lesley *(Celtic)* 'Keeper of the grey fort'
Les, Lesli, Leslie, Lesly

Lesli *see* Lesley

Leslie *see* Lesley

Leta *see* Letha or Letitia

Letha *(Greek)* 'Sweet oblivion'. Lethe was the river of forgetfulness in Greek mythology
Leda, Leta, Leithia, Lethia, Lethitha

Lethia *see* Letha

Lethitha *see* Letha

Leticia *see* Letitia

Letisha *see* Letitia

Letitia *(Latin)* 'Joyous gladness'
Laetitia, Leda, Leshia, Leta, Leticia, Letisha, Letizia, Lettice, Lettie, Loutitia, Tish

Letizia *see* Letitia

Lettice *see* Letitia

Lettie *see* Letitia

Levana *(Latin)* 'The sun of the dawn'. The goddess of childbirth
Levania

Levania *see* Levana

Levina *(English)* 'A bright flash'. One who passes like a comet

Lewanna *(Hebrew)* 'As pure as the white moon'
Luanna

Lexie *see* Alexandra

Lexine *see* Alexandra

Leya *(Spanish)* 'Loyalty to the law'. A strict upholder of morals and principles

Leyla *(Turkish)* 'Born at night'

Lia *(Greek)* 'The bringer of good news'

Lian *(Chinese)* 'The graceful willow'

Liana *(French)* 'The climbing vine'
Leana, Leane, Leanna, Lianna, Lianne

Lianna *see* Liana

Lianne *see* Liana

Libb *see* Elizabeth

Libby *see* Elizabeth

Liberata *(Latin)* 'Freed'

Libusa *(Russian)* 'Beloved'

Lida *(Slavic)* 'Beloved of the people'

Lidia *see* Lydia

Lidie *see* Lydia

Lien *(Chinese)* 'Lotus blossom'
Lienne

Lienne *see* Lien

Ligia *(Greek)* 'Silver voice'

Lila *see* Delilah, Leila or Lilian

Lilac *(Persian)* 'Dark mauve flower'

Lilah *see* Leila

Lilais *see* Lilian

Lili *see* Lilian

Lilia *see* Leila or Lilian

Lilian *(Latin)* 'A lily'. One who is pure in thought, word and deed
Lela, Lelah, Lelia, Leila, Lila, Lilah, Lilais, Lili, Lilia, Liliana, Liliane, Lilias, Lilla, Lilli, Lillian, Liliana, Lilliane, Lillis, Lily, Lilly, Lilyan, Lillyan

Liliana *see* Lilian

Liliane *see* Lilian

Lilias *see* Lilian

Lilith *(Arabic)* 'Woman of the night'. According to Eastern belief, Lilith was the first wife of Adam and the first woman in the world; Eve was his second wife

Lilla *see* Lilian

Lilli *see* Lilian

Lillian *see* Lilian

Lilliana *see* Lilian

Lilliane *see* Lilian

Lillis *see* Lilian

Lilly *see* Lilian

Lillyan *see* Lilian

Lily *see* Lilian

Lilyan *see* Lilian

Lin *(Chinese)* 'Beautiful jade'

Lina *see* Caroline, Helen or Lena

Lind *see* Linda

Linda *(Spanish)* 'Pretty one'. Also diminutive of Belinda, Rosalinda, etc Lind, Linde, Lindie, Lindy, Lynd, Lynda *see also* Belinda

Linde *see* Linda

Lindie *see* Belinda or Linda

Lindsay *(Old English)* 'From the linden tree island' Lindsey

Lindsey *see* Lindsay

Lindy *see* Belinda or Linda

Line *see* Caroline

Linetta *see* Linnet

Linette *see* Linnet

Ling *(Chinese)* 'Delicate' or 'dainty'

Linnea *(Norse)* 'The lime blossom' Lynnea

Linnet *(French)* 'Sweet bird' Linetta, Linette, Linnetta, Linnette, Lynette, Lynnette

Linnetta *see* Linnet

Linnette *see* Linnet

Liorah *(Hebrew)* 'I have light'

Lira *(Greek)* 'Lyre'

Liria *(Greek)* 'Tender one'

Lisa *see* Elizabeth or Melissa

Lisandra *(Greek)* Feminine variation of Alexander

Lisbeth *see* Elizabeth

Lisha *(Arabic)* 'The darkness before midnight'
Lishe

Lishe *see* Lisha

Lissie *see* Alida

Lita *see* Alida

Liusade *see* Louise

Livi *see* Olga

Livia *see* Olga or Olive

Livie *see* Olga

Livvi *see* Olga

Liyna *(Arabic)* 'Tender'

Liza *see* Elizabeth

Lizabeta *see* Elizabeth

Lizbeth *see* Elizabeth

Lizzy *see* Elizabeth

Llawela *(Welsh)* 'Like a ruler'
Llawella

Llawella *see* Llawela

Lodema *(English)* 'Leader or guide'

Lodie *see* Melody

Loella *see* Luella

Logan *(Celtic)* 'Little hollow'

Loietu *(Native American)* 'Flower'

Lois *see* Louise

Lola *(Spanish)* 'Strong woman'
Loleta, Lolita, Lollie, Lulita *see also* Dolores or Theola

Loleta *see* Lola

Lolita *see* Dolores or Lola

Lollie *see* Lola

Lomasi *(Native American)* 'Pretty flower'

Lona *(Anglo-Spanish)* 'Solitary watcher'

Lora *see* Helen or Laura

Loraine *see* Lorraine

Loralie *see* Laura

Loree *see* Laura

Lorelei *(Teutonic)* 'Siren of the river'. The Rhine maiden who lured unwary mariners to their death
Lorelia, Lorelie, Lorilyn, Lurleen

Lorelia *see* Lorelei

Lorelie *see* Lorelei

Lorelle *(Latin/Old German)* 'Little'

Loren *see* Laura

Lorena *see* Laura

Lorene *see* Laura

Lorenza *see* Laura

Loretta *see* Laura

Lorette *see* Laura

Lori *see* Laura

Lorie *see* Laura

Lorilyn *see* Lorelei

Lorinda *see* Laura

Lorine *see* Laura

Loris *see* Chloris

Lorita *see* Laura

Lorna *see* Laura

Lorne *see* Laura

Lorraine *(French)* 'The Queen'
Larina, Larine, Laraine, Larayne, Larraine, Loraine

Lorraine *(Teutonic)* 'Renowned in battle' Loraine, Laraine, Larraine, Larayne, Larine, Larina

Lorrie *see* Laura

Lotus *(Greek)* 'Flower of the sacred Nile'

Louanna *see* Luana

Louanne *see* Luana

Louella *(Teutonic)* 'Shrewd in battle' *see also* Luella

Louisa *see* Louise

Louise *(Teutonic)* 'Famous battle maid'. One who leads victorious armies into battle
Alison, Allison, Aloisa, Aloisia, Aloysia, Eloisa, Eloise, Heloise, Labhaoise, Liusade, Lois, Loise, Louisa, Louisitte, Loyce, Luise

Louisitte *see* Louise

Loutitia *see* Letitia

Love *(English)* 'Tender affection'

Loveday *(English)* 'Reconciliation'

Lowena *(English)* 'Joy'

Loyce *see* Louise

Luana *(Teutonic)* 'Graceful army maiden'
Luane, Louanna, Louanne, Luwana, Luwanna, Luwanne

Luane *see* Luana

Luanna *see* Lewanna

Luba *(Russian)* 'Love' Lubmila

Lubmila *see* Luba

Lubna *(Arabic)* 'Flexible'

Lucette *see* Lucy

Lucia *see* Lucy

Luciana *see* Lucy

Lucianna *(Combination Lucy/Anna)*

Lucida *see* Lucy

Lucie *see* Lucinda

Lucile *see* Lucy

Lucille *see* Lucy

Lucinda *see* Lucy

Lucita *see* Lucy

Lucrece *see* Lucretia

Lucrecia *see* Lucretia

Lucretia *(Latin)* 'A rich reward'.
Lucrece, Lucrecia, Lucrezia

Lucrezia *see* Lucretia

Lucy *(Latin)* 'Light'. One who brings the lamp of learning to the ignorant
Lacinia, Lucette, Lucia, Luciana, Lucida, Lucie, Lucile, Lucille, Lucinda, Lucita, Luighseach, Luisadh

Ludella *(Anglo-Saxon)* 'Pixie maid'

Ludmila *see* Ludmilla

Ludmilla *(Slavic)* 'Beloved of the people'
Ludmila

Luella *(Anglo-Saxon)* 'The appeaser'
Loella, Louella, Luelle

Luelle *see* Luella

Luighseach *see* Lucy

Luisadh *see* Lucy

Lulita *see* Lola

Lulu *(Arabic)* 'Pearl'

Luna *see* Lunetta

Luneda *(Celtic)* 'With a beautiful figure'

Luneta *see* Lunetta

Lunetta *(Latin)* 'Little Moon'
Luna, Luneta

Lupe *(Spanish)* 'She wolf. A fierce guardian of the home

Lura *see* Lurline

Lurleen *see* Lorelei or Lurline

Lurlene *see* Lurline

Lurlette *see* Lurline

Lurlina *see* Lurline

Lurline *(Teutonic)* 'Siren'
Lura, Lurleen, Lurlene, Lurlette, Lurlina *see also* Lorelei

Luvena *(Latin)* 'Little beloved one'

Luwana *see* Luana

Luwanna *see* Luana

Luwanne *see* Luana

Lycoris *(Greek)* 'Twilight'

Lydia *(Greek)* 'Cultured one'
Lidia, Lidie, Lydie

Lydie *see* Lydia

Lyn *see* Jocelyn or Lynette

Lynd *see* Linda

Lynda *see* Linda

Lynette *(English)* 'Idol'
Linnet, Lyn, Lynn, Lynne

Lynn *(Celtic)* 'A waterfall'. Also diminutive of Carolyn, Evelyn, etc
Lynne *see also* Lynette

Lynne *see* Jocelyn or Lynette

Lynnea *see* Linnea

Lynnette *see* Linnet

Lyonelle *(Old French)* 'Young lion'

Lyra *see* Lyris

Lyris *(Greek)* 'She who plays the harp'
Lyra

Lysandra *(Greek)* 'The liberator'. The prototype of feminism

Mab *(Gaelic)* 'Mirthful joy'
Mave, Mavis, Meave

Mabel *(Latin)* 'Amiable and
loving'. An endearing
companion
Mable, Maible,
Maybelle, Moibeal

Mable *see* Mabe

Mackenzie *(Gaelic)*
'Handsome'

Mada *see* Madeleine

Madalaine *see* Madeleine

Madaleine *see* Madeleine

Madalena *see* Madeleine

Madaline *see* Madeleine

Maddalena *see* Madeleine

Maddalene *see* Madeleine

Maddy *see* Madeleine

Madel *see* Madeleine

Madelaine *see* Madeleine

Madeleine *(Greek)* 'Tower
of strength'. A girl of
great physical and
moral courage who will
support others in
difficult times
Lena, Mada, Madalaine,
Madaleine, Madalena,
Madaline, Maddalena,
Maddalene, Maddy,
Madel, Madelaine,
Madelia, Madeline,
Madella, Madelle,
Madelon, Madlin,
Magdaa, Magdala,
Magdalane, Magdalen,
Magdalene, Magdalyn,
Maighdlin, Mala,
Malena, Malina,
Marleen, Marlena,
Marlene, Marline,
Melina

Madelia *see* Madeleine

Madeline *see* Madeleine

Madella *see* Madeleine

Madelle *see* Madeleine

Madelon *see* Madeleine

Madge *see* Margaret

Madhuk *(Sanskrit)* 'Honey bee'

Madhulika *(Sanskrit)* 'Honey'

Madhur *(Hindi)* 'Sweet'
Madhura

Madhur *(Sanskrit)* 'Sweetness'
Madhura, Madhuri

Madhura *see* Madhur

Madhuri *see* Madhur

Madison *(Teutonic)* 'Child of Maud'

Madlin *see* Madeleine

Madona *(Latin)* *'Mother'*

Madora *see* Medea

Madra *(Spanish)* 'Matriarch'

Mady *see* Maida

Mae *see* May

Maeve *(Irish)* The warrior queen of Connaught
Mave, Meave

Mag *see* Magnilda or Magnolia

Magaski *(Native American)* 'White swan'

Magdaa *see* Madeleine

Magdala *see* Madeleine

Magdalane *see* Madeleine

Magdalen *see* Madeleine

Magdalene *see* Madeleine

Magdalyn *see* Madeleine

Magdi *(Arabic)* 'My glory'

Magena *(Native American)* 'The coming moon'

Maggie *see* Magnilda, Magnolia or Margaret

Magnhilda *see* Magnilda

Magnhilde *see* Magnilda

Magnilda *(Teutonic)* 'Great battle maid'
Mag, Maggie, Magnhilda, Magnhilde, Magnilde, Nilda, Nillie

Magnilde *see* Magnilda

Magnolia *(Latin)* 'Magnolia flower'
Mag, Maggie, Nola, Nolie

Maha *(Arabic)* 'Wild oxen'

Mahala *(Hebrew)* 'Tenderness'
Mahalah, Mahalia

Mahalah *see* Mahala

Mahalia *see* Mahala

Mahira *see* Mehira

Maia *see* May

Maida *(Anglo-Saxon)* 'The maiden'
Mady, Maidel, Maidie, Mayda, Mayde, Maydena

Maidel *see* Maida

Maidie *see* Maida

Maighdlin *see* Madeleine

Maigrghread *see* Margaret

Maire *see* Mary

Mairi *see* Mary

Maisie *see* Margaret

Maitilde *see* Mathilda

Majesta *(Latin)* 'Majestic one'

Makala *(Hawaiian)* 'Myrtle'

Makana *(Hawaiian)* 'Gift'

Makani *(Hawaiian)* 'Wind'

Makara *(Hindi)* 'Born under the constellation of Capricorn'

Mala *see* Madeleine

Malan *see* Melanie

Malena *see* Madeleine

Malika *(Sanskrit)* 'Garland of flowers'

Malina *see* Madeleine

Malinda *see* Melinda

Malini *(Hindi)* 'Gardener'

Malise *(Gaelic)* 'Servant of God'

Malita *see* Melita

Mallika *(Sanskrit)* 'Jasmine flower'

Mallory *(French)* 'Unlucky'

Malva *(Greek)* 'Soft and tender'
Melba, Melva *see also* Malvina or Mauve

Malvie *see* Malvina

Malvina *(Gaelic)* 'Polished chieftain'
Malva, Malvie, Melva, Melvina, Melvine

Mamie *see* Mary

Manda *see* Amanda

Mandie *see* Amanda

Mandy *see* Amanda

Manette *see* Mary

Mani *(Chinese)* 'Mantra'

Manon *see* Mary

Manpreet *(Punjabi)* 'Full of love'

Manuela *(Spanish)* 'God with us'
Manuella

Manuella *see* Manuela

Mara *see* Damara or Mary

Maraam *(Arabic)*
'Aspiration'

Maralla *see* Mareria

Marcela *see* Marcella

Marcelia *see* Marcella

Marcella *(Latin)* 'Belonging
to Mars'
Marcela, Marcelia,
Marcelle, Marcelline,
Marchella, Marchelle,
Marchelline, Marchita,
Marcia, Marcie,
Marcile, Marcille,
Marcy, Marilda,
Marquita, Marsha

Marcelle *see* Marcella

Marcelline *see* Marcella

Marchella *see* Marcella

Marchelle *see* Marcella

Marchelline *see* Marcella

Marchita *see* Marcella

Marcia *see* Marcella

Marcie *see* Marcella

Marcile *see* Marcella

Marcille *see* Marcella

Marcy *see* Marcella

Mardi *(French)* 'Born on
Tuesday'

Marelda *(Teutonic)* 'Famous
battle maiden

Mareria *(Latin)* 'Of the sea'
Maralla

Maretta *see* Mary

Marette *see* Mary

Margalo *see* Margaret

Margao *see* Margaret

Margaret *(Latin)* 'A pearl'
Daisy, Greta, Grete,
Gretchen, Grethe,
Maggie, Maigrghread,
Maisie, Margalo,
Margao, Margareta,
Margaretha,
Margarethe, Margaretta,
Margarita, Marge,
Margerie, Margerita,
Margery, Marget,
Margethe, Margetta,
Margette, Margharita,
Margo, Margorie,
Margory, Margot,
Marguerita, Marguerite,
Margueritta, Marjery,
Marjorie, Meg, Meta,
Pearl, Peggy, Rita

Margareta *see* Margaret

Margaretha *see* Margaret

Margarethe *see* Margaret

Margaretta *see* Margaret

Margarita *see* Margaret

Marge *see* Margaret

Margerie *see* Margaret

Margerita *see* Margaret

Margery *see* Margaret

Marget *see* Margaret

Margethe *see* Margaret

Margetta *see* Margaret

Margette *see* Margaret

Margharita *see* Margaret

Margo *see* Margaret

Margorie *see* Margaret

Margory *see* Margaret

Margot *see* Margaret

Marguerita *see* Margaret

Marguerite *see* Margaret

Margueritta *see* Margaret

Maria *see* Mary

Mariah *see* Mary

Mariam *see* Marian

Marian *(Hebrew)* 'Bitter and graceful'
Mariam, Mariana, Marianna, Marianne, Mariom, Marion, Maryanne

Mariana *see* Marian

Marianna *see* Marian

Marianne *see* Marian

Maribell *see* Marybelle

Marie *see* Mary

Mariel *see* Mary

Marietta *see* Mary

Mariette *see* Mary

Marigold *(English)* 'Golden flower girl'
Marygold

Mariko *(Japanese)* 'Circle'

Marilda *see* Marcella

Marilla *see* Amaryllis or Mary

Marilyn *see* Mary

Marina *(Latin)* 'Lady of the sea'
Marnie

Marini *(Swahili)* 'Healthy and pretty'

Mariom *see* Marian

Marion *see* Marian

Mariposa *(Spanish)* 'Butterfly'

Maris *(Latin)* 'Of the seá'
Marisa, Marissa, Marris
see also Damara

Marisa *see* Maris

Marissa *see* Maris

Maritza *(Arabic)* 'Blessed'

Marjery *see* Margaret

Marjorie *see* Margaret

Marla *see* Mary

Marleen *see* Madeleine

Marlena *see* Madeleine

Marlene *see* Madeleine

Marline *see* Madeleine

Marnie *see* Marina

Marola *(Latin)* 'Woman who lives by the sea'

Marola *(Latin)* 'Little dark girl'

Marquita *see* Marcella

Marris *see* Maris

Marsha *see* Marcella

Marta *see* Martha or Martina

Martella *see* Martha

Martha *(Arabic)* 'The mistress'
Marta, Martella, Marthe, Marti, Martie, Martita, Marty, Martynne, Mattie, Matty

Marthe *see* Martha

Marti *see* Martha

Martie *see* Martha

Martina *(Latin)* 'War-like one'. Feminine of Martin
Marta, Martine, Tina

Martine *see* Martina

Martita *see* Martha

Marty *see* Martha

Martynne *see* Martha

Marva *see* Marve

Marvel *(Latin)* 'A wondrous miracle'
Marva, Marvela, Marvella, Marvelle

Marvela *see* Marvel

Marvella *see* Marvel

Marvelle *see* Marvel

Mary *(Hebrew)* 'Bitterness'. One of the most consistently popular girl's names in Christian countries
Maire, Mairi, Mamie, Manette, Manon, Mara, Maretta, Marette, Maria, Mariah, Marie, Mariel, Marietta, Mariette, Marilla, Marilyn, Marla, Marya, Marylin, Marylyn, Maryse, Maureen, May, Mearr, Mimi, Miriam, Mitzi, Molly, Moya, Polly

Marya *(Arabic)* 'Purity, whiteness' *see also* Mary

Maryam *(Arabic)* 'Purity'

Maryanne *see* Marian

Marybelle A combination of Mary and Belle
Maribell

Maryellen A combination of Mary and Ellen

Marygold *see* Marigold

Maryjo A combination of Mary and Joanne

Marylin *see* Mary

Marylou A combination of Mary and Louise

Marylyn *see* Mary

Maryse *see* Mary

Masa *(Japanese)* 'Straightforward, upright'

Massa *(Arabic)* 'Uplifting'

Massima *(Italian/Latin)* 'Greatest'

Matelda *see* Mathilda

Mathea *see* Mattea

Mathena *(Hebrew)* 'Gift from God'

Mathia *see* Mattea

Mathilda *(Teutonic)* 'Brave little maid'. One as courageous as a lion
Maitilde, Matelda, Mathilde, Matilda, Matilde, Mattie, Tilda, Tilly

Mathilde *see* Mathilda

Matilda *see* Mathilda

Matilde *see* Mathilda

Matsu *(Japanese)* 'Pine tree'
Matsuko

Matsuko *see* Matsu

Mattea *(Hebrew)* 'Gift of God'. Feminine of Matthew
Mathea, Mathia, Matthea, Matthia

Matthea *see* Mattea

Matthia *see* Mattea

Mattie *see* Mathilda or Martha

Matty *see* Martha

Maud *(Teutonic)* 'Brave girl'

Maude *see* Maud

Mauralia *see* Maurilla

Maureen *see* Mary

Maurilia *see* Maurilla

Maurilla *(Latin)* 'Sympathetic woman'
Mauralia, Maurilia

Maurise *(French)* 'Dark-skinned'

Mauve *(Latin)* 'Lilac-coloured bird'
Malva

Mave *see* Mab or Maeve

Mavis *(French)* 'Song thrush' *see also* Mab

Maxene *see* Maxine

Maxie *see* Maxine

Maxima *see* Maxine

Maxine *(French)* 'The greatest'. Feminine of Maximilian
Maxene, Maxie, Maxima

May *(Latin)* 'Born in May'
Maia, May *see also* Mary

Maya *(Sanskrit)* 'Illusion'

Maybelle *see* Mabel

Mayda *see* Maida

Mayde *see* Maida

Maydena *see* Maida

Mead *(Greek)* 'Honey wine'
Meade

Meade *see* Mead

Meagan *see* Megan

Meaghan *see* Megan

Meara *(Gaelic)* 'Mirth'

Mearr *see* Mary

Meave *see* Mab or Maeve

Meda *see* Halimeda

Medea *(Greek)* 'The middle child' or 'enchantress'
Madora, Media, Medora

Media *see* Medea

Medora *(Literary)* Poetic character of Lord Byron *see also* Medea

Medwenna *(Welsh)* 'Maiden, princess'
Modwen, Modwenna

Meena *(Hindi)* 'Bird'. Blue semi-precious stone

Meera *see* Meira

Meg *see* Margaret

Megan *(Celtic)* 'The strong one'. A popular name in Wales
Meagan, Meaghan, Meghan, Meghann

Megara *(Greek)* 'First'. Hercules' first wife

Meghan *see* Megan

Meghann *see* Megan

Mehetabel *see* Mehitabel

Mehetabelle *see* Mehitabel

Mehetabie *see* Mehitabel

Mehira *(Hebrew)* 'Energetic and quick'
Mahira

Mehitabel *(Hebrew)*
'Favoured of God'
Hetty, Hitty,
Mehetabel,
Mehetabelle,
Mehetabie, Mehitabelle,
Mehitable, Metabel

Mehitabelle *see* Mehitabel

Mehitable *see* Mehitabel

Mehri *(Persian)* 'Lovable
and kind

Mei *see* Meiying

Meinwen *(Welsh)* 'Slim'

Meira *(Hebrew)* 'Light'
Meera

Meiying *(Chinese)*
'Beautiful flower' Mei

Mel *see* Melanie or Melissa

Melada *(Greek)* 'Honey'

Melan *see* Melanie

Melania *see* Melanie

Melanie *(Greek)* 'Clad in
darkness'. Lady of the
night
Malan, Mel, Melan,
Melania, Melany,
Mellie, Melloney, Melly

Melantha *(Greek)* 'Dark
flower'
Melanthe

Melanthe *see* Melantha

Melany *see* Melanie

Melba *see* Malva

Melda *see* Imelda

Melia *(Greek)* 'The ash tree'

Melicent *see* Milicent

Melina *(Latin)* 'Yellow
canary' *see also* Carmel
or Madeleine

Melinda *(Greek)* 'Mild and
gentle'. A quiet, home-
loving girl
Malinda

Melior *(Latin)* 'Better'

Melisanda *see* Millicent

Melisande *see* Millicent

Melisandra *see* Millicent

Melisenda *see* Milicent

Melisende *see* Milicent

Melissa *(Greek)* 'Honey
bee' or 'nymph of the
forest'
Lisa, Mel, Melisa

Melita *(Greek)* 'Little honey
flower'
Elita, Malita, Melitta

Melitta *see* Melita

Mell *see* Amelia

Melle *(Celtic/French)*
'Princess'

Mellicent *see* Milicent

Mellie *see* Amelia or
  Melanie

Melloney *see* Melanie

Melly *see* Melanie

Melodia *see* Melody

Melodie *see* Melody

Melody *(Greek)* 'Like a
  song'
  Lodie, Melodia,
  Melodie

Melva *see* Malva or
  Malvina

Melvina *see* Malvina

Melvine *see* Malvina

Mcraud *(Greek)* 'Emerald'

Mercedes *(Spanish)*
  'Compassionate,
  merciful'. One who
  forgives and does not
  condemn
  Merci, Mercy

Merci *see* Mercedes

Mercia *(Anglo-Saxon)* 'Lady
  of Mercia'. One from
  the old Saxon kingdom
  in central England

Mercy *(Middle English)*
  'Compassion, mercy'
  see also Mercedes

Merdyce *see* Mertice

Meredeth *see* Meredith

Meredith *(Celtic)* 'Protector
  from the sea'. A popular
  name for both boys and
  girls in Wales
  Meredeth, Meredydd,
  Meredyth, Merideth,
  Meridith, Meridyth,
  Merrie, Merry

Meredydd *see* Meredith

Meredyth *see* Meredith

Meri *see* Merrie

Merideth *see* Meredith

Meridith *see* Meredith

Meridyth *see* Meredith

Meriel *see* Muriel

Meris *(Latin)* 'Of the sea'

Meritt *see* Merritt

Meritta *see* Merritt

Merl *see* Merle

Merla *see* Merle

Merle *(Latin)* 'The
  blackbird'
  Merl, Merla, Merlina,
  Merline, Merola, Meryl,
  Myrlen

Merlina *see* Merle or
  Merlyn

Merline *see* Merle

Merlyn *(Celtic/Spanish)*
  'Sea hill'
  Merlina

Merna *see* Myrna

Merola *see* Merle

Merri *see* Merrie

Merrie *(Anglo-Saxon)*
'Mirthful, joyous'
Meri, Merri, Merry *see
also* Meredith

Merrila *(Greek)* 'Fragrant'

Merrilees *(Old English)* 'St.
Mary's field'
Merrilie

Merrilie *see* Merrilees

Merrit *see* Merritt

Merritt *(Anglo-Saxon)*
'Worthy, of merit'
Meritt, Meritta, Merrit,
Merritta

Merritta *see* Merritt

Merry *see* Meredith or
Merrie

Mertice *(Anglo-Saxon)*
'Famous and pleasant'.
One who has not been
spoiled by praise or
fame
Merdyce, Mertyce *see
also* Myrtle

Mertie *see* Myrtle

Mertyce *see* Mertice

Merula *(Latin)* 'Blackbird'

Meryl *see* Merle

Mesha *(Hindi)* 'Born under
the constellation of
Aries'

Messina *(Latin)* 'The
middle child'

Meta *(Latin)* 'Ambition
achieved' *see also*
Margaret

Metabel *see* Mehitabel

Metea *(Greek)* 'Gentle'

Metis *(Greek)* 'Wisdom and
skill'
Metys

Metys *see* Metis

Mevena *(Celtic/French)*
'Agile'

Mia *(Latin)* 'Mine'

Micaela *see* Michaela

Michaela *(Hebrew)*
'Likeness to God'.
Feminine of Michael
Micaela, Michaelina,
Michaeline, Michaella,
Michel, Micheline,
Michella, Michelle,
Michelline, Mikaela

Michaelina *see* Michaela

Michaeline *see* Michaela

Michaella *see* Michaela

Michal *(Hebrew)* 'God is
perfect'

Michel *see* Michaela

Micheline *see* Michaela

Michella *see* Michaela

Michelle *see* Michaela

Michelline *see* Michaela

Michi *(Japanese)* 'The way'

Michiko *(Japanese)* 'Three thousand'

Midori *(Japanese)* 'Green'

Mignon *(French)* 'Little, dainty darling'. A kitten-like girl of charm and grace
Mignonette

Mignonette *see* Mignon

Mihewi *(Native American)* 'Woman of the sun'

Mikaela *see* Michaela

Miki *(Japanese)* 'Stem'

Mildred *(Anglo-Saxon)* 'Gentle counsellor'. The diplomatic power behind the throne
Mildrid, Milli, Millie, Milly

Mildrid *see* Mildred

Milicent *see* Millicent

Milicia *see* Amelia

Milisent *see* Millicent

Milissent *see* Millicent

Mill *see* Amelia

Milli *see* Mildred or Millicent

Millicent *(Teutonic)* 'Strong and industrious'. The hard-working girl
Melicent, Melisanda, Melisande, Melisandra, Melisenda, Melisende, Mellicent, Milicent, Milisent, Milissent, Milli, Millie, Milly

Millie *see* Amelia, Mildred or Millicent

Milly *see* Mildred or Millicent

Mimi *see* Mary

Mimosa *(Latin)* 'Imitative'

Mina *see* Adamina, Jemina, Minta or Wilhelmina

Minda *(Indian)* 'Knowledge' *see also* Minta

Mindora *(Teutonic)* 'Gift of love'

Mindy *see* Minta

Minerva *(Latin)* 'Wise, purposeful one'. The goddess of wisdom

Minetta *see* Minette or Minta

Minette *(French)* 'Little kitten'
Minetta *see also* Henrietta

Minna *(Old German)* 'Tender affection'

Minnie *see* Minta or Wilhelmina

Minny *see* Wilhelmina

Minta *(Greek/Teutonic)* 'Remembered with love'. From the plant Mina, Minda, Mindy, Minetta, Minnie, Mintha, Minthe *see also* Araminta

Mintha *see* Minta

Minthe *see* Minta

Mione *(Greek)* 'Small'

Mira *(Latin)* 'Wonderful one'
Mireilla, Mireille, Mirella, Mirilla, Myra, Myrilla

Mirabel *(Latin)* 'Admired for her beauty'
Mirabella, Mirabelle

Mirabella *see* Mirabel

Mirabelle *see* Mirabel

Miranda *(Latin)* 'Greatly admired'
Randa

Mireilla *see* Mira

Mireille *see* Mira

Mirella *see* Mira

Miriam *see* Mary

Mirle *see* Myrtle

Mirna *see* Myrna

Mirta *(Greek/Spanish)* 'Crown of beauty'
Mirtala, Myrta

Mirtala *see* Mirta

Misty *(Old English)* 'Shrouded with mist'

Mitra *(Persian)* 'Name of angel'

Mitzi *see* Mary

Miya *(Japanese)* 'Temple'

Miyuki *(Japanese)* 'Snow'

Mocita *(Sanskrit)* 'The one who is set free'

Modana *(Sanskrit)* 'One who makes people happy'

Modesta *see* Modesty

Modeste *see* Modesty

Modestia *see* Modesty

Modestine *see* Modesty

Modesty *(Latin)* 'Shy, modest'. The retiring and bashful girl
Desta, Modesta, Modeste, Modestia, Modestine

Modwen *see* Medwenna

Modwenna *see* Medwenna

Mohala *(Hawaiian)* 'Flowers in bloom'

Moibeal *see* Mabel

Moina *(Celtic)* 'Soft' *see also* Myrna

Moira *see* Morag

Molly *see* Mary

Mona *see* Monica or Ramona

Monca *see* Monica

Monica *(Latin)* 'Advice giver'
Mona, Monca, Monika, Monique, Moyna

Monika *see* Monica

Monique *see* Monica

Mora *(Gaelic)* 'Sun'

Morag *(Celtic)* 'Great'
Moira, Moyra

Morette *see* Amorette

Morgan *see* Morgana

Morgana *(Welsh)* 'From the sea shore'
Morgan, Morgen

Morganica *see* Morgan

Morganne *see* Morgan

Morgen *see* Morgana

Morna *see* Myrna

Morwena *(Welsh)* 'Maiden'

Mosella *see* Moselle

Moselle *(Hebrew)* 'Taken from the water'. Feminine of Moses
Mosella, Mozel, Mozella, Mozelle

Mosera *(Hebrew)* 'Bound to men'

Motaza *(Arabic)* 'Proud'

Moto *(Japanese)* 'Source'

Moya *see* Mary

Moyna *see* Monica or Myrna

Moyra *see* Morag

Moza *(Hebrew)* 'Fountain'

Mozel *see* Moselle

Mozella *see* Moselle

Mozelle *see* Moselle

Muire *see* Muriel

Munira *(Arabic)* 'Illuminating, light'

Muriel *(Celtic)* 'Sea bright'
Meriel, Muire, Murielle

Murielle *see* Muriel

Musa *(Latin)* 'Song'

Musetta *(French)* 'Child of
the Muses'
Musette

Musette *see* Musetta

Musidore *(Greek)* 'Gift of
the Muses'

Mwynen *(Welsh)* 'Gentle'

Mya *(Burmese)* 'Emerald'

Myfanwy *(Welsh)* 'My rare
one'
Myvanwy

Myla *(English)* 'Merciful'

Myra *(Latin)* 'Admired',
'wonderful one' *see also*
Mira

Myrilla *see* Mira

Myrlene *see* Merle

Myrna *(Gaelic)* 'Beloved'
Merna, Mirna, Moina,
Morna, Moyna

Myrta *see* Mirta or Myrtle

Myrtia *see* Myrtle

Myrtis *see* Myrtle

Myrtle *(Greek)* 'Victorious
crown'. The hero's
laurel wreath
Mertice, Mertle, Mirle,
Myrta, Myrtia, Myrtis

Myvanwy *see* Myfanwy

GIRLS

Naamah *(Hebrew)*
'Pleasant, beautiful'
Namana

Naashom *(Hebrew)*
'Enchantress'
Nashom, Nashoma

Naava *(Hebrew)* 'Beautiful'

Nabeela *(Arabic)* 'Noble'
Nabila

Nabila *see* Nabeela

Nabrissa *(French/Greek)*
'Peace'

Nada *see* Nadine

Nadda *see* Nadine

Nadeen *see* Nadine

Nadia *see* Nadine

Nadine *(French)* 'Hope'
Nada, Nadda, Nadeen,
Nadia

Nadira *(Arabic)* 'Rare,
precious'

Nafisa *(Arabic)* 'Precious'

Nahtanha *(Native
American)* 'Cornflower'

Naiada *see* Naida

Naida *(Latin)* 'The water
nymph'. From the
streams of Arcadia
Naiada

Naima *(Arabic)* 'Contented'

Nairne *(Gaelic)* 'From the
river'

Najila *(Arabic)* 'One with
beautiful eyes'

Nalani *(Hawaiian)*
'Calmness of the
heavens'

Nama *see* Namah

Namah *(Hebrew)*
'Beautiful, pleasant'
Nama

Namana *see* Naamah

Nan *see* Anne

Nana *see* Anne

Nancy *see* Anne

Nandelle *(German)*
'Adventuring life'

Nandita *(Sanskrit)* 'Happy'

Nanetta *see* Anne

Nanette *see* Anne

Nani *(Hawaiian)* 'Beautiful'

Nanice *see* Anne

Nanine *see* Anne

Nanna *see* Anne

Nanon *see* Anne

Naoma *see* Naomi

Naomi *(Hebrew)* 'The
pleasant one'
Naoma, Noami, Nomi,
Nomie

Napaea *see* Napea

Napea *(Latin)* 'Girl of the
valley'
Napaea, Napia

Napia *see* Napea

Nara *(English)* 'Nearest and
dearest' *see also* Narda

Narda *(Latin)* 'Fragrant
perfume'
Nara

Narelle *(Australian)*
'Woman from the sea'

Narmada *(Hindi)* 'Gives
pleasure'

Nashom *see* Naashom

Nashoma *see* Naashom

Nasiba *(Arabic)* 'Love,
poetry'

Nasima *(Arabic)* 'Gentle
breeze'

Nastasya *see* Natalie

Nasya *(Hebrew)* 'Miracle of
God'

Nata *(Sanskrit)* 'Dancer'

Natacha *see* Natalie

Natala *see* Natalie

Natale *see* Natalie

Natalia *see* Natali

Natalie *(Latin)* 'Born at
Christmas tide'
Nastasya, Natacha,
Natala, Natale, Natalia,
Natalina, Natasha,
Nathalie, Natica,
Natika, Natividad,
Nattie, Netta, Nettie,
Netty, Noel, Noelle,
Novella

Natalina *see* Natalie

Natasha *(Latin)* 'Born at
Christmas' *see also*
Natalie

Natene *see* Nathania

Natesa *(Hindi)* 'God-like'.
Another name for the
Hindu goddess Shakti

Nathalie *see* Natalie

Nathane *see* Nathania

Nathania *(Hebrew)* 'Gift of God'
Natene, Nathane, Nathene

Nathene *see* Nathania

Natica *see* Natalie

Natika *see* Natalie

Natividad *see* Natalie

Natsu *(Japanese)* 'Summer'

Nattie *see* Natalie

Nayana *(Sanskrit)* 'Lovely eyes'

Nazima *(Sanskrit)* 'Beautiful song'

Neala *(Gaelic)* 'The champion'. Feminine of Neale, Neil

Neale *see* Neala

Nebula *(Latin)* 'A cloud of mist'

Neda *(Slav)* 'Born on Sunday'
Nedda, Nedi

Nedda *see* Neda

Nedi *see* Neda

Neila *(Irish)* 'Champion'

Nela *see* Cornelia or Nila

Nelda *(Anglo-Saxon)* 'Born under the elder tree'

Nelie *see* Cornelia

Nell *see* Helen

Nelli *see* Cornelia

Nellwyn *(Greek)* 'Bright friend and companion'

Neola *(Greek)* 'The young one'

Neoma *(Greek)* 'The new moon'

Nerice *see* Nerima

Nerima *(Greek)* 'From the sea'
Nerice, Nerine, Nerissa, Nerita

Nerine *see* Nerima

Nerissa *(Greek)* 'Of the sea'
Nerita *see also* Nerima

Nerita *see* Nerima or Nerissa

Nerys *(Welsh)* 'Lordly one'

Nessa *see* Agnes

Nessi See Agnes

Nessie *see* Agnes

Nesta *see* Agnes

Netania *(Hebrew)* 'Gift of God'

Netie *see* Henrietta

Netta *see* Antonia,
Henrietta, Natalie etc

Nettie *see* Antonia or
Natalie

Netty *see* Antonia or
Natalie

Neva *(Spanish)* 'As white as
the moon'
Nevada

Nevada *see* Neva

Nevina *(Irish)* 'Worshipper
of Saint Nevin'

Neysa *see* Agnes

Niamh *(Irish)* 'Brightness'

Nichola *see* Nicole

Nicholina *see* Nicole

Nickie *see* Nicole

Nicky *see* Nicole

Nicol *see* Nicole

Nicola *see* Nicole

Nicole *(Greek)* 'The
people's victory'
Nichola, Nicholina,
Nickie, Nicky, Nicol,
Nicola, Nicolina,
Nicoline, Nikki, Nikola,
Nikoletta

Nicolina *see* Nicole

Nicoline *see* Nicole

Nidia *(Latin)* 'Nest'

Nieta *(Spanish)*
'Granddaughter'

Nigella *(Latin)* 'Black'

Nike *(Greek)* 'Victorious'

Nikhita *(Sanskrit)* 'The
earth'

Nikki *see* Nicole

Nikola *see* Nicole

Nikoletta *see* Nicole

Nila *(Latin)* 'From the Nile'
Nela

Nilaya *(Sanskrit)* 'Home'

Nilda *see* Magnilda

Nilde *see* Magnilda

Nillie *see* Magnilda

Nima *(Hebrew)* 'Thread'

Nina *(Spanish)* 'The
daughter'
Nineta, Ninetta, Ninette
see also Anne

Nineta *see* Nina

Ninetta *see* Nina

Ninette *see* Anne or Nina

Ninon *see* Anne

Nipha *(Greek)* 'Snowflake'

Nirah *(Hebrew)* 'Light'

Nirel *(Hebrew)* 'Light of
God'

Nisha *(Sanskrit)* 'Night'

Nissa *(Scandinavian)*
'Friendly elf. A fairy
who can be seen only
by lovers

Nissie *see* Nixie

Nissy *see* Nixie

Nita *see* Anne, Jane or
Bonita

Nixie *(Teutonic)* 'Water
sprite'
Nissie, Nissy

Nizana *(Hebrew)* 'Flower
bud'

Noami *see* Naomi

Noel *see* Natalie

Noelle *see* Natalie

Nokomis *(American Indian)*
'The grandmother'.
From the legend of
Hiawatha

Nola *(Gaelic)* 'Famous one'
see also Magnolia or
Olive

Noleta *(Latin)* 'Unwilling'
Nolita

Nolie *see* Magnolia

Nolita *see* Noleta

Nollie *see* Olive

Nomi *see* Naomi

Nomie *see* Naomi

Nona *(Latin)* 'Ninth-born'

Nonnie *see* Annona

Nora *see* Honora, Eleanor
or Helen

Norah *see* Helen or
Honora

Norberta *(Teutonic)* 'Bright
heroine'
Norberte, Norbertha,
Norberthe

Norberte *see* Norberta

Norbertha *see* Norberta

Norberthe *see* Norberta

Nordica *(Teutonic)* 'Girl
from the North'
Nordika

Nordika *see* Nodica

Noreen *see* Honora or
Norma

Norinc *see* Honora

Norma *(Latin)* 'A pattern
or rule'. The template
of the perfect girl
Noreen, Normi, Normie

Normi *see* Norma

Normie *see* Norma

Norna *(Norse)* 'Destiny'.
The goddess of fate

Norrey *see* Honora

Norrie *see* Honora

Norry *see* Honora

Nova *see* Novia

Novella *see* Natalie

Novia *(Latin)* 'The newcomer'
Nova

Nuala *(Gaelic)* 'One with beautiful shoulders'

Numidia *(Latin)* 'The traveller'

Nuna *(Native American)* 'Our land'

Nunciata *(Italian)* 'She has good news' *see also* Annunciata

Nuru *(Swahili)* 'Daylight'

Nydia *(Latin)* 'A refuge' or 'nest'

Nyssa *(Greek)* 'Starting point'

Nyx *(Greek)* 'White-haired'

Obelia *(Greek)* 'A pointed pillar'

Octavia *(Latin)* 'The eighth child'
Octavie, Ottavia, Ottavie, Tavi, Tavia, Tavie, Tavy

Octavie *see* Octavia

Oda *(Teutonic)* 'Rich'

Odele *see* Odelia

Odelet *see* Odelette

Odelette *(French)* 'A small lyric'
Odelet

Odelia *(Teutonic)* 'Prosperous one'
Odele, Odelie, Odelinda, Odella, Odilia, Odilla, Otha, Othilla, Ottilie

Odelie *see* Odelia

Odelinda *see* Odelia

Odeline *see* Odile

Odella *see* Odelia

Odessa *(Greek)* 'A long journey'

Odette *(French)* 'Home-lover'. One who makes a house a home

Odila *see* Odile

Odile *(French/German)* 'Rich'
Odeline, Odila

Odilia *see* Odelia

Odilla *see* Odelia

Ofelia *see* Ophelia

Ofilia *see* Ophelia

Ofrah *(Hebrew)* 'Young mind, lively maiden'

Ola *(Scandinavian)* 'Descendant'. The daughter of a chief
Olaa

Olaa *see* Ola

Olaathe *(Native American)* 'Beautiful'

Olatta *(Native American)* 'Lagoon'

Olave *(Teutonic)* 'Ancestor's relic'

Olenka *see* Olga

Oleta *see* Olethea

Olethea *(Latin)* 'Truth'
Alethea, Oleta

Olga *(Teutonic)* 'Holy'. One
who has been
annointed in the
service of God
Helga, Livi, Livia, Livie,
Livvi, Olenka, Olive,
Olivia, Ollie, Olva *see
also* Elga

Olien *(Russian)* 'Deer'

Olimpie *see* Olympia

Olina *(Hawaiian)* 'Filled
with happiness'

Olinda *(Latin)* 'Fragrant
herb'

Olive *(Latin)* 'Symbol of
peace'
Livia, Nola, Nollie,
Olivette, Olivia, Ollie,
Olva *see also* Olga

Olivette *see* Olive

Olivia *see* Olga or Olive

Ollie *see* Olga or Olive

Olva *see* Olga or Olive

Olwen *see* Olwyn

Olwyn *(Welsh)* 'White
clover'
Olwen

Olympe *see* Olympia

Olympia *(Greek)* 'Heavenly
one'
Olimpie, Olympe,
Olympie *see also* Pia

Olympie *see* Olympia

Oma *(Hebrew)* 'Reverent'.
Feminine of Omar

Ona *see* Una

Onawa *(American Indian)*
'Maiden who is wide
awake'

Ondina *see* Ondine

Ondine *(Latin)* 'Wave',
'wave of water'
Ondina, Undine

Oneida *(Native American)*
'Expected'
Onida

Onida *see* Oneida

Oola *see* Ula

Oona *see* Una

Oonagh *see* Una

Opal *(Sanskrit)* 'Precious
jewel'
Opalina, Opaline

Opalina *see* Opal

Opaline *see* Opal

Ophelia *(Greek)* 'Wise and
immortal'
Ofelia, Ofilia, Phelia

Ora *(Latin)* 'Golden one'
Orabel, Orabella,
Orabelle *see also* Aura,
Aurelia or Ursula

Orabel *see* Ora

Orabella *see* Ora

Orabelle *see* Ora

Oralee *(Hebrew)* 'My light'
Orali, Orli

Orali *see* Oralee

Oralia *see* Aurelia

Oralie *see* Aurelia

Orane *(French)* 'Rising'

Ordelia *(Teutonic)* 'Elf's
spear'

Orea *(Greek)* 'Of the
mountain'. The original
maid of the mountains

Orel *see* Bambi

Orela *(Latin)* 'Divine
pronouncement'. The
oracle

Orella *(Latin)* 'Girl who
listens'

Orenda *(American Indian)*
'Magic power'

Oria *see* Oriana

Oriana *(Latin)* 'Golden
one'
Oria, Oriane

Oriane *see* Oriana

Oriel *see* Aurelia

Oriole *see* Aurelia

Orla *(Irish)* 'Golden lady'

Orlanda *see* Rolanda

Orlande *see* Rolanda

Orlena *(French)* 'Gold'

Orli *see* Orali

Orna *(Gaelic)* 'Pale-
coloured'

Orpah *(Hebrew)* 'A fawn'.
From *The Song of
Solomon*, in the Bible

Orquidea *(Spanish)*
'Orchid'

Orsa *see* Ursula

Orsola *see* Ursula

Ortrud *(Teutonic)* 'Golden
girl'

Orva *(Teutonic)* 'Spear
friend'

Orvala *(Latin)* 'Worthy of
gold'

Osanna *(Latin)* 'Filled with
mercy'

Osnat *(Hebrew)* 'Favourite
of the deity'

Otha *see* Odelia

Othilla *see* Odelia

Ottavia *see* Octavia

Ottavie *see* Octavia

Ottilie *see* Odelia

Ovina *(Latin)* 'Like a lamb'

Owena *(Welsh)* 'Well-born'

Owissa *(Native American)* 'Bluebird'. The bringer of spring

Ozana *(Hebrew)* 'Treasure' or 'wealth'

Ozora *(Hebrew)* 'Strength of the Lord'

Paciane *(French from Latin)* 'Peace'

Pacifica *(Latin)* 'Peaceful one'

Page *see* Paige

Paige *(Anglo-Saxon)* 'Young child'
Page

Paka *(Swahili)* 'Kitten'

Pakhi *see* Pakshi

Pakshi *(Sanskrit)* 'Bird'
Pakhi

Pallas *(Greek)* 'Wisdom and knowledge'

Palma *(Latin)* 'Palm tree'
Palmer, Palmira

Palmer *see* Palma

Palmira *see* Palma

Paloma *(Spanish)* 'The dove'. Gentle, tender
Palometa, Palomita

Palometa *see* Paloma

Palomita *see* Paloma

Pam *see* Pamela

Pamela *(Greek)* 'All sweetness and honey'. A loving person of great kindness
Pam, Pamelina, Pamella, Pammie, Pammy

Pamelina *see* Pamela

Pamella *see* Pamela

Pammie *see* Pamela

Pammy *see* Pamela

Pamphila *(Greek)* 'All loving'. One who loves all humanity

Pandora *(Greek)* 'Talented, gifted one'

Pansy *(Greek)* 'Fragrant, flower-like'

Panthea *(Greek)* 'Of all the Gods'
Panthia

Panthia *see* Panthea

Panya *(Swahili)* 'Little mouse'

Paola *(Italian)* 'Little' *see also* Paula

Parasha *see* Paschasia

Parnella *(French)* 'Little rook'
Parnelle, Pernella, Pernelle

Parnelle *see* Parnella

Parthenia *(Greek)* 'Sweet virgin'

Parvaneh *(Persian)* 'Butterfly'

Paschasia *(Latin)* 'Born at Easter'
Parasha

Pat *see* Patricia

Patience *(Latin)* 'Patient one'
Patienza, Pattie, Patty

Patienza *see* Patience

Patrice *see* Patricia

Patricia *(Latin)* 'Well-born girl'
Pat, Patrice, Patrizia, Patsy, Patti, Patty

Patrizia *see* Patricia

Patsy *see* Patricia

Patti *see* Patricia

Pattie *see* Patience

Patty *see* Patience or Patricia

Paula *(Latin)* 'Little'.
Feminine of Paul
Paola, Paule, Paulena, Pauletta, Paulette, Pauli, Paulie, Paulina, Pauline, Paulita, Pavia

Paule *see* Paula

Paulena *see* Paula

Pauletta *see* Paula

Paulette *see* Paula

Pauli *see* Paula

Paulie *see* Paula

Paulina *see* Paula

Pauline *see* Paula

Paulita *see* Paula

Pavla *see* Paula

Peace *(Latin)* 'Tranquillity, calm'

Pearl *(Latin)* 'Precious jewel'. One of unmatched beauty
Pearle, Pearlie, Perl, Perle, Perlie, Perlina, Perline *see also* Margaret

Pearle *see* Pearl

Pearlie *see* Pearl

Peggy *see* Margaret

Peirrette *see* Petrina

Pelagia *(Greek)* 'Mermaid'

Pen *see* Penelope

Penelope *(Greek)* 'The
weaver'. The patient
wife of Ulysses
Pen, Penny

Peni *see* Peninah

Penina *see* Peninah

Peninah *(Hebrew)* 'Pearl'
Peni, Penina, Peninnah

Peninnah *see* Peninah

Penny *see* Penelope

Penta *see* Penthea

Penthea *(Greek)* 'Fifth
child'
Penta, Penthia

Penthia *see* Penthea

Peony *(Latin)* 'The gift of
healing'

Pepita *see* Josephine

Perdita *(Latin)* 'The lost
one'

Perfecta *(Spanish)* 'The
most perfect being'

Perizada *(Persian)* 'Born of
the fairies'

Perl *see* Pearl

Perle *see* Pearl

Perlie *see* Pearl

Perlina *see* Pearl

Perline *see* Pearl

Pernella *see* Parnella

Pernelle *see* Parnella

Peronel *(Latin)* 'A rock'
Peronelle

Peronelle *see* Peronel

Perpetua *(Latin)*
'Everlasting'

Perrine *see* Petrina

Persephone *(Greek)*
'Goddess of the
Underworld'

Persis *(Latin)* 'Woman from
Persia'

Peta *(Greek)* 'A rock'

Petica *(Latin)* 'Noble one'

Petra *see* Petrina

Petrina *(Greek)* 'Steadfast
as a rock'. Feminine of
Peter
Perrine, Petra,
Petronella, Petronelle,
Petronia, Petronilla,
Petronille, Petula,
Pierette, Pierrette,
Pietra

Petronella *see* Petrina

Petronelle *see* Petrina

Petronia *see* Petrina

Petronilla *see* Petrina

Petronille *see* Petrina

Petula *(Latin)* 'Seeker' *see also* Petrina

Petunia *(Indian)* 'Reddish flower'

Phaidra *see* Phedra

Phebe *see* Phoebe

Phedra *(Greek)* 'Bright one'. The daughter of King Minos of Crete
Phaidra, Phedre

Phedre *see* Phedra

Phelia *see* Ophelia

Phemie *see* Euphemia

Philadelphia *(Greek)* 'Brotherly love'

Philana *(Greek)* 'Friend of humanity'
Filana

Philantha *(Greek)* 'Lover of flowers'. Child of the blossoms
Filantha, Philanthe

Philanthe *see* Philantha

Philberta *(Teutonic)* 'Exceptionally brilliant'
Filberta, Filberte, Filbertha, Filberthe, Philberthe, Philertha

Philbertha *see* Philberta

Philberthe *see* Philbertha

Philippa *(Greek)* 'Lover of horses'. Feminine of Philip
Filipa, Filippa, Phillie, Phillipa, Phillippa, Pippa

Philis *see* Phyllis

Phillida *(Greek)* 'Loving woman' *see also* Phyllis

Phillie *see* Philippa

Phillipa *see* Philippa

Phillippa *see* Philippa

Phillis *see* Phyllis

Philmen *see* Filma

Philomela *(Greek)* 'Lover of song'

Philomena *(Greek)* 'Lover of the Moon'. The nightingale

Philothra *(Greek)* 'Pious'

Phoebe *(Greek)* 'Bright, shining sun'. Feminine of Phoebus (Apollo)
Phebe

Phoenix *(Greek)* 'The phoenix' or 'the eagle'. Legendary bird of which only one ever exists. A new bird rises from the ashes of the old
Fenix

Pholma *see* Filma

Photina *(Greek)* 'Light'

Phylis *see* Phyllis

Phyllida *see* Phyllis

Phyllis *(Greek)* 'A green
bough'
Filida, Filis, Fillida,
Fillis, Philis, Phillis,
Phylis, Phyllida *see also*
Phillida

Pia *(Latin)* 'Pious' *see also*
Olympia

Pierette *see* Petrina

Pietra *see* Petrina

Pilar *(Spanish)* 'A
foundation or pillar'

Ping *(Chinese)* 'Duckweed'

Pinon *(Greek)* 'Pearl'

Piper *(English)* 'Player of
the pipes'

Pippa *see* Philippa

Placida *(Latin)* 'Peaceful
one'
Placidia

Placidia *see* Placida

Platona *(Greek)* 'Broad
shouldered'. Feminine
of Plato. A woman of
wisdom

Polly *see* Mary

Pomona *(Latin)* 'Fruitful
and fertile'

Poppaea *see* Poppy

Poppy *(Latin)* 'Red flower'
Poppaea

Porcia *see* Portia

Portia *(Latin)* 'An offering
to God'
Porcia

Poupée *(French)* 'Doll'

Prabha *(Hindi)* 'Light'

Precious *(French)*
'Precious' or 'dear'

Preeti *(Hindi)* 'Love'

Prem *see* Prema

Prema *(Sanskrit)* 'Love'
Prem, Premala

Premala *see* Prema

Prima *(Latin)* 'First-born'

Primalia *(Latin)* 'Like the
springtime'

Primavera *(Spanish)* 'Child
of the spring'

Primmie *see* Primrose

Primrose *(Latin)* 'The first
flower of spring'
Primmie, Primula,
Rosa, Rose

Primula *see* Primrose

Pris *see* Priscilla

Prisca *see* Priscilla

Priscilla *(Latin)* 'Of ancient lineage'. The descendant of princes Pris, Prisca, Prisilla, Prissie *see also* Cilla

Prisilla *see* Priscilla

Prissie *see* Priscilla

Proba *(Latin)* 'Honest'

Prospera *(Latin)* 'Favourable'

Prud *see* Prudence

Prudence *(Latin)* 'Cautious foresight' Prud, Prudentia, Prudie, Prudy, Prue

Prudentia *see* Prudence

Prudie *see* Prudence

Prudy *see* Prudence

Prue *see* Prudence

Prunella *(French)* 'Plum-coloured' Prunelle

Prunelle *see* Prunella

Psyche *(Greek)* 'Of the soul or mind'

Pulcheria *(Latin)* 'Very beautiful'

Purity *(Middle English)* 'Purity'

Pyrena *(Greek)* 'Fiery one'. The warmth of home Pyrenia

Pyrenia *see* Pyrena

Pythea *see* Pythia

Pythia *(Greek)* 'A prophet'. The oracle Pythea

Qadira *(Arabic)* 'Powerful'

Qing *(Chinese)* 'Blue'

Qiturah *(Arabic)*
'Fragrance'

Queena *(Teutonic)* 'The
queen'. The supreme
woman
Queenie

Queenie *see* Queena

Quenberga *(Latin)*
'Queen's pledge'

Quenby *(Scandinavian)*
'Womanly' or 'perfect
wife'

Quendrida *(Latin)* 'One
who threatens the
queen'

Querida *(Spanish)* 'Beloved
one'
Cherida

Questa *(French)* 'Searcher'

Quinta *(Latin)* 'The fifth
child'
Quintana, Quintella,
Quintilla, Quintina

Quintana *see* Quinta

Quintella *see* Quinta

Quintessa *(Latin)* 'Essence'

Quintilla *see* Quinta

Quintina *see* Quinta

Quisha *(African)* 'Physical
and spiritual beauty'

Quita *(French)* 'Tranquil'

Rabi *(Arabic)* 'The harvest' or 'breeze'

Rabiah *(Arabic)* 'Garden'

Rachel *(Hebrew)* 'Innocent as a lamb'. One who suffers in silence Rachele, Rachelle, Rae, Rahel, Raoghnailt, Raquel, Ray, Shelly *see also* Rochelle or Shelley

Rachele *see* Rachel

Rachelle *see* Rachel

Rachida *(Arabic)* 'Wise'

Radella *(Anglo-Saxon)* 'Elf-like adviser'. A fairy-like creature whose advice is weighty

Radinka *(Slavic)* 'Alive and joyful'

Radmilla *(Slavic)* 'Worker for the people'

Rae *(Middle English)* 'A doe deer' *see also* Rachel

Rafa *(Arabic)* 'Happy and prosperous'

Rafaela *see* Raphaela

Rafaella *see* Raphaela

Ragan *see* Regina

Ragini *(Sanskrit)* 'A melody'

Rahel *see* Rachel

Rahima *(Arabic)* 'Merciful'

Raina *see* Regina

Rainbow *(English)* 'Bow of light'

Raine *see* Regina

Raissa *(French)* 'The believer' Raisse

Raisse *see* Raissa

Raja *(Arabic)* 'Hopeful'

Rajani *(Sanskrit)* 'Night'

Rama *see* Ramona

Ramona *(Teutonic)* 'Wise protector'. Feminine of Raymond Mona, Rama, Ramonda, Ramonde *see also* Raymonda

Ramonda *see* Ramona

Ramonde *see* Ramona

Ran *(Japanese)* 'Water lily'

Rana *(Sanskrit)* 'Of royal
  birth, a queen'
  Ranee, Rani, Rania,
  Ranique, Rayna

Randa *see* Miranda

Ranee *see* Rana or Rani

Rani *(Sanskrit)* 'Queen'
  Ranee *see also* Rana

Rania *see* Rana

Ranique *see* Rana

Ranita *(Hebrew)* 'Joyful
  song'
  Ranite

Ranite *see* Ranita

Raoghnailt *see* Rachel

Raphaela *(Hebrew)*
  'Blessed healer'. One
  who has a God-given
  healing touch
  Rafaela, Rafaella,
  Raphaella

Raphaella *see* Raphaela

Raquel *see* Rachel

Rasha *(Arabic)* 'Young
  gazelle'

Rashida *(African)*
  'Righteous'

Rashmi *(Sanskrit)*
  'Sunlight'

Rasia *see* Rose

Raven *(English)* 'Sleek,
  black bird'

Ray *see* Rachel

Raymonda *(Teutonic)* 'Wise
  protector'. Feminine of
  Raymond
  Raymonde *see also*
  Ramona

Rayna *see* Rana or Regina

Rea *see* Rhea

Reba *see* Rebecca

Rebeca *see* Rebecca

Rebecca *(Hebrew)* 'The
  captivator'
  Beckie, Becky, Bekky,
  Reba, Rebeca, Rebeka,
  Rebekah, Rebekka, Riba
  see also Riva

Rebeka *see* Rebecca

Rebekah *see* Rebecca

Rebekka *see* Rebecca

Rechaba *(Hebrew)* 'Horse
  woman'

Reena *see* Rena

Regan *see* Regina

Regina *(Latin)* 'A queen,
  born to rule'
  Gina, Ragan, Raina,
  Raine, Rayna, Regan,
  Regine, Reina, Reine,
  Rina, Rioghnach

Regine *see* Regina

Rehka *(Sanskrit)* 'Art'

Reiko *(Japanese)* 'Gratitude'

Reina *see* Regina

Reine *see* Regina

Reini *see* Irene

Rena *(Hebrew)* 'Song'
Reena *see also* Irene

Renata *(Latin)* 'Born again'.
The spirit of
reincarnation
Renate, Rene, Renee,
Rennie *see also* Irene

Renate *see* Renata

Rene *see* Irene, Renata

Renee *(French)* 'Born again'

Renee *see* Renata

Renita *(Latin)* 'A rebel'

Rennie *see* Irene or
Renata

Renny *see* Irene

Reseda *(Latin)* 'Mignonette
flower'

Reshma *(Sanskrit)* 'Silken'
Reshmam, Reshmi

Reshmam *see* Reshma

Reshmi *see* Reshma

Retha *see* Areta

Reva *(Latin)* 'Strength
regained'

Rexana *(Latin)* 'Regally
graceful'. One whose
bearing is regal
Rexanna

Rexanna *see* Rexana

Reyhan *(Turkish)* 'Sweet-
smelling flower'

Reynalda *(Teutonic)* 'King's
advisor'

Rhea *(Greek)* 'Mother' or
'poppy'. The mother of
the Greek gods
Rea

Rhedyn *(Welsh)* 'Fern'

Rheta *(Greek)* 'An orator'

Rhiana *see* Rihana

Rhianna *see* Rihana

Rhiannon *(Welsh)*
'Nymph'

Rhianwen *(Welsh)* 'Blessed
maiden'

Rhoda *(Greek)* 'Garland of
roses' or 'girl from
Rhodes'
Rhodia, Rodina *see also*
Rose

Rhodanthe *(Greek)* 'The
rose of roses'

Rhodia *see* Rhoda or Rose

Rhona *see* Rona

Rhonda *(Welsh)* 'Grand'

Rhonwen *(Welsh)* 'White lance'

Ria *(Spanish)* 'The river'

Riana *see* Rihana

Rianna *see* Rihana

Riba *see* Rebecca

Rica *see* Roderica or Ulrica

Ricadonna *(Italian)* 'Ruling lady'. One who rules in her own right or on behalf of her son

Ricarda *(Teutonic)* 'Powerful ruler'. Feminine of Richard Dickie, Dicky, Richarda, Richarde, Rickie, Ricky

Richarda *see* Ricarda

Richarde *see* Ricarda

Rickie *see* Ricarda or Roderica

Ricky *see* Ricarda

Rihana *(Arabic)* 'Sweet basil herb' Rhiana, Rhianna, Riana, Rianna

Riju *(Sanskrit)* 'Innocent' Rijuta

Rijuta *see* Rijul

Rika (Swedish) 'Ruler'

Rilla *(Teutonic)* 'A stream or brook' Rille, Rillette

Rille *see* Rilla

Rillette *see* Rilla

Rina *see* Regina

Rinah *(Hebrew)* 'Song' or 'joy'

Rioghnach *see* Regina

Risa *(Latin)* 'Laughter'

Risha *(Hindi)* 'Born under the constellation of Taurus'

Rita *see* Margaret

Riva *(French)* 'Riverbank' *see also* Rebecca

Ro *see* Rolanda

Roanna *(Latin)* 'Sweet and gracious' Rohanna, Rohanne

Roberta *(Anglo-Saxon)* 'Of shining fame'. Feminine of Robert Bertie, Bobbie, Bobby, Bobette, Bobina, Robertha, Roberthe, Robinette, Robina, Robinia, Ruberta, Ruperta

Robertha *see* Roberta

Roberthe *see* Roberta

Robia *(Teutonic)* 'Famous'

Robin *(Old English)* 'Bright or shining with fame'
Robina, Robyn

Robina *see* Roberta or Robin

Robinette *see* Roberta

Robinia *see* Roberta

Robyn *see* Robin

Rochalla *see* Rochelle

Rochalle *see* Rochelle

Rochana *(Persian)* 'Sunrise'

Rochella *see* Rochelle

Rochelle *(French)* 'From the small rock'
Rochalla, Rochalle, Rochella, Rochette *see also* Rachel

Rochette *see* Rochelle

Roddie *see* Roderica

Roddy *see* Roderica

Roderica *(Teutonic)* 'Famous ruler'.
Feminine of Roderick
Rica, Roddie, Roddy, Rodericka, Rickie

Rodericka *see* Roderica

Rodina *see* Rhoda

Rohana *(Hindu)* 'Sandalwood' or 'sweet incense'
Rohane, Rohanna

Rohane *see* Rohana

Rohanna *see* Roanna or Rohana

Rohanne *see* Roanna or Rohana

Rohesia *see* Rose

Rois *see* Rose

Rola *see* Rolanda

Rolanda *(Teutonic)* 'From the famed land'.
Feminine of Roland
Orlanda, Orlande, Ro, Rola, Rolande

Rolande *see* Rolanda

Roma *see* Romola

Romella *see* Romola

Romelle *see* Romola

Romhilda *see* Romilda

Romhilde *see* Romilda

Romilda *(Teutonic)* 'Glorious warrior maiden'
Romhilda, Romhilde, Romilde

Romilde *see* Romilda

Romola *(Latin)* 'Lady of
Rome'
Roma, Romella,
Romelle, Romula

Romula *see* Romola

Romy *see* Rosemary

Rona *(Scandinavian)*
'Mighty power'
Rhona, Ronalda

Ronalda *(Teutonic)* 'All
powerful'. Feminine of
Ronald
Ronalde, Ronnie,
Ronny *see also* Rona

Ronalde *see* Ronalda

Ronnie *see* Ronalda or
Veronica

Ronny *see* Ronalda or
Veronica

Ros *see* Rosalind

Rosa *see* Primrose or Rose

Rosabel *(Latin)* 'Beautiful
rose'
Rosabella, Rosabelle

Rosabella *see* Rosabel

Rosabelle *see* Rosabel

Rosalee *see* Rose

Rosaleen *see* Rose

Rosalia *see* Rose

Rosalie *see* Rose

Rosalind *(Latin)* 'Fair and
beautiful rose'
Ros, Rosalinda,
Rosaline, Rosalyn,
Rosalynd, Roseline,
Roselyn, Roslyn, Roz,
Rozalind, Rozaline,
Rozeline

Rosalinda *see* Rosalind

Rosaline *see* Rosalind

Rosalyn *see* Rosalind

Rosalynd *see* Rosalind

Rosamond *(French)* 'Rose
of the world'
Rosamonda, Rosamund,
Rosamunda, Rosemond,
Rosemonde, Rosemund,
Rosmunda, Rozamond

Rosamonda *see* Rosamond

Rosamund *see* Rosamond

Rosamunda *see* Rosamond

Rosanna *(English)*
'Graceful rose'
Rosanne

Rosanne *see* Rosanna

Rosarana *(Celtic)* 'Rose
bush'

Rose *(Greek)* 'The rose'
Rasia, Rhodia, Rohesia,
Rois, Rosa, Rosalee,
Rosaleen, Rosalia,
Rosalie, Rosel, Rosella,
Roselle, Rosena,
Rosene, Rosetta,
Rosette, Rosia, Rosie,
Rosina, Rosy, Rozalina,
Rozella, Rozello *see also*
Primrose or Rhoda

Rosel *see* Rose

Roseline *see* Rosalind

Rosella *see* Rose

Roselle *see* Rose

Roselyn *see* Rosalind

Rosemary *(Latin)* 'Dew of
the sea'
Romy, Rosie,
Rosemarie, Rosy

Rosemond *see* Rosamond

Rosemonde *see* Rosamond

Rosemund *see* Rosamond

Rosena *see* Rose

Rosene *see* Rose

Rosetta *see* Rose

Rosette *see* Rose

Rosgrana *(Celtic)*
'Sunbeam'

Rosia *see* Rose

Rosie *see* Rose or
Rosemary

Rosina *see* Rose

Roslyn *see* Rosalind

Rosmunda *see* Rosamond

Rosslyn *(Welsh)* 'Moorland
lake'

Rosy *see* Rose or Rosemary

Roux *see* La Roux

Rowena *(Anglo-Saxon)*
'Friend with white hair'
Rowenna

Rowenna *see* Rowena

Rox *see* Roxana

Roxana *(Persian)* 'Brilliant
dawn'
Rox, Roxane, Roxanna,
Roxanne, Roxie, Roxina,
Roxine, Roxy

Roxane *see* Roxana

Roxanna *see* Roxana

Roxanne *see* Roxana

Roxie *see* Roxana

Roxina *see* Roxana

Roxine *see* Roxana

Roxy *see* Roxana

Royale *(French)* 'Regal
being'. Feminine of Roy

Roz *see* Rosalind

Rozalina *see* Rose

Rozalind *see* Rosalind

Rozamond *see* Rosamond

Rozeline *see* Rosalind

Rozella *see* Rose

Rozene *(Native American)* 'Rose'

Ruberta *see* Roberta

Rubetta *see* Ruby

Rubette *see* Ruby

Rubia *see* Ruby

Rubie *see* Ruby

Rubina *see* Ruby

Ruby *(Latin)* 'Precious red jewel'
Rubetta, Rubette, Rubia, Rubie, Rubina

Rucita *(Sanskrit)* 'Shining'

Rudella *see* Rudelle

Rudelle *(Teutonic)* 'Famous person'
Rudella

Ruella *(Hebrew)*
Combination of Ruth and Ella

Rufina *(Latin)* 'Red-haired one'

Rugina *(Latin)* 'Girl with bright red hair'

Rula *(Latin)* 'A sovereign'. One who rules by right

Rupak *(Sanskrit)* 'Beautiful'
Rupali, Rupashi, Rupashri

Rupali *see* Rupak

Rupashi *see* Rupak

Rupashri *see* Rupak

Ruperta *see* Roberta

Ruri *(Japanese)* 'Emerald'

Ruth *(Hebrew)* 'Compassionate and beautiful'
Ruthie

Ruthie *see* Ruth

Rutilia *(Latin)* 'Fiery red'

GIRLS

Saba *(Greek)* 'Woman of Sheba'
Sheba

Sabella *(Latin)* 'The wise'
Sabelle

Sabelle *see* Sabella

Sabina *(Latin)* 'Woman of Sabine'
Bina, Binnie, Sabine, Saidhbhain, Savina *see also* Bina

Sabine *see* Sabina

Sabira *(Arabic)* 'Patient'

Sabra *(Hebrew)* 'The restful one'

Sabrina *(Latin)* 'A princess'
Brina, Sabrine

Sabrine *see* Sabrina

Sacha *(Greek)* 'Helpmate'
Sasha

Sacharissa *(Greek)* 'Sweet'

Sadella *see* Sarah

Sadhbh *see* Sophia

Sadhbha *see* Sophia

Sadie *see* Sarah

Sadira *(Persian)* 'The lotus-eater'

Sadye *see* Sarah

Saffron *(English)* From the plant

Safia *(Arabic)* 'Pure'

Sahlah *(Arabic)* 'Smooth'

Sai *(Japanese)* 'Intelligence'

Saidhbhain *see* Sabina

Sajal *see* Sajala

Sajala *(Sanskrit)* 'Clouds'
Sajal

Sakhi *(Sanskrit)* 'Friend'
Sakina

Sakina *see* Sakhi

Sal *see* Sarah

Salaidh *see* Sarah

Salema *(Hebrew)* 'Girl of peace'
Selemas, Selima *see also* Selima

Salene *see* Selena

Saliha *(Arabic)* 'Goodness'

Salima *(Arabic)* 'Safe' or 'unharmed'

Salina *(Greek)* 'From the salty place'

Sallie *see* Sarah

Sally *see* Sarah

Saloma *see* Salome

Salome *(Hebrew)* 'Peace'. 'Shalom' is the traditional Hebrew greeting, meaning 'peace'
Saloma, Salomi

Salomi *see* Salome

Salvia *(Latin)* 'Sage herb'
Salvina

Salvina *see* Salvia

Samala *(Hebrew)* 'Asked of God'

Samantha *(Aramaic)* 'A listener'

Samara *(Hebrew)* 'Watchful, cautious', 'guarded by God'

Samella *see* Samuela

Samelle *see* Samuela

Samira *(Arabic)* 'Entertaining'

Samuela *(Hebrew)* 'His name is God'. Feminine of Samuel
Samella, Samelle, Samuella, Samuelle

Samuelle *see* Samuela

Sancha *see* Sancia

Sanchia *see* Sancia

Sancia *(Latin)* 'Sacred'
Sancha, Sanchia

Sandeep *(Punjabi)* 'Enlightened'

Sandip *(Sanskrit)* 'Beautiful one'

Sandra *see* Alexandra

Sandy *see* Alexandra

Sanjay *(Sanskrit)* 'Charioteer'

Santina *(Spanish)* 'Little saint'

Sapphira *(Greek)* 'Eyes of sapphire colour'
Sapphire

Sapphire *see* Sapphira

Sara *see* Sarah

Sarah *(Hebrew)* 'Princess'
Morag, Sadella, Sadie, Sadye, Sal, Salaidh, Sallie, Sally, Sara, Sarene, Sarette, Sari, Sarine, Sarita, Sharie, Sorcha, Zara, Zarah, Zaria *see also* Morag and Zara

Saree *(Arabic)* 'Most noble'

Sarene *see* Sarah

Sarette *see* Sarah

Sari *see* Sarah

Sarila *(Turkish)* 'Waterfall'

Sarine *see* Sarah

Sarita *see* Sarah

Sasha *see* Alexandra or
Sacha

Sashenka *see* Alexandra

Saskia *(Norse)* 'Protector of
humankind' *see also*
Alexandra

Savanna *(Spanish)* 'An
open plain'

Savannah *see* Savanna

Savina *see* Sabina

Saxona *(Teutonic)* 'A sword
bearer'

Scarlet *see* Scarlett

Scarlett *(Middle English)*
'Scarlet coloured'
Scarlet, Scarletta

Scarletta *see* Scarlett

Scholastica *(Latin)*
'Scholar'

Sean *see* Jane

Sebastiane *(Latin)* 'Revered'
Sebastianan, Sebastianna,
Sebastianne, Sebastienna,
Sebastienne

Sebastianna *see* Sebastiane

Sebastianne *see* Sebastiane

Sebastienna *see* Sebastiane

Sebastienne *see* Sebastiane

Sebestianan *see* Sebastiane

Sebila *(Latin)* 'Wise old
woman'

Secunda *(Latin)* 'Second
born'

Seema *(Hebrew)* 'Treasure'

Seirian *(Welsh)* 'Sparkling'

Seiriol *(Welsh)* 'Bright'
Siriol

Sela *see* Selena

Selam *(Sudanese)* 'Peaceful'

Selda *see* Griselda

Selemas *see* Salema

Selena *(Greek)* 'The Moon'
Celene, Celie, Celina,
Celinda, Lena, Salene,
Sela, Selene, Selia,
Selie, Selina, Selinda,
Sena

Selene *see* Selena

Selia *see* Selena or Sheila

Selie *see* Selena

Selima *(Hebrew)* 'Peaceful'
see also Salema

Selina *see* Selena

Selinda see Selena

Selma (Celtic) 'The fair' see also Anselma

Semele (Latin) 'The single one'
Semelia

Semelia see Semele

Semira (Hebrew) 'Height of the heavens'

Sena see Selena

Senalda (Spanish) 'A sign'

Seon see Jane

Seonaid see Jane

Septima (Latin) 'Seventh born'

Sera see Seraphina

Serafina see Seraphina

Serafine see Seraphina

Seraphina (Hebrew) 'The ardent believer'. One with a burning faith
Sera, Serafina, Serafine, Seraphine

Seraphine see Seraphina

Serena (Latin) 'Bright tranquil one'

Serhilda see Serilda

Serhilde see Serilda

Serica (Latin) 'Silken'

Serilda (Teutonic) 'Armoured battle maid'
Serhilda, Serhilde, Serilde

Serilde see Serilda

Shafira (Arabic) 'Eminent', 'honourable'

Shahdi (Persian) 'Happiness'

Shahla (African) 'Beautiful eyes'

Shaina (Hebrew) 'Beautiful'
Shayna, Shayne

Shaira (Arabic) 'Thankful'
Shakira

Shakira see Shaira

Shakra see Chakra

Shama (Sanskrit) 'A flame'

Shamara (Arabic) 'Ready for battle'
Shamari, Shamora

Shamari see Shamara

Shamita (Sanskrit) 'Peace-maker'

Shamora see Shamara

Shani (African) 'Marvellous'

Shanley (Gaelic) 'Child of the old hero'

Shannah see Shannon

Shannon *(Gaelic)* 'Small but wise'
Shannah

Shari *see* Sharon

Sharie *see* Sarah

Sharleen *see* Charlotte or Caroline

Sharlene *see* Caroline

Sharline *see* Caroline

Sharon *(Hebrew)* 'A princess of exotic beauty'
Shari, Sharri, Sharron, Sharry, Sherry, Sheryl

Sharri *see* Sharon

Sharron *see* Sharon

Sharry *see* Sharon

Shava *see* Shelah

Shayna *see* Shaina

Shayne *see* Shaina

Shea *(Gaelic)* 'From the fairy fort' *see also* Shelah

Sheba *see* Saba

Shedea *(Native American)* 'Wild geese'

Sheela *see* Sheena or Sheila

Sheelah *see* Sheena or Sheila

Sheena *(Gaelic)* 'Dim-sighted'
Sheela, Sheelah, Sheilah *see also* Jane

Sheila *(Celtic)* 'Musical'
Selia, Sheela, Shelagh, Sheelah, Sheilah *see also* Cecilia

Sheilah *see* Sheena or Sheila

Shela *see* Shelah

Shelagh *see* Sheila

Shelah *(Hebrew)* 'Asked for'
Shava, Shea, Shela, Sheva, Sheya

Shelby *(Old English)* 'From the estate'

Shelley *(English)* 'From the edge of the meadow' *see also* Rachel

Shelly *see* Rachel

Shena *see* Jane

Sher *see* Cher

Shereen *(Arabic)* 'Sweet'

Sheri *see* Shirley

Sherrie *see* Cherie

Sherry *see* Charlotte, Cherie or Sharon

Sheryl *see* Charlotte, Cherie or Sharon

Sheva *see* Shelah

Sheya *see* Shelah

Shifra *(Hebrew)* 'Beautiful'

Shina *(Japanese)* 'Good virtue'

Shiri *(Hebrew)* 'My song'

Shirlee *see* Shirley

Shirleen *see* Shirley

Shirlene *see* Shirley

Shirley *(Anglo-Saxon)* 'From the white meadow'
Sheri, Sherry, Sheryl, Shirlee, Shirleen, Shirlene, Shirlie

Shirlie *see* Shirley

Shoshana *(Hebrew)* 'Rose'

Shula *(Arabic)* 'Flame, brightness'

Shulamith *(Hebrew)* 'Peace'

Siân *see* Jane

Sib *see* Sybil

Sibbie *see* Sybil

Sibby *see* Sybil

Sibel *see* Sybil

Sibell *see* Sybil

Sibella *see* Sybil

Sibie *see* Sybil

Sibil *see* Sybil

Sibilla *see* Sybil

Sibille *see* Sybil

Sibyl *see* Sybil

Sibylle *see* Sybil

Sida *(Greek)* 'Water lily'

Sidney *see* Sydney

Sidonia *see* Sydney

Sidonie *see* Sydney

Sidra *(Latin)* 'Glittering lady of the stars'
Sidria

Sidria *see* Sidra

Sicrna *(Greek)* 'A sweetly singing mermaid'

Sierra *(Irish)* 'Black'

Sigfreda *(Teutonic)* 'Victorious and peaceful'
Sigfrieda, Sigfriede

Sigfrieda *see* Sigfreda

Sigfriede *see* Siegfreda

Signa *(Latin)* 'Signed on the heart'

Sigourney *(English)* 'Victorious'

Sigrath *see* Sigrid

Sigrid *(Norse)* 'Victorious counsellor'
Sigrath, Sigrud, Sigurd

Sigrud *see* Sigrid

Sigurd *see* Sigrid

Sile *see* Julia

Sileas *see* Cecilia or Julia

Silva *see* Sylvia

Silvana *(Latin)* 'Wood-dweller' *see also* Sylvia

Silvie *see* Sylvia

Simona *see* Simone

Simone *(Hebrew)* 'Heard by the Lord'. Feminine of Simon/Simeon Simona, Simonetta, Simonette

Simonetta *see* Simone

Simonette *see* Simone

Sine *see* Jane

Sinead *(Welsh) see* Jane

Siobhan *(Gaelic)* 'Gift of God' *see also* Jane

Sireen *see* Sirena

Sirena *(Greek)* 'Sweet-singing mermaid'. Originally from the sirens who lured mariners to their deaths on the rocks with their beautiful singing. Used sometimes in World War II for babies born during an air raid Sireen, Sirene

Sirene *see* Sirena

Siriol *see* Seiriol

Sisile *see* Cecilia

Sisle *see* Cecilia

Sisley *see* Cecilia

Sissie *see* Cecilia

Siuban *see* Judith

Skye *see* Skylar

Skylar *(Dutch)* 'Sheltering' Skye

Smita *(Sanskrit)* 'Smiling'

Snowdrop *(English)* From the plant

Sofia *see* Sophia

Sofie *see* Sophia

Solah *(Latin)* 'Alone' Solita

Solana *(Spanish)* 'Sunshine'

Solange *(Latin)* 'Good shepherdess'

Solita *see* Solah

Solvig *(Teutonic)* 'Victorious battle maid'

Sonia *see* Sophia

Sonja *see* Sophia

Sonya *see* Sophia

Sophia *(Greek)* 'Wisdom' Beathag, Sadhbh, Sadhbha, Sofia, Sofie, Sonia, Sonja, Sonya, Sophie, Sophy

Sophie *see* Sophia

Sophronia *(Greek)* 'Sensible one'

Sophy *see* Sophia

Sorcha *(Gaelic)* 'Bright one' *see also* Sarah

Sparkle *(Dutch)* 'Gleaming'

Sperata *(Latin)* 'Hoped for'

Spring *(English)* 'Joyous season'

Stacey *see* Anastasia or Eustacia

Stacia *see* Anastasia or Eustacia

Stacie *see* Anastasia or Eustacia

Stacy *see* Anastasia or Eustacia

Star *see* Starr

Starr *(English)* 'A star' Star

Stefa *see* Stephanie

Steffie *see* Stephanie

Stella *see* Estelle

Stelle *see* Estelle

Stepha *see* Stephanie

Stephania *see* Stephanie

Stephanie *(Greek)* 'A crown, garland'. Feminine of Stephen
Stefa, Steffie, Stepha, Stephania, Stephena, Stephenia, Stephenie, Stevana, Stevania, Stevena, Stevenia, Stevie

Stephena *see* Stephanie

Stephenia *see* Stephanie

Stephenie *see* Stephanie

Stevana *see* Stephanie

Stevania *see* Stephanie

Stevena *see* Stephanie

Stevenia *see* Stephanie

Stevie *see* Stephanie

Storm *(Anglo-Saxon)* 'A tempest'. One of turbulent nature

Sucheta *(Sanskrit)* 'With a beautiful mind'
Suchi, Suchira, Suchita, Suchitra

Suchi *see* Sucheta

Suchira *see* Sucheta

Suchita *see* Sucheta

Suchitra *see* Sucheta

Sue *see* Susan

Sukey *see* Susan

Suki *(Japanese)* 'Loved one' *see also* Susan

Suky *see* Susan

Sulia *(Latin)* 'Downy, youthful'

Suliana *see* Sulia

Sulwyn *(Welsh)* 'Beautiful as the sun'

Sumalee *(Thai)* 'Beautiful flower'

Sumi *(Japanese)* 'Refined'

Sunita *(Hindi)* 'Good conduct and deeds'

Sunny *(Anglo-Saxon)* 'Bright and cheerful'. The brightness of the sun after the storm

Supriti *see* Supriya

Supriya *(Sanskrit)* 'Loved' Supriti

Susan *(Hebrew)* 'Graceful lily' Sue, Sukey, Suki, Suky, Susana, Susanna, Susannah, Susanne, Susette, Susi, Susie, Susy, Suzanna, Suzanne, Suzetta, Suzette, Suzie, Suzy, Zsa, Zsa-Zsa

Susana *see* Susan

Susanna *see* Susan

Susannah *see* Susan

Susanne *see* Susan

Susette *see* Susan

Sushila *(Sanskrit)* 'Well-behaved'

Susi *see* Susan

Susie *see* Susan

Susy *see* Susan

Suzanna *see* Susan

Suzanne *see* Susan

Suzetta *see* Susan

Suzette *see* Susan

Suzie *see* Susan

Suzy *see* Susan

Swetlana *(German)* 'A star'

Sybella *see* Sybil

Sybil *(Greek)* 'Prophetess'. The female soothsayer of ancient Greece Cybil, Sib, Sibbie, Sibby, Sibel, Sibell, Sibella, Sibie, Sibil, Sibilla, Sibille, Sibyl, Sibylle, Sybella, Sybille, Sybyl

Sybille *see* Sybil

Sybyl *see* Sybil

Syd *see* Sydney

Sydel *(Hebrew)* 'That enchantress'
Sydelle

Sydney *(Hebrew)* 'The enticer' *(French)* 'From St. Denis'. Feminine of Sidney
Sid, Sidney, Sidonia, Sidonie, Syd

Syl *see* Sylvia

Sylgwyn *(Welsh)* 'Born on Whit Sunday'

Sylvana *(Latin)* 'From the woods'

Sylvia *(Latin)* 'From the forest'
Sil, Silva, Silvana, Silvia, Silvie, Slyvana, Syl, Sylva, Zilva, Zilvia

Syna *(Greek)* 'Together'
Syne

Syne *see* Syna

Syntyche *(Greek)* 'With good fortune'

GIRLS

Tabbie *see* Tabitha

Tabby *see* Tabitha

Tabina *(Arabic)* 'Muhammed's follower'

Tabitha *(Aramaic)* 'The gazelle'. One of gentle grace
Tabbie, Tabby, Tabithe

Tabithe *see* Tabitha

Tacita *see* Tacitah

Tacitah *(Latin)* 'Silence'
Tacita

Tacy *(Latin)* 'Peace'

Tahani *(Arabic)* 'Congratulations'

Tahira *(Arabic)* 'Pure'

Takara *(Japanese)* 'Treasure'

Talia *(Greek)* 'Blooming'

Taliba *(Arabic)* 'Student'

Talitha *(Aramaic)* 'The maiden'

Tallie *see* Tallulah

Tallu *see* Tallulah

Tallula *see* Tallulah

Tallulah *(Native American)* 'Laughing water'. One who bubbles like a spring
Tallie, Tallu, Tallula, Tally

Tally *see* Tallulah

Tama *(Japanese)* 'Jewel'

Tamali *(Sanskrit)* 'Tree with the black bark'
Tamalika

Tamalika *see* Tamali

Tamar *see* Tamara

Tamara *(Hebrew)* 'Palm tree'
Tamar, Tammie, Tammy

Tammie *see* Tamara

Tammy *(Hebrew)* 'Perfection' *see also* Tamara

Tamsin *see* Thomasina

Tandi *see* Tansy

Tangerine *(Anglo-Saxon)* 'Girl from Tangiers'

Tangwystl *(Welsh)* 'Peace pledge'

Tani *(Japanese)* 'Valley'

Tania *see* Tatiana

Tansy *(Latin)* 'Tenacious'. A woman of determination. Also the name of a herb
Tandi

Tanuka *(Sanskrit)* 'Slender'

Tanya *see* Tania or Titania

Tara *(Gaelic)* 'Towering rock'. The home of the ancient kings of Ireland
Tarah, Terra

Tarah *see* Tara

Tate *(Old English)* 'To be cheerful'
Tatum

Tatiana *(Russian)* 'Silver-haired one'

Tatum *see* Tate

Tavi *see* Octavia

Tavia *see* Octavia

Tavie *see* Octavia

Tavy *see* Octavia

Taylor *(Middle English)* 'A tailor'

Tecla *see* Thecla

Teddie *see* Theodora

Tegan *(Welsh)* 'Beautiful'

Tegwen *(Welsh)* 'Beautiful and blessed'

Temira *(Hebrew)* 'Tall'
Timora

Tempest *(French)* 'Stormy one'
Tempesta, Tempeste

Tempesta *see* Tempest

Tempeste *see* Tempest

Teodora *see* Theodora

Teodore *see* Theodora

Terencia *see* Terentia

Terentia *(Greek)* 'Guardian'. Feminine of Terence
Terencia, Teri, Terri, Terrie, Terry

Teresa *(Greek)* 'The harvester'
Terese, Teresina, Teresita, Teressa, Terri, Terrie, Terry, Tess, Tessa, Tessie, Tessy, Theresa, Therese, Toireasa, Tracie, Tracy, Trescha, Zita *see also* Tessa and Tracy

Terese *see* Teresa

Teresina *see* Teresa

Teresita *see* Teresa

Teressa see Teresa

Teri see Terentia

Terra see Tara

Terri see Terentia

Terrie see Terentia or
Teresa

Terry see Terentia or
Teresa

Tertia (Latin) 'Third child'

Terza (Greek) 'Girl from the
farm'

Tess see Teresa

Tessa (Greek) 'Fourth child'
see also Teresa

Tessie see Teresa

Tessy see Teresa

Tewdews (Welsh) 'Divinely
given'

Thada see Thaddea

Thadda see Thaddea

Thaddea (Greek)
'Courageous being'. A
girl of great bravery
and endurance
Thada, Thadda

Thalassa (Greek) 'From the
sea'

Thalia (Greek) 'Luxurious
blossom'

Thea (Greek) 'Goddess' see
also Althea, Anthea,
Dorothea or Theodora

Theadora see Theodora

Theadosia see Theodora

Theafania see Theophila

Theana see Theano

Theano (Greek) 'Divine
name'
Theana

Theaphania see Theophila

Thecla (Greek) 'Divine
follower'. A disciple of
St Paul
Tecla, Thekla

Theda see Theodora

Thekla see Thecla

Thelma (Greek) 'The
nursling'

Theo see Theodora or
Theola

Theodora (Greek) 'Gift of
God'
Dora, Feadora, Feadore,
Fedora, Fedore,
Feodora, Feodore,
Teddie, Teodora,
Teodore, Thea,
Theadora, Theadosia,
Theda, Theo,
Theodosia see also
Dorothy

Theodosia *see* Theodora

Theofanie *see* Theophila

Theofila *see* Theophania

Theofilia *see* Theophania

Theola *(Greek)* 'Sent from God'
Theo, Lola

Theona *see* Theone

Theone *(Greek)* 'In the name of God'
Theona

Theophania *(Greek)* 'Beloved of God'
Theofila, Theofilia, Theophilia *see also* Theophila

Theophanie *see* Theophila

Theophila *(Greek)* 'Appearance of God'
Theafania, Theofanie, Theaphania, Theophanie, Tiffanie, Tiffy

Theophilia *see* Theophania

Theora *(Greek)* 'Watcher for God'

Thera *(Greek)* 'Wild, untamed one'

Theresa *see* Teresa

Therese *see* Teresa

Thetis *(Greek)* 'Positive one'. One who knows her own mind
Thetys

Thetys *see* Thetis

Thia *see* Anthea

Thirza *(Hebrew)* 'Pleasantness'
Thyrza, Tirza

Thomasa *see* Thomasina

Thomase *see* Thomasina

Thomasina *(Hebrew)* 'The twin'. Feminine of Thomas
Tamsin, Thomasa, Thomase, Thomasine, Tomasa, Tomase, Tomasina, Tomasine

Thomasine *see* Thomasina

Thora *(Norse)* 'Thunder'. From the Norse God of Thunder, Thor

Thorberta *(Norse)* 'Brilliance of Thor'
Thorberte, Thorbertha, Thorberthe

Thorberte *see* Thorberta

Thorbertha *see* Thorberta

Thorberthe *see* Thorberta

Thordia *see* Thordis

Thordie *see* Thordis

Thordis *(Norse)* 'Spirit of Thor'. The sound of thunder
Thordia, Thordie

Thyra *(Greek)* 'Shield-bearer'

Thyrza *see* Thirza

Tia *(Greek)* 'Princess'

Tiana *(Greek)* 'Princess'

Tiara *(Latin)* 'Crowned'

Tibelda *(Teutonic)* 'Boldest person'

Tiberia *(Latin)* 'From the Tiber'. The river of ancient Rome

Tierney *(Gaelic)* 'Grandchild of the lordly'

Tiffanie *see* Theophila

Tiffany *(Greek)* 'Manifestation of God'
Tiphani

Tiffy *see* Theophila

Tilda *see* Mathilda

Tilly *see* Mathilda

Tim *see* Timothea

Timandra *(Greek)* 'Honour'
Tymandra

Timmie *see* Timothea

Timmy *see* Timothea

Timora *see* Temira

Timothea *(Greek)* 'Honouring God'
Tim, Timmie, Timmy

Tina *see* Christine or Martina

Tiphani *see* Tiffany

Tirza *(Spanish)* 'Cypress' *see also* Thirza

Tish *see* Letitia

Tita *(Latin)* 'Honoured title'

Titania *(Greek)* 'Giantess'. Also the name of the Queen of the Fairies

Tizane *(Hungarian)* 'A gypsy' *see also* Gitana

Tobe *see* Tobey

Tobey *(Hebrew)* 'God is good'
Tobe, Tobi, Toby

Tobi *see* Tobey

Toby *see* Tobey

Toinette *see* Antonia

Toireasa *see* Teresa

Tomasa *see* Thomasina

Tomase *see* Thomasina

Tomasina *see* Thomasina

Tomasine *see* Thomasina

Tomi *(Japanese)* 'Riches'

Toni *see* Antonia

Tonia *see* Antonia

Topaz *(Latin)* 'The topaz gem'

Tory *see* Victoria

Tourmalina *see* Tourmaline

Tourmaline *(Sri Lankan)* 'A Carnelian' Tourmalina

Tracey *see* Tracy

Tracie *see* Teresa

Tracy *(Gaelic)* 'Battler' Tracey *see also* Teresa

Traviata *(Italian)* 'The frail one'

Trescha *see* Teresa

Triantafilia *(Greek)* 'Rose'

Trilby *(Italian)* 'A singer who trills'

Trina *(Greek)* 'Girl of purity'

Triphena *see* Tryphena

Triphenia *see* Tryphena

Trista *(Latin)* 'Melancholia, sorrow'

Trix *see* Beatrice

Trixie *see* Beatrice

Trixy *see* Beatrice

Trudey *see* Trudy

Trudi *see* Trudy

Trudie *see* Gertrude or Trudy

Trudy *(Teutonic)* 'Loved one' Trudey, Trudi, Trudie *see also* Gertrude

Tryphena *(Latin)* 'The delicate one' Triphena, Triphenia, Tryphenia

Tryphenia *see* Tryphena

Tuesday *(Anglo-Saxon)* 'Born on Tuesday'

Tullia *(Gaelic)* 'Peaceful one'

Turaya *(Arabic)* 'Star'

Twyla *(Middle English)* 'Woven of double thread'

Tymandra *see* Timandra

Tyne *(Old English)* 'River'

Tyra *(Scandinavian)* 'Battler'

Uda *(Teutonic)* 'Prosperous'.
A child of fortune
Udella, Udelle

Udella *see* Uda

Udelle *see* Uda

Ula *(Celtic)* 'Jewel of the
sea' *(Teutonic)* 'The
inheritor'
Oola

Ulima *(Arabic)* 'The
learned one'. A woman
who gives good advice

Ulrica *(Teutonic)* 'Ruler of
all'
Elrica, Rica, Ulrika

Ulrika *see* Ulrica

Ultima *(Latin)* 'The most
distant'

Ulva *(Teutonic)* 'The she-
wolf. A symbol of
bravery

Umar *(Arabic)* 'Flourishing'

Umeko *(Japanese)* 'Plum-
blossom child'

Una *(Latin)* 'One'. The one
and only girl *(Irish)*
'United'
Ona, Oona, Oonagh

Undine *see* Ondine

Unity *(Middle English)*
'Unity'

Urania *(Greek)* 'Heavenly'.
The muse of astronomy

Urania *(Greek)* 'One from
heaven'

Urbana *(Latin)* 'Born in
the town'

Urith *(Old German)*
'Deserving'

Ursa *see* Ursula

Ursel *see* Ursula

Ursie *see* Ursula

Ursola *see* Ursula

Ursula *(Latin)* 'The she-
bear'
Ora, Orsa, Orsola, Ursa,
Ursel, Ursie, Ursola,
Ursule, Ursulette,
Ursuline, Ursy

Ursule *see* Ursula

Ursulette *see* Ursula

Ursuline *see* Ursula

Ursy *see* Ursula

Usha *(Sanskrit)* 'Dawn'

Ushakiran *(Sanskrit)* 'The first rays of the sun'

Ushashi *(Sanskrit)* 'Morning'

Uta *(German)* 'Rich'

Utano *(Japanese)* 'Field of song'

Utina *(Native American)* 'Woman from my country'

Utsa *(Sanskrit)* 'Spring'

Vahsti *(Persian)* 'Beautiful one'

Val *see* Valentina or Valerie

Vala *(Teutonic)* 'The chosen one'. Ideal name for an adopted daughter

Valborga *(Teutonic)* 'Protecting ruler' Valburga, Walborga, Walburga

Valburga *see* Valborga

Valda *(Teutonic)* 'Ruler' Walda, Welda

Valeda *see* Valentina

Valencia *see* Valentina

Valentia *see* Valentina

Valentina *(Latin)* 'Strong and vigorous' Val, Valeda, Valencia, Valentia, Valentine, Valera, Valida, Vallie

Valentine *see* Valentina

Valera *see* Valentina

Valeria *see* Valerie

Valerie *(French)* 'Strong' Val, Valeria, Valery, Vallie, Valora, Valorey, Valorie, Valory

Valery *see* Valerie

Valeska *(Slavic)* 'Glorious ruler' Waleska

Valida *see* Velda or Valentina

Vallie *see* Valentina or Valerie

Valma *(Welsh)* 'Mayflower' Valmai

Valmai *see* Valma

Valona *see* Valonia

Valonia *(Latin)* 'From the vale' Valona

Valora *see* Valerie

Valorey *see* Valerie

Valorie *see* Valerie

Valory *see* Valerie

Van *see* Vanessa

Vancy *see* Evangeline

Vanda *(Teutonic)* 'Family'

Vanessa *(Greek)* 'The butterfly'
Van, Vania, Vanna, Vanni, Vannie, Vanny, Vanya

Vangie *see* Evangeline

Vania *(Hebrew)* 'God's precious gift'
Vanina *see also* Vanessa

Vanina *see* Vania

Vanita *(Sanskrit)* 'Desired'

Vanna *see* Vanessa

Vanni *see* Vanessa

Vannie *see* Vanessa

Vanny *see* Vanessa

Vanora *see* Genevieve

Vanya *see* Vanessa

Varina *(Slavic)* 'Stranger'

Vashti *(Persian)* 'The most beautiful'

Veda *(Sanskrit)* 'Wisdom and knowledge'
Vedis

Vedetta *see* Vedette

Vedette *(Italian)* 'The sentinel'
Vedetta

Vedis *see* Veda

Vega *(Arabic)* 'The great one'

Velda *(Teutonic)* 'Very wise'
Valida

Velda (Dutch) 'Field'

Velica *see* Velika

Velika *(Slavic)* 'The falling one'
Velica

Velma *see* Wilhelmina

Velvet *(English)* 'Soft as velvet'

Venetia *(Latin)* 'Lady of Venice'

Venita *see* Venus

Ventura *(Spanish)* 'Happiness and good luck'

Venus *(Latin)* 'Loveliness, beauty'. The Roman Goddess of Beauty and Love
Venita, Vinita, Vinnie, Vinny

Vera *(Latin)* 'Truth'. One who is honest and steadfast
Vere, Verena, Verene, Veria, Verina, Verine

Verbena *(Latin)* 'The sacred bough'

Verda *(Latin)* 'Fresh youth'. Possessing the verdant qualities of spring *see also* Verna

Vere *see* Vera

Verena *see* Vera or Verna

Verene *see* Vera

Veria *see* Vera

Verina *see* Vera

Verine *see* Vera Verity *(Latin)* 'Truth'

Verla *see* Vera

Vern *see* Laverne

Verna *(Latin)* 'Spring-like' Verda, Verena, Verneta, Vernice, Vernis, Vernita, Virina, Virna *see also* Laverne

Verne *see* Laverne

Verneta *see* Verna

Vernice *see* Verna

Vernis *see* Verna

Vernita *see* Verna

Verona *(Latin)* 'Lady of Verona'

Veronica *(Latin)* 'True image' Ronnie, Ronny, Veronique, Vonnie, Vonny, and all variations of Bernice *see also* Bernice

Veronique *see* Veronica

Vesna *(Slavic)* 'Spring'

Vespera *(Latin)* 'The evening star'

Vesta *(Latin)* 'Guardian of the sacred flame' or 'melodious one'. The vestal virgins tended the temples of ancient Greece

Veta *see* Vita

Vevila *(Gaelic)* 'Melodious one'

Vi *see* Violet

Vicenta *see* Vincentia

Vicki *see* Victoria

Vicky *see* Victoria

Victoria *(Latin)* 'The victorious one'. Became very popular in Britain during the long reign of Queen Victoria Tory, Vicki, Vicky, Victorine, Victorie, Vitoria, Vittoria

Victorie *see* Victoria

Victorine *see* Victoria

Vida *(Hebrew)* 'Beloved one'. Feminine of David

Vidette *(Hebrew)* 'Beloved'

Vidonia *(Portuguese)* 'Vine branch'

Vidula *(Sanskrit)* 'The moon'

Vienna *(Latin)* 'Geography'. The capital of Austria

Vigilia *(Latin)* 'The alert, vigilant'

Vignette *(French)* 'The little vine'

Vijaya *(Sanskrit)* 'Victory'

Villette *(French)* 'From the village'

Vina *(Spanish)* 'From the vineyard' *see also* Alviona or Lavinia

Vinaya *(Sanskrit)* 'Modest'

Vincencia *see* Vincentia

Vincentia *(Latin)* 'The conqueror'. Feminine of Vincent
Vicenta, Vincencia

Vinia *see* Lavinia

Vinita *see* Venus

Vinnie *see* Venus

Vinny *see* Venus

Viola *see* Violet

Violante *see* Violet

Violet *(Latin)* 'Modest flower'. Shy and retiring, like the flower
Eolande, Vi, Viola, Violante, Violetta, Violette, Yolanda, Yolande, Yolanthe *see also* Iolanthe

Violetta *see* Violet

Violette *see* Violet

Virdis *(Latin)* 'Fresh, blooming'

Virgi *see* Virginia

Virgie *see* Virginia

Virgilia *(Latin)* 'The staff-bearer'

Virginia *(Latin)* 'The virgin, maidenly and pure'
Ginger, Ginnie, Ginny, Jinny, Virgi, Virgie, Virginie, Virgy

Virginie *see* Virginia

Virgy *see* Virginia

Viridis *(Latin)* 'The green bough'

Virina *see* Verna

Virna *see* Verna

Vita *(Latin)* 'Life'. One who likes living
Evita, Veta, Vitia

Vitia *see* Vita

Vitoria *see* Victoria

Vittoria *see* Victoria

Viv *see* Vivian

Viveca *(Latin/ Scandinavian)* 'Living voice'

Vivi *see* Vivian

Vivia *see* Vivian

Vivian *(Latin)* 'Alive'. Vivid and vibrant with life Viv, Vivi, Vivia, Viviana, Viviane, Vivie, Vivien, Viviene, Vivienna, Vivienne, Vivyan, Vyvyan

Viviana *see* Vivian

Viviane *see* Vivian

Vivie *see* Vivian

Vivien *see* Vivian

Viviene *see* Vivian

Vivienna *see* Vivian

Vivienne *see* Vivian

Vivyan *see* Vivian

Volante *(Latin)* 'The flying one'. One who steps so lightly that she seems to fly

Voleta *(French)* 'A floating veil' Voletta

Voletta *see* Voleta

Von *see* Yvonne

Vonnie *see* Veronica or Yvonne

Vonny *see* Veronica

Vyvyan *see* Vivian

GIRLS

Wahilda *(Arabic)* 'Unique'

Wahkuna *(Native American)* 'Beautiful'

Walborga *see* Valborga

Walburga *see* Valborga

Walda *see* Valda

Waleska *see* Valeska

Walida *(Arabic)* 'New-born girl'

Wallace *see* Wallis

Wallie *see* Wallis

Wallis *(Anglo-Saxon)* 'The Welshwoman', 'the stranger'
Wallace, Wallie, Wally

Wally *see* Wallis

Wanda *(Teutonic)* 'The wanderer'. The restless roamer
Wandie, Wandis, Wenda, Wendeline, Wendy

Wandie *see* Wanda

Wandis *see* Wanda

Wanetta *(Anglo-Saxon)* 'The pale one'
Wanette

Wanette *see* Wanetta

Warda *(Teutonic)* 'The guardian'

Wasima *(Arabic)* 'Pretty'

Welda *see* Valda

Welma *see* Wilhelmina

Wenda *see* Wanda

Wendeline *see* Wanda

Wendy *(English)* Character created in *Peter Pan* by J.M. Barrie *see also* Gwendoline or Wanda

Wenona *see* Winona

Wenonah *see* Winona

Wesla *(Old English)* 'From the west meadow'

Whitney *(Old English)* 'From the white island'

Wilf *see* Wilfreda

Wilfreda *(Teutonic)* 'The peacemaker'. Feminine of Wilfred
Freda, Freddie, Wilf, Wilfreida, Wilfrieda

Wilfreida *see* Wilfreda

Wilfrieda *see* Wilfreda

Wilhelmina *(Teutonic)* 'The protectress'. One who guards resolutely what is her own
Billie, Billy, Guilla, Helma, Mina, Minnie, Minny, Velma, Welma, Willa, Willie, Willy, Wilma *see also* Helma

Willa *(Anglo-Saxon)* 'Desirable' *see also* Billie or Wilhelmina

Willie *see* Wilhelmina

Willow *(English)* Plant name

Willy *see* Wilhelmina

Wilma *see* Wilhelmina

Wilona *(Old English)* 'Desired'

Win *see* Edwina or Wynne

Wina *see* Edwina

Winema *(Native American)* 'Chief of the tribe'

Winifred *(Teutonic)* 'Peaceful friend'. A restful person to have around
Winifreida, Winifrida, Winifrieda, Winnie, Winny, Wynn

Winifreida *see* Winifred

Winifrida *see* Winifred

Winifrieda *see* Winifred

Winna *(African)* 'Friend'
Winnah

Winnah *see* Winna

Winnie *see* Edwina or Winifred

Winny *see* Winifred

Winola *(Teutonic)* 'Gracious friend'

Winona *(American-Indian)* 'First born daughter'
Wenona, Wenonah, Winonah

Winonah *see* Winona

Winsome *(English)* 'Pleasant, attractive'

Wren *(Old English)* 'Wren'

Wyanet *(Native American)* 'Very beautiful'

Wylda *(Teutonic)* 'Rebellious'

Wylma *(Teutonic)* 'Resolute'

Wyne *see* Wynne

Wynn *see* Winifred

Wynne *(Celtic)* 'Fair, white maiden'
Win, Wyne

GIRLS

Xanthe *(Greek)* 'Golden blonde'

Xanthippe *(Greek)* The wife of Socrates

Xaverie *(Aramaic)* 'Bright'

Xaviera *(Spanish)* 'Owner of the home'

Xena *(Greek)* 'Hospitality'
Xene, Xenia, Zenia

Xene *see* Xena

Xenia *see* Xena

Xiaoli *(Chinese)* 'Small and beautiful'

Xiiaoying *(Chinese)* 'Small flower'

Ximena *(Greek)* 'Heroine'

Xylia *(Greek)* 'From the woods'
Xyline, Xylona

Xyline *see* Xylia

Xylona *see* Xylia

GIRLS

Yaffa *(Hebrew)* 'Beautiful'

Yakira *(Hebrew)* 'Valuable'

Yasmeen *(Persian)* 'Flower'

Yasmin *see* Jasmin

Yasmina *see* Jasmin

Yasmine *see* Jasmin

Yasu *(Japanese)* 'Tranquil'

Yedda *(Anglo-Saxon)* 'One with a melodious voice'

Yeira *(Hebrew)* 'Light'

Yepa *(Native American)* 'Snow girl'

Yerusha *see* Jerusha

Yesima *(Hebrew)* 'Right hand', 'strength'

Yetta *(Anglo-Saxon)* 'To give, the giver' *see also* Henrietta

Yevetta *see* Yvonne

Ynes *see* Agnes

Ynez *see* Agnes

Yoanna *see* Jane

Yolanda *see* Iolanthe or Violet

Yolande *see* Iolanthe or Violet

Yolanthe *see* Violet

Yona *(Korean)* 'Lotus blossom'

Yosepha *see* Josephine

Yoshe *(Japanese)* 'Beautiful'

Yoshiko *(Japanese)* 'Good'

Yovela *(Hebrew)* 'Rejoicing'

Ysabeau *see* Isabel

Ysabel *see* Isabel

Ysabella *see* Isabel

Ysabelle *see* Isabel

Yseult *see* Isolde

Ysobel *see* Isabel

Ysolda *see* Isolde

Ysolde *see* Isolde

Yusepha *see* Josephine

Yvetta *see* Yvonne

Yvette *see* Yvonne

Yvona *see* Yvonne

Yvonne *(French)* 'Archer
with the yew bow'
Evette, Evonne, Ivonne,
Von, Vonnie, Yevetta,
Yevette, Yvetta, Yvette,
Yvona

GIRLS

Zabrina *(Anglo-Saxon)* 'Noble maiden'

Zada *(Arabic)* 'Lucky one'. Fortune's favourite

Zahra *(Arabic)* 'Blossom'

Zakira *(Arabic)* 'Remembrance'

Zamira *(Hebrew)* 'Song'

Zana *(Persian)* 'Woman'

Zandra *see* Alexandra

Zaneta *see* Jane

Zara *(Hebrew)* 'Brightness of dawn'
Zarah, Zaria *see also* Sarah

Zarah *see* Sarah or Zara

Zaria *see* Azaria, Sarah or Zara

Zarifa *(Arabic)* 'Graceful'

Zea *(Latin)* 'Ripened grain'

Zebada *(Hebrew)* 'Gift of the Lord'

Zelda *see* Griselda

Zele *see* Zelia

Zelia *(Greek)* 'Devoted to duty'
Zele, Zelie, Zelina

Zelie *see* Zelia

Zelina *see* Zelia

Zella *(Hebrew)* 'Shadow'

Zelma *see* Anselma

Zelosa *(Greek)* 'Jealous one'

Zena *(Greek)* 'The hospitable one' *see also* Zenobia or Zian

Zenaida *see* Zenobia

Zenda *see* Zenobia

Zenia *see* Xena or Zenobia

Zenina *see* Zenobia

Zenna *see* Zenobia

Zennie *see* Zenobia

Zenobia *(Greek)* 'Zeus gave life' *(Arabic)* 'Ornament to her father'
Zena, Zenaida, Zenda, Zenia, Zenina, Zenna, Zennie, Zenorbie

Zenorbie *see* Zenobia

Zephirah *(Hebrew)* 'Dawn'

Zera *(Hebrew)* 'Seeds'

Zerelda *(Old German)*
'Armoured warrior maid'

Zerla *see* Zerlina

Zerlina *(Teutonic)* 'Serene
beauty'
Zerla, Zerline

Zerlinda *(Hebrew)*
'Beautiful as the dawn'

Zerline *see* Zerlina

Zetta *(Anglo-Saxon)* 'Sixth
born'. The sixth letter
of the Greek alphabet
Zita, Zitao

Zeva *(Greek)* 'Sword'

Zia *(Sanskrit)* 'Enlightened'
(Latin) 'Kind of grain'

Zian *(Hebrew)* 'Abundance'
Zena, Zinah

Zila *(Sanskrit)* 'A shady
place'

Zilla *(Hebrew)* 'Shadow'
Zillah

Zillah *see* Zilla

Zilpah *(Hebrew)* 'Dropping'

Zinah *see* Zian

Zinia *see* Zinnia

Zinnia *(Latin)* 'The zinnia
flower'
Zinia

Zippora *(Hebrew)*
'Trumpet' or 'sparrow'
Zipporah

Zipporah *see* Zippora

Zita *see* Teresa or Zetta

Zitao *see* Zetta

Ziva *(Hebrew)* 'Brightness'

Zoë *(Greek)* 'Life'

Zofeyah *(Hebrew)* 'God
sees'

Zohara *(Hebrew)* 'The
bright child'

Zona *(Latin)* 'A girdle'. The
belt of Orion
Zonie

Zonie *see* Zona

Zora *(Latin)* 'The dawn'
Zorah, Zorana, Zorina,
Zorin

Zorah *see* Zora

Zorana *see* Zora

Zorina *see* Zora

Zorine *see* Zora

Zosima *(Greek)* 'Wealthy
woman'

Zsa *see* Susan

Zsa-Zsa *see* Susan

Zuleika *(Arabic)* 'Fair'

Zulema *(Arabic/Hebrew)*
'Peace'

Aadi *(Sanskrit)* 'First, most important'

Aahmes *(Egyptian)* 'Child of the moon'

Aaron *(Hebrew)* 'Exalted'. Brother of Moses
Ari, Arnie, Aron, Erin, Haroun

Abba *(Hebrew)* 'Father'
Abbe *see also* Abbott

Abbe *see* Abbott

Abbey *see* Abbott, Abelard or Abner

Abbot *see* Abbott

Abbott *(Anglo-Saxon)* 'Father of the abbey'
Abba, Abbe, Abbey, Abbot, Abott

Abdel *see* Abdul

Abdi *(Hebrew)* 'My servant'

Abdiel *(Hebrew)* 'Servant of God'

Abdon *(Hebrew)* 'Son of'

Abdul *(Arabic)* 'Son of'
Abdel

Abdullah *(Arabic)* 'Servant of Allah'

Abe *see* Abraham or Abelard

Abel *(Hebrew)* 'Breath'. The first recorded murder victim according to the Bible

Abelard *(Teutonic)* 'Nobly resolute'
Abbey, Abe

Abiah *(Hebrew)* 'The Lord is my father'
Abija, Abijah

Abie *see* Abraham

Abijah *see* Abiah

Abir *(Hebrew)* 'Strong'
Abiri

Abiri *see* Abir

Abisha *(Hebrew)* 'God's gift'

Abner *(Hebrew)* 'Father of light'
Abbey, Eb

Abott *see* Abbott

Abraham *(Hebrew)* 'Father of multitudes'. The original patriarch
Abe, Abie, Abram, Abran, Avram, Bram, Ibrahim

Abram *see* Abraham

Abran *see* Abraham

Abric *(Teutonic)* 'Above authority'

Abros *(Greek)* 'Elegant'

Absalom *(Hebrew)* 'Father of peace'
Absolom

Absolom *see* Absalom

Ace *(Latin)* 'Unity'
Acey

Acelin *(French)* 'Noble'
Aceline, Acelot

Aceline *see* Ascelin

Acelot *see* Acelin

Acey *see* Ace

Achates *(Greek)* 'Faithful companion'

Achilles *(Greek)* 'Swift'

Acima *(Hebrew)* 'The Lord's judgement'

Ackerley *(Anglo-Saxon)* 'From the acre meadow'
Ackley

Ackley *see* Ackerley

Acton *(Old English)* 'Town near oak trees'

Ad *see* Adolph

Adair *(Gaelic)* 'From the oak tree near the ford'

Adal *(Teutonic)* 'Regal, noble'

Adalard *(Teutonic)* 'Noble and brave'
Adelard, Adhelard

Adalric *(Old German)* 'Noble ruler'
Adelric

Adam *(Hebrew)* 'Of the red earth'. The first man, according to the Bible
Adamo, Adan, Adao, Adhamh

Adamo *see* Adam

Adams *see* Adamson

Adamson *(Hebrew)* 'Son of Adam'
Adams

Adan *see* Adam, Adin or Aidan

Adao *see* Adam

Adar *(Hebrew)* 'Fiery'

Addison *(Anglo-Saxon)* 'Adam's son'

Addo (*Teutonic*) 'Happy, cheerful'

Addy (*Teutonic*) 'Awesome, noble'

Ade *see* Adrian

Adelard *see* Adalard

Adelbert *see* Albert

Adelgar (*Hebrew*) 'Bright spear'

Adelpho (*Greek*) 'Brother'

Adelric *see* Adalric

Adelwine *see* Audwin

Ademar (*Teutonic*) 'Fierce, noble, famous'
Ademaro

Ademaro *see* Ademar

Adesh (*Sanskrit*) 'Command'

Adham (*Arabic*) 'Black'

Adhamh *see* Adam

Adhar (*Arabic*) 'Waiting'

Adhelard *see* Adalard

Adiel (*Hebrew*) 'One who is favoured by God'

Adin (*Hebrew*) 'Sensual'
Adan

Adlai (*Hebrew*) 'My witness, my ornament'

Adler (*Teutonic*) 'Eagle'. One of keen perception

Adley (*Hebrew*) 'Fair-minded'

Adney (*Anglo-Saxon*) 'One who lives on the island

Adolf *see* Adolph

Adolfus *see* Adolph

Adolph (*Teutonic*) 'Noble wolf'
Ad, Adolf, Adolfus, Adolphe, Adolpho, Adolphus, Dolf, Dolph

Adolphe *see* Adolph

Adolpho *see* Adolph

Adolphus *see* Adolph

Adon (*Hebrew*) 'Lord'. The sacred Hebrew word for God

Adonis (*Greek*) 'Manly and handsome'

Adrian (*Latin*) 'Dark one' or 'man from the sea'
Ade, Adriano, Adrien, Hadrian

Adriano *see* Adrian

Adriel (*Hebrew*) 'From God's congregation'

Adrien *see* Adrian

Aeldred *see* Alfred

Aelhaearn (*Welsh*) 'Iron brow'

Aeneas *(Greek)* 'The much-praised one'. The defender of Troy
Eneas

Aethelard *see* Allard

Aethelhard *see* Allard

Afdal *(Arabic)* 'Excellent'

Afif *(Arabic)* 'Virtuous'

Agamemnon *(Greek)* 'Resolute'

Agilard *(Teutonic)* 'Formidably bright'

Agosto *see* August

Aguistin *see* August

Agur *(Hebrew)* 'Gatherer'

Ahanu *(Native American)* 'Laughing one'

Ahearn *see* Ahern

Aherin *see* Ahern

Ahern *(Gaelic)* 'Horse lord' or 'horse owner'
Ahearn, Aherin, Aherne, Hearn, Hearne

Aherne *see* Ahern

Ahmed *(Arabic)* 'Most highly praised'

Ahren *(Teutonic)* 'The eagle'

Aickin *see* Aiken

Aidan *(Gaelic)* 'Little fiery one'
Adan, Eden

Aijaz *(Sanskrit)* 'Favour'

Aiken *(Anglo-Saxon)* 'Little Adam'
Aickin, Aokin

Ailbert *see* Albert

Ailean *see* Alan

Ailfrid *see* Alfred

Ailin *see* Alan

Aimery *(Teutonic)* 'Industrious ruler'

Aimon *(French from Teutonic)* 'House'

Aindreas *see* Andrew

Aineislis *see* Stanislaus

Ainsley *(Anglo-Saxon)* 'Meadow of the respected one'

Airell *(Celtic)* 'Free man'

Airleas *see* Arlen

Ajax *(Greek)* 'Eagle'

Ajay *(Sanskrit)* 'Invincible'

Akbar *(Arabic)* 'Great'

Akim *see* Joachim

Akira *(Japanese)* 'Intelligent one'

Akmal *(Arabic)* 'Perfect'

Akram *(Arabic)* 'Noble, generous'

Akule *(Native American)* 'One who looks to the sky'

Al *see* Alfred, Algernon or Alison

Alaam *(Sanskrit) see* Alam

Alabhaois *see* Aloysius

Aladdin *(Arabic)* 'Servant of Allah'

Alain *see* Alan

Alair *(Gaelic)* 'Cheerful' *see also* Alan

Alam *(Arabic/Sanskrit)* 'Universe'
Alaam

Alan *(Gaelic)* 'Cheerful harmony'
Ailean, Ailin, Alain, Alair, Aland, Alano, Alanson, Allan, Allen, Allie, Allyn

Aland *see* Alan

Alano *see* Alan

Alanson *see* Alan

Alanus *(Latin)* 'Cheerful one'

Alard *(German)*'Noble ruler' *see also* Allard

Alaric *(Teutonic)* 'Ruler of all'
Alarick, Alric, Rich, Richie, Rick, Rickie, Ricky, Ricy, Ulric, Ulrich, Ulrick

Alarick *see* Alaric

Alasdair *see* Alexander

Alastair *see* Alexander

Alasteir *see* Alexander

Alaster *see* Alexander

Alban *(Latin)* 'White complexion'. A man of outstandingly fair colouring
Alben, Albin, Aleb, Alva, Aubin

Alben *(Hebrew)* Fair, blond
Alban, Albin

Alberik *see* Aubrey

Albern *(Anglo-Saxon)* 'Noble warrior'

Albert *(Teutonic)* 'Noble and illustrious'. Name which became popular in Britain after the marriage of Queen Victoria to Prince Albert of Saxe-Coborg-Gotha
Adelbert, Ailbert, Aldabert, Aubert, Bert, Bertie, Berty, Delbert, Elbert

Albin see Alban or Alben

Albor (Latin) 'Dawn'

Alburn (Latin) 'Pale complexion'

Alcander (Greek) 'Strong'

Alcott (Anglo-Saxon) 'One who lives at the old cottage'

Aldabert see Albert

Alden (Anglo-Saxon) 'Wise old friend'. One on whom friends can rely Aldin, Aldwin, Aldwyn, Elden, Eldin

Alder (Anglo-Saxon) 'At the alder tree'

Aldin see Alden

Aldis (Anglo-Saxon) 'From the old house' Aldo, Aldous, Aldus

Aldo (Teutonic) 'Old, wise and rich' see also Aldis

Aldous see Aldis

Aldred (Teutonic) 'Wise advisor'

Aldric see Aldrich

Aldrich (Anglo-Saxon) 'Wise old ruler' Aldric, Aldridge, Alric, Eldric, Eldrich, Eldridge

Aldridge see Aldrich

Aldus see Aldis

Aldwin see Alden, Alvin or Audwin

Aldwyn see Alden or Audwin

Aleb see Alban

Alec see Alexander

Aleck see Alexander

Aled (Welsh) Name of a Welsh river

Aleem (Sanskrit) 'Knowledgeable'

Alejandro see Alexander

Alejo see Alexander

Aleksandr see Alexander

Alem (Arabic) 'Wise man'

Aleron (Latin) 'The eagle'

Alessandro see Alexander

Alex see Alexander

Alexander (Greek) 'Protector of mankind' Alasdair, Alastair, Alasteir, Alaster, Alec, Aleck, Alejandro, Alejo, Aleksandr, Alessandro, Alex, Alexis, Alick, Alister, Allister, Alsandair, Sander, Sandie, Sandy, Sasha, Saunders

Alexis *see* Alexander

Alf *see* Alfred

Alfie *see* Alfred

Alfons *see* Alphonso

Alfonse *see* Alphonso

Alfonso *see* Alphonso

Alford *(Anglo-Saxon)* 'The old ford' *see* also Alphonso

Alfred *(Anglo-Saxon)* 'The wise counsel of the elf' Aelfred, Ailfrid, Al, Alf, Alfie, Alfredo, Alfy, Avery, Fred, Freddie, Freddy

Alfredo *see* Alfred

Alfy *see* Alfred

Algar *see* Alger

Alger *(Teutonic)* 'Noble spearman' Algar, Elgar *see also* Algernon

Algernon *(French)* 'The whiskered one'. A man with a moustache or beard Al, Alger, Algie, Algy

Algie *see* Algernon

Algis *(French from Teutonic)* 'Spear'

Algy *see* Algernon

Ali *(Sanskrit/Arabic)* 'Protected by god' *(Sanskrit)* or 'greatest, noble, sublime' *(Arabic)*

Alick *see* Alexander

Alim *(Arabic)* 'Scholar'

Alison *(Anglo-Saxon)* 'Son of a nobleman' or 'Alice's son' Al, Allie, Allison

Alister *see* Alexander

Allan *see* Alan

Allard *(Anglo-Saxon)* 'Noble and brave' Aethelard, Aethelhard, Alard, Ethelard *see also* Alard

Allen *see* Alan

Allie *see* Alan or Alison

Allison *see* Alison

Allister *see* Alexander

Allyn *see* Alan

Almer *(Arabic)* 'Prince' or 'ruler'

Almerick *(Teutonic)* 'Working ruler'

Almo *(Anglo-Saxon)* 'Noble and famous'

Almund *(Teutonic)* 'Protection'

Aloin *see* Alvin

Alonso *see* Alphonso

Alonzo *see* Alphonso

Aloys *see* Aloysius

Aloysius *(Latin)* 'Famous warrior'
Alabhaois, Aloys, Lewis, Louis, Ludwig

Alpha *(Greek)* 'First-born'

Alpheus *(Greek)* 'God of the river'

Alphonse *see* Alphonso

Alphonso *(Teutonic)* 'Noble and ready'
Alfons, Alfonse, Alfonso, Alford, Alonso, Alonzo, Alphonse, Alphonsus, Fonz

Alphonsus *see* Alphonso

Alpin *(Early Scottish)* 'Blond one'. Name borne by the descendants of the earliest Scottish clan McAlpin

Alric *see* Alaric, Aldrich or Ulric

Alroy *(Gaelic)* 'Red-haired boy'

Alsandair *see* Alexander

Alston *(Anglo-Saxon)* 'From the old village'

Altman *(Teutonic)* 'Old, wise man'

Alton *(Anglo-Saxon)* 'One who lives in the old town'

Aluin *see* Alvin

Aluino *see* Alvin

Alva *see* Alban or Alvin

Alvah *(Hebrew)* 'The exalted one'
Alvar

Alvan *see* Alvin

Alvar *see* Alvah

Alvin *(Teutonic)* 'Friend of all' or 'noble friend'
Aldwin, Aloin, Aluin, Aluino, Alva, Alvan, Alwin, Alwyn

Alward *(Teutonic)* 'Everyone's protector'

Alwin *see* Alvin

Alworth *(Teutonic)* 'Respected by everyone'

Alwyn *see* Alvin

Amadeo *(Spanish)* 'Beloved of God'
Amadeus, Amando

Amadeus *see* Amadeo, Amadour

Amadour *(French from Latin)* 'Lovable' Amadeus

Amal *(Sanskrit)* 'Pure', *(Arabic)* 'hope' or *(Hebrew)* 'work'

Amand *see* Amandus

Amando *see* Amadeo or Amandus

Amandus *(Latin)* 'Worthy of love' Amand, Amando

Amaro *(Portuguese)* 'Dark, moor'

Amasa *(Hebrew)* 'Burden bearer'

Ambar *(Hindi)* 'Sky'

Ambert *(Teutonic)* 'Shining, bright light'

Ambler *(English)* 'Stable-keeper'

Ambroise *see* Ambrose

Ambros *see* Ambrose

Ambrose *(Latin)* 'Belonging to the divine immortals' Ambroise, Ambros, Ambrosi, Ambrosio, Ambrosius, Amby, Brose, Emrys, Gino

Ambrosi *see* Ambrose

Ambrosio *see* Ambrose

Ambrosius *see* Ambrose

Amby *see* Ambrose

Ameen *see* Amin

Amerigo *see* Emery

Amery *see* Amory

Amhlaoibh *see* Olaf

Amiel *(Hebrew)* 'Lord of my people'

Amijad *(Arabic)* 'Glorious'

Amil *(Arabic/Sanskrit)* 'Industrious, invaluable'

Amin *(Arabic/Hebrew)* 'Trustworthy, honest' or *(Sanskrit)* 'divine grace' Ameen, Aman

Amirov *(Hebrew)* 'My people are great'

Amitan *(Hebrew)* 'True, faithful'

Amiya *(Sanskrit)* 'Nectar'

Amlan *(Sanskrit)* 'Unfading'

Ammon *(Egyptian)* 'The hidden'

Amnon *(Hebrew)* 'Faithful'

Amol *(Sanskrit)* 'Priceless' Anmol

Amon *see* Amin

Amory *(Teutonic)* 'Famous ruler'
Amery

Amos *(Hebrew)* 'A burden'. One used to tackling difficult problems

Amram *(Arabic)* 'Life'

Amrit *(Sanskrit)* 'Water of life'

Amund *(Scandinavian)* 'Divine protection'

Amyot *(French)* 'Beloved'

Anand *(Hindi)* 'Peaceful'

Ananias *(Hebrew)* 'Grace of the Lord'

Anarawd *(Welsh)* 'Eloquent'

Anastasius *(Greek)* 'One who shall rise again'

Anatol *see* Anatole

Anatole *(Greek)* 'From the East'
Anatol, Anatolio

Anatolio *see* Anatole

Ancel *(German)* 'God-like'
Ancell

Ancell *see* Ansel

Anders *see* Andrew

Anderson *see* Andrew

Andie *see* Andrew

Andonis *see* Andrew

Andras *see* Andrew

Andre *see* Andrew

Andreas *see* Andrew

Andrej *see* Andrew

Andrew *(Greek)* 'Strong and manly'. The patron saint of Scotland
Aindreas, Anders, Anderson, Andie, Andonis, Andre, Andreas, Andrej, Andrien, Andris, Andy, Drew

Andrias *(Greek)* 'Courageous one'

Andrien *see* Andrew

Andris *see* Andrew

Androcles *(Greek)* 'Male glory'

Andy *see* Andrew

Aneurin *(Celtic)* 'Truly golden'
Nye

Ange *see* Angelo

Angell *see* Angelo

Angelo *(Italian)* 'Saintly messenger'
Ange, Angel

Angus *(Celtic)* 'Outstanding and exceptional man'. One of unparalleled strength
Ennis, Gus

Angwyn *(Welsh)* 'Very handsome'

Anil *(Sanskrit)* 'God of the wind'

Anmol *see* Amol

Annan *(Celtic)* 'From the stream'

Anniss *(Arabic)* 'Charming'

Anntoin *see* Anthony

Ansari *(Arabic)* 'Helper'

Anscom *(Anglo-Saxon)* 'One who lives in the secret valley'. An awe-inspiring, solitary man
Anscomb

Anscomb *see* Anscom

Anse *see* Anselm

Ansel *(French)* 'Nobleman's follower'
Ancell, Ansell *see also* Anselm

Ansell *see* Ansel

Anselm *(Teutonic)* 'Divine helmet'
Anse, Ansel, Anselme, Anshelm, Elmo

Anselme *see* Anselm

Anshar *(Teutonic)* 'Divine spear'

Anshelm *see* Anselm

Ansley *(Anglo-Saxon)* 'From Ann's meadow'

Anson *(Anglo-Saxon)* 'Ann's son'

Anstice *(Greek)* 'The resurrected'. One who returns to life after death
Anstiss

Anstiss *see* Anstice

Anthony *(Latin)* 'Of inestimable worth'. A man without peer
Anntoin, Antin, Antoine, Anton, Antonino, Antonio, Antons, Antony, Tony

Antin *see* Anthony

Antinous *(Greek)* 'Contradictory'

Antoine *see* Anthony

Antol *(Hungarian)* 'Estimable one'

Anton *see* Anthony

Antonino *see* Anthony

Antonio *see* Anthony

Antons *see* Anthony

Antony *see* Anthony

Anwell *(Celtic)* 'Beloved one'
Anwyl, Anwyll

Anwyl *see* Anwell

Anwyll *see* Anwell

Anyon *(Celtic)* 'The anvil'. One on whom all the finest characteristics have been forged

Aodh *(Celtic)* 'Fire' *see also* Hubert

Aoidh *see* Hubert

Aokin *see* Aiken

Apollo *(Greek)* 'Beautiful man'

Aquila *(Latin)* 'Eagle'

Ara *(Arabic)* 'Rainmaker'

Araldo *see* Harold

Arch *see* Archibald

Archaimbaud *see* Archibald

Archambault *see* Archibald

Archard *(Teutonic)* 'Sacred and powerful'
Archerd

Archer *(Anglo-Saxon)* 'The bowman' *see also* Archibald

Archerd *see* Archard

Archibald *(Teutonic)* 'Noble and truly bold'. A brave and sacred warrior
Arch, Archaimbaud, Archambault, Archer, Archibaldo, Archie, Archimbald, Archy, Arkady, Gilleasbuig

Archibaldo *see* Archibald

Archie *see* Archibald

Archimbald *see* Archibald

Archimedes *(Greek)* 'Master mind'

Archy *see* Archibald

Arden *(Latin)* 'Ardent, fiery, fervent, sincere'. One of intensely loyal nature
Ardin

Ardin *see* Arden

Ardley *(Anglo-Saxon)* 'From the domestic meadow'

Ardolf *see* Ardolph

Ardolph *(Anglo-Saxon)* 'The home-loving wolf'. The roamer who longs only for home
Ardolf

Arel *see* Ariel

Aretino *(Greek)* 'Victorious'

Argus *(Greek)* 'The watchful one'. The giant with one hundred eyes, who saw everything at once

Argyle *(Gaelic)* 'From the land of the Gaels'

Ari *(Teutonic)* 'Eagle' *see also* Aaron

Aric *(Anglo-Saxon)* 'Sacred ruler'
Rick, Rickie, Ricky

Ariel *(Hebrew)* 'Lion of God'
Arel

Aries *(Latin)* 'A ram'. One born in April, from the sign of the Zodiac – Aries

Ario *see* Arrio

Aristo *(Greek)* 'The best'

Aristol *(Greek)* 'Excellence'

Aristotle *(Greek)* 'Best thinker'

Arjit *(Sanskrit)* 'Earned'

Arka *(Sanskrit)* 'The sun'

Arkady *see* Archibald

Arledge *(Anglo-Saxon)* 'One who lives by the lake where the rabbit dances'

Arlen *(Gaelic)* 'Pledge'
Airleas, Arlin

Arley *see* Arlie or Harley

Arlie *(Anglo-Saxon)* 'From the rabbit meadow'
Arley, Arly, Harley, Harly *see also* Harley

Arlin *see* Arlen

Arlo *(Spanish)* 'The barberry'

Arly *see* Arlie

Arlyn *(Greek)* 'Swift one'

Armand *(Teutonic)* 'Man of the army'. The military man personified
Armando, Armin, Armond *see also* Herman

Armando *see* Armand

Armin *see* Armand or Herman

Armon *(Hebrew)* 'Castle'

Armond *see* Armand or Herman

Armstrong *(Anglo-Saxon)* 'Strong arm'. The tough warrior who could wield a battle axe

Armyn *see* Herman

Arnald *see* Arnold

Arnaldo *see* Arnold

Arnall *(Teutonic)* 'Gracious eagle'. The nobleman who is also a gentleman

Arnatt *see* Arnett

Arnaud *see* Arnold

Arne *see* Arney or Arnold

Arnett *(French)* 'Little eagle'
Arnatt, Arnott

Arney *(Teutonic)* 'The eagle'
Arne, Arnie

Arnie *see* Aaron, Arney or Arnold

Arno *see* Arnold

Arnold *(Teutonic)* 'Strong as an eagle' Arnald, Arnaldo, Arnaud, Arne, Arnie, Arno

Arnott *see* Arnett

Aron *see* Aaron

Arpad *see* Arvad

Arrio *(Spanish)* 'Warlike'
Ario

Art *see* Arthur

Artair *see* Arthur

Artemas *see* Artemis

Artemis *(Greek)* 'Gift of Artemis'
Artemas

Arthfael *(Welsh)* 'Strong as a bear'

Arthur *(Celtic)* 'The noble bear man' or 'strong as a rock'. The semi-legendary King of Britain, who founded the Round Table
Art, Artair, Artie, Artur, Arturo, Artus, Aurthur

Artie *see* Arthur

Artur *see* Arthur

Arturo *see* Arthur

Artus *see* Arthur

Arundel *(Anglo-Saxon)* 'One who lives with eagles'. Man who shares their keen sight

Arvad *(Hebrew)* 'The wanderer'
Arpad

Arval *(Latin)* 'Much lamented'
Arvel

Arvel *see* Arval

Arvin *(Teutonic)* 'Friend of the people'. The first true socialist

Asa *(Hebrew)* 'The healer'

Asaph *(Hebrew)* 'Gatherer'

Ascelin *(German)* 'Of the moon'
Aceline

Ascot *(Anglo-Saxon)* 'Owner of the east cottage'
Ascott

Ascott *see* Ascot

Aseem *see* Ashim

Ashbey *see* Ashby

Ashburn *(Anglo-Saxon)* 'The brook by the ash tree'

Ashby *(Anglo-Saxon)* 'Ash tree farm'
Ashbey, Ashton

Asher *(Hebrew)* 'The laughing one'

Ashford *(Anglo-Saxon)* 'One who lives in the ford by the ash tree'

Ashim *(Sanskrit)* 'Without limit'
Aseem

Ashley *(Anglo-Saxon)* 'One who lives in the ash tree meadow'
Ashlin *see also* Lee

Ashlin *(Anglo-Saxon)* 'One who lives by the ash tree pool' *see also* Ashley

Ashok *(Hindi)* 'Without sadness'

Ashraf *(Arabic)* 'More noble' or 'more honourable'

Ashton *(Anglo-Saxon)* 'One who lives at the ash tree farm' *see also* Ashby

Ashur *(Semitic)* 'The martial one'. One of war-like tendencies

Ashwani *(Hindi)* 'First of 27 galaxies revolving round the moon'

Aslam *(Sanskrit/Arabic)* 'Greeting' *(Sanskrit)* or 'safe' *(Arabic)*

Astrophel *(Greek)* 'Star-lover'

Aswin *(Anglo-Saxon)* 'Spear comrade'
Aswine

Aswine *see* Aswin

Athanasius *(Greek)* 'Immortal'

Atherton *(Anglo-Saxon)* 'One who lives at the spring farm'

Athol *(Scottish)* Place name

Atley *(Anglo-Saxon)* 'One who lives in the meadow'

Attwood *see* Atwood

Atwater *(Anglo-Saxon)* 'One who lives by the water'

Atwell *(Anglo-Saxon)* 'From the spring'. One who built his home by a natural well

Atwood *(Anglo-Saxon)* 'From the forest' Attwood, Atwoode

Atwoode *see* Atwood

Atworth *(Anglo-Saxon)* 'From the farm'

Aube *see* Aubrey

Auberon *(Teutonic)* 'Noble' Oberon *see also* Aubrey

Aubert *see* Albert

Aubin *see* Alban

Aubrey *(Teutonic)* 'Elf ruler'. The golden-haired king of the spirit world
Alberik, Aube, Auberon, Avery

Audley *(Old English)* 'Prospering'

Audric *(Teutonic)* 'Noble ruler'

Audun *(Scandinavian)* 'Deserted, desolate'

Audwin *(Teutonic)* 'Noble friend'
Adalwine, Aldwin, Aldwyn

Augie *see* August

August *(Latin)* 'Exalted one'
Agosto, Aguistin, Augie, Auguste, Augustin, Augustine, Augustus, Austen, Austin, Gus, Gussy

Auguste *see* August

Augustin *see* August

Augustine *see* August

Augustus *see* August

Aurelius *(Latin)* 'Golden friend'

Aurthur *see* Arthur

Auryn *(Welsh)* 'Gold'

Austen *see* August

Austin *see* August

Avan *(Hebrew)* 'Proud' Evan

Avenall *(French)* 'One who lives in the oak field' Avenel, Avenell

Avenel *see* Avenall

Avenell *see* Avenall

Averel *see* Averill

Averell *see* Averill

Averia *(Teutonic)* 'One who is assertive'

Averil *see* Averill

Averill *(Anglo-Saxon)* 'Boar-like' or 'born in April' Averel, Averell, Averil, Everild

Avery *(Anglo-Saxon)* 'Ruler of the elves' *see also* Alfred or Aubrey

Avidor *(Hebrew)* 'Father of a generation'

Avila *(Spanish)* 'Brave and reckless'

Aviv *(Hebrew)* 'Spring'

Avram *see* Abraham

Axel *(Teutonic)* 'Father of peace'

Axton *(Anglo-Saxon)* 'Stone of the sword fighter'. The whetstone of the warrior's sword

Aylmer *(Anglo-Saxon)* 'Noble and famous' *see also* Elmer

Aylward *(Anglo-Saxon)* 'Awe-inspiring guardian'

Aylwin *(Teutonic)* 'Devoted friend'

Aylworth *(Anglo-Saxon)* 'Farm belonging to the awe-inspiring one'

Aymon *(Old French)* 'Home'

Ayward *(Old English)* 'Noble guardian'

Azal *(Hebrew)* 'The heart of the mountain'

Azarias *(Hebrew)* 'One whom the Lord helps'

Azriel *(Hebrew)* 'Angel of the Lord'

Bachir *(Arabic)* 'Welcome'

Bahar *(Arabic)* 'Sailor'

Bahram *(Persian)* 'Ancient king'

Bailey *(French)* 'Steward'. The trusted guardian of other men's properties Baillie, Baily, Bayley

Baillie *see* Bailey

Baily *see* Bailey

Bainbridge *(Anglo-Saxon)* 'Bridge over the white water'

Baird *(Celtic)* 'The minstrel'. The ancient bard Bard, Barde, Barr

Balbo *(Latin)* 'The mutterer'

Baldemar *(Teutonic)* 'Bold, famous prince'

Balder *(Norse)* 'Prince'. The god of peace Baldhere, Baldur

Baldhere *see* Balder

Baldric *(Teutonic)* 'Princely ruler' Baudric *see also* Bardrick

Baldrick *see* Bardrick

Balduin *see* Baldwin

Baldur *see* Balder

Baldwin *(Teutonic)* 'Bold, noble protector' Balduin, Baudouin, Baudowin

Balfour *(Gaelic)* 'From the pasture'

Ballard *(Teutonic)* 'Strong and bold'

Balraj *(Hindi)* 'Strongest'

Balthasar *(Greek)* 'May the Lord protect the King' Belshazzar

Bancroft *(Anglo-Saxon)* 'From the bean field'

Banning *(Gaelic)* 'The little golden-haired one'

Banquo *(Gaelic)* 'White'

Barak *(Hebrew)* 'Flash of lightning'

Baram *(Hebrew)* 'Son of the nation'

Barclay *(Anglo-Saxon)* 'One who lives by the birch tree meadow'
Berk, Berkeley, Berkley

Bard *see* Baird

Barde *see* Baird

Barden *(Old English)* 'One who lives near the boar's den'

Bardo *(Danish) see* Bartholomew

Bardolf *(Anglo-Saxon)* 'Axe wolf'
Bardolph, Bardolphe, Bardulf, Bardulph

Bardolph *see* Bardolf

Bardolphe *see* Bardolf

Bardon *(Anglo-Saxon)* 'Barley valley'

Bardrick *(Anglo-Saxon)* 'Axe ruler'. One who lived by the battle axe
Baldric, Baldrick

Bardulf *see* Bardolf

Bardulph *see* Bardolf

Barend *(Dutch)* 'Firm bear'

Bari *(Arabic)* 'The maker'

Barker *(Old English)* 'Birch tree'

Barlow *(Anglo-Saxon)* 'One who lives on the barren hills'

Barnaba *see* Barnaby

Barnabe *see* Barnaby

Barnabus *see* Barnaby

Barnaby *(Hebrew)* 'Son of consolation'
Barnaba, Barnabe, Barnabus, Barney, Barny, Burnaby

Barnard *see* Bernard

Barnes *(Old English)* 'Bear'

Barnet *see* Barnett or Bernard

Barnett *(Anglo-Saxon)* 'Noble leader'
Barnet, Barney, Barron, Barry *see also* Bernard

Barney *see* Barnaby, Barnett or Bernard

Barnum *(Anglo-Saxon)* 'Nobleman's house'

Barny *see* Barnaby or Bernard

Baron *(Anglo-Saxon)* 'Noble warrior'. The lowest rank of the peerage
Barron *see also* Barnett

Barr *(Anglo-Saxon)* 'A gateway' *see also* Baird

Barret *(Teutonic)* 'As mighty as the bear'
Barrett

Barrett *see* Barret

Barrie *see* Barry or Baruch

Barris *(Celtic)* 'Barry's son' *see also* Barry

Barron *see* Baron

Barry *(Gaelic)* 'Spear-like'. One whose intellect is sword-sharp
Barrie *see also* Barris, Barnett, Baruch

Bart *see* Bartholomew, Barton or Bertram

Bartel *see* Bartholomew

Barth *see* Bartholomew

Barthel *see* Bartholomew

Barthelmey *see* Bartholomew

Barthol *see* Bartholomew

Bartholomeo *see* Bartholomew

Bartholomeus *see* Bartholomew

Bartholomew *(Hebrew)* 'Son of the furrows, ploughman'. One of the 12 apostles
Bardo, Bart, Bartel, Barth, Barthel, Barthelmey, Barthol, Bartholomeo, Bartholomeus, Bartlett, Bartley, Bartolome, Bat, Parlan

Bartie *see* Barton

Bartlett *see* Bartholomew

Bartley *(Anglo-Saxon)* 'Bartholomew's meadow' *see also* Bartholomew

Bartolome *see* Bartholomew

Barton *(Anglo-Saxon)* 'Barley farmer'
Bart, Bartie

Bartram *(Old German)* 'Bright raven' *see also* Bertram

Baruch *(Hebrew)* 'Blessed'
Barrie, Barry

Barulai *(Hebrew)* 'Man of iron'

Base *see* Basil

Bashir *(Sanskrit)* 'Bringer of good news'

Basil *(Greek)* 'Kingly'. St Basil was the founder of the Greek Orthodox Church
Base, Basile, Basilio, Basilius, Vassily

Basile *see* Basil

Basilio *see* Basil

Basilius *see* Basil

Basilyr *(Arabic)* 'Insight'

Basir *(Turkish)* 'Intelligent', 'discerning'

Basum *(Arabic)* 'Smiling'

Bat *see* Bartholomew

Baudouin *see* Baldwin

Baudowin *see* Baldwin

Baudric *see* Baldric

Bax *see* Baxter

Baxter *(Teutonic)* 'The baker of bread'
Bax

Bay *see* Bayard

Bayard *(Anglo-Saxon)* 'Red-haired and strong'. The personification of knightly courtesy
Bay

Bayley *see* Bailey

Baylor *(Anglo-Saxon)* 'Horse-trainer'

Beach *see* Beacher

Beacher *(Anglo-Saxon)* 'One who lives by the oak tree'
Beach, Beech, Beecher

Beagan *(Gaelic)* 'Little one'
Beagen

Beagen *see* Beagan

Beal *(French)* 'Handsome'. In the form 'Beau' used to identify the smart, well-dressed, personable men of the 17th and early 18th centuries
Beale, Beall, Beau, Beaufort

Beale *see* Beal

Beall *see* Beal

Beaman *(Anglo-Saxon)* 'The bee-keeper'

Bearnard *see* Bernard

Beasley *(Old English)* 'Field of peas'

Beathan *see* Benjamin

Beatie *see* Beattie

Beattie *(Gaelic)* 'Public provider'. One who supplies food and drink for the inhabitants of a town
Beatie, Beatty, Beaty

Beatty *see* Beattie

Beaty *see* Beattie

Beau *see* Beal or Beauregard

Beaufort *(French)*
'Beautiful stronghold'.
The name adopted by
the descendants of the
union of John of Gaunt
and Katharine
Swynford *see also* Beal

Beaumont *(French)*
'Beautiful mountain'

Beauregard *(Old French)*
'Beautiful in expression'
Beau, Bo

Beavan *see* Bevan

Beaven *see* Bevan

Bec *see* Beck

Beck *(Anglo-Saxon)* 'A
brook'
Bec

Bede *(Old English)* 'A
prayer'

Bedell *(Old English)*
'Messenger'

Beech *see* Beacher

Beecher *see* Beacher

Behram *(Persian)*
'Mythological figure'

Behzad *(Persian)* 'Noble'

Belden *(Anglo-Saxon)* 'One
who lives in the
beautiful glen'
Beldon

Beldon *see* Belden

Bellamy *(French)*
'Handsome friend'

Belshazzar *see* Balthasar

Belton *(Old French)*
'Beautiful town'

Beltran *(German)*'Brilliant'
see also Bertram

Bemus *(Greek)* 'Platform'

Ben *see* Benedict or
Benjamin

Bendick *see* Benedict

Bendix *see* Benedict

Benedetto *see* Benedict

Benedic *see* Benedict

Benedick *see* Benedict

Benedict *(Latin)* 'Blessed'.
One blessed by God
Ben, Bendick, Bendix,
Benedetto, Benedic,
Benedick, Benedicto,
Benedikt, Benedix,
Bengt, Benito, Bennet,
Bennett, Bennie,
Benny, Benoit, Benot
see also Dixon

Benedicto *see* Benedict

Benedikt *see* Benedict

Benedix *see* Benedict

Bengt *see* Benedict

Beniah *(Hebrew)* 'Son of the Lord'

Beniamino *see* Benjamin

Benito *see* Benedict

Benjamin *(Hebrew)* 'Son of my right hand'. The beloved youngest son Beathan, Ben, Beniamino, Benjie, Benjy, Bennie, Benny, Benyamin

Benjie *see* Benjamin

Benjy *see* Benjamin

Bennet *see* Benedict

Bennett *see* Benedict

Bennie *see* Benedict or Benjamin

Benny *see* Benedict or Benjamin

Benoit *see* Benedict

Benoni *(Hebrew)* 'Son of my sorrow'. The former name of the Biblical Benjamin

Benot *see* Benedict

Benroy *(Hebrew)* 'Son of a lion'

Benson *(Hebrew)* 'Son of Benjamin' *see also* Benjamin

Bentley *see* Bently

Bently *(Anglo-Saxon)* 'From the farm where the grass sways' Bentley

Benton *(Anglo-Saxon)* 'From the town on the moors'

Benyamin *see* Benjamin

Berard *see* Bernard

Béraud *(French)* 'Strong leader' Beraut

Beraut *see* Béraud

Berenger *(Teutonic)* 'Bear spear'

Beresford *(Anglo-Saxon)* 'From the barley ford'

Berg *(Teutonic)* 'The mountain' *see also* Bergren, Burgess

Berger *(French)* 'The shepherd' *see also* Burgess

Bergess *see* Burgess

Bergren *(Scandinavian)* 'Mountain stream' Berg

Berk *see* Barclay or Burke

Berke *see* Burke

Berkeley *see* Barclay

Berkley *see* Barclay

Berman *(Teutonic)* 'Bear-like one'

Bern *see* Bernard

Bernado *see* Bernard

Bernard *(Teutonic)* 'As brave as a bear'. A courageous warrior Barnard, Barnet, Barnett, Barney, Barny, Bearnard, Berard, Bern, Bernado, Bernhard, Bernie, Berny, Burnard

Bernhard *see* Bernard

Bernie *see* Bernard

Berny *see* Bernard

Bert *see* Albert, Berthold, Bertram, Burton, Egbert, Gilbert, Herbert, Hubert, Humbert or Osbert

Berthold *(Teutonic)* 'Brilliant ruler' Bert, Berthoud, Bertie, Bertold, Berty

Berthoud *see* Berthold

Bertie *see* Albert, Berthold, Berton, Bertram, Humbert or Osbert

Bertold *see* Berthold

Berton *(Anglo-Saxon)* 'Brilliant one's estate' Bertie, Burt, Burton *see also* Burton or Bertram

Bertram *(Anglo-Saxon)* 'Bright raven' Bart, Bartram, Beltran, Bert, Bertran, Bertrand, Bertrando, Berty

Bertrand *see* Bertram

Bertrando *see* Bertram

Bertwin *(Teutonic)* 'Bright friend'

Berty *see* Albert, Berthold, Bertram, Humbert or Osbert

Berwick *(Old English)* 'Barley grange'

Berwin *(Teutonic)* 'Warrior friend'

Bevan *(Welsh)* 'Son of a noble man' Beavan, Beaven, Beven

Beven *see* Bevan

Beverley *(Anglo-Saxon)* 'From the beaver meadow' Beverly

Beverly *see* Beverley

Bevis *(French)* 'Fair view'
Beavais

Bhagat *(Arabic)* 'Joy'

Bibiano *(Spanish)* Spanish
variation of Vyvyan

Bickford *(Anglo-Saxon)*
'Hewer's ford'

Bienvenido *(Spanish)*
'Welcome'

Bildad *(Hebrew)* 'Beloved'

Bill *see* William

Billie *see* William

Billy *see* William

Bing *(Teutonic)* 'Kettle-
shaped hollow'

Bion *(Greek)* 'Life'

Birch *(Anglo-Saxon)* 'At the
birch tree'
Birk, Burch

Birk *see* Birch or Burke

Birke *see* Burke

Birket *see* Birkett

Birkett *(Anglo-Saxon)* 'One
who lives by the birch
headland'
Birket

Birley *(Anglo-Saxon)* 'Cattle
shed in the field'

Birney *(Anglo-Saxon)* 'One
who lives on the island
in the brook'

Birtle *(Anglo-Saxon)* 'From
the bird hill'

Bishop *(Anglo-Saxon)* 'The
bishop'

Bjorn *(Scandinavian)* 'Bear'

Black *(Anglo-Saxon)* 'Of
dark complexion'

Blade *(Anglo-Saxon)*
'Prosperity, glory'

Blagden *(Anglo-Saxon)*
'From the dark valley'

Blagoslav *(Polish)* 'Good
glory'

Blain *see* Blaine

Blaine *(Gaelic)* 'Thin,
hungry-looking'
Blane, Blain, Blayn,
Blayne

Blair *(Gaelic)* 'A place' or
'from the plain'

Blaise *(Latin)* 'Stammerer'
or 'firebrand'
Blase, Blayze, Blaze

Blake *(Anglo-Saxon)* 'Of fair
complexion'

Blakeley *(Anglo-Saxon)*
'From the black
meadow'

Blakey *(Anglo-Saxon)* 'Little fair one'

Bland *(Latin)* 'Mild and gentle'

Blandford *see* Blanford

Blane *see* Blaine

Blanford *(Anglo-Saxon)* 'River crossing belonging to one with grey hair'
Blandford

Blase *see* Blaise

Blayn *see* Blaine

Blayne *see* Blaine

Blayze *see* Blaise

Blaze *see* Blaise

Bliss *(Anglo-Saxon)* 'Joyful one'. One who always sees the cheerful side

Blythe *(Anglo-Saxon)* 'The merry person'
Blyth

Bo *see* Beauregard or Bogart

Boas *see* Boaz

Boase *see* Boaz

Boaz *(Hebrew)* 'Strength is in the Lord'
Boas, Boase

Bob *see* Robert

Bobbie *see* Robert

Bobby *see* Robert

Boden *(French)* 'The herald'. The bringer of news

Bogart *(Teutonic)* 'Strong bow'
Bo

Bogdan *(Polish)* 'God's gift'

Bolton *(French)* 'Manor farm'

Bonamy *(French)* 'Good friend'

Bonar *(French)* 'Good, gentle and kind'

Bonaro *(Italian/Spanish)* 'Friend'

Bond *(Anglo-Saxon)* 'Tiller of the soil'
Bondie, Bondon

Bondie *see* Bond

Bondon *see* Bond

Boniface *(Latin)* 'One who does good'

Booker *(Anglo-Saxon)* 'Beech tree'

Boone *(Norse)* 'The good one'
Boonie

Boonie *see* Boone

Boot *see* Booth

Boote *see* Booth

Booth *(Teutonic)* 'From a market' or 'herald' Both, Boot, Boote, Boothe

Boothe *see* Booth

Bord *see* Borden

Borden *(Anglo-Saxon)* 'From the valley of the boar' Bord

Borg *(Norse)* 'One who lives in the castle'

Boris *(Slavic)* 'A fighter'. A born warrior

Bosley *(Old English)* 'Grove of trees'

Boswell *(French)* 'Forest town'

Bosworth *(Anglo-Saxon)* 'At the cattle enclosure'

Both *see* Booth

Botolf *(Anglo-Saxon)* 'Herald wolf' Botolph, Botolphe

Botolph *see* Botolf

Botolphe *see* Botolf

Boucard *(French/Teutonic)* 'Beech tree' Bouchard

Bouchard *see* Boucard

Bourke *see* Burke

Bourn *see* Bourne

Bourne *(Anglo-Saxon)* 'From the brook' Bourn, Burn, Burne, Byrne

Bow *see* Bowie

Bowen *(Celtic)* 'Descendant of Owen'. A proud Welsh name borne by descendants of the almost legendary Owen *see also* Bowie

Bowie *(Gaelic)* 'Yellow-haired' Bow, Bowen, Boyd

Bowman *(Old English)* 'Archer'

Boyce *(French)* 'From the woods'. A forester Boycie

Boycie *see* Boyce

Boyd *(Gaelic)* 'Light haired'. The blond Adonis *see also* Bowie

Boydell *(Celtic)* 'Wise and fair'

Boyden *(Celtic)* 'Herald'

Boyle *(Teutonic)* 'Spirited' or 'nervous'

Boyne *(Gaelic)* 'White cow'. A very rare person

Brad *see* Bradford or Bradley

Bradan *see* Braden

Bradburn *(Anglo-Saxon)* 'Broad brook'

Brade *see* Braden

Braden *(Anglo-Saxon)* 'From the wide valley' Bradan, Brade

Bradford *(Anglo-Saxon)* 'From the broad crossing' Brad, Ford

Bradley *(Anglo-Saxon)* 'From the broad meadow' Brad, Bradly, Bradney, Lee, Leigh

Bradly *see* Bradley

Bradney *see* Bradley

Bradshaw *(Old English)* 'Large virginal forest'

Brady *(Gaelic)* 'Spirited one' or 'from the broad island'

Brage *(Nordic)* Norse god of poetry

Braham *(Hindi)* 'Creator'

Brainard *(Anglo-Saxon)* 'Bold as a raven'. One who knows no fear Brainerd

Brainerd *see* Brainard

Bram *see* Abraham, Bramwell or Bran

Bramwell *(Anglo-Saxon)* 'From the bramble bush spring' Bram

Bran *(Celtic)* 'Raven'. The spirit of eternal youth Bram *see also* Brand

Branch *(Latin)* 'Paw, claw', 'branch of a tree'

Brand *(Anglo-Saxon)* 'Firebrand'. The grandson of the god Woden Bran, Brander, Brandt, Brandyn, Brannon, Brantley

Brander *(Norse)* 'Sword of fire' *see also* Brand

Brandon *(Anglo-Saxon)* 'From the beacon on the hill' Brandyn, Brannon

Brandt *see* Brand

Brandyn *see* Brandon

Brannon *see* Brandon *or also* Brand

Brant *(Anglo-Saxon)* 'Fiery or proud one'

Brantley *see* Brand

Brawley *(Anglo-Saxon)* 'From the meadow on the hill slope'

Braxton *(Anglo-Saxon)* 'Brock's town'

Bren *see* Brendan

Brendan *(Gaelic)* 'Little raven' or 'from the fiery hill'
Bren, Brendis, Brendon, Brennan, Bryn

Brendis *see* Brendan

Brendon *see* Brendan

Brennan *see* Brendan

Brent *(Anglo-Saxon)* 'Steep hill'
Brenton

Brenton (Old English) 'From the steep hill'
Brent

Bret *see* Brett

Brett *(Celtic)* 'Native of Brittany' or 'from the island of Britain'. One of the original Celts
Bret, Britt

Brevis *(Latin)* 'Short' or 'thrifty'

Brew *see* Brewster

Brewster *(Anglo-Saxon)* 'The brewer'
Brew, Bruce

Brian *(Celtic)* 'Powerful strength with virtue and honour'. Brian Boru, the great Irish king
Briano, Briant, Brien, Brion, Bryan, Bryant, Bryon

Briand *(French)* 'Castle'

Briano *see* Brian

Briant *see* Brian

Brice *(Celtic)* 'Quick, ambitious and alert'
Bryce

Bridger *(Anglo-Saxon)* 'One who lives by the bridge'

Brien *see* Brian

Brigg *see* Brigham

Brigham *(Anglo-Saxon)* 'One who lives where the bridge is enclosed'
Brigg

Brinsley *(Anglo-Saxon)* 'Brin's meadow'

Brion *see* Brian

Brisbane *(Gaelic)* 'Noble or royal mount'

Britt *see* Brett

Broc *see* Brock

Brock *(Anglo-Saxon)* 'The badger'
Broc, Brockie, Brok

Brockie *see* Brock

Brockley *(Anglo-Saxon)* 'From the badger meadow'

Broderic *see* Broderick or Roderick

Broderick *(Anglo-Saxon)* 'From the broad ridge' or 'son of Roderick' Broderic *see also* Roderick

Brodie *(Gaelic)* 'A ditch' Brody

Brodrick *see* Roderick

Brody *see* Brodie

Brok *see* Brock

Bromley *(Anglo-Saxon)* 'One who lives in the broom meadow'

Bromwell *(Teutonic)* 'One who lives by the spring where the wild broom grows'

Bronislav *(Slavonic)* 'Weapon of glory'

Bronnie *see* Bronson

Bronson *(Anglo-Saxon)* 'The brown-haired one's son' Bronnie, Sonny

Brook *(Anglo-Saxon)* 'One who lives by the brook' Brooke, Brooks

Brooke *see* Brook

Brooks *see* Brook

Brose *see* Ambrose

Brough *see* Brougher

Brougher *(Anglo-Saxon)* 'The fortified residence'

Brough Broughton *(Anglo-Saxon)* 'From a fortified town'

Bruce *(French)* 'From the thicket'. From Robert the Bruce, Scotland's hero king *see also* Brewster

Bruno *(Teutonic)* 'Brown-haired man'

Brutus *(Latin)* 'Coarse, stupid'

Bryan *see* Brian

Bryant *see* Brian

Bryce *see* Brice

Brychan *(Welsh)* 'Freckled'

Brymer *(Anglo-Saxon)* 'Bright one'

Bryn *(Welsh)* 'Hill' *see also* Brendan

Bryon *see* Brian

Buck *(Anglo-Saxon)* 'The buck deer'. A fast-running youth

Buckley *(Anglo-Saxon)* 'One who dwells by the buck-deer meadow'

Bud *see* Budd

Budd *(Anglo-Saxon)* 'Herald'. The welcome messenger

Buddy *see* Budd

Bundy *(Anglo-Saxon)* 'Free man'. An enfranchised serf

Burbank *(Anglo-Saxon)* 'One who lives on the castle hill slope'

Burch *see* Birch

Burchard *(Anglo-Saxon)* 'Strong as a castle' Burckhard, Burgard, Burkhart

Burckhard *see* Burchard

Burdett *(French)* 'Little shield'

Burdon *(Anglo-Saxon)* 'One who lives by the castle on the hill'

Burford *(Anglo-Saxon)* 'One who lives at the river crossing by the castle'

Burg *see* Burgess

Burgard *see* Burchard

Burgess *(Anglo-Saxon)* 'One who lives in a fortified town' Berg, Berger, Bergess, Burg, Burr

Burk *see* Burke

Burke *(French)* 'From the stronghold' Berk, Berke, Birk, Birke, Bourke, Burk

Burkett *(French)* 'From the little fortress'

Burkhart *see* Burchard

Burl *(Anglo-Saxon)* 'The cup-bearer'. The wine server Byrle

Burleigh *see* Burley

Burley *(Anglo-Saxon)* 'One who lives in the castle by the meadow' Burleigh

Burn *see* Bourne

Burnaby *(Norse)* 'Warrior's estate' *see also* Barnaby

Burnard *see* Bernard

Burne *see* Bourne

Burnell *(French)* 'Little one with brown hair'

Burnett *(Anglo-Saxon)* 'Little one with brown complexion'

Burney *(Anglo-Saxon)* 'One who lives on the island in the brook'

Burr *(Norse)* 'Youth' *see also* Burgess

Burrell *(French)* 'One of light brown complexion'

Burris *(Old English)* 'Of the town'

Burt *see* Berton or Burton

Burton *(Anglo-Saxon)* 'Of bright and glorious fame' or 'one who lives at the fortified town' Bert, Berton, Burt *see also* Berton

Busby *(Norse)* 'One who lives in the thicket'

Butch Familiar form of Bert or Burt

Byford *(Anglo-Saxon)* 'One who lives by the ford'

Byram *(Anglo-Saxon)* 'One who lives at the cattle pen' Byrom *see also* Byron

Byran *see* Byron

Byrd *(Anglo-Saxon)* 'Like a bird'

Byrle *see* Burl

Byrne *see* Bourne

Byrom *see* Byram

Byron *(French)* 'From the cottage' or 'the bear' Byram, Byran

Cadby *(Norse)* 'Warrior's settlement'

Cadda *see* Chad

Caddaric *see* Cedric

Caddock *(Celtic)* 'Keenness in battle'

Cadell *(Celtic)* 'Battle spirit'

Cadeyrn *(Welsh)* 'Battle king'

Cadfael *(Welsh)* 'Battle metal'

Cadfan *(Welsh)* 'Battle peak'

Cadman *(Celtic)* 'Battle man'

Cadmus *(Greek)* 'Man from the east'. The legendary scholar who devised the Greek alphabet

Cadogan *(Celtic)* 'War'

Cadwallader *(Celtic)* 'Battle leader'

Caedmon *(Celtic)* 'Wise warrior'

Caesar *(Latin)* 'Emperor'. Source of all names meaning Emperor – Tsar, Kaiser, Shah, etc Cesar, Cesare

Cailean *see* Colin

Cain *(Hebrew)* 'The possessed'. The original Biblical murderer

Cal *see* Caleb or Calvin

Calder *(Anglo-Saxon)* 'The brook'

Caldwell *(Anglo-Saxon)* 'The cold spring'

Cale *see* Caleb

Caleb *(Hebrew)* 'The bold one'. Impetuous Cal, Cale

Caley *(Gaelic)* 'Thin, slender'

Calhoun *(Gaelic)* 'From the forest strip'

Callum *(Celtic)* 'Dove' *see also* Columba

Calvert *(Anglo-Saxon)* 'One who looks after the calves' *see also* Calvin

Calvin *(Latin)* 'Bald' Cal, Calvino *see also* Calvert

Calvino *see* Calvin

Cam *see* Cameron or Campbell

Camden *(Gaelic)* 'From the valley which winds'

Cameron *(Celtic)* 'Crooked nose'. The founder of the Scottish clan Cam, Camey, Camm

Camey *see* Cameron

Camilo *(Spanish)* 'Free born'

Camm *see* Cameron

Campbell *(Celtic)* 'Crooked mouth'. Founder of Campbell clan Cam

Candan *(Turkish)* 'Sincerely, heartily'

Cannon *see* Channing

Canute *(Norse)* 'The knot'. King who tried to hold back the waves Knut, Knute

Caradoc *(Celtic)* 'Beloved' *see also* Craddock

Caradock *see* Craddock

Care *see* Carey

Carey *(Celtic)* 'One who lives in a castle' Care, Cary *see also* Charles

Carl *see* Carleton, Carlin or Charles

Carleton *(Anglo-Saxon)* 'Farmers' meeting place' Carl, Carlton, Charlton

Carlile *see* Carlisle

Carlin *(Gaelic)* 'Little champion' Carl, Carling, Carlyle

Carling *see* Carlin

Carlisle *(Anglo-Saxon)* 'Tower of the castle' Carlile, Carlyle, Carlysle

Carlo *see* Charles

Carlos *see* Charles

Carlton *see* Carleton

Carlyle *see* Carlin or Carlisle

Carlysle *see* Carlisle

Carmichael *(Celtic)* 'From St Michael's castle'

Carmine *(Latin)* 'Song'

Carney *(Gaelic)* 'Victorious'. The warrior who never lost a battle
Carny, Kearney

Carny *see* Carney

Carol *(Gaelic)* 'The champion'
Carolus, Carrol, Carroll, Caryl *see also* Charles

Carollan *(Gaelic)* 'Little champion'

Carolus *see* Carol

Carr *(Norse)* 'One who dwells beside a marsh'
Karr, Kerr

Carrick *(Gaelic)* 'The rocky cape'

Carrol *see* Charles

Carroll *see* Carol

Carson *(Anglo-Saxon)* 'Son of the man who lives by the marsh'

Carswell *(Anglo-Saxon)* 'The watercress grower'

Carter *(Anglo-Saxon)* 'The cart driver'. One who transports cattle and goods

Cartland *(Celtic)* 'The land between the rivers'

Carvel *see* Carvell

Carvell *(French)* 'Estate in the marshes'
Carvel

Carver *(Old English)* 'Woodcarver'

Carvey *(Gaelic)* 'The athlete'
Carvy

Carvy *see* Carvey

Cary *see* Carey or Charles

Caryl *see* Carol

Case *see* Casey

Casey *(Gaelic)* 'Brave and watchful'. The warrior who never slept
Case

Cash *see* Cassius

Casimir *(Slavic)* 'The proclaimer of peace'
Cass, Cassie, Cassy, Kasimir, Kazimir

Caspar *(Persian)* 'Master of the treasure'. Guard of the most precious possessions
Casper, Gaspar, Gasper *see also* Gaspar

Casper *see* Caspar or Gaspar

Cass *see* Casimir, Cassidy or Cassius

Cassidy *(Gaelic)* 'Ingenuity' or 'curly haired'
Cass, Cassy

Cassie *see* Casimir

Cassius *(Latin)* 'Vain and conceited'
Cash, Cass, Cassie, Cassy

Cassy *see* Casimir, Cassidy or Cassius

Castor *(Greek)* 'The beaver'. An industrious person

Cathmor *(Gaelic)* 'Great warrior'

Cato *(Latin)* 'The wise one'. One with great worldly knowledge

Cavan *(Gaelic)* 'Handsome'. The Irish Adonis
Kavan

Cavell *(French)* 'Little lively one'. Always active

Cawley *(Norse)* 'Ancestral relic'

Cece *see* Cecil

Cecil *(Latin)* 'The unseeing one'
Cece, Cecilio, Cecilius, Celio, Sissil

Cecilio *see* Cecil

Cecilius *see* Cecil

Cedric *(Celtic)* 'Chieftain'
Caddaric, Rick, Rickie, Ricky

Cedron *(Latin)* 'Cedar tree'

Celio *see* Cecil

Cephas *(Aramaic)* 'Rock'

Cerwyn *(Welsh)* 'Fair love'

Cesar *see* Caesar

Cesare *see* Caesar

Chad *(Anglo-Saxon)* 'Warlike, bellicose'
Cadda, Chadda, Chaddie *see also* Chadwick and Charles

Chadda *see* Chad

Chaddie *see* Chad

Chadwick *(Anglo-Saxon)* 'Town of the warrior'
Chad

Chaim *(Hebrew)* 'Life'
Hy, Hyman, Mannie, Manny

Chalmer *(Celtic)* 'The chamberlain's son' or 'king of the household'
Chalmers

Chalmers *see* Chalmer

Chan *see* Chandler, Channing or Chauncey

Chance *(Anglo-Saxon)* 'Good fortune' *see also* Chauncey

Chanceller *see* Chancellor

Chancellor *(Anglo-Saxon)* 'King's counsellor'. A man trusted with the highest state secrets Chanceller, Chaunceler, Chaunceller

Chancey *see* Chauncey

Chander *(Sanskrit)* 'The moon who outshines the stars'

Chandler *(French)* 'The candle-maker' Chan, Chane

Chane *see* Chandler or Channing

Chaney *see* Cheney

Channing *(French)* 'The canon' Cannon, Chan, Chane

Chapman *(Anglo-Saxon)* 'The merchant'. The travelling salesmen of medieval times Mannie, Manny

Charles *(Teutonic)* 'The strong man'. The personification of all that is masculine Carey, Carl, Carlo, Carlos, Carol, Carrol, Cary, Charlie, Charley, Charlton, Chas, Chic, Chick, Chuck, Karl, Karlan, Karlens, Karol, Tearlach *see also* Carol

Charleton *see* Charlton

Charley *see* Charles

Charlie *see* Charles

Charlton *(Anglo-Saxon)* 'Charles's farm' Charleton *see also* Carlton and Charles

Chas *see* Charles

Chase *(French)* 'The hunter'. One who enjoys the chase

Chatham *(Anglo-Saxon)* 'Land of the soldier'

Chaunce *see* Chauncey

Chaunceler *see* Chancellor

Chaunceller *see* Chancellor

Chauncey *(French)* 'Chancellor, record-keeper' Chancey, Chaunce *see also* Chance or Chancellor

Cheiro *(Greek)* 'Hand'

Chelton *see* Chilton

Chen *(Chinese)* 'Great'

Cheney *(French)* 'One who lives in the oak wood'. A woodman
Chaney, Cheyney

Ches *see* Chester

Chester *(Latin)* 'The fortified camp'
Ches, Cheston *see also* Chet

Cheston *see* Chester

Chet *(Thai)* 'Brother' *see also* Chester

Chetwin *(Anglo-Saxon)* 'Cottage dweller by the winding path'
Chetwyn

Chetwyn *see* Chetwin

Cheung *(Chinese)* 'Good luck'

Chevalier *(French)* 'Knight'
Chevy

Chevy *see* Chevalier

Cheyney *see* Cheney

Chic *see* Charles

Chick *see* Charles

Chico *(Spanish)* Familiar form of Francis, from Francisco

Chilt *see* Chilton

Chilton *(Anglo-Saxon)* 'From the farm by the spring'
Chelton, Chilt

Chretien *see* Christian

Chris *see* Christian or Christopher

Christian *(Latin)* 'Believer in Christ, a Christian'
Chretien, Chris, Christiano, Christie, Christy, Kit, Kristian, Kristin

Christiano *see* Christian

Christie *see* Christian

Christoforo *see* Christopher

Christoper *see* Christopher

Christoph *see* Christopher

Christophe *see* Christopher

Christopher *(Greek)* 'The Christ carrier'. The man who carried the infant Christ across the river
Chris, Christoforo, Christoper, Christoph, Christophe, Christophorus, Cristobal, Gillecirosd, Kit, Kester, Kris, Kriss

Christophorus *see* Christopher

Christy *see* Christian

Chrysander *(Greek)* 'Golden man'

Chuck *see* Charles

Chung *(Chinese)* 'Intelligent'

Churchill *(Anglo-Saxon)* 'One who lives by the church on the hill'

Cian *(Gaelic)* 'The ancient one'. Long-living

Ciaran (Irish) 'Dark-haired'
Keiran

Cicero *(Latin)* 'The chick-pea'

Cid (Spanish) 'A lord'. El Cid was an 11th-Century Spanish hero and soldier of fortune
Cyd

Cillan *see* Cullen

Ciprian *see* Cyprian

Cirilo *see* Cyril

Ciro *see* Cyrus

Claiborn *see* Clayborne

Clair *see* Clare

Clare *(Latin)* 'Famous one' or *(Anglo-Saxon)* 'bright, illustrious'
Clair *see also* Clarence

Clarence *(Latin/Anglo-Saxon)* 'Famous, illustrious one'
Clare, Clavance

Clark *(French)* 'Wise and learned scholar'
Clarke, Clerk

Clarke *see* Clark

Claud *(Latin)* 'The lame one'
Chlaudio, Claude, Claudian, Claudianus, Claus

Claude *see* Claud

Claudian *see* Claud

Claudianus *see* Claud

Claudio *see* Claud

Claus *see* Claud or Nicholas

Clavance *see* Clarence

Clay *(Anglo-Saxon)* 'From the clay pit' *see also* Clayborne

Clayborne *(Anglo-Saxon)* 'From the brook by the clay pit'
Claiborn, Clay, Claybourne

Claybourne *see* Clayborne

Clayson *see* Clayton

Clayton *(Anglo-Saxon)*
'From the clay town' or
'mortal man'
Clayson

Cleary *(Gaelic)* 'The
scholar'

Cleavon *(Old English)* 'Cliff'

Cledwyn *(Welsh)* 'Blessed
sword'

Cleeve *see* Clive

Clem *see* Clement

Clemence *see* Clement

Clemens *see* Clement

Clement *(Latin)* 'Kind and
merciful'
Clem, Clemence,
Clemens, Clementius,
Clemmy, Clim

Clementius *see* Clement

Clemmy *see* Clement

Cleon *(Greek)* 'Famous'

Clerk *see* Clark

Cletis *see* Cletus

Cletus *(Greek)* 'Summoned'
Cletis

Cleve *see* Cleveland or
Clive

Cleveland *(Anglo-Saxon)*
'From the cliff land'
Cleve, Clevey

Clevey *see* Cleveland

Clif *see* Clifford

Cliff *see* Clifford *see also*
Clive

Clifford *(Anglo-Saxon)*
'From the ford by the
cliff'
Clif, Cliff

Clift *see* Clifton

Clifton *(Anglo-Saxon)*
'From the farm by the
cliff'
Clift

Clim *see* Clement

Clint *see* Clinton

Clinton *(Anglo-Saxon)*
'From the farm on the
headland'
Clint

Clive *(Anglo-Saxon)* 'Cliff'
Cleeve, Cleve, Clyve

Clovis *(Teutonic)* 'Famous
warrior'. An early form
of Lewis (Louis)

Cluny *(Gaelic)* 'From the
meadow'

Cly *see* Clyde

Clydai *(Welsh)* 'Fame'

Clyde *(Celtic)* 'Warm' *(Welsh Celtic)* or 'heard from the distance' *(Scots Celtic)*
Cly, Clywd

Clydias *(Greek)* 'Glorious'

Clyve *see* Clive

Clywd *see* Clyde

Cobb *see* Jacob

Coburn *(Old English)* 'Small stream'

Cody *(Old English)* 'A cushion'

Coel *(Welsh)* 'Trust'
Cole

Coile *see* Coyle

Col *see* Coleman

Colan *see* Colin

Colbert *(Anglo-Saxon)* 'Brilliant seafarer' or 'cool and calm'
Cole, Colvert, Culbert

Colby *(Norse)* 'From the dark country'
Cole

Cole *see* Coel, Colbert, Colby, Coleman or Nicholas

Coleman *(Celtic)* 'Keeper of the doves' or *(Anglo-Saxon)* 'follower of Nicholas'
Col, Cole, Colman

Colier *see* Collier

Colin *(Gaelic)* 'Strong and virile' or 'the young child' or 'victorious army'
Colan, Cailean, Collin and all derivatives of Nicholas

Colis *see* Collier

Colley *(Old English)* 'Swarthy' *see also* Nicholas

Collier *(Anglo-Saxon)* 'Charcoal merchant'
Colier, Colis, Collyer, Colton, Colyer

Collin *see* Colin

Collyer *see* Collier

Colm *see* Columba

Colman *see* Coleman

Colter *(Anglo-Saxon)* 'The colt herder'

Colton *(Anglo-Saxon)* 'From the dark town' *see also* Colier

Colum *see* Columba

Columba *(Latin)* 'Dove'
Colm, Colum *see also*
Callum

Colver *see* Culver

Colvert *see* Colbert

Colyer *see* Collier

Con *see* Conan, Conrad or
Conroy

Conal *see* Conan

Conan *(Celtic)* 'High and
mighty' or 'wisely
intelligent'
Con, Conal, Conant,
Conn, Connall, Connel,
Kynan, Quinn

Conant *see* Conan

Conlan *(Gaelic)* 'The hero'
Conlin, Conlon

Conlin *see* Conlan

Conlon *see* Conlan

Conn *see* Conan, Conroy
or Constantine

Connall *see* Conan or
Conroy

Connel *see* Conan

Connie *see* Conrad,
Conroy or Cornelius

Connor *(Old English)* 'Wise
aid'

Conrad *(Teutonic)* 'Brave
counsellor'
Con, Conn, Connie,
Conrade, Conrado,
Cort, Curt, Konrad,
Kort, Kurt

Conrade *see* Conrad

Conrado *see* Conrad

Conroy *(Gaelic)* 'The wise
one'
Con, Conn, Connie,
Roy

Constant *see* Constantine

Constantin *see* Constantin

Constantine *(Latin)* 'Firm
and unwavering'.
Always constant
Conn, Connie,
Constant, Constantin,
Constantino, Costa,
Konstantin,
Konstantine

Constantino *see*
Constantine

Conway *(Gaelic)* 'Hound of
the plain'

Coop *see* Cooper

Cooper *(Anglo-Saxon)*
'Barrel-maker'
Coop

Corbet *see* Corbett

Corbett *(French)* 'The raven'. From the raven device worn by the ancient Vikings
Corbet, Corbie, Corbin, Corby

Corbie *see* Corbett

Corbin *see* Corbett

Corby *see* Corbett

Corcoran *(Gaelic)* 'Reddish complexion'
Corquoran

Cord *see* Cordell

Cordell *(French)* 'Rope-maker'
Cord, Cory

Corey *(Gaelic)* 'One who lives in a ravine'
Cory

Cormac *see* Cormick

Cormack *see* Cormick

Cormick *(Gaelic)* 'The charioteer'
Cormac, Cormack

Cornal *see* Cornelius

Cornall *see* Cornelius

Cornel *see* Cornelius

Cornelius *(Latin)* 'Battle horn'
Connie, Cornal, Cornall, Cornel,

Cornell, Neal, Neel, Neil

Cornell *see* Cornelius

Corquoran *see* Corcoran

Cort *see* Conrad or Courtenay

Cortie *see* Courtenay

Corty *see* Courtenay

Corwen *see* Corwin

Corwin *(French)* 'Friend of the heart'
Corwen

Cory *see* Cordell, Corey, Cornelius or Corydon

Corydon *(Greek)* 'The helmeted man'
Cory

Cosimo *see* Cosmo

Cosme *see* Cosmo

Cosmo *(Greek)* 'The perfect order of the universe'
Cosimo, Cosme

Costa *see* Constantine

Court *see* Courtenay or Courtland

Courtenay *(French)* 'A place'
Cort, Cortie, Corty, Court, Courtney, Curt

Courtland *(Anglo-Saxon)*
'One who dwelt on the
court land'
Court

Courtney *see* Courtenay

Covell *(Anglo-Saxon)* 'One
who lives in the cave
on the hill'
Covill

Covill *see* Covell

Cowan *(Gaelic)* 'Hollow in
the hillside'

Coyle *(Gaelic)* 'Battle
flower'
Coile

Craddock *(Celtic)*
'Abundance of love'
Caradoc, Caradock

Craggie *see* Craig

Craig *(Celtic)* 'From the
stony hill'
Craggie

Crandall *see* Crandell

Crandell *(Anglo-Saxon)*
'One who lives in the
valley of the crane'
Crandall

Crane *(Old English)* 'Cry'

Cranley *(Anglo-Saxon)*
'From the crane
meadow'

Cranog *(Welsh)* 'Heron'

Cranston *(Anglo-Saxon)*
'From the farmstead
where the cranes
gather'

Crawford *(Anglo-Saxon)*
'From the crow ford'
Crowford

Crayton *see* Creighton

Creigh *see* Creighton

Creight *see* Creighton

Creighton *(Anglo-Saxon)*
'From the farm by the
creek'
Crayton, Creigh,
Creight, Crichton

Crepin *see* Crispin

Crichton *see* Creighton

Crisp *see* Crispin

Crispen *see* Crispin

Crispin *(Latin)* 'Curly
haired'. Patron saint of
shoemakers
Crepin, Crisp, Crispen

Cristobal *see* Christopher

Cromwell *(Anglo-Saxon)*
'One who lives by a
winding spring'. The
small rivulet that winds
through the countryside

Crosbey *see* Crosby

Crosbie *see* Crosby

Crosby *(Anglo-Saxon/ Norse)* 'One who lives at the crossroads' Crosbey, Crosbie

Crosley *(Anglo-Saxon)* 'From the meadow with the cross'

Crowford *see* Crawford

Culbert *see* Colbert

Cullen *(Gaelic)* 'Handsome one' Cullan, Cullin, Cully

Culley *(Gaelic)* 'From the woodland' Cully

Cullin *see* Cullen

Cully *see* Cullen or Culver

Culver *(Anglo-Saxon)* 'Gentle as the dove' peaceful'. The symbol of peace Colver, Cully

Curelo *see* Curtis

Curran *(Gaelic)* 'The resolute hero' Curren, Currey, Currie, Curry

Curren *see* Curran

Currey *see* Curran

Currie *see* Curran

Curry *see* Curran

Curt *see* Conrad, Courtney or Curtis

Curtis *(French)* 'The courteous one'. A gentleman with perfect manners Curelo, Curt, Kurt

Cuthbert *(Anglo-Saxon)* 'Famous and brilliant'

Cutler *(Old English)* 'Knife-maker' Cuttie

Cuttie *see* Cutler

Cy *see* Cyril or Cyrus

Cyd *see* Cid

Cybard *(French)* 'Ruler'

Cyndeyrn *(Welsh)* 'Chief lord'

Cynfael *(Welsh)* 'Chief metal'

Cynfor *(Welsh)* 'Great chief'

Cyngen *(Welsh)* 'Chief son'

Cynric *(Anglo-Saxon)* 'From the royal line of kings'

Cynyr *(Welsh)* 'Chief hero'

Cyprian *(Greek)* 'Man from Cyprus' Ciprian, Cyprien

Cyprien *see* Cyprian

Cyrano *(Greek)* 'From
Cyrene'
Cyrenaica

Cyrenaica *see* Cyrano

Cyril *(Greek)* 'The lord'
Cirilo, Cy, Cyrill,
Cyrille, Cyrillus

Cyrill *see* Cyril

Cyrille *see* Cyril

Cyrillus *see* Cyril

Cyrus *(Persian)* 'The sun
god'. The founder of the
Persian Empire
Ciro, Cy, Russ

D'Arcy *see* Darcy

Dabert *(French)* 'Bright action'

Dacey *(Gaelic)* 'The southerner'
Dacy

Dacy *see* Dacey

Daegal *(Scandinavian)* 'Boy born at dawn'

Dael *see* Dale

Dag *(Norse)* 'Day of brightness'
Dagny

Dagan *(Semitic)* 'The earth' or 'the small fish'
Dagon

Dagny *(Teutonic)* 'Fresh as day'
Dagobert *see also* Dag

Dagobert *see* Dagny

Dagon *see* Dagan

Dagwood *(Anglo-Saxon)* 'Forest of the shining one'

Dahab *(Arabic)* 'Gold'

Daimon *(Latin)* 'Guardian angel'

Dakota *(Native American)* 'Friend, partner'. Tribal name

Dal *see* Dale, Dallas or Dalton

Dalbert *(Anglo-Saxon)* 'From the shining valley'
Delbert

Dale *(Teutonic)* 'One who lives in the valley'
Dael, Dal

Dallas *(Celtic)* 'Skilled' or 'from the water field'
Dal, Dallia

Dallia *see* Dallas

Dallon *see* Dalston

Dalston *(Old English)* 'From Daegal's place'
Dallon

Dalt *see* Dalton

Dalton *(Anglo-Saxon)* 'From the farm in the valley'
Dal, Dalt, Tony

Daly *(Gaelic)* 'The counsellor'

Dalziel *(Celtic)* 'From the little field'
Dalziell

Dalziell *see* Dalziel

Daman *(Sanskrit)* 'One in control'
Damian

Damek *(Slavic)* 'Man of the earth'

Damian *see* Daman or Damon

Damiano *see* Damon

Damien *see* Damon

Damon *(Greek)* 'Tame and domesticated'. The true friend
Damian, Damiano, Damien

Dan *see* Daniel

Dana *(Anglo-Saxon)* 'Man from Denmark'
Dane

Danby *(Norse)* 'From the settlement of the Danish'

Dane *see* Dana or Daniel

Daniel *(Hebrew)* 'The lord is my judge'
Dan, Dane, Daniell, Danielle, Danny *see also* Darnell

Daniell *see* Daniel

Danielle *see* Daniel

Danny *see* Daniel

Dante *see* Durant

Darby *(Gaelic)* 'Freeman'
Derby

Darcie *see* Darcy

Darcy *(French)* 'From the fortress'
Darcie, D'Arcy, Darsey, Darsy

Dare *see* Darius

Daren *see* Darren

Darien *(Spanish)* A place name

Darin *see* Darren

Dario *see* Darius

Darius *(Persian)* 'The wealthy man'
Dare, Dario *see also* Derek or Derry

Darnall *see* Darnell

Darnell *(French)* 'From the hidden nook'
Darnall *see also* Daniel

Daron *see* Darren

Darrell *(French)* 'Beloved one'
Darryl, Daryl, Derril

Darren *(Gaelic)* 'Little great one'
Daren, Darin, Daron, Derron

Darrick *see* Derek

Darryl *see* Darrel

Darsey *see* Darcy

Darsy *see* Darcy

Darton *(Anglo-Saxon)* 'From the deer forest'

Darwin *(Old English)* 'Beloved friend'
Derwin

Daryl *see* Darrel

Dave *see* David

Daven *see* David

David *(Hebrew)* 'The beloved one'. The patron saint of Wales
Dave, Daven, Davidson, Davie, Davin, Davon, Davy *see also* Davis or Dov

Davidson *see* David

Davie *see* David

Davin *(Scandinavian)* 'Brightness of the Finns' *see also* David

Davis *(Anglo-Saxon)* David's son *see also* David

Davon *see* David

Davorin *(Slavonic)* 'God of war'

Davy *see* David

De Witt *(Flemish)* 'Fair-haired one'
Dwight

Dean *(Anglo-Saxon)* 'From the valley'
Deane, Dene, Dino

Deane *see* Dean

Dearborn *(Anglo-Saxon)* 'Beloved child' or 'from the deer brook'

Decca *see* Dexter

Deck *see* Dexter

Declan *(Irish)* 'Man of prayer'

Dedrick *(Teutonic)* 'Ruler of the people'

Deems *(Anglo-Saxon)* 'The judge's son'

Dekkel *(Arabic)* 'Palm tree'

Delaney *(Gaelic)*
'Descendant of the
challenger'

Delano *(French)* 'From the
nut tree woods'

Delbert *see* Albert or
Dalbert

Delling *(Norse)* 'Very
shining one'

Delmar *(Latin)* 'From the
sea'
Delmer, Delmor,
Delmore

Delmer *see* Delmar

Delmor *see* Delmar

Delmore *see* Delmar

Delwin *see* Delwyn

Delwyn *(Anglo-Saxon)*
'Bright friend from the
valley'
Delwin

Demas *(Greek)* 'The
popular person'

Demetri *see* Demetrius

Demetris *see* Demetrius

Demetrius *(Greek)*
'Belonging to Demeter'
Demetri, Demetris,
Demmy, Dimitri,
Dmitri

Demmy *see* Demetrius

Demos *(Greek)* 'The
spokesman of the
people'

Demosthenes *(Greek)*
'Strength of the people'

Dempsey *(Gaelic)* 'The
proud one'

Dempster *(Anglo-Saxon)*
'The judge'

Den *see* Dennis and other
names beginning with
Den

Denby *(Norse)* 'From the
Danish settlement'
Den

Dene *see* Dean

Denholm *(Scottish)* 'Island
valley'

Denis *see* Dennis

Denison *see* Dennison

Denley *(Anglo-Saxon)* 'One
who lives in the
meadow in the valley'

Denman *(Anglo-Saxon)*
'Resident in the valley'

Dennie *see* Dennis

Dennis *(Greek)* 'Wine
lover'. From Dionysus,
the God of Wine
Den, Denis, Dennie,

Dennison, Denny, Deny, Denys, Denzil, Dion, Dionisio, Dionysus, Ennis *see also* Denzil

Dennison *(Anglo-Saxon)* 'Son of Dennis' Denison *see also* Dennis

Denny *see* Dennis

Denton *(Anglo-Saxon)* 'From the farm in the valley' Den, Dennie, Denny

Denver *(Anglo-Saxon)* 'From the edge of the valley'

Deny *see* Dennis

Denys *see* Dennis

Denzil *(Cornish)* 'High stronghold' Dennis

Deodatus *(Latin)* 'God-given'

Derby *see* Darby

Derek *(Teutonic)* 'Ruler of the people' Darrick, Derk, Derrick, Derry, Dirk *see also* Derry or Theodoric

Derk *see* Derek or Theodoric

Dermot *(Gaelic)* 'Free man' Diarmid *see also* Kermit

Derrick *see* Derek or Theodoric

Derron *see* Darren

Derry *(Gaelic)* 'The red one' *see also* Darius, Derek or Kermit

Derward *(Anglo-Saxon)* 'Guardian of the deer'

Derwin *see* Darwin

Desmond *(Gaelic)* 'Man of the world, sophisticated' Desmund

Desmund *see* Desmond

Deverell *(Celtic)* 'From the river bank'

Devin *(Celtic)* 'A poet'

Devland *see* Devlin

Devlin *(Gaelic)* 'Fierce bravery' Devland

Devon *(English)* 'From Devon'. Someone born in that county, the name of which means 'people of the deep valley'

Dew *see* Dewey

Dewain *see* Dwayne

Dewar *(Celtic)* 'Hero'

Dewey *(Celtic)* 'The beloved one'. The Celtic form of David
Dew

Dex *see* Dexter

Dexter *(Latin)* 'The right-handed man, dextrous'
Decca, Deck, Dex

Diamond *(Anglo-Saxon)* 'The shining protector'

Diarmid *see* Dermot

Diccon *see* Richard

Dick *see* Richard

Dickie *see* Richard

Dickon *see* Richard

Dickson *see* Dixon

Dicky *see* Richard

Diego *see* Jacob

Dieter *(German)* 'From strong people'

Dietrich *see* Theodoric

Digby *(Norse)* 'From the settlement by the dyke'

Diggory *(French)* 'Strayed, lost'

Dilan *see* Dylan

Dillon *(Gaelic)* 'Faithful'. A true and loyal man

Dilly *see* Dylan

Dilwin *(Teutonic)* 'Serene friend'

Dimitri *see* Demetrius

Dinar *(Sanskrit)* 'Golden coin'

Dino *see* Dean

Dinsdale *(English)* 'Settlement surrounded by a moat'

Dinsmore *(Gaelic)* 'From the fortified hill'

Diomede *(Greek)* 'Divine ruler'

Dion *see* Dennis

Dionisio *see* Dennis

Dionysus *see* Dennis

Dirk *see* Derek or Theodoric

Dixon *(Anglo-Saxon)* 'Son of Richard' (Dick's son) Dickson *see also* Benedict

Dmitri *see* Demetrius

Doane *(Celtic)* 'From the sand dune'

Dodd *(Teutonic)* 'Of the people'

Dolan *(Gaelic)* 'Black haired'

Dolf *see* Adolph or Rudolph

Dolph *see* Adolph or Rudolph

Dom *see* Dominic

Domenico *see* Dominic

Domingo *see* Dominic

Dominic *(Latin)* 'Belonging to the Lord, born on the Lord's day' Dom, Domenico, Domingo, Dominic, Dominik, Dominy, Nic, Nick, Nickie, Nicky

Dominik *see* Dominic

Dominy *see* Dominic

Don *see* Donahue or Donald

Donaghan *(Celtic)* 'Dark skinned'

Donahue *(Gaelic)* 'Warrior dressed in brown' Don, Donn, Donnie, Donny

Donal *see* Donald

Donald *(Celtic)* 'Ruler of the world'. The founder of the MacDonald clan Don, Donal, Donn, Donnall, Donalt, Donaugh, Donnell, Donnie, Donny

Donalt *see* Donald

Donato *(Latin)* 'A gift'

Donaugh *see* Donald or Donnelly

Donn *see* Donahue or Donald

Donnall *see* Donald

Donnell *see* Donald or Donnelly

Donnelly *(Gaelic)* 'Brave, dark man' Don, Donn, Donnell, Donaugh, Donny

Donnie *see* Donald or Donahue

Donny *see* Donald or Donahue

Donovan *(Irish)* 'Dark brown' Don, Donn, Donnie, Donny

Doogan *see* Dugan

Doran *(Celtic)* 'The stranger' Dore

Dorcas *(Hebrew)* 'From the forest'

Dore *see* Doran, Theodore

Dorian *(Greek)* 'Man from Doria'

Dory *(French)* 'The golden-haired boy'

Doug *see* Douglas

Dougal *see* Douglas

Dougan *see* Dugan

Douggie *see* Douglas

Douggy *see* Douglas

Douglas *(Celtic)* 'From the dark stream'. One of the largest Scottish clans
Doug, Dougal, Douggie, Douggy, Dugal, Dugald, Duggie, Duggy, Duglass

Dov *see* David or Dovev

Dovev (Hebrew) 'To whisper'
Dov

Dow *(Gaelic)* 'Black haired'

Doyle *(Gaelic)* 'The dark-haired stranger'

Drake *(Anglo-Saxon)* 'The dragon'

Drew *(Celtic)* 'The wise one'
Drud *see also* Andrew

Driscol *see* Driscoll

Driscoll *(Celtic)* 'The interpreter'
Driscol

Drostan *see* Tristan

Druce *(Celtic)* 'Son of Drew'

Drud *see* Drew

Drummond *(Celtic)* 'One who lives on the hill'

Drury *(French)* 'The dear one'

Dryden *(Anglo-Saxon)* 'From the dry valley'

Duane *see* Dwayne

Dubert *(Teutonic)* 'Bright knight'

Dud *see* Dudley

Duddie *see* Dudley

Duddy *see* Dudley

Dudley *(Anglo-Saxon)* 'From the people's meadow'
Dud, Duddie, Duddy, Dudly

Dudly *see* Dudley

Duff *(Gaelic)* 'Dark complexion'

Dugal *see* Douglas

Dugald *see* Douglas

Dugan *(Gaelic)* 'Dark skinned'. The sun-tanned man
Doogan, Dougan

Duggie *see* Douglas

Duggy *see* Douglas

Duglass *see* Douglas

Duke *(French)* 'The leader' *see also* Marmaduke

Dulal *(Sanskrit)* 'Precious one'

Dunbar *(Celtic)* 'Dark branch'

Dunc *see* Duncan

Duncan *(Celtic)* 'Brown warrior'
Dunc, Dunn

Dunham *(Celtic)* 'Dark man'

Dunlea *(Teutonic)* 'From the dark field'

Dunley *(Anglo-Saxon)* 'From the meadow on the hill'

Dunmore *(Celtic)* 'From the fortress on the hill'

Dunn *(Anglo-Saxon)* 'Dark skinned' *see also* Duncan

Dunstan *(Anglo-Saxon)* 'From the brown stone hill'

Durand *see* Durant

Durant *(Latin)* 'Enduring'. One whose friendship is lasting
Dante, Durand

Durward *(Anglo-Saxon)* 'The gate-keeper'. The guardian of the drawbridge
Ward

Durwin *(Anglo-Saxon)* 'Dear friend'
Durwyn

Durwyn *see* Durwin

Dustan *see* Dustin

Dustin *(Old German)* 'Valiant fighter'
Dustan, Dusty

Dusty *see* Dustin

Dwain *see* Dwayne

Dwayne *(Celtic)* 'The singer' or *(Gaelic)* 'the small, dark man'
Dewain, Duane, Dwain

Dwight *(Teutonic)* 'The light-haired one' *see also* De Witt

Dyfan *(Welsh)* 'Ruler of the tribe'

Dyfrig *(Welsh)* 'Princely hero'

Dylan *(Welsh)* 'Man from the sea'
Dilan, Dilly

Dynami *(Native American)* 'Eagle'

Dynawd *(Welsh)* 'Given'

Eachan *(Gaelic)* 'Little horse'
Eacheann *see also* Hector

Eachann *see* Hector

Eachunn *see* Hector

Eamon *see* Edmund

Eamonn *see* Edmund

Eanruig *see* Henry

Earl *(Anglo-Saxon)* 'Nobleman' chief'
Erle, Earle, Erl, Errol, Early, Rollo

Earle *see* Earle

Early *see* Earl

Earn *(Teutonic)* 'One who is like the eagle'

Eaton *(Anglo-Saxon)* 'From the estate by the river'

Eb *see* Aber, Ebenezer or Everard

Eben *see* Ebenezer

Ebenezer *(Hebrew)* 'Stone of help'
Eb, Eben

Eberard *(Teutonic)* 'Strong and steadfast' *see also* Everard

Eberhard *see* Everard

Eberhart *see* Everard

Ed *see* Edgar, Edmund or Edward

Edan *(Celtic)* 'Flame'

Edbert *(Anglo-Saxon)* 'Prosperous' or 'brilliant'

Edd *see* Edwin

Eddie *see* Edgar, Edmund, Edward or Edwin

Eddy *see* Edgar, Edmund, Edward or Edwin

Edel *(Teutonic)* 'The noble one'

Edelmar *(Anglo-Saxon)* 'Noble and famous'

Eden *(Hebrew)* 'Place of delight and pleasure'. The original paradise *see also* Aidan

Edgar *(Anglo-Saxon)* 'Lucky spear warrior'
Ed, Eddie, Eddy, Edgard, Ned, Neddie, Neddy, Ted, Teddie, Teddy

Edgard *see* Edgar

Edison *see* Edson

Edlin *(Anglo-Saxon)* 'Prosperous friend' *see also* Edwin

Edmon *see* Edmund

Edmond *see* Edmund

Edmondo *see* Edmund

Edmonn *see* Edmund

Edmund *(Anglo-Saxon)* 'Rich guardian'
Eamon, Eamonn, Ed, Eddie, Eddy, Edmon, Edmond, Edmondo, Edmonn, Ned, Neddie, Ted, Teddie, Teddy

Edolf *(Anglo-Saxon)* 'Prosperous wolf'

Edouard *see* Edward

Edred *(Teutonic)* 'Wise adviser'

Edric *(Anglo-Saxon)* 'Fortunate ruler'

Edryd *(Welsh)* 'Restoration'

Edsel *(Anglo-Saxon)* 'A prosperous man's house' or 'profound thinker'

Edson *(Anglo-Saxon)* 'Edward's son'
Edison

Eduard *see* Edward

Eduino *see* Edwin

Edwald *(Anglo-Saxon)* 'Prosperous ruler'

Edward *(Anglo-Saxon)* 'Prosperous guardian'
Ed, Eddie, Eddy, Edouard, Eduard, Ewart, Ned, Neddie, Neddy, Ted, Teddy

Edwin *(Anglo-Saxon)* 'Prosperous friend'
Edd, Eddie, Eddy, Edlin, Eduino

Edwy *(Old English)* 'Richly beloved'

Efrem *see* Ephraim

Egan *(Gaelic)* 'Formidable, fiery'
Egon

Egbert *(Anglo-Saxon)* 'Bright, shining sword'. The name of the first king of all England
Bert

Egerton *(Old English)*
'Town on ridge'

Egmont *(Anglo-Saxon)*
'Protected by a sword'

Egon *see* Egan

Ehren *(Teutonic)*
'Honourable one'

Einar *(Norse)* 'Warrior
leader'

Eiros *(Welsh)* 'Bright'

Elaeth *(Welsh)* 'Intelligent'

Elan *(Hebrew)* 'Tree'

Elazar *(Hebrew)* 'God
helps'

Elbert *see* Albert

Elden *(Anglo-Saxon)* 'Elf
valley'
Eldon *see also* Alden

Elder *(Anglo-Saxon)* 'One
who lives by an elder
tree'

Eldin *see* Alden

Eldo *(Greek)* 'A wish'

Eldon *(Teutonic)* 'Respected
elder' or *(Anglo-Saxon)*
'from the holy hill' *see
also* Elden

Eldoris *(Teutonic)* 'The
point of a spear'

Eldred *see* Eldridge

Eldredge *see* Eldridge

Eldric *see* Aldrich

Eldrich *see* Aldrich

Eldrid *see* Eldridge

Eldridge *(Anglo-Saxon)*
'Wise adviser'
Eldred, Eldredge,
Eldrid, Eldwin, Eldwyn
see also Aldrich

Eldwin *(Old English)* 'Old
friend' *see also* Eldridge

Eldwyn *see* Eldridge

Eleazar *(Hebrew)* 'Helped
by God'
Elizer, Lazar, Lazarus

Elery *see* Ellery

Eleutherios *(Greek)* 'A free
man'

Elfed *(Welsh)* 'Autumn'

Elford *(Teutonic)* 'One who
lives by the ford'

Elgar *see* Alger

Elgin *(Gaelic)* 'Earldom of
the Bruces of Scotland'

Elhanan *(Hebrew)* 'God is
gracious'

Eli *(Hebrew)* 'The highest'
Ely

Elia *(Hebrew)* 'God's own
man'

Elian *(Hebrew)* 'Bright'

Elias *(Hebrew)* 'The Lord is God'
Elihu, Elijah, Eliot, Elliott, Ellis

Elidr *(Welsh)* 'Brass'

Elihu *see* Elias

Elijah *see* Elias

Elika *(Hebrew)* 'Sanctified by God'

Elim *(Hebrew)* 'Oak tree'

Eliot *see* Elias

Elisha *(Hebrew)* 'God is my salvation'

Elizer *see* Eleazar

Elkan *(Hebrew)* 'Created by God'

Elkanah *(Hebrew)* 'God has created'

Elki *(Native American)* 'Bear'

Ellard *(Anglo-Saxon)* 'Noble, brave'

Ellerey *see* Ellery

Ellery *(Teutonic)* 'From the elder tree'
Elery, Ellerey

Elliot *see* Elias

Ellis *see* Elias

Ellison *(Anglo-Saxon)* 'Son of Elias'
Elson

Ellsworth *(Anglo-Saxon)* 'A farmer' or 'lover of the land'

Elmen *(Teutonic)* 'Sturdy' or 'built like an oak tree'

Elmer *(Anglo-Saxon)* 'Noble' or 'famous'
Aylmer

Elmo *(Greek/Italian)* 'Friendly protector' *see also* Anselm

Elmore *(Anglo-Saxon)* 'One who lives by the elm tree on the moor'

Elnathan *(Hebrew)* 'God gives'

Elner *(Teutonic)* 'Famous'

Elon *(Teutonic)* 'The strong oak tree'

Elrad *(Hebrew)* 'God is my ruler'

Elred *(Anglo-Saxon)* 'Wise advice'

Elrod *(Teutonic)* 'Famous'

Elroy *(French)* 'The king'. The name is supposed to be an anagram of 'le roi' or it may be from the Spanish 'el rey', both meaning 'the king'

Elsdon *(Anglo-Saxon)* 'Hill belonging to the noble one'

Elson *see* Ellison

Elston *(Anglo-Saxon)* 'Estate of the noble one'

Elsworth *(Anglo-Saxon)* 'Estate of the noble one'

Elton *(Anglo-Saxon)* 'From the old farm'

Elvan *(Teutonic)* 'Strong willed'

Elvis *(Norse)* 'All wise'. The prince of wisdom

Elvy *(Anglo-Saxon)* 'Elfin warrior'. Though small in stature he had the heart of a lion

Elwell *(Anglo-Saxon)* 'From the old well'

Elwin *(Anglo-Saxon)* 'Friend of the elves'

Elwood *(Anglo-Saxon)* 'From an ancient forest'

Ely *see* Eli

Emanuel *see* Emmanuel

Emelen *see* Emil

Emeria *(Teutonic)* 'One who works hard'

Emerson *see* Emery

Emery *(Teutonic)* 'Industrious ruler' or 'joint ruler' Amerigo, Emerson, Emmerich, Emmery, Emory, Merrick

Emil *(Teutonic)* 'Industrious' Emelen, Emile, Emilio, Emlen, Emlyn

Emile *see* Emil

Emilio *see* Emil

Emlen *see* Emil

Emlyn *(Welsh)* 'One who lives on the border' *see also* Emil

Emmanuel *(Hebrew)* 'God is with us' Emanuel, Immanuel, Mannie, Manny, Mano, Manolo, Manuel

Emmerich *see* Emery

Emmery *see* Emery

Emmet *(Anglo-Saxon)* 'The industrious ant' Emmett, Emmit, Emmot, Emmott, Emmy

Emmett *see* Emmet

Emmit *see* Emmet

Emmot *see* Emmet

Emmott *see* Emmet

Emmy *see* Emmet

Emory *see* Emery

Emry *(Welsh)* 'Honorable'

Emry *(Welsh)* 'Honour'

Emrys *see* Ambrose

Emyr *(Welsh)* 'Honour'

Enan *(Welsh)* 'Firm and unyielding'

Endemon *(Greek)* 'Fortunate'

Endimion *(Greek)* Mythological figure, son of Jupiter and Calyce (nymph), so beautiful, honest and just, Jupiter made him immortal

Eneas *see* Aeneas

Engelbert *(Old German)* 'Bright as an angel' *see also* Inglebert

Englebert *see* Inglebert

Ennis *(Gaelic)* 'The only choice' *see also* Angus or Dennis

Enoch *(Hebrew)* 'Consecrated', 'dedicated' or 'devoted'

Enos *(Hebrew)* 'The mortal'

Enrico *see* Henry

Ensley *(Celtic)* 'Watchword'

Enzio *see* Ezio

Eoghan *(Celtic)* 'Young warrior'

Eoin *see* John

Eph *see* Ephraim

Ephraim *(Hebrew)* 'Abounding in fruitfulness' Efrem, Eph

Erasme *see* Erasmus

Erasmus *(Greek)* 'Worthy of being loved' Erasme, Ras, Rasmus

Erastus *(Greek)* 'The beloved' Ras

Erdogan *(Turkish)* 'Son is born'

Erhard *(Old German)* 'Honour' Erhart

Erhart *see* Erhard

Eric *(Norse)* 'All-powerful ruler' or 'kingly'
Erich, Erick, Erik, Rick, Ricky

Erich *see* Eric

Erick *see* Eric

Erik *see* Eric

Erin *(Gaelic)* 'Peace' *see also* Aaron

Erl *see* Earle

Erland *(Anglo-Saxon)* 'Land of the nobleman'

Erle *see* Earl

Erling *(Anglo-Saxon)* 'Son of the nobleman'

Erlon *(Teutonic)* 'Like an elf'

Ermin *see* Herman

Ermos *(Teutonic)* 'Popular one'

Ernest *(Anglo-Saxon)* 'Sincere and earnest'
Ernesto, Ernestus, Ernie, Ernst, Erny

Ernesto *see* Ernest

Ernestus *see* Ernest

Ernie *see* Ernest

Ernst *see* Ernest

Erny *see* Ernest

Errol *see* Earl

Erskine *(Celtic)* 'From the cliff's height'

Ervand *(Scandinavian)* 'Sea warrior'

Ervin *see* Erwin or Irving

Erwin *(Old English)* 'Army friend' *see also* Ervin, Irving

Esau *(Hebrew)* 'The one who finishes the job' or 'the hairy one'

Esbern *(Teutonic)* 'Divine ruler'

Esdras *(Hebrew)* 'Rising light'

Esmond *(Anglo-Saxon)* 'Gracious protector'

Esra *see* Ezra

Este *(Italian)* 'Man from the East'
Estes

Estes *see* Este

Estevan *(Greek)* 'Crown'

Etan *see* Ethan

Ethan *(Hebrew)* 'Steadfast and firm'
Etan

Ethelard *see* Allard

Ethelbert *(Teutonic)* 'Noble, bright'

Ethelred *(Teutonic)* 'Noble counsel'

Etienne *see* Stephen

Euclid *(Greek)* 'True glory'

Eudon *(Greek)* 'Rich ruler'

Eugene *(Greek)* 'Nobly born'
Eugenio, Eugenius, Gene

Eugenio *see* Eugene

Eugenius *see* Eugene

Eurwyn *(Welsh)* 'Golden and fair'

Eusebius *(Greek)* 'Honourable'

Eustace *(Greek)* 'Stable, tranquil' or 'fruitful'
Eustazio, Eustis

Eustazio *see* Eustace

Eustis *see* Eustace

Ev *see* Everard

Evan *(Gaelic)* 'Well-born young warrior'. Also Welsh form of John
Evyn, Ewan, Ewen, Owen *see also* Avan, John or Owen

Evaristus *(Greek)* 'Most excellent'

Evelin *see* Evelyn

Evelyn *(English)* From a surname
Evelin

Everard *(Anglo-Saxon)* 'Strong as a boar'
Eb, Eberhard, Eberhart, Ev, Evelin, Evered, Everettt, Ewart

Evered *see* Everard

Everett *see* Everard

Everild *see* Averill

Everley *(Anglo-Saxon)* 'Field of the wild boar'

Evner *(Turkish)* 'House'

Evyn *see* Evan

Ewald *(Anglo-Saxon)* 'The power of the law'

Ewan *see* Evan

Ewart *see* Edward or Everard

Ewen *see* Evan

Ewert *(Anglo-Saxon)* 'Ewe herder'. One who tended the ewes in lamb

Ewing *(Anglo-Saxon)* 'Friend of the law'

Eymer *(Teutonic)* 'Royal worker'

Ez *see* Ezra

Ezekiel *(Hebrew)* 'Strength
   of God'
   Zeke

Ezio *(Italian)* 'Aquiline
   nose'
   Enzio

Ezra *(Hebrew)* 'The one
   who helps'
   Esra, Ez

Fabe *see* Fabian

Faber *see* Fabian or Fabron

Fabian *(Latin)* 'The bean-grower' or 'prosperous farmer'
Fabe, Faber, Fabiano, Fabien, Fabio

Fabiano *see* Fabian

Fabien *see* Fabian

Fabio *see* Fabian

Fabre *see* Fabron

Fabron *(French)* 'The little blacksmith'
Faber, Fabre

Fadoul *(Arabic)* 'Honest'

Fagan *(Gaelic)* 'Little, fiery one'
Fagin

Fagin *see* Fagan

Fai *(Chinese)* 'Beginning'

Fairburn *(Teutonic)* 'Handsome boy'

Fairchild *(Teutonic)* 'Blond or fair-haired boy'

Fairfax *(Anglo-Saxon)* 'Fair-haired one'

Fairhold *(Teutonic)* 'Powerful one'

Fairleigh *see* Farley

Fairley *(Anglo-Saxon)* 'From the far meadow'
Fairly, Fairlie, Farl, Farley

Fairlie *see* Fairley

Fairly *see* Fairley

Faisal *(Arabic)* 'Wise judge'

Falah *(Arabic)* 'Success'

Falkner *(Anglo-Saxon)* 'Falcon trainer'. One who trained the birds used in the hunt
Faulkener, Faulkner, Fowler

Fane *(Anglo-Saxon)* 'Glad, joyful'

Faramond *(Teutonic)* 'Journey protection'

Farand *(Teutonic)* 'Pleasant and attractive'
Farant, Farrand, Ferrand

Farant *see* Farand

Farl *see* Fairley

Farland *(Old English)* 'Land near road'

Farleigh *see* Farley

Farley *(Old English)* 'From the bull meadow'
Fairleigh, Farleigh *see also* Fairley

Farman *see* Firman

Farnall *see* Farnell

Farnell *(Anglo-Saxon)* 'From the fern slope'
Farnall, Fernald, Fernall

Farnham *(Teutonic)* 'Village among the ferns'

Farnley *(Anglo-Saxon)* 'From the fern meadow'
Fernley

Farold *(Anglo-Saxon)* 'Mighty traveller'

Farquhar *(Celtic)* 'Man' or 'friendly'

Farr *(Anglo-Saxon)* 'The traveller'

Farrand *see* Farand

Farrel *see* Farrell

Farrell *(Celtic)* 'The valorous one'
Farrel, Ferrell

Farris *see* Ferris

Faulkener *see* Falkner

Faulkner *see* Falkner

Faust *(Latin)* 'Lucky, auspicious'

Favian *(Latin)* 'A man of understanding'

Fawaz *(Arabic)* 'Victorious'

Faxon *(Teutonic)* 'Thick haired'

Fay *(Gaelic)* 'The raven'. Symbol of great wisdom
Fayette

Fayad *(Arabic)* 'Generous'

Fayette *see* Fay

Faysal *(Arabic)* 'Decision-maker'

Fayza *(Arabic)* 'Victorious'

Feargus *see* Fergus

Felice *see* Felix

Felicio *see* Felix

Felips *see* Phillips

Felix *(Latin)* 'Fortunate'
Felice, Felicio, Felizio

Felizio *see* Felix

Fellips *see* Phillips

Felton *(Anglo-Saxon)* 'From the town estate'

Fenton *(Anglo-Saxon)* 'One who lives of the marshland'

Fenwick *(Teutonic)* 'From the marshlands'

Fenwood *(Teutonic)* 'From the low-lying forest'

Feodor *see* Theodore

Feodore *see* Theodore

Ferand *see* Ferrand

Ferant *see* Ferrand

Ferd *see* Ferdinand

Ferdie *see* Ferdinand

Ferdinand *(Teutonic)* 'Bold, daring adventurer'
Ferd, Ferdie, Ferdy, Fernand, Fernando, Hernando

Ferdusi *(Persian)* 'Paradisical'

Ferdy *see* Ferdinand

Fergie *see* Fergus

Fergus *(Gaelic)* 'The best choice'
Feargus, Fergie, Ferguson

Ferguson *see* Fergus

Fermin *(Latin/Spanish)* 'Firm, steadfast'

Fernald *see* Farnell

Fernall *see* Farnell

Fernand *see* Ferdinand

Fernando *see* Ferdinand

Ferner *(Teutonic)* 'Far away'

Fernley *see* Farnley

Ferrand *(French)* 'One with iron grey hair'
Ferand, Ferant, Ferrant *see also* Farand

Ferrant *see* Ferrand

Ferrell *see* Farrell

Ferris *(Gaelic)* 'The rock' or *(Latin)* 'man of iron'
Farris

Festus *(Latin)* 'Happy and joyful'

Fidel *(Latin)* 'Advocate of the poor'
Fidele, Fidelio

Fidele *see* Fidel

Fidelio *see* Fidel

Fielding *(Anglo-Saxon)* 'One who lives near the field'

Fife *see* Fyfe

Filbert *(Anglo-Saxon)* 'Very brilliant one'
Filberto, Philbert

Filberto *see* Filbert

Filib *see* Philip

Filip *see* Philip

Filli *see* Philip

Fillmore *see* Filmer

Filmer *(Anglo-Saxon)* 'Very famous one'
Fillmore, Filmore

Filmore *see* Filmer

Fin *see* Finlay

Findal *(Teutonic)* 'Inventive one'

Findlay *see* Finlay

Findley *see* Finlay

Fingal *(Scottish)* 'Blond stranger'

Finlay *(Gaelic)* 'Fair soldier'
Fin, Findlay, Findley, Finley, Lee

Finley *see* Finlay

Finn *(Gaelic)* 'Fair haired'

Finnegan *(Celtic)* 'Fair one'

Firman *(Anglo-Saxon)* 'Long-distance traveller'
Farman

Firmin *(French)* 'The firm, strong one'

Fiske *(Anglo-Saxon)* 'Fish'

Fitch *(Anglo-Saxon)* 'The marten'

Fitz (Anglo-French) 'Son'. Originally in the form of 'fils' (French for son), the present form was introduced into Britain by the Normans *see also* names beginning with 'Fitz'

Fitzgerald *(Anglo-Saxon)* 'Son of Gerald'
Fitz

Fitzhugh *(Anglo-Saxon)* 'Son of Hugh'
Fitz

Fitzpatrick (Old English) 'Son of a nobleman'
Fitz, Pat, Patrick

Fitzroy *(French)* 'King's son'

Flann *(Gaelic)* 'Lad with red hair'

Flavian *see* Flavius

Flavius *(Latin)* 'Yellow-haired one'
Flavian

Flem *see* Fleming

Fleming *(Anglo-Saxon)*
'The Dutchman'
Flem

Fletch *see* Fletcher

Fletcher *(French)* 'The
arrow-maker'
Fletch

Flinn *(Gaelic)* 'Son of the
red-haired one'
Flynn

Flint *(Anglo-Saxon)* 'A
stream'

Florean *(Latin)* 'Beautiful
as a flower'

Florian *(Latin)* 'Flowering,
blooming'
Flory

Flory *see* Florian

Floyd *see* Lloyd

Flynn *see* Flinn

Fonz *see* Alphonso

Forbes *(Gaelic)* 'Man of
prosperity, owner of
many fields'. A great
landowner

Ford *(Anglo-Saxon)* 'The
river crossing' *see also*
Bradford or Crawford

Forest *see* Forrest

Forester *see* Forrest

Forrest *(Teutonic)*
'Guardian of the forest'
Forest, Forester,
Forrester, Forrie,
Forster, Foss, Foster

Forrester *see* Forrest

Forrie *see* Forrest

Forster *see* Forrest

Fortescue *(Teutonic)*
'Sturdy shield'

Fortune *(French)* 'The
lucky one'. Child of
many blessings

Foss *see* Forrest

Foster *see* Forrest

Fowler *see* Falkner

Fraine *see* Frayne

Fran *see* Francis

Franchot *see* Francis

Francis *(Latin)* 'Free man'
Chico, Fran, Franchot,
Frank, Frankie, Franz

Francklin *see* Franklin

Francklyn *see* Franklin

Frank *see* Francis or
Franklin

Frankie *see* Francis or
Franklin

Franklin *(Anglo-Saxon)*
'Free-holder of
property'. One who
owns his own land to
use as he wished
Francklin, Francklyn,
Frank, Frankie,
Franklyn

Franklyn *see* Franklin

Franz *see* Francis

Fraser *(French)*
'Strawberry' or 'curly-
haired one'
Frasier, Frazer, Frazier

Frasier *see* Fraser

Frayne *(Anglo-Saxon)*
'Stranger'
Fraine, Frean, Freen,
Freyne

Frazer *see* Fraser

Frazier *see* Fraser

Frean *see* Frayne

Fred *see* Alfred, Frederick
or Wilfred

Freddie *see* Alfred,
Frederick or Wilfred

Freddy *see* Alfred,
Frederick or Wilfred

Frederic *see* Frederick

Frederick *(Teutonic)*
'Peaceful ruler'. One
who uses diplomacy
not war
Fred, Freddie, Freddy,
Frederic, Frederik,
Fredric, Fredrick,
Friedrich, Fritz

Frederik *see* Frederick

Fredric *see* Frederick

Fredrick *see* Frederick

Freeborn *(Old English)*
'Child of freedom'

Freedman *see* Freeman

Freeland *(Old English)*
'From free land'

Freeman *(Anglo-Saxon)*
'Born a free man'
Freedman

Freen *see* Frayne

Fremont *(Teutonic)* 'Free
and noble protector'

Frewen *see* Frewin

Frewin *(Anglo-Saxon)* 'Free,
noble friend'
Frewen

Frey *(Anglo-Saxon)* 'The
lord of peace and
prosperity'. From the
ancient Norse god

Freyne *see* Frayne

Frick *(Anglo-Saxon)* 'Bold man'

Fridolf *(Anglo-Saxon)* 'Peaceful wolf'

Friedrich *see* Frederick

Frith *(Anglo-Saxon)* 'One who lives in the woods'

Fritz *see* Frederick

Frysa *(Anglo-Saxon)* 'One with curly hair'

Fulbert *see* Fulbright

Fulbright *(Old German)* 'Very bright' Fulbert

Fuller *(Anglo-Saxon)* 'One who works with cloth' Tucker

Fulton *(Anglo-Saxon)* 'From the field' or 'living by the chicken pen'

Fyfe *(Scottish)* 'Man from Fife' Fife, Fyffe

Fyffe *see* Fyfe

Gabbie *see* Gabriel

Gabby *see* Gabriel

Gabe *see* Gabriel

Gabie *see* Gabriel

Gable *(French)* 'The small Gabriel'

Gabriel *(Hebrew)* 'Messenger of God'. The archangel who announced the birth of Christ
Gabbie, Gabby, Gabe, Gabie, Gabriello

Gabriello *see* Gabriel

Gadiel *(Hebrew)* 'God is my fortune'

Gadman *(Hebrew)* 'The lucky one'
Gadmann

Gadmann *see* Gadman

Gaelen *see* Galen

Gage *(French)* 'A pledge'. The glove that was given as an earnest pledge of good faith

Gail *see* Gale

Gair *(Gaelic)* 'Short one'

Gaius *(Latin)* 'Rejoiced'

Galahad *(Hebrew)* 'Gilead'

Galdemar *(French/Old German)* 'Famous ruler'

Gale *(Celtic)* 'The lively one'
Gail, Gayle

Galen *(Gaelic/Greek)* 'Little bright one' or 'helper'
Gaelen

Gallagher *(Gaelic)* 'Eager helper from overseas'

Gallard *see* Gaylord

Galloway *(Celtic)* 'Man from the stranger lands'
Gallway, Galway

Gallway *see* Galloway

Galor *see* Gaylord

Galpin *(French)* 'Swift runner'

Galt *(Old English)* 'High land'

Galton *(Anglo-Saxon)* 'Lease holder of an estate'

Galvan *see* Galvin

Galven *see* Galvin

Galvin *(Gaelic)* 'Bright, shining white' or 'the sparrow'
Galvan, Galven

Galway *see* Galloway

Gamal *(Arabic)* 'Camel'
Gammali, Jamaal, Jammal

Gamalat *(Arabic)* 'Beautiful one'

Gamali *see* Gamal

Gamaliel *(Hebrew)* 'The recompense of the Lord'

Gannon *(Gaelic)* 'Little blond one'

Ganymede *(Greek)* 'Rejoicing in mankind'

Gardener *see* Gardiner

Gardiner *(Teutonic)* 'A gardener, a flower-lover'
Gardener, Gardner

Gardner *see* Gardiner

Gare *see* Gary

Garek *see* Garrick

Gareth *(Welsh)* 'Gentle'

Garett *see* Garrett

Garey *see* Gary

Garfield *(Anglo-Saxon)* 'War or battlefield'

Gari *see* Gary

Garland *(Anglo-Saxon)* 'From the land of the spears'

Garman *(Anglo-Saxon)* 'The spearman'

Garmon *see* Garmond

Garmond *(Anglo-Saxon)* 'Spear protector'
Garmon, Garmund

Garmund *see* Garmond

Garner *(Teutonic)* 'Army guard, noble defender'

Garnet *(Latin)* 'A red seed, pomegranate seed'

Garnett *(Anglo-Saxon)* 'Compulsive spear man'. He struck first and challenged afterwards

Garnock *(Celtic)* 'One who dwells by the river alder'

Garold *see* Gerald

Garrard *see* Garrett

Garraway *see* Garroway

Garrek *see* Garrick

Garret *see* Garrett

Garrett *(Anglo-Saxon)*
'Mighty spear warrior'
Garett, Garrard, Garret,
Garritt, Gerard, Jarrett

Garrick *(Anglo-Saxon)*
'Spear ruler'
Garek, Garrek

Garritt *see* Garrett

Garroway *(Anglo-Saxon)*
'Spear warrior'
Garraway

Garry *see* Gary

Garson *(French)* 'Young
man' or 'garrison'

Garth *(Norse)* 'From the
garden'

Garton *(Anglo-Saxon)* 'The
one who lives by the
triangular-shaped farm'

Garvey *(Gaelic)* 'Rough
peace'. Peace obtained
after victory
Garvie

Garvie *see* Garvey

Garvin *(Teutonic)* 'Spear
friend'
Garwin

Garwin *see* Garvin

Garwood *(Anglo-Saxon)*
'From the fir trees'

Gary *(Anglo-Saxon)*
'Spearman'
Gare, Garey, Gari,
Garry

Gaspar *(Persian)* 'Master of
the treasure'. One of
the Magi
Caspar, Casper, Gasper,
Jasper, Kaspar, Kasper
see also Caspar

Gasper *see* Caspar or
Gaspar

Gaston *(French)* 'Man from
Gascony'

Gaubert *(Old German)*
'Brilliant ruler'

Gauderic *(Old German)*
'Ruler, king'

Gavan *see* Gawain

Gaven *see* Gawain

Gavin *see* Gawain

Gawain *(Celtic)* 'The battle
hawk'
Gavan, Gaven, Gavin,
Gawaine, Gawen

Gawaine *see* Gawain

Gawen *see* Gawain

Gayle *see* Gale

Gayler *see* Gaylord

Gaylor *see* Gaylord

Gaylord *(French)* 'The happy noble man' Gallard, Galor, Gayler

Gaynell *(Teutonic)* 'One who makes a profit'

Gaynor *(Gaelic)* 'Son of the blond-haired one'

Gearalt *see* Gerald

Gearard *see* Gerard

Gearey *see* Geary

Geary *(Anglo-Saxon)* 'Changeable' Gearey, Gery

Gemmel *(Scandinavian)* 'Old'

Gene *see* Eugene

Genesius *(Latin)* 'Welcome newcomer'

Geno *see* John

Gentilis *(Latin)* 'Kind man'

Geof *see* Geoffrey

Geoff *see* Geoffrey

Geoffrey *(Teutonic)* 'God's divine peace' Geof, Geoff, Godfrey, Jeff, Jeffers, Jeffery, Jeffrey, Jeffry

Geordie *see* George

Georg *see* George

George *(Greek)* 'The farmer'. The patron saint of England Geordie, Georg, Georges, Georgie, Georgy, Giorgio, Gordie, Gordy, Jorge, Jorgen, Jorin, Joris, Jurgen, Yorick

Georges *see* George

Georgie *see* George

Georgy *see* George

Ger *see* Gerald or Gervase

Geraint *(Welsh)* 'Old'

Gerald *(Teutonic)* 'Mighty spear ruler' Garold, Gearalt, Ger, Geraud, Gereld, Gerrald, Gerry, Gery, Giraldo, Giraud, Jer, Jerald, Jereld, Jerold, Jerrold, Jerry

Gerard *(Anglo-Saxon)* 'Spear strong, spear brave' Gearard, Gerardo, Gerhard, Gerhardt, Gerrard, Gerry *see also* Garrett

Gerardo *see* Gerard

Geraud *see* Gerald

Gereld *see* Gerald

Gerhard *see* Gerard

Gerhardt *see* Gerald

Gerius *(Latin)* 'Reliable'

Germain *(Middle English)* 'Sprout, bud'

Gerome *see* Jerome

Gerrald *see* Gerald

Gerrard *see* Gerard

Gerry *see* Gerald or Gerard

Gersham *see* Gershom

Gershom *(Hebrew)* 'Exile Gersham

Gervais *see* Gervase

Gervase *(Teutonic)* 'Spear vassal'
Ger, Gervais, Jarv, Jarvey, Jarvis, Jervis, Jervoise

Gerwyn *(Welsh)* 'Fair love'

Gery *see* Geary or Gerald

Gethin *(Welsh)* 'Dark skinned'

Ghislaine *(French)* 'A pledge'

Giacomo *see* Jacob

Gian *see* John

Gianni *see* John

Gib *see* Gilbert

Gibb *see* Gilbert

Gibson *(Anglo-Saxon)* 'Son of Gilbert'

Gideon *(Hebrew)* 'Brave indomitable spirit' or 'the destroyer'

Giffard *see* Gifford

Gifferd *see* Gifford

Gifford *(Teutonic)* 'The gift' Giffard, Gifferd

Gil *see* Gilbert or Giles

Gilber *see* Gilby

Gilbert *(Anglo-Saxon)* 'Bright pledge' or 'a hostage'
Bert, Gib, Gibb, Gil, Gilibeirt, Gill, Gilleabart, Gillie

Gilbey *see* Gilby

Gilby *(Norse)* 'The pledge' or 'a hostage'
Gilbey

Gilchrist *(Gaelic)* 'The servant of Christ' Gilecriosd

Gildas *(Latin)* 'Servant of the Lord'

Gilecriosd *see* Gilchrist

Giles *(Latin/French)* 'Shield-bearer'
Gil, Gilles

Gilford *(Teutonic)* 'One who lives by the big ford'

Gilibeirt *see* Gilbert

Gill *see* Gilbert

Gilland *(Teutonic)* 'Bold young man'

Gilleabart *see* Gilbert

Gilleasbuig *see* Archibald

Gillecirosd *see* Christopher

Gilles *see* Giles

Gillet *(French)* 'Little Gilbert'

Gillie *see* Gilbert

Gillmore *see* Gilmore

Gilman *(Teutonic)* 'Tall man'

Gilmer *(Anglo-Saxon)* 'Famous hostage'. An eminent knight taken captive in battle

Gilmore *(Gaelic)* 'Mary's servant'
Gillmore, Gilmour

Gilmour *see* Gilmore

Gilroy *(Latin/Gaelic)* 'The king's servant'

Gino *see* Ambrose

Giorgio *see* George

Giovanni *see* John

Giraldo *see* Gerald

Giraud *see* Gerald

Girvan *see* Girvin

Girven *see* Girvin

Girvin *(Gaelic)* 'Little rough one'
Girvan, Girven

Giuseppe *see* Joseph

Gladwin *(Anglo-Saxon)* 'Kind friend'

Glanmor *(Welsh)* 'Seashore'

Glanvil *see* Glanville

Glanville *(French)* 'One who lives on the oak tree estate'
Glanvil

Glen *(Celtic)* 'From the valley'
Glenn, Glyn, Glynn

Glenden *see* Glendon

Glendon *(Celtic)* 'From the fortress in the glen'
Glenden

Glenn *see* Glen

Gleve *(Teutonic)* 'The point of a spear'

Glyn *see* Glen

Glynn *see* Glen

Godard *see* Goddard

Godart *see* Goddard

Goddard *(Teutonic)*
'Divinely firm'. Firm in
belief and trust in God
Godard, Godart, Goddart

Goddart *see* Goddard

Godewyn *see* Goodwin

Godfrey *see* Geoffrey

Godwin *see* Goodwin

Godwine *see* Goodwin

Golding *(Anglo-Saxon)* 'Son
of the golden one'

Goldwin *(Anglo-Saxon)*
'Golden friend'
Goldwyn

Goldwyn *see* Goldwin

Gomez *(Spanish)* 'Man'

Gonzalo *(Spanish)* 'Wolf'

Goodman *(Anglo-Saxon)*
'Good man'

Goodwin *(Anglo-Saxon)*
'Good friend, God's
friend'
Godewyn, Godwin,
Godwine

Gordan *see* Gordon

Gorden *see* Gordon

Gordie *see* George or
Gordon

Gordon *(Anglo-Saxon)*
'From the cornered hill'
Gordan, Gorden,
Gordie, Gordy

Gordy *see* George or
Gordon

Gorhan *(Old English)* 'One
who lives in the mud
hut'

Gorman *(Gaelic)* 'Small,
blue-eyed boy'

Gouveneur *(French)* 'The
governor, the ruler'

Gower *(Celtic)* 'The pure
one'

Grady *(Gaelic)* 'Illustrious
and noble'

Graeme *see* Graham

Graham *(Teutonic)* 'From
the grey lands'. One
from the country
beyond the mists
Graeme

Grandvil *see* Granville

Grandville *see* Granville

Grange *see* Granger

Granger *(Anglo-Saxon)*
'The farmer'
Grange

Grant *(French)* 'The great one'
Grantley, Grenville

Grantham *(Old English)* 'From the big meadow'

Grantland *(Anglo-Saxon)* 'From the great lands'

Grantley *see* Grant

Granvil *see* Granville

Granville *(French)* 'One who lives in the large town'
Grandvil, Grandville, Granvil, Greville

Grayson *(Anglo-Saxon)* 'The bailiff's son'

Greagoir *see* Gregory

Greeley *(Anglo-Saxon)* 'From the grey meadow'

Greg *see* Gregory

Gregg *see* Gregory

Gregor *see* Gregory

Gregorio *see* Gregory

Gregorius *see* Gregory

Gregory *(Greek)* 'The watchful one'. Someone ever vigilant
Greagoir, Greg, Gregg, Gregor, Gregorio, Gregorius, Greiogair

Greiogair *see* Gregory

Grenville *see* Grant

Gresham *(Anglo-Saxon)* 'From the grazing meadow'

Greville *see* Granville

Griff *see* Rufus

Griffin *see* Griffith or Rufus

Griffith *(Celtic)* 'Fierce red-haired warrior'
Griffin, Gruffydd, Rufus
see also Rufus

Grimbald *(Teutonic)* 'Fierce power'

Griswold *(Teutonic)* 'From the grey forest'

Grosvenor *(Old French)* 'Great hunter'

Grover *(Anglo-Saxon)* 'One who comes from the grove'

Gruffydd *see* Griffith

Guido *see* Guy

Guillermo *see* William

Guillym *(Welsh)* Form of William

Guin *see* Gwynn

Gunar *see* Gunther

Gunnar *see* Gunther

Gunner *see* Gunther

Guntar *see* Gunther

Gunter *see* Gunther

Gunthar *see* Gunther

Gunther *(Teutonic)* 'Bold
warrior'
Gunar, Gunnar,
Gunner, Guntar,
Gunter, Gunthar

Gurion *(Hebrew)* 'Dwelling
place of God'

Guru *(Sanskrit)* 'Teacher'

Gus *see* Angus, August or
Gustave

Gussy *see* August

Gustaf *see* Gustave

Gustav *see* Gustave

Gustave *(Scandinavian)*
'Staff of the Goths'
Gus, Gustaf, Gustav,
Gustavo, Gustavus

Gustavo *see* Gustave

Gustavus *see* Gustave

Guthrie *(Celtic)* 'War
serpent', 'war hero' or
'from the windy
country'
Guthry

Guthry *see* Guthrie

Guy *(Latin)* 'Life', *(French)*
'guide' or *(Teutonic)*
'warrior'
Guido, Guyon, Wiatt,
Wyatt

Guyon *see* Guy

Gwion *(Welsh)* 'Elf'

Gwylim *see* William

Gwynfor *(Welsh)* 'Fair
place'

Gwynllyw *(Welsh)* 'Blessed
leader'

Gwynn *(Celtic)* 'The blond
one'
Guin

Haakon *(Scandinavian)*
'Noble kin' *see also*
Hakon

Haaris *(Arabic)* 'Vigilant'

Haarwyn *see* Hardwin

Habakkuk *(Hebrew)*
'Embrace'

Habib *(Sanskrit/Arabic)*
'Beloved'

Habor *(Teutonic)*
'Dexterous'

Hachmann *(Hebrew)* 'Wise
or learned one'

Hacket *see* Hackett

Hackett *(Teutonic)* 'The
small woodsman'. The
apprentice forester
Hacket

Hacon *(Old Norse)* 'Useful'

Had *see* Hadley

Hadar *(Hebrew)*
'Ornament'

Haddan *see* Hadden

Hadden *(Anglo-Saxon)*
'From the heath valley'
Haddan, Haddon

Haddon *see* Hadden

Hadi *(Arabic)* 'Guide'

Hadlee *see* Hadley

Hadleigh *see* Hadley

Hadley *(Anglo-Saxon)*
'From the hot meadow'
Had, Hadlee, Hadleigh

Hadrian *see* Adrian

Hadwin *(Anglo-Saxon)*
'Battle companion'

Hafiz *(Arabic)* 'He who
remembers'

Hagan *see* Hagen

Hagen *(Gaelic)* 'The young
one'
Hagan, Haggan,
Haggen

Haggai *(Hebrew)* 'Festive'

Haggan *see* Hagen

Haggen *see* Hagen

Hagley *(Anglo-Saxon)*
'From the hedged
meadow'

Hagos *(Ethiopian)* 'Happy'

275

Haig *(Anglo-Saxon)* 'One who lives in an enclosure'. Popular name for boys during early part of 20th century in compliment to the Field Marshal Lord Haig

Haines *(Old German)* 'From a vined cottage'

Hakan *(Native American)* 'Fiery'

Hakeem *(Arabic)* 'Wise' Hakim

Hakim *see* Hakeem

Hako *see* Hakon

Hakon *(Norse)* 'From an exalted race' Haakon, Hako *see also* Haakon

Hal *see* Harold or Henry

Halbert *(Anglo-Saxon)* 'Brilliant hero'

Haldan *see* Halden

Haldane *see* Halden

Halden *(Norse)* 'Half Danish' Haldan, Haldane, Halfdan

Hale *(Anglo-Saxon)* 'From the hall'

Haley *(Gaelic)* 'The ingenious one'. One with a scientific intelligence

Halfdan *see* Halden

Halford *(Anglo-Saxon)* 'From the ford by the manor house'

Halim *(Arabic)* 'Patient'

Hall *(Anglo-Saxon)* 'One who lives at the manor house'

Hallam *(Anglo-Saxon)* 'One who lives on the hill slopes'

Halley *(Anglo-Saxon)* 'From the manor house meadow' or 'holy'

Halliwell *(Anglo-Saxon)* 'The one who lives by the holy well'

Hallward *(Anglo-Saxon)* 'Guardian of the manor house' Halward

Halsey *(Anglo-Saxon)* 'From Hal's island' Halsy

Halstead *(Anglo-Saxon)* 'From the manor house' Halsted

Halsted *see* Halstead

Halsy *see* Halsey

Halton *(Anglo-Saxon)* 'From the estate on the hill slope'

Halward *see* Hallward

Ham *(Hebrew)* 'South'

Hamal *(Arabic)* 'The lamb'. A very gentle person

Hamar *(Norse)* 'Symbol of ingenuity'. A great gift for invention
Hammar

Hamdan *(Arabic)* 'Thankful'

Hamed *(Arabic)* 'One who receives praise'

Hamelin *see* Hamlin

Hamelyn *see* Hamlin

Hamford *(Teutonic)* 'From the old ford'

Hamid *(Sanskrit)* 'Friend' or *(Arabic)* 'thanking God

Hamil *see* Hamilton

Hamilton *(French/Anglo-Saxon)* 'From the mountain village'
Hamil

Hamish *see* Jacob

Hamlet *(Teutonic)* 'Little village'

Hamlin *(Teutonic)* 'Small home-lover'
Hamelin, Hamelyn, Hamlyn *see also* Henry

Hamlyn *see* Hamlin

Hammar *see* Hamar

Hamon *(Greek)* 'Faithful'

Hanafi *(Arabic)* 'Orthodox'

Hanan *(Hebrew)* 'Grace'

Hananel *(Hebrew)* 'God is gracious'

Handley *see* Hanley

Hanford *(Anglo-Saxon)* 'From the high ford'

Hanif *(Arabic)* 'Orthodox, true'

Hank *see* Henry

Hanley *(Anglo-Saxon)* 'From the high meadow'
Handley, Henleigh, Henley

Hannibal *(Greek)* The hero of Carthage

Hanraoi *see* Henry

Hans *see* John

Hansel *(Scandinavian)* 'Gift from the Lord'

Harailt *see* Harold

Harald *see* Harold

Harbert *see* Herbert

Harbin *see* Herbert

Harcourt *(French)* 'From a fortified court'

Harden *(Anglo-Saxon)* 'From the valley of the hare' *see also* Harley

Hardey *see* Hardy

Hardi *see* Hardy

Hardie *see* Hardy

Hardik *(Sanskrit)* 'Heartfelt'

Harding *(Anglo-Saxon)* 'Son of the hero'

Hardwin *(Anglo-Saxon)* 'Brave friend' Haarwyn, Hardwyn, Harwin

Hardwyn *see* Hardwin

Hardy *(Teutonic)* 'Bold and daring' Hardey, Hardi, Hardie

Hareford *see* Harford

Harem *(Hebrew)* 'One who climbs mountains'

Harford *(Anglo-Saxon)* 'From the hare ford' Hareford, Hereford, Herford

Hargrave *see* Hargrove

Hargreave *see* Hargrove

Hargreaves *see* Hargrove

Hargrove *(Anglo-Saxon)* 'From the hare grove' Hargrave, Hargreave, Hargreaves

Harim *(Hebrew)* 'Boy with a flat nose'

Hark *see* Henry

Harl *see* Harley

Harlan *see* Harlon

Harland *see* Harlon

Harleigh *see* Harley

Harley *(Anglo-Saxon)* 'From the hare meadow' Arley, Arlie, Harden, Harl, Harleigh, Hart, Hartleigh, Hartley *see also* Arlie or Hartwell

Harlon *(Teutonic)* 'From the battle land' Harlan, Harland

Harlow *(Anglo-Saxon)* 'The fortified hill'. An army camp on the hillside

Harly *see* Arlie

Harman *see* Herman

Harmon *see* Herman

Harold *(Anglo-Saxon)*
'Army commander'. A
mighty general
Araldo, Hal, Harailt,
Harald, Harry, Herald,
Hereld, Herold,
Herrick

Haroun *see* Aaron

Harper *(Anglo-Saxon)* 'The
harp player'. The
wandering minstrel

Harris *(Anglo-Saxon)*
'Harold's son'
Harrison

Harrison *see* Harris

Harry *see* Harold or Henry

Harshad *(Sanskrit)* 'Joy
bringer'

Harshil *see* Harshit

Harshit *(Sanskrit)* 'Joyful',
'happy'
Harshil

Hart *(Anglo-Saxon)* 'The
hart deer' *see also*
Harley or Hartwell

Hartford *(Anglo-Saxon)*
'The river crossing of
the deer'
Hertford

Hartleigh *see* Harley

Hartley *(Anglo-Saxon)*
'Meadow of the hart
deer' *see also* Harley

Hartman *(Anglo-Saxon)*
'Keeper of the stags' or
(Teutonic) 'strong and
austere'
Hartmann

Hartmann *see* Hartman

Hartwell *(Anglo-Saxon)*
'Well where the deer
drink'
Harwell, Hart, Hartwill,
Harwill

Hartwill *see* Hartwell

Hartwood *(Anglo-Saxon)*
'Forest of the hart deer'
Harwood

Harv *see* Harvey

Harve *see* Harvey

Harvey *(Teutonic/French)*
'Army warrior'
Harv, Harve, Herv,
Herve, Hervey

Harwell *see* Hartwell

Harwill *see* Hartwell

Harwin *see* Hardwin

Harwood *see* Hartwood

Hasaka *(Sanskrit)* 'Jester'

Hasheem *see* Hashim

Hashim *(Arabic)*
'Destroyer of evil'
Hasheem

Hasin *(Sanskrit)* 'Laughing
one'

Haskel *(Hebrew)*
'Understanding'
Haskell

Haskell *see* Haskel

Haslett *(Anglo-Saxon)*
'Hazel tree grove on
the headland'
Haslitt, Hazlett, Hazlitt

Haslitt *see* Haslett

Hassan *(Arabic)*
'Handsome'

Hastings *(Anglo-Saxon)*
'Son of violence'

Havelock *(Norse)* 'Sea
battle'
Havlock

Haven *(Anglo-Saxon)* 'A
place of safety'

Havlock *see* Havelock

Hawley *(Anglo-Saxon)*
'From the hedged
meadow'

Hayden *(Teutonic)* 'From
the hedged valley'
Haydon

Haydon *see* Hayden

Hayes *(Old English)* 'From
the hedged forest'

Hayward *(Anglo-Saxon)*
'Keeper of the hedged
field'
Heyward

Haywood *(Anglo-Saxon)*
'From the hedged
forest'
Heywood

Hazlett *see* Haslett

Hazlitt *see* Haslett

Hearn *see* Ahern

Hearne *see* Ahern

Hearst *see* Hurst

Heath *(Anglo-Saxon)*
'Heathland'

Heathcliff *(Anglo-Saxon)*
'From the heather cliff'
Heathcliffe

Heathcliffe *see* Heathcliff

Hebert *see* Herbert

Heck *see* Hector

Hector *(Greek)* 'Steadfast,
unswerving, holds fast'
Eachan, Eachann,
Eachunn, Heck

Heddwyn *(Welsh)* 'Blessed
peace'

Hedley *(Old English)*
'Blessed peace'

Heer *(Sanskrit)* 'Diamond'

Heilyn *(Welsh)* 'Cup-bearer'

Heinrich *see* Henry

Heinrick *see* Henry

Henderson *(Old English)* 'Son of Henry'

Hendrick *see* Henry

Hendry *(Teutonic)* 'Manly'

Hendy *(Teutonic)* 'Skilful one'

Henleigh *see* Hanley

Henley *see* Hanley

Henri *see* Henry

Henrik *see* Henry

Henry *(Teutonic)* 'Ruler of the estate'. Lord of the manor
Eanruig, Hal, Hamlin, Hank, Hanraoi, Hark, Harry, Heinrich, Heinrick Hendrick, Henri, Henrik

Herald *see* Harold

Herb *see* Herbert

Herbert *(Teutonic)* 'Brilliant warrior'
Bert, Harbert, Harbin, Hebert, Herb, Herbie, Heriberto, Hoireabard

Herbie *see* Herbert

Hercules *(Latin)* 'Glory of Hera'

Hereford *see* Harford

Hereld *see* Harold

Herford *see* Harford

Heriberto *see* Herbert

Herm *see* Herman

Herman *(Teutonic)* 'Army warrior'
Armand, Armin, Armond, Armyn, Ermin, Harman, Harmon, Herm, Hermann, Hermie, Hermon

Hermann *see* Herman

Hermie *see* Herman

Hermon *see* Herman

Hernando *see* Ferdinand

Herold *see* Harold

Herrick *(Teutonic)* 'Army ruler' *see also* Harold

Herschel *(Hebrew)* 'Deer'

Hertford *see* Hartford

Herv *see* Harvey

Herve *see* Harvey

Hervey *see* Harvey

Herwin *(Teutonic)* 'Lover of war, battle companion'

Hewe *see* Hugh

Hewett *(Anglo-Saxon)* 'Little Hugh'

Heyward *see* Hayward

Heywood *see* Haywood

Hezekiah *(Hebrew)* 'God is strength'. Belief in God arms this man against all adversity

Hi *see* Hiram

Hiatt *see* Hyatt

Hilaire *see* Hilary

Hilary *(Latin)* 'Cheerful and merry' Hilaire, Hillary, Hillery

Hildebrand *(Teutonic)* 'Sword of war'

Hillard *see* Hilliard

Hillary *see* Hilary

Hillel *(Hebrew)* 'Greatly praised'

Hillery *see* Hilary

Hilliard *(Teutonic)* 'War guardian' or 'brave in battle' Hillard, Hillier, Hillyer

Hillier *see* Hilliard

Hillyer *see* Hilliard

Hilton *(Anglo-Saxon)* 'From the hill farm' Hylton

Himmet *(Turkish)* 'Support, help'

Hiram *(Hebrew)* 'Most noble and exalted one' Hi, Hy, Hyram

Hiroshi *(Japanese)* 'Generous man'

Hisham *(Arabic)* 'Generosity'

Hobart *see* Hubert

Hobbard *see* Hubert

Hogan *(Celtic)* 'Youth' Hoibeard *see* Hubert

Hoireabard *see* Herbert or Hubert

Holbrook *(Anglo-Saxon)* 'From the brook in the valley'

Holcomb *(Anglo-Saxon)* 'Deep valley' Holcombe, Holecomb, Holecombe

Holcombe *see* Holcomb

Holden *(Anglo-Saxon/Teutonic)* 'From the valley' or 'kind'

Holecomb *see* Holcomb

Holecombe *see* Holcomb

Holgate *(Anglo-Saxon)* 'Gatekeeper'

Holger *(Scandinavian)* 'Faithful warrior'

Hollis *(Anglo-Saxon)* 'One who lives in the holly grove'

Holman *(Dutch)* 'Man from the hollow'

Holmes *(Anglo-Saxon)* 'From the island in the river'

Holt *(Anglo-Saxon)* 'From the forest'

Homer *(Greek)* 'A pledge'

Horace *(Latin)* 'Time keeper, hours of the sun' Horatio, Horatius, Race

Horatio *see* Horace Horatius *see* Horace

Horst *(German)* 'From the thickct'

Horton *(Anglo-Saxon)* 'From the grey farm'

Hosea *(Hebrew)* 'Salvation'

Houghton *(Anglo-Saxon)* 'From the estate on the cliff'

Houston *(Anglo-Saxon)* 'From the town in the mountains'

Howard *(Anglo-Saxon)* 'Chief guardian' Howie

Howe *(Teutonic)* 'The eminent one'. A person of high birth

Howell *(Celtic)* 'Little, alert one' Hywel, Hywell

Howie *see* Howard

Howland *(Anglo-Saxon)* 'One who lives on the hill'

Hoyt *see* Hubert

Hubbard *see* Hubert

Hube *see* Hubert

Hubert *(Teutonic)* 'Brilliant, shining mind' Aodh, Aoidh, Bert, Hobart, Hobbard, Hoibeard, Hoireabard, Hoyt, Hubbard, Hube, Huey, Hughes, Hugo

Huburd *see* Hulbert

Hudson *(Anglo-Saxon)* 'Son of the hoodsman'

Huey *see* Hubert

Hugh *(Teutonic)* 'Brilliant
mind'
Hewe, Hughie, Hughy

Hughes *see* Hubert

Hughie *see* Hugh

Hughy *see* Hugh

Hugo *see* Hubert

Hulbard *see* Hulbert

Hulbert *(Teutonic)*
'Graceful'
Hulbard, Hulburd,
Hulburt

Hulburt *see* Hulbert

Humbert *(Teutonic)*
'Brilliant Hun' or
'bright home'
Bert, Bertie, Berty,
Humbie, Umberto

Humbie *see* Humbert

Humfrey *see* Humphrey

Humfry *see* Humphrey

Hump *see* Humphrey

Humph *see* Humphrey

Humphrey *(Teutonic)*
'Protector of the peace'
Humfrey, Humfry,
Hump, Humph

Hunt *see* Hunter

Hunter *(Anglo-Saxon)* 'A
hunter'
Hunt

Huntingdon *(Anglo-Saxon)*
'Hill of the hunter'

Huntington *(Anglo-Saxon)*
'Hunting estate'

Huntley *see* Huntly

Huntly *(Anglo-Saxon)*
'From the hunter's
meadow'
Huntley

Hurlbert *(Teutonic)*
'Brilliant army leader'

Hurley *(Gaelic)* 'Sea tide'

Hurst *(Anglo-Saxon)* 'One
who lives in the forest'
Hearst

Hussain *(Sanskrit)* Islamic
saint

Hussein *(Arabic)* 'Small
and handsome'

Hutton *(Anglo-Saxon)*
'From the farm on the
ridge'

Huxford *(Anglo-Saxon)*
'Hugh's ford'

Huxley *(Anglo-Saxon)*
'Hugh's meadow'

Hy *see* Chaim, Hiram or
Hyman

Hyatt *(Anglo-Saxon)* 'From
the high gate'
Hiatt

Hyde *(Anglo-Saxon)* 'From the hide of land'. An old unit of measurement of land

Hylton *see* Hilton

Hyman *(Hebrew)* 'Life'. The divine spark Hy, Hymen, Hymie *see also* Chaim

Hymen *see* Hyman

Hymie *see* Hyman

Hyram *see* Hiram

Hywel *see* Howell

Hywell *see* Howell

BOYS

Iago *(Hebrew)* 'Supplanter'

Iaian *see* Ian or John

Iain *see* Ian or John

Ian *(Celtic)* 'God is gracious'
Iaian, Iain *see also* John

Ibald *(Teutonic)* 'Noble archer'

Ibrahim *see* Abraham

Icabod *(Hebrew)* 'Departed glory'

Icarus *(Greek)* 'Dedicated to the moon'

Ichabod *(Hebrew)* 'The glory has departed'

Iddo *(Hebrew)* 'Loving and kind'

Iden *(Anglo-Saxon)* 'Prosperous'

Idris *(Welsh)* 'Fiery lord'

Idwal *(Welsh)* 'Wall lord'

Iestin *see* Iestyn or Justin

Iestyn *(Welsh)* 'Just man' Iestin

Ieuan *(Welsh)* Form of John

Ifor *see* Ivor

Ignace *see* Ignatius

Ignacio *see* Ignatius

Ignate *see* Ignatius

Ignatius *(Latin)* 'The ardent one'. A fiery patriot
Ignace, Ignacio, Ignate, Ignazio, Inigo

Ignazio *see* Ignatius

Igor *(Scandinavian)* 'The hero'

Ikar *(Russian)* 'Ancient legendary hero'

Ike *see* Isaac

Ikey *see* Isaac

Ikie *see* Isaac

Ilia *(Russian)* 'Equivalent of Elias'

Illan *(Basque)* 'Equivalent of Julian'

Illaris *(Greek)* 'Happy one'

Illtyd *(Welsh)* 'Ruler of a district'

Imala *(Native American)* 'The one who imposes discipline'

Immanuel *see* Emmanuel

Imo *(Greek)* 'Beloved one'

Imran *(Arabic)* 'Host' or *(Sanskrit)* 'strong'

Indra *(Hindi)* 'Raindrop' or 'god-like'

Ingar *see* Inger

Ingeborg *(Scandinavian)* 'Protection'

Ingemar *(Norse)* 'Famous son'
Ingmar

Inger *(Norse)* 'A son's army'
Ingar, Ingvar

Inglebert *(Teutonic)* 'Brilliant angel'
Engelbert, Englebert

Ingmar *see* Ingemar

Ingraham *see* Ingram

Ingram *(Teutonic)* 'The raven' or 'the raven's son'
Ingraham

Ingvar *see* Inger

Inigo *see* Ignatius

Inir *(Welsh)* 'Honour'

Iniss *see* Inness

Innes *see* Inness

Inness *(Celtic)* 'From the island in the river'
Iniss, Innes, Innis

Innis *see* Inness

Ionwyn *(Welsh)* 'Fair-skinned ruler'

Iorweth *(Welsh)* 'Lord Worth'

Iorwyn *(Welsh)* 'Fair lord'

Iqbal *(Sanskrit)* 'Prosperity'

Ira *(Hebrew)* 'The watcher' or *(Arabic)* 'the stallion'

Iram *(Arabic)* 'Mountain peak' or 'crown of the head'

Irfon *(Welsh)* 'Annointed one'

Irvin *see* Irving

Irvine *see* Irving

Irving *(Anglo-Saxon)* 'Friend of the sea' or *(Celtic)* 'white river'
Ervin, Erwin, Irvin, Irvine, Irwin

Irwin *see* Irving

Isa *(Greek)* 'Equal'

Isaac *(Hebrew)* 'The laughing one'
Ike, Ikey, Ikie, Isaak, Izaak

Isaak *see* Isaac

Isaam *(Arabic)* 'Noble'

Isador *see* Isidore

Isaiah *(Hebrew)* 'God is my helper'

Isas *(Japanese)* 'Worthy of praise'

Isham *(Anglo-Saxon)* 'From the estate of the iron man'

Ishi *(Hebrew)* 'Husband'

Ishmael *(Hebrew)* 'The wanderer'

Isidor *see* Isidore

Isidore *(Greek)* 'The gift of Isis'
Isador, Isidor, Issy, Iz, Izzie, Izzy

Iskander *(Ethiopian)* Equivalent of Alexander *see also* Alexander

Isman *(Hebrew)* 'Faithful husband'

Isoep *see* Joseph

Israel *(Hebrew)* 'The Lord's soldier'. The warrior of God
Issie, Izzie

Issie *see* Israel

Issy *see* Isidore

Istvan *(Hungarian)* Equivalent of Stephen *see also* Stephen

Ithel *(Welsh)* 'Generous ruler'

Ithnan *(Hebrew)* 'Strong seafarer'

Ivan *see* John

Ivander *(Hebrew)* 'Divine'

Ivar *(Norse)* 'Battle archer'. The warrior with the long bow
Iven, Iver, Ives, Ivo, Ivon, Ivor

Iven *see* Ivar

Iver *see* Ivar

Ives *(Anglo-Saxon)* 'Son of the archer'
Yves *see also* Ivar

Ivo *see* Ivar

Ivon *see* Ivar

Ivor *(Welsh)* 'Lord'
Ifor *see also* Ivar

Ixara *(Sanskrit)* 'Master' or 'prince'

Iz *see* Isidore

Izaak *see* Isaac

Izod *(Celtic)* 'Fair-haired one'

Izzie *see* Isidore or Israel

Izzy *see* Isidore

BOYS

Jabez *(Hebrew)* 'Cause of sorrow'

Jabin *(Hebrew)* 'Born of god'

Jacinto *(Spanish)* 'Purple flower'

Jack *see* John

Jackie *see* John

Jackson *(Old English)* 'Son of Jack'

Jacob *(Hebrew)* 'The supplanter'
Cobb, Diego, Giacomo, Hamish, Jacobus, Jacques, Jakc, James, Jamie, Jas, Jem, Jemmie, Jemmy, Jim, Jimmie, Jimmy, Jock, Jocko, Koby

Jacobus *see* Jacob

Jacques *see* Jacob

Jadda *(Hebrew)* 'Wise man'

Jael *(Hebrew)* 'To ascend'

Jagger *(Northumbrian)* 'A carter'

Jaime *see* James

Jair *see* Jairus

Jairus *(Hebrew)* 'Enlightened by God' Jair

Jake *see* Jacob

Jakeh *(Hebrew)* 'Pious one'

Jalaad *(Arabic)* 'Glory'

Jalal *(Sanskrit)* 'Glory'

Jaleel *(Arabic)* 'Majestic'

Jamaal *see* Gamal and Jamal

Jamal *(Arabic)* 'Beauty' Jamaal

James *(Hebrew)* 'The supplanter'. Derivative of Jacob
Hamish, Jamie, Jim, Jock, Seamus, Seumas, Shamus

Jamie *see* Benjamin, Jacob or James

Jamil *(Arabic)* 'Handsome'

Jan *see* John

Janitra *(Sanskrit)* 'Of noble origin'

Janiuszck *see* Jarek

Januarius *see* Jarek

Januisz *see* Jarek

Janos *see* John

Janus *(Latin)* 'One who opens doors'

Japhet *(Hebrew)* 'Youthful, beautiful'

Jareb *(Hebrew)* 'He will contend'
Jarib

Jared *(Hebrew)* 'The descendant'
Jarid, Jarrad, Jarrod

Jarek *(Slavic)* 'January'
Janiuszck, Januarius, Januisz

Jarib *see* Jareb

Jarid *see* Jared

Jarlath *(Latin)* 'Man of control'
Jarlen

Jarlen *see* Jarlath

Jarman *(Teutonic)* 'The German'
Jerman, Jermyn

Jaron *(Hebrew)* 'Sing out, cry out'

Jaroslav *(Slavic)* 'Praise of spring'

Jarrad *see* Jared

Jarratt *(Teutonic)* 'Strong spear'

Jarrett *see* Garrett

Jarrod *see* Jared

Jarv *see* Gervase

Jarvey *see* Gervase

Jarvis *see* Gervase

Jas *see* Jacob

Jashan *(Sanskrit)* 'Celebration'

Jason *(Greek)* 'The healer'
Jasun

Jasper *see* Gaspar

Jasun *see* Jason

Javas *(Sanskrit)* 'Swift'

Javier *see* Xavier

Jawahar *(Sanskrit)* 'Jewel'

Jay *(Anglo-Saxon)* 'Jay or crow'. Diminutive for any name beginning with J

Jean *see* John

Jed *see* Jedediah

Jeddy *see* Jedediah

Jedediah *(Hebrew)* 'Beloved by the Lord'
Jed, Jeddy, Jedidiah

Jedidiah *see* Jedediah

Jeff *see* Geoffrey

Jeffers *see* Geoffrey

Jefferson *(Anglo-Saxon)*
'Jeffrey's son'

Jeffery *see* Geoffrey

Jeffrey *see* Geoffrey

Jeffry *see* Geoffrey

Jehiel *(Hebrew)* 'May God
live'

Jehoshaphat *(Hebrew)*
'The Lord judges'

Jem *see* Jacob

Jemmie *see* Jacob

Jemmy *see* Jacob

Jer *see* Gerald

Jerald *see* Gerald

Jeramey *see* Jeremy

Jere *see* Jeremy

Jereld *see* Gerald

Jeremiah *see* Jeremy

Jeremias *see* Jeremy

Jeremy *(Hebrew)* 'Exalted
by the Lord'
Jeramey, Jere,
Jeremiah, Jeremias,
Jerry

Jerman *see* Jarman

Jermyn *see* Jarman

Jerold *see* Gerald

Jerome *(Latin)* 'Sacred,
holy'. A man of God
Gerome, Jerry

Jerrold *see* Gerald

Jerry *see* Gerald, Jeremy
or Jerome

Jervis *see* Gervase

Jervoise *see* Gervase

Jess *see* Jesse

Jesse *(Hebrew)* 'God's gift'
Jess

Jesus *(Hebrew)* 'God will
help'

Jethro *(Hebrew)* 'Excellent,
without equal'

Jevon *see* John

Jim *see* Jacob

Jimmie *see* Benjamin,
Jacob or James

Jimmy *see* Jacob

Jivin *(Sanskrit)* 'Life-giving'

Joab *(Hebrew)* 'Praise the
lord'
Jacob

Joachim *(Hebrew)*
'Judgement of the Lord'
Akim, Joaquin

Joan *(Hebrew)* 'Praise the
lord'

Joaquin *see* Joachim

Job *(Hebrew)* 'The persecuted'

Jock *see* Jacob or John

Jocko *see* Jacob

Jodel *(Latin)* 'Sportive'

Jodi *see* Joseph

Jodu *see* Joseph

Joe *see* Joel or Joseph

Joel *(Hebrew)* 'The Lord is God'
Joe, Joey

Joey *see* Joel or Joseph

Johan *see* John

Johann *see* John

John *(Hebrew)* 'God's gracious gift'
Eoin, Evan, Geno, Gian, Gianni, Giovanni, Hans, Iaian, Iain, Ian, Ivan, Jack, Jackie, Jan, Janos, Jean, Jevon, Jock, Johan, Johann, Johnnie, Johnny, Jon, Juan, Seain, Sean, Seann, Shane, Shawn, Sian, Siân, Zane

Johnnie *see* John

Johnny *see* John

Joliet *see* Julius

Jolyon *see* Julius

Jon *see* John or Jonathan

Jonah *(Hebrew)* 'Peace'

Jonas *(Hebrew)* 'Dove'. A man of tranquillity

Jonathan *(Hebrew)* 'Gift of the Lord'
Jon, Jonathon

Jonathon *see* Jonathan

Jordan *(Hebrew)* 'The descending river'
Jordon, Jourdain

Jordon *see* Jordan

Jorens *(Norse)* 'Laurel'

Jorge *see* George

Jorgen *see* George

Jorin *(Spanish from Hebrew)* 'Child of freedom' *see also* George

Joris *see* George

Jose *see* Joseph

Joseph *(Hebrew)* 'He shall add'
Guiseppe, Isoep, Jodi, Jodu, Joe, Joey, Jose, Josiah, Jozef, Seosaidh

Josh *see* Joshua

Joshua *(Hebrew)* 'God's salvation'
Josh

Josiah *see* Joseph

Jotham *(Hebrew)* 'God is perfect'

Jourdain *see* Jordan

Jozef *see* Joseph

Juan *see* John

Juaud *(Arabic)* 'Generous'

Judah *see* Judd

Judd *(Hebrew)* 'Praised, extolled'
Judah, Jude

Jude *see* Judd

Jule *see* Julius

Jules *see* Julius

Julian *see* Julius

Julie *see* Julius

Julius *(Latin)* 'Youthful shaveling'
Joliet, Jolyon, Jule, Jules, Julian, Julie

Junayd *(Arabic)* 'Warrior'

Junius *(Latin)* 'Born in June'

Jurgen *see* George

Jurisa *(Scandinavian)* 'Storm'

Just *see* Justin

Justin *(Latin)* 'The just one'. One of upright principles and morals
Iestin, Just, Justinian, Justino, Justus

Justinian *see* Justin

Justino *see* Justin

Justis *(French)* 'Justice'. Upholder of moral laws

Justus *see* Justin

Kabir *(Sanskrit)* Name of a saint

Kadmiel *(Hebrew)* 'God is the ancient one'

Kadrri *(Arabic)* 'My destiny'

Kahaleel *see* Kalil

Kaleva *(Scandinavian)* 'Hero'

Kalil *(Arabic)* 'Good friend' Kahaleel

Kalo *(Greek)* 'Royal, noble' Kalon

Kalon *see* Kalo

Kamal *(Arabic)* 'Perfect'

Kamper *(Teutonic)* 'Fighter'

Kamran *(Sanskrit)* 'Successful'

Kane *(Celtic)* 'Little, war-like one' or 'radiant brightness' Kayne

Kaniel *(Arabic)* 'Spear'

Kano *(Japanese)* 'God of waters'

Kareem *(Arabic)* 'Noble' Karim

Karim *see* Kareem

Karl *see* Charles

Karlan *see* Charles

Karlens *see* Charles

Karney *see* Kearney

Karol *see* Charles

Karr *see* Carr

Karsten *(Slavonic)* 'Christian'

Kasimir *see* Casimir

Kaspar *see* Gaspar

Kasper *see* Gaspar

Kavan *see* Cavan

Kay *(Celtic)* 'Rejoiced in'. Also diminutive for any name beginning with K

Kayne *see* Kane

Kazimir *see* Casimir

Kean *(Irish)* 'Fast'

Keane *(Anglo-Saxon)* 'Bold and handsome'. A sharp-witted man Kearney

Karney *see* Carney

Kedar *(Arabic)* 'Powerful'

Keefe *(Celtic)* 'Handsome, noble and admirable'

Keegan *(Celtic)* 'Little fiery one'

Keelan *(Celtic)* 'Little slender one'

Keelby *see* Kelby

Keeley *(Celtic)* 'Little handsome one'

Keen *see* Keenan

Keenan *(Celtic)* 'Little ancient one' Keen, Kienan

Keir *(Teutonic)* 'Ever king'

Keira *(Scandinavian)* 'Regal'

Keiran *see* Ciaran

Keith *(Celtic)* 'A place' or 'from the forest'

Kelbee *see* Kelby

Kelby *(Old German)* 'From the farm by the spring' Keelby, Kelbee

Kell *(Norse)* 'From the well'

Kellen *see* Kelly

Keller *(Gaelic)* 'Little companion'

Kelley *see* Kelly

Kelly *(Gaelic)* 'The warrior' Kellen, Kelley

Kelsey *(Norse/Teutonic)* 'One who lives on the island'

Kelton *(Celtic)* 'Celtic town'

Kelvan *see* Kelvin

Kelven *see* Kelvin

Kelvin *(Gaelic)* 'From the narrow stream' Kelvan, Kelven, Kelwin

Kelwin *see* Kelvin

Kembell *see* Kimball

Kemble *see* Kimball

Kemp *(Anglo-Saxon)* 'The warrior champion'

Ken *see* Kendall or Kenneth

Kenaz *(Hebrew)* 'The hunter'

Kendal *see* Kendall

Kendall *(Celtic)* 'Chief of the valley' Ken, Kendal, Kendell

Kendell *see* Kendall

Kendrick *(Anglo-Saxon/Gaelic)* 'Royal ruler, son of Henry'

Kenelm *(Anglo-Saxon)* 'Brave helmet'. A courageous protector

Keneth *see* Kenneth

Kenley *(Anglo-Saxon)* 'Owner of a royal meadow'

Kenn *(Celtic)* 'Clear as bright water'
Kennan, Kenon

Kennan *see* Kenn

Kennard *(Anglo-Saxon)* 'Bold and vigorous'

Kennedy *(Gaelic)* 'The helmeted chief'

Kennet *see* Kenneth

Kenneth *(Celtic)* 'The handsome' or 'royal oath'
Ken, Keneth, Kennet, Kennith, Kenny, Kent

Kennith *see* Kenneth

Kenny *see* Kenneth

Kenon *see* Kenn

Kenrick *(Anglo-Saxon)* 'Bold ruler'

Kensell *(Teutonic)* 'Royal and brave'

Kent *(Celtic)* 'Bright and white' *see also* Kenneth

Kenton *(Anglo-Saxon)* 'From the royal estate'

Kenward *(Anglo-Saxon)* 'Bold guardian'

Kenway *(Anglo-Saxon)* 'Bold or royal warrior'

Kenyon *(Celtic)* 'White haired'

Kerby *see* Kirby

Kermit *(Celtic)* 'A free man'
Dermot, Derry, Kerry

Kern *(Gaelic)* 'Little dark one'

Kerr *see* Carr or Kirby

Kerry *(Gaelic)* 'Son of the dark one' *see also* Kermit or Kieran

Kerwin *(Gaelic)* 'Small black-haired one'
Kirwin

Kester *(Anglo-Saxon/Latin)* 'From the army camp' *see also* Christopher

Keung *(Chinese)* 'Universe'

Kev *see* Kevin

Kevan *see* Kevin

Keven *see* Kevin

Kevin *(Gaelic)* 'Gentle, kind and lovable'
Kev, Kevan, Keven, Kevon

Kevon *see* Kevin

Key *(Gaelic)* 'Son of the fiery one'

Khalid *(Arabic)* 'Immortal'

Khalil *(Arabic)* 'Friend'

Khalipha *(Arabic)* 'Successor'

Khayam *(Arabic)* 'Tent-maker'

Kiel *see* Kyle

Kienan *see* Keenan

Kieran *(Gaelic)* 'Small and dark skinned'
Kerrin, Kerry, Kiernan, Kieron

Kiernan *see* Kieran

Kieron *see* Kieran

Kilby *(Teutonic)* 'Farm by the spring'

Kilian *(Celtic)* 'Innocent'

Killian *(Gaelic)* 'Little war-like one'
Killie

Killie *see* Killian

Kim *see* Kimball

Kimball *(Celtic)* 'Royally brave' or 'warrior chief'
Kembell, Kemble, Kim, Kimbell, Kimble

Kimbell *see* Kimball

Kimble *see* Kimball

Kincaid *(Celtic)* 'Battle chief'

King *(Anglo-Saxon)* 'The sovereign'. The ruler of his people

Kingdom *(Old English)* 'King's hill'

Kingsley *(Anglo-Saxon)* 'From the king's meadow'
Kinsley

Kingston *(Anglo-Saxon)* 'From the king's farm'

Kingswell *(Anglo-Saxon)* 'From the king's well'

Kinnaird *see* Kinnard

Kinnard *(Gaelic)* 'From the high mountain'
Kinnaird

Kinnell *(Gaelic)* 'One who lives on the top of the cliff'

Kinsey *(Anglo-Saxon)* 'Royal victor'

Kinsley see Kingsley

Kipp (Anglo-Saxon) 'One who lives on the pointed hill'
Kippar, Kippie

Kippar see Kipp

Kippie see Kipp

Kirby (Teutonic) 'From the church village'
Kerby, Kerr

Kirin (Latin) 'Spearman'

Kirk (Norse) 'One who lives at the church'

Kirkley (Anglo-Saxon) 'From the church meadow'

Kirkwood (Anglo-Saxon) 'From the church wood'

Kirwin see Kerwin

Kit see Christian or Christopher

Kitron (Hebrew) 'Crown'

Klaus see Nicholas

Knight (Anglo-Saxon) 'Mounted soldier'

Knox (Anglo-Saxon) 'From the hills'

Knut see Canute

Knute see Canute

Koby see Jacob

Kong (Chinese) 'Glorious' or 'sky'

Konrad see Conrad

Konstantin see Constantine

Konstantine see Constantine

Kosey (African) 'Son'
Kosse

Kosse see Kosey

Kris see Christopher

Krisha see Krishna

Krishna (Hindi) 'Delightful'
Krisha

Kriss see Christopher

Kristian see Christian

Kristin see Christian

Kurt see Conrad or Curtis

Kwasi (African) 'Born on Sunday'

Kyle (Gaelic) 'From the strait'
Kiel

Kynan see Conan

Kyne (Anglo-Saxon) 'The royal one'

Laban *(Hebrew)* 'White'

Labhras *see* Lawrence

Labhruinn *see* Lawrence

Labid *(Arabic)* 'Intelligent'

Lach *(Celtic)* 'One who lives by the water'
Lache

Lache *see* Lach

Lachlan *(Celtic)* 'War-like'

Lacy *(Latin)* 'From the Roman manor house'

Ladd *(Anglo-Saxon)* 'Attendant, page'
Laddie

Laddie *see* Ladd

Ladislas *(Slavic)* 'A glory of power'

Laibrook *(Anglo-Saxon)* 'Path by the brook'

Laidley *(Anglo-Saxon)* 'From the water meadow'

Laird *(Celtic)* 'The land owner'. The lord of the manor

Lakshman *(Hindi)* 'Younger brother of Ram'

Lamar *(Teutonic)* 'Famous throughout the land'

Lambert *(Teutonic)* 'Rich in land'. An owner of vast estates

Lamech *(Hebrew)* 'Strong young man'

Lammond *see* Lamont

Lammont *see* Lamont

Lamond *see* Lamont

Lamont *(Norse)* 'A lawyer'
Lamond, Lammond, Lammont

Lance *see* Lancelot

Lancelot *(French)* 'Spear attendant'
Lance, Lancey, Launce, Launcelot

Lancey *see* Lancelot

Lander *(Anglo-Saxon)* 'Owner of a grassy plain'
Landers, Landor, Launder

Landers *see* Lander

Landon *(Anglo-Saxon)* 'One who lives on the long hill'
Langdon, Langston

Landor *see* Lander

Landric *(Old German)* 'Land ruler'

Lane *(Anglo-Saxon)* 'From the narrow road'
Laina, Layne

Lanfrance *(Italian from Teutonic)* 'Free country'

Lang *(Teutonic)* 'Tall or long-limbed man'

Langdon *see* Landon

Langford *(Anglo-Saxon)* 'One who lives by the long ford'

Langley *(Anglo-Saxon)* 'One who lives by the long meadow'

Langsdon *see* Langston

Langston *(Anglo-Saxon)* 'The farm belonging to the tall man'
Langsdon *see also* Landon

Langworth *(Anglo-Saxon)* 'From the long enclosure'

Lann *(Celtic)* 'Sword'

Lanny *see* Roland

Laris *(Latin)* 'Cheerful'

Larkin *(Latin)* 'Laurel bush'

Larrance *see* Lawrence

Larry *see* Lawrence

Lars *see* Lawrence

Larson *(Norse)* 'Son of Lars'

Latham *(Norse)* 'From the barns'

Lathrop *(Anglo-Saxon)* 'From the barn farmstead'

Latimer *(Anglo-Saxon)* 'The interpreter' or 'the language teacher'

Laughton *see* Lawton

Launce *see* Lancelot

Launcelot *see* Lancelot

Launder *see* Lander

Lauren *see* Lawrence

Laurence *see* Lawrence

Laurent *see* Lawrence

Lauric *see* Lawrence

Lauritz *see* Lawrence

Lawford *(Anglo-Saxon)* 'One who lives at the ford by the hill'

Lawler *(Gaelic)* 'The mumbler'

Lawley *(Anglo-Saxon)* 'From the meadow on the hill'

Lawrance *see* Lawrence

Lawrence *(Latin)* 'Crowned with laurels'. The victor's crown of bay leaves
Labhras, Labhruinn, Larrance, Larry, Lars, Lauren, Laurence, Laurent, Lauric, Lauritz, Lawrance, Lawry, Lon, Lonnie, Loren, Lorenz, Lorenze, Lorenzo, Lori, Lorin, Lorne, Lorrie, Lorry

Lawry *see* Lawrence

Lawson *(Anglo-Saxon)* 'Son of Lawrence'

Lawton *(Anglo-Saxon)* 'From the town on the hill'
Laughton

Layton *see* Leighton

Lazar *see* Eleazar

Lazaro *see* Eleazar

Lazarus *see* Eleazar

Lazhar *(Arabic)* 'Best appearance'

Leal *(Anglo-Saxon)* 'Loyal, true and faithful'
Loyal

Lealand *see* Leland

Leander *(Greek)* 'Like a lion'
Leandro

Leandro *see* Leander

Lear *(Celtic)* 'One who keeps cattle'

Lech *(Polish)* 'Woodland spirit'

Ledyard *(Teutonic)* 'Nation's guardian'

Lee *(Anglo-Saxon)* 'From the meadow' or *(Gaelic)* 'poetic'
Leigh *see also* Ashley, Bradley, Finlay or Leroy

Leger *(Teutonic)* 'People's spear'

Leggett *(French)* 'Envoy or ambassador'
Leggitt, Liggett

Leggitt *see* Leggett

Leicester *see* Lester

Leif *(Norse)* 'The beloved one'

Leigh *see* Lee or *also* Bradley

Leighton *(Anglo-Saxon)*
'One who lives at the
farm by the meadow'
Layton

Leith *(Celtic)* 'Broad, wide
river'

Leland *(Anglo-Saxon)* 'One
who lives by the
meadow land'
Lealand, Leyland

Lem *see* Lemuel

Lemmie *see* Lemuel

Lemuel *(Hebrew)*
'Consecrated to God'
Lem, Lemmie

Len *see* Leonard

Lenard *see* Leonard

Lennard *see* Leonard

Lennie *see* Leonard

Lenno *(Native American)*
'Man'

Lennon *(Gaelic)* 'Little
cloak'

Lennox *(Celtic)* 'Grove of
elm trees'

Lenny *see* Leonard

Leo *(Latin)* 'Lion'
Lev *see also* Leopold

Leon *(French)* 'Lion-like'

Leonard *(Latin)* 'Lion
brave'. One with all the
courage and tenacity of
the king of beasts
Len, Lenard, Lennard,
Lennie, Lenny, Leoner,
Leonardo, Leonhard,
Leonid, Leonidas,
Lonnard

Leonardo *see* Leonard

Leoner *see* Leonard

Leonhard *see* Leonard

Leonid *see* Leonard

Leonidas *(Greek)* 'Son of
the lion' *see also*
Leonard

Leopold *(Teutonic)* 'Brave
for the people'. One
who fights for his
countryman
Leo, Lepp

Lepp *see* Leopold

Leroi *see* Leroy

Leroy *(French)* 'The king'
Lee, Leroi, Roy Les *see*
Leslie

Lesley *see* Leslie

Leslie *(Celtic)* 'From the
grey fort'
Les, Lesley

Lester *(Anglo-Saxon)* 'From the army camp' Leicester

Lev *see* Leo

Leverett *(French)* 'The young hare'

Leverton *(Anglo-Saxon)* 'From the rush farm'

Levi *(Hebrew)* 'United' Levin

Levin *see* Levi

Lew *see* Lewis

Lewes *see* Lewis

Lewis *(Teutonic)* 'Famous battle warrior' Lew, Lewes, Lou, Louis, Ludo, Ludovic, Ludovick, Ludwig, Lugaidh, Luigi, Luis, Luthais *see also* Aloysius or Clovis

Leyland *see* Leland

Leyman *see* Lyman

Liall *see* Lyle

Liam *(Celtic)* 'Determined protector' *see also* William

Liggett *see* Leggett

Lin *see* Lynn

Lincoln *(Celtic)* 'From the place by the pool'

Lind *(Anglo-Saxon)* 'From the lime tree' Linden, Lindon, Lyndon *see also* Lindsey

Lindberg *(Teutonic)* 'Lime tree hill'

Lindell *(Anglo-Saxon)* 'One who lives by the lime tree in the valley'

Linden *see* Lind

Lindley *(Anglo-Saxon)* 'By the lime tree in the meadow'

Lindo *(Latin)* 'Handsome man'

Lindon *see* Lind

Lindsay *see* Lindsey

Lindsey *(Anglo-Saxon)* 'Pool island' Lind, Lindsay, Linsay, Linsey

Linford *(Anglo-Saxon)* 'From the lime tree ford'

Linfred *(Teutonic)* 'Gentle and gracious'

Lingard *(Celtic)* 'The sea guard'

Link *(Anglo-Saxon)* 'From the bank or edge'

Linley *(Anglo-Saxon)* 'From the flax field'

Linn *see* Lynn

Linsay *see* Lindsey

Linsey *see* Lindsey

Linton *(Anglo-Saxon)* 'From the flax farm'

Linus *(Greek)* 'Flax-coloured hair'

Lion *see* Lionel

Lionel *(French)* 'The young lion'
Lion, Lionello

Lionello *see* Lionel

Lisle *see* Lyle

Litton *(Anglo-Saxon)* 'Farm on the hillside'

Livingston *(Old English)* 'From Leif's town'

Lleufer *(Welsh)* 'Splendid'

Llewellyn *(Welsh)* 'Lion-like' or 'like a ruler'

Lloyd *(Welsh)* 'Grey haired'
Floyd

Locke *(Anglo-Saxon)* 'One who lives in the stronghold'
Lockwood

Lockwood *see* Locke

Logan *(Celtic)* 'Little hollow'

Lok *(Chinese)* 'Happiness'

Loman *(Celtic)* 'Enlightened'

Lombard *(Latin)* 'Long-bearded one'

Lon *(Gaelic)* 'Strong, fierce' *see also* Lawrence

London *(Middle English)* 'Fortress of the moon'

Lonnard *see* Leonard

Lonnie *see* Lawrence

Lonny *see* Zebulon

Loren *see* Lawrence

Lorenz *see* Lawrence

Lorenze *see* Lawrence

Lorenzo *see* Lawrence

Lori *see* Lawrence

Lorimer *(Latin)* 'Harness-maker'

Lorin *see* Lawrence

Loring *(Teutonic)* 'Man from Lorraine'

Lorne *see* Lawrence

Lorrie *see* Lawrence

Lorry *see* Lawrence

Lort *see* Conrad

Lorus *(Latin)* 'Laurel bush'

Lothaire *see* Luther

Lothar *see* Luther

Lothario *see* Luther

Lou *see* Lewis

Louis *see* Lewis or Aloysius

Lovel *see* Lowell

Lovell *see* Lowell

Lowe *see* Lowell

Lowell *(Anglo-Saxon)* 'The beloved one'
Lovel, Lovell, Lowe

Loyal *see* Leal

Lubin *(Old English)* 'Dear friend'

Luc *see* Lucius

Lucais *see* Lucius

Lucas *see* Lucius

Luce *see* Lucius

Lucian *see* Lucius

Lucio *see* Lucius

Lucius *(Latin)* 'Light'
Luc, Lucais, Lucas, Luce, Lucian, Lucio, Luck, Lukas, Luke, Lukey

Luck *see* Lucius

Ludlow *(Anglo-Saxon)* 'From the hill of the prince'

Ludo *see* Lewis

Ludolf *(Old German)* 'Famous wolf'

Ludovic *see* Lewis

Ludovick *see* Lewis

Ludwig *see* Aloysius or Lewis

Lugaidh *see* Lewis

Luigi *see* Lewis

Luis *see* Lewis

Lukas *see* Lucius

Luke *(Latin)* 'Light' *see also* Lucius

Lukey *see* Lucius

Luman *(Latin)* 'Radiant'

Lundy *(French)* 'Born on Monday'

Lunn *(Gaelic)* 'From the grove'

Lunt *(Norse)* 'Strong and fierce'

Lute *see* Luther

Luthais *see* Lewis

Luther *(Teutonic)* 'Famous warrior'
Lothaire, Lothar, Lothario, Lute

Lyall *see* Lyle

Lycidas *(Greek)* 'Wolf son'

Lydell *(Greek)* 'Man from
Lydia'

Lyell *see* Lyle

Lyle *(French)* 'From the
island'
Liall, Lisle, Lyall, Lyell

Lyman *(Anglo-Saxon)* 'Man
from the meadow'
Leyman

Lyn *see* Lynn

Lyndon *see* Lind

Lynfa *(Welsh)* 'From the
lake'

Lynn *(Welsh)* 'From the
pool or waterfall'
Lin, Linn, Lyn

Lysander *(Greek)* 'The
liberator'
Sandy

Mabon *(Welsh)* 'Youth'

Mac *(Celtic)* Used in many Scots and Irish names and meaning 'son of'. Also used in the form 'Mc'. For instance Macadam (son of Adam), McDonald (son of Donald) and so on

Macaire *(Greek)* 'Happy one'

Macarius *(Latin)* 'Blessed'

Mack *see* Mackenzie

Mackenzie *(Irish Gaelic)* 'Son of the wise leader' Mack

Macnair *(Celtic)* 'Son of the heir'

Macy *(French)* 'From Matthew's estate'

Madaan *(Arabic)* 'Striving'

Maddison *see* Madison

Maddock *(Welsh)* 'Beneficent' Maddox, Madoc, Madock, Madog

Maddox *see* Maddock

Madhur *(Sanskrit)* 'Sweet'

Madison *(Anglo-Saxon)* 'Mighty in battle' Maddison

Madjid *(Arabic)* 'Glorious'

Madoc *see* Maddock

Madock *see* Maddock

Madog *see* Maddock

Maelgwyn *(Welsh)* 'Metal chief'

Magee *(Gaelic)* 'Son of the fiery one'

Magloire *(French)* 'My glory'

Magna *(Native American)* 'The coming moon'

Magnus *(Latin)* 'The great one'. One who excels all others

Maher *(Hebrew/Arabic)* 'Clever, industrious and skilful'

Mahfuz *(Arabic)* 'Guardian'

Mahin *(Sanskrit)* 'Royal'
Mahish

Mahish *see* Mahin

Mahon *(Celtic)* 'Chief'

Maitland *(Anglo-Saxon)*
'One who lives in the
meadow land'

Majnoon *(Persian)*
Legendary hero like
Romeo (from the story
of Majnoon and Leila)

Major *(Latin)* 'Greater'.
Anything you can do,
he can do better!

Mal *see* Malvin

Malachi *(Hebrew)* 'Angel'

Malchus *(Hebrew)* 'King'

Malcolm *(Celtic)* 'The dove'
or 'follower of St
Columba'

Malik *(Muslim)* 'Master'

Malin *(Anglo-Saxon)* 'Little
warrior'

Malise *(Gaelic)* 'Servant of
Jesus'

Malkawn *(Hebrew)* 'Their
king'

Mallard *(Teutonic)* 'Strong
advisor'

Mallory *(Anglo-Saxon)*
'Army counsellor' or
(Latin) 'unlucky' *see also*
Malory

Maloney *(Gaelic)* 'Believer
in the Sabbath'

Malory *(Old French)*
'Unfortunate'
Mallory

Malvin *(Celtic)* 'Polished
chief'
Mal, Mel, Melva,
Melvin

Mamoun *(Arabic)*
'Trustworthy'

Manassa *(Arabic)* 'Causes
to forget'

Manasseh *(Hebrew)*
'Making one forget'

Manchu *(Chinese)* 'Pure
one'

Mandel *(Teutonic)* 'Almond'

Mander *(Old French)*
'Stable lad'

Manfred *(Anglo-Saxon)*
'Peaceful hero'
Manfried

Manfried *see* Manfred

Manik *(Sanskrit)* 'Precious
ruby'

Manish *(Sanskrit)* 'Intelligent'

Manleich *see* Manley

Manley *(Anglo-Saxon)* 'The hero's meadow' Manleich

Mannie *see* Chaim, Chapman or Emmanuel

Manning *(Anglo-Saxon)* 'Hero's son'

Manny *see* Chaim, Chapman or Emmanuel

Mano *see* Emmanuel

Manolo *see* Emmanuel

Mansfield *(Anglo-Saxon)* 'Hero's field'

Mansoor *(Arabic)* 'Victorious'

Manton *(Anglo-Saxon)* 'Hero's farm'

Manuel *see* Emmanuel

Manvil *see* Manville

Manville *(French)* 'From the great estate' Manvil

Marc *see* Mark

Marcel *(Latin)* 'Little follower of Mars'. A war-like person Marcello, Marcellus

Marcello *see* Marcel

Marcellus *see* Marcel

Marcius *(Latin)* 'Martial'

Marco *see* Mark

Marcus *see* Mark

Marden *(Anglo-Saxon)* 'From the pool in the valley'

Mardon *(Teutonic)* 'Famous leader'

Marino *(Italian from Latin)* 'Sea'

Mario *see* Marius

Marion *(French)* 'Bitter'. A French form of Mary, often given as a boy's name in compliment to the Virgin

Marius *(Latin)* 'The martial one' Mario

Marjan *(Arabic)* 'Small pearls'

Mark *(Latin)* 'Follower of Mars, the warrior' Marc, Marco, Marcus

Marl *see* Merlin

Marland *(Anglo-Saxon)*
'One who lives in the
lake land'

Marlen *see* Merlin

Marley *(Anglo-Saxon)*
'From the lake in the
meadow'
Marly

Marlin *see* Merlin

Marlon *see* Merlin

Marlow *(Anglo-Saxon)*
'From the lake on the
hill'
Marlowe

Marlowe *see* Marlow

Marly *see* Marley

Marmaduke *(Celtic)* 'Sea
leader'
Duke

Marmion *(French)* 'Very
small one'

Marques *(Portuguese)*
'Nobleman'

Marsden *(Anglo-Saxon)*
'From the marshy
valley'
Marsdon

Marsdon *see* Marsden

Marsh *(Anglo-Saxon)* 'From
the marsh'

Marshall *(Anglo-Saxon)*
'The steward'. The man
who looked after the
estate of a nobleman

Marston *(Anglo-Saxon)*
'From the farm by the
lake'

Mart *see* Martin

Martainn *see* Martin

Martel *(Old French)*
'Hammer of war'

Marten *see* Martin

Martial *(Latin)* 'War-like'

Martie *see* Martin

Martin *(Latin)* 'War-like
person'. A follower of
Mars
Mart, Martainn,
Marten, Martie,
Martino, Marton, Marty

Martino *see* Martin

Marton *see* Martin

Marty *see* Martin

Marvin *(Anglo-Saxon)*
'Famous friend'
Marwin, Mervin,
Merwin, Merwyn

Marwin *see* Marvin

Marwood *(Anglo-Saxon)*
'From the lake in the
forest'

Maska *(Native American)* 'Powerful one'

Maskil *(Hebrew)* 'Enlightened, educated'

Maslen *see* Maslin

Maslin *(French)* 'Small Thomas'
Maslen, Maslon

Maslon *see* Maslin

Mason *(Latin)* 'Worker in stone'
Massey

Massey *see* Mason or Thomas

Mat *see* Matthew

Mata *see* Matthew

Math *(Welsh)* 'Treasure'

Mather *(Anglo-Saxon)* 'Powerful army'

Mathew *see* Matthew

Mathias *see* Matthew

Matmon *(Hebrew)* 'Treasure'

Matt *see* Matthew

Matthew *(Hebrew)* 'Gift of God'. One of the 12 apostles
Mat, Mata, Mathew, Mathias, Matt, Mattie, Matty, Matthias, Mattias

Matthias *see* Matthew

Mattias *see* Matthew

Mattie *see* Matthew

Matty *see* Matthew

Maurey *see* Maurice

Maurice *(Latin)* 'Moorish-looking, dark-complexioned'
Maury, Maurey, Mauricio, Maurizio, Mo, Morel, Morey, Morice, Moritz, Morrell, Morrie, Morris, Morry

Mauricio *see* Maurice

Maurizio *see* Maurice

Maury *see* Maurice

Max *see* Maximilian or Maxwell

Maxey *see* Maximilian

Maxi *see* Maxwell

Maxie *see* Maximilian or Maxwell

Maxim *see* Maximilian

Maximilian *(Latin)* 'The greatest, the most excellent'. One without equal
Max, Maxey, Maxie, Maxim, Maximilien, Maxy

Maximilien *see*
Maximilian

Maxwell *(Anglo-Saxon)*
'Large spring of fresh
water'
Max, Maxi, Maxie

Maxy *see* Maximilian

Mayer *(Latin)* 'Greater'
Myer

Mayfield *(Anglo-Saxon)*
'From the field of the
warrior'

Mayhew *(French)* 'Gift of
God'. Another form of
Matthew

Maynard *(Teutonic)*
'Powerfully strong and
brave'
Menard

Mayne *(Teutonic)* 'Mighty
one'

Mayo *(Gaelic)* 'From the
plain of the yew trees'

Mead *(Anglo-Saxon)* 'From
the meadow'

Medwin *(Teutonic)* 'Strong
and powerful friend'

Megha *(Sanskrit)* 'Star'

Mehrdad *(Persian)* 'Gift of
the sun'

Meilyr *(Welsh)* 'Man of
iron'

Mekuria *(Ethiopian)* 'Pride'

Mel *see* Malvin or Melville

Melbourne *(Anglo-Saxon)*
'From the mill stream'
Melburn, Melburne,
Milbourn, Milbourne,
Milburn, Milburne,
Pierrot

Melburn *see* Melbourne

Melburne *see* Melbourne

Melchior *(Persian)* 'King of
light'

Meldon *(Anglo-Saxon)*
'From the mill on the
hill'

Melmoth *(Celtic)* 'Servant
of Math'

Melva *see* Malvin

Melvern *(Native American)*
'Great leader'

Melvil *see* Melville

Melville *(French)* 'From the
estate of the
industrious'
Mel, Melvil

Melvin *see* Malvin

Menachin *(Hebrew)*
'Comforter'
Menahem

Menahem *see* Menachin

Menard *see* Maynard

Mendel *(Semitic)* 'Wisdom'

Mercer *(Anglo-Saxon)* 'Merchant'

Meredith *(Welsh)* 'Guardian from the sea' Meredydd, Meredyth, Merideth, Meridith, Meridyth, Merry

Meredydd *see* Meredith

Meredyth *see* Meredith

Merideth *see* Meredith

Meridith *see* Meredith

Meridyth *see* Meredith

Merl *see* Merlin

Merle *(Latin)* 'The blackbird' or 'the black-haired one'

Merlin *(Anglo-Saxon)* 'The falcon'. The legendary wizard of King Arthur's court Marl, Marlin, Marlen, Marlon, Merl

Meron *(Hebrew)* 'Army'

Merrick *see* Emery

Merrill *(French)* 'Little famous one' Merritt *see also* Myron

Merritt *see* Merrill

Merry *see* Meredith

Merton *(Anglo-Saxon)* 'From the farm by the sea'

Mervin *see* Marvin

Merwin *see* Marvin

Merwyn *see* Marvin

Meryll *(French from Old German)* 'King'

Methuselah *(Hebrew)* 'Man of the javelin'

Metis *(Greek)* 'Counsellor, adviser'

Meven *(Celtic/French)* 'Agile'

Meyer *(Teutonic)* 'Steward'

Micah *see* Michael

Mich *see* Michael

Michael *(Hebrew)* 'Like the Lord' Micah, Mich, Michel, Mickie, Micky, Mike, Mischa, Mitch, Mitchell, Mithell

Michel *see* Michael

Mickie *see* Michael

Micky *see* Michael

Midyan *(Arabic)* 'Rule'

Mihriban *(Turkish)* 'Tender, affectionate'

Mike *see* Michael

Mikki *see* Nicholas or
Nicodemus

Milan *(Slavic)* 'Beloved'

Milbourn *see* Melbourne

Milbourne *see* Melbourne

Milburn *(Old English)* 'Mill
stream' *see also*
Melbourne

Milburne *see* Melbourne

Miles *(Greek/Latin)* 'The
soldier'
Myles

Milford *(Anglo-Saxon)*
'From the mill ford'
Millford

Millard *(French)* 'Strong
and victorious'

Miller *(Anglo-Saxon)* 'Grain
grinder'

Millford *see* Milford

Milo *(Latin)* 'The miller'
Mylo

Milt *see* Milton

Milton *(Anglo-Saxon)* 'From
the mill town'
Milt

Milward *(Anglo-Saxon)*
'The mill-keeper'

Miner *(Latin/French)*
'Young person'
Minor

Minor *see* Miner

Miroslav *(Slavonic)* 'Peace'
or 'glory'

Mischa *see* Michael

Mitch *see* Michael

Mitchell *see* Michael

Mithell *see* Michael

Mo *see* Maurice

Modred *(Anglo-Saxon)*
'Brave counsellor'. One
who advised honestly
without fear of reprisal

Moe *see* Moses

Moelwyn *(Welsh)* 'Fair
haired'

Mohamad *(Sanskrit)*
'Prophet of Islam'
Mohammed

Mohammed *(Arabic/
Sanskrit)* 'Praised'

Moise *see* Moses

Mokbil *(Arabic)* 'The
approaching one'

Mokhtar *(Arabic)* 'Chosen'

Monro *see* Monroe

Monroe *(Celtic)* 'From the
red swamp'
Monro, Munro, Munroe

Montagu *see* Montague

Montague *(French)* 'From the jagged mountain' Montagu, Monte, Monty

Monte *see* Montague or Montgomery

Montega *(Native American)* 'New arrows'

Montgomery *(French)* 'The mountain hunter' Monte, Monty

Monty *see* Montague or Montgomery

Moore *(French)* 'Dark complexioned, a Moor' More

Mordecai *(Hebrew)* 'Belonging to Marduk' Mort

More *see* Moore

Morel *see* Maurice

Moreland *(Anglo-Saxon)* 'From the moors'

Morell *see* Morrell

Morfin *see* Morven

Morey *see* Maurice

Morgan *(Welsh)* 'White sea'. The foam-flecked waves Morganica, Morganne, Morgen

Morgen *see* Morgan

Moriah *(Hebrew)* 'Man chosen by Jehovah'

Morice *see* Maurice

Morison *see* Morrison

Moritz *see* Maurice

Morley *(Anglo-Saxon)* 'From the moor meadow'

Morrell *(Latin)* 'Dark' Morell *see also* Maurice

Morrie *see* Maurice

Morris *see* Maurice

Morrison *(Anglo-Saxon)* 'Maurice's son' Morison

Morry *see* Maurice

Morse *(Anglo-Saxon)* 'Maurice's son'

Mort *see* Mordecai

Mortemer *see* Mortimer

Morten *see* Morton

Mortermer *see* Mortimer

Morthermer *see* Mortimer

Mortimer *(French)* 'From the quiet water' Mortemer, Mortermer, Morthermer

Morton *(Anglo-Saxon)*
'From the farm on the moor'
Morten

Morven *(Gaelic)* 'Blond giant'
Morfin

Morys *(Welsh)* Form of Maurice

Mose *see* Moses

Moses *(Hebrew)* 'Saved from the water'. The great prophet of Israel
Moe, Moise, Mose, Mosie, Moss

Mosie *see* Moses

Moss *see* Moses

Mostyn *(Welsh)* 'Fortress'

Moustapha *(Arabic)* 'Chosen'
Mustapha

Mubarak *(Arabic)* 'Blessed'

Muhammad *(Arabic)* 'Praised'

Muir *(Celtic)* 'From the moor'

Mungo *(Gaelic)* 'Lovable'

Munir *(Arabic)* 'Illuminating, light'

Munro *see* Monroe

Munroe *see* Monroe

Murad *(Arabic)* 'Desired' or 'wanted'

Murdoch *(Celtic)* 'Prosperous from the sea'
Murdock, Murtagh

Murdock *see* Murdoch

Murphy *(Gaelic)* 'Sea warrior'

Murray *(Celtic)* 'The mariner, a sea fighter'

Murtagh *see* Murdoch

Mustapha *see* Moustapha

Myer *see* Mayer

Myles *see* Miles

Mylo *see* Milo

Mylor *(Celtic)* 'Ruler, prince'

Myron *(Greek)* 'Sweet-smelling'

Myron *(Greek)* 'The fragrant oil'
Merrill

BOYS

Naaman *(Hebrew)* 'Pleasant one'

Nabil *(Arabic)* 'Noble'

Nadabb *(Hebrew)* 'One with wide-ranging ideas'

Nadim *(Arabic)* 'Repentant'

Nadir *(Arabic/Sanskrit)* 'Rare, precious, the pinnacle'

Nadiv *(Hebrew)* 'Noble'

Nahum *(Hebrew)* 'Comfort'

Naim *(Arabic)* 'Contented'

Nairn *(Celtic)* 'One who lives by the alder tree'

Najibullah *(Arabic)* 'God-given intelligence'

Naldo *see* Reginald

Namir *(Hebrew)* 'Leopard'

Napoleon *(Greek)* 'Lion of the woodland dell'

Narcissus *(Greek)* 'Daffodil'. A Greek youth who fell in love with his own image

Nash *(Old French)* 'Cliff'

Nashif *(Arabic)* 'Hard'

Nasim *(Persian)* 'Breeze'

Nat *see* Nathan

Natal *see* Noel

Natale *see* Noel

Nataniel *see* Nathan

Nate *see* Nathan

Nathan *(Hebrew)* 'Gift of God'
Nat, Nataniel, Nate, Nathaniel, Nattie

Nathaniel *see* Nathan

Nattie *see* Nathan

Nayan *(Sanskrit)* 'Lovely eyes'

Neacail *see* Nicholas

Neal *(Gaelic)* 'The champion'
Neale, Neall, Neel, Neil, Neill, Nels, Niall, Niels, Niles, Nils *see also* Cornelius

Neale *see* Neal

Neall *see* Neal

317

Ned Diminutive of many names beginning with Ed *see* Edgar, Edmund or Edward

Neddie Diminutive of many names beginning with Ed *see* Edgar or Edward

Neddy Diminutive of many names beginning with Ed *see* Edgar or Edward

Needham *(Teutonic)* 'Tyrant'

Neel *see* Cornelius or Neal

Nefen *see* Nevin

Nehemiah *(Hebrew)* 'Consolation of the Lord'

Neil *see* Neal

Neill *see* Neal

Nels *see* Neal or Nelson

Nelson *(Celtic)* 'Son of Neal'
Nels, Nils, Nilson

Nemo *(Greek)* 'From the glen'

Nennog *(Welsh)* 'One from heaven'

Neo *(Greek)* 'Born'

Nero *(Latin)* 'Dark complexioned, black haired'
Neron

Neron *see* Nero

Nestor *(Greek)* 'Ancient wisdom'

Nev *see* Neville

Nevil *see* Neville

Nevile *see* Neville

Neville *(Latin)* 'From the new town'
Nev, Nevil, Nevile

Nevin *(Gaelic)* 'Worshipper of saints' or *(Anglo-Saxon)* 'nephew'
Nefen, Nevins, Niven, Nivens

Nevins *see* Nevin

Nevlin *(Celtic)* 'Sailor'

Newall *see* Newell

Newbern *(Teutonic)* 'The new leader'

Newbold *(Old English)* 'From the new building'

Newcomb *(Anglo-Saxon)* 'Stranger'

Newel *see* Noel

Newell *(Anglo-Saxon)* 'From the new hall'
Newall *see also* Noel

Newland *(Anglo-Saxon)*
'From the new lands'
Newlands

Newlands *see* Newland

Newlin *(Celtic)* 'One who
lives by the new pool'
Newlyn

Newlyn *see* Newlin

Newman *(Anglo-Saxon)*
'The newcomer, the
new arrival'

Newton *(Anglo-Saxon)*
'From the new estate'

Niall *see* Neal

Nic *see* Dominic

Nicander *(Greek)* 'Man of
victory'

Niccolo *see* Nicholas

Nichol *see* Nicholas

Nicholas *(Greek)*
'Victorious people's
army'. The leader of
the people
Claus, Cole, Colin,
Colley, Klaus, Neacail,
Niccolo, Nichol,
Nicholl, Nick, Nickie,
Nicky, Nicol, Nicolai,
Nicolas, Nik, Nikki,
Nikos, Niles *see also*
Colin

Nicholl *see* Nicholas

Nick *see* Dominic,
Nicholas or
Nicodermus

Nickie *see* Dominic,
Nicholas or Nicodemus

Nickson *see* Nixon

Nicky *see* Dominic,
Nicholas or Nicodemus

Nico *(Greek)* 'Victory'

Nicodemus *(Greek)*
'Conqueror for the
people'
Nick, Nickie, Nicky,
Nik, Nikki, Nikky

Nicol *see* Nicholas

Nicolai *see* Nicholas

Nicolas *see* Nicholas

Nicomede *(Greek)*
'Victorious leader'

Niels *see* Neal

Nigel *(Latin)* 'Black-haired
one'

Niger *(Latin)* 'Black'

Nik *see* Nicholas or
Nicodemus

Nikhat *(Sanskrit)* 'Fragrant'

Nikos *see* Nicholas

Nilay *(Sanskrit)* 'Home'

Niles *see* Nicholas or Neal

Nils *see* Neal or Nelson

Nilson *see* Nelson

Nimrod *(Hebrew)* 'Valiant'

Ninian *see* Vivien

Niran *(Thai)* 'Eternal'

Niven *see* Nevin

Nivens *see* Nevin

Nixon *(Anglo-Saxon)*
'Nicholas's son'
Nickson

Noach *see* Noah

Noah *(Hebrew)* 'Rest,
comfort and peace'
Noach

Noam *(Hebrew)* 'Sweetness,
friendship'

Nobel *see* Noble

Noble *(Latin)* 'Noble and
famous'
Nobel, Nolan, Noland

Noda *(Hebrew)* 'Famous'

Nodas *(Hebrew)* 'Son of the
leader'

Nodin *(Native American)*
'Wind'

Noel *(French)* 'Born at
Christmas'. A suitable
name for a boy born on
Christmas Day
Natal, Natale, Newel,
Newell, Nowell

Nolan *see* Noble

Noland *see* Noble

Noll *see* Oliver

Nollie *see* Oliver

Nolly *see* Oliver

Norbert *(Teutonic)* 'Brilliant
sea hero'. The coura-
geous commander of
ships'
Norbie

Norbie *see* Norbert

Norm *see* Norman

Norman *(French)* 'Man
from the north, a
Northman'. The bold
Viking from
Scandinavia
Norm, Normand,
Normie, Norris

Normand *see* Norman

Normie *see* Norman

Norris *see* Norman

North *see* Northrop

Northcliff *see* Northcliffe

Northcliffe *(Anglo-Saxon)*
'Man from the north
cliff'
Northcliff

Northrop *(Anglo-Saxon)*
'From the northern
farm'
North, Northrup,
Nortrop, Nortrup

Northrup *see* Northrop

Norton *(Anglo-Saxon)*
'From the north farm'

Nortrop *see* Northrop

Nortrup *see* Northrop

Norua *(Teutonic)* 'Divine
strength'

Norval *(Old French)*
'Northern valley'

Norvel *see* Norville

Norvie *see* Norville

Norvil *see* Norville

Norville *(French)* 'From the
north town'
Norvel, Norvie, Norvil

Norvin *(Anglo-Saxon)*
'Friend from the north'
Norwin, Norwyn

Norward *(Anglo-Saxon)*
'Guardian from the
north'

Norwell *(Anglo-Saxon)*
'From the north well'

Norwin *see* Norvin

Norwood *(Anglo-Saxon)*
'From the north forest'

Norwyn *see* Norvin

Notos *(Greek)* 'The south
wind'

Nova *(Latin)* 'New'

Nowell *see* Noel

Nuncio *(Italian from Latin)*
'Messenger'
Ninzio

Nunzio *see* Nuncio

Nuri *(Hebrew)* 'Fire'
Nuriel, Nuris

Nuriel *see* Nuri

Nuris *see* Nuri

Nye *see* Aneurin

Oakes *(Anglo-Saxon)* 'One who lives by the oak tree'

Oakley *(Anglo-Saxon)* 'From the oak tree meadow'
Okely

Oates *see* Otis

Obadiah *(Hebrew)* 'Servant of the Lord'. The obedient one
Obadias

Obadias *see* Obadiah

Obed *(Hebrew)* 'Worshipper of the Lord'

Oberon *see* Auberon

Obert *(Teutonic)* 'Wealthy and brilliant'

Octave *see* Octavius

Octavian *see* Octavius

Octavius *(Latin)* 'The eighth born'
Octavian, Octave, Octavus, Tavey

Octavus *see* Octavius

Odagoma *(Native American)* 'One with iron nerves'

Odell *(Teutonic)* 'Wealthy one'
Odie, Odin, Odo

Odie *see* Odell

Odin *see* Odell

Odmar *(Teutonic)* 'Rich and famous'

Odo *see* Odell

Odolf *(Teutonic)* 'The wealthy wolf'

Odwin *(Teutonic)* 'Rich friend'
Ortwin

Ogdan *see* Ogden

Ogden *(Anglo-Saxon)* 'From the oak valley'
Ogdan

Ogilvie *(Celtic)* 'From the high peak'

Oglesby *(Anglo-Saxon)* 'Awe-inspiring'

Ogmund *(Teutonic)* 'Impressive protector'

Okely *see* Oakley

Ola *(Hebrew)* 'Eternity'

Olaf *(Scandinavian)*
'Ancestral relic' or
'peaceful reminder'
Amhlaoibh, Olav, Olen,
Olin

Olav *see* Olaf

Olave *(Scandinavian)* 'Relic
of our ancestors'

Olcott *(Teutonic)* 'One who
lives in the old cottage'

Ole *(Scandinavian)* 'Squire'

Olen *see* Olaf

Olin *see* Olaf

Oliver *(Latin)* 'Symbol of
peace'. The olive
branch
Noll, Nollie, Nolly,
Olivero, Oliviero, Ollie,
Olvan

Olivero *see* Oliver

Oliviero *see* Oliver

Ollie *see* Oliver

Olney *(Anglo-Saxon)* 'Olla's
island'

Olvan *see* Oliver

Olvidio *(Spanish)* 'The
forgetful one'

Oman *(Scandinavian)*
'High protector'

Omanisa *(Native American)*
'The wanderer'

Omar *(Arabic/Sanskrit)*
'The first son' or 'most
high follower of the
prophet'

On *(Chinese)* 'Peace'

Onilwyn *(Welsh)* 'Ash
grove'

Onllwyn *(Welsh)* 'The ash
grove'

Onslow *(Anglo-Saxon)* 'Hill
of the zealous one'

Oram *(Anglo-Saxon)* 'From
the enclosure by the
riverbank'

Oran *(Gaelic)* 'Pale-skinned
man'
Oren, Orin, Orran,
Orren, Orrin

Orban *(French from Latin)*
'Globe'

Ordway *(Anglo-Saxon)* 'The
spear fighter'

Orel *(Latin)* 'The one who
listens'

Oren *see* Oran

Orestes *(Greek)* 'The
mountain climber'

Orford *(Anglo-Saxon)* 'One
who lives at the cattle
ford'

Orien *(Latin)* 'The dawn'

Orin *see* Oran

Orion *(Greek)* 'The son of light'

Orlan *(Anglo-Saxon)* 'From the pointed land'

Orlando
Roland *see* Lanny

Orlin *(Latin)* 'Golden and bright'

Orman *see* Ormond

Ormand *see* Ormond

Ormen *see* Ormond

Ormin *see* Ormond

Ormond *(Teutonic)* 'Spearman' or 'shipman'
Orman, Ormand, Ormen, Ormin

Ornette *(Hebrew)* 'Light, cedar tree'

Oro *(Spanish)* 'Golden-haired one'

Orran *see* Oran

Orren *see* Oran

Orrick *(Anglo-Saxon)* 'One who lives by the ancient oak tree'

Orrin *see* Oran

Orris *(Old French)* 'Gold or silver lace'

Orson *(Anglo-Saxon)* 'Son of the spearman' or *(Latin)* 'little bear'
Urson

Ortensio *(Latin)* 'The gardener'

Orton *(Anglo-Saxon)* 'From the shore-farmstead'

Ortwin *see* Odwin

Orval *(Anglo-Saxon)* 'Mighty with a spear'

Orvil *see* Orville

Orville *(French)* 'From the golden town'
Orvil

Orvin *(Anglo-Saxon)* 'Spear friend'

Os *see* Oscar

Osbert *(Anglo-Saxon)* 'Divinely bright warrior'
Bert, Bertie, Berty, Oz, Ozzie

Osborn *(Anglo-Saxon)* 'Divine warrior'
Osborne, Osbourn, Osbourne, Osburn, Osburne

Osborne *see* Osborn

Osbourn *see* Osborn

Osbourne *see* Osborn

Osburn *see* Osborn

Osburne *see* Osborn

Oscar *(Anglo-Saxon)* 'Divine spearman'. A fighter for God
Os, Oskar, Ossie, Oz, Ozzie

Osgood *(Scandinavian)* 'The divine Goth'

Oskar *see* Oscar

Oslac *(Scandinavian)* 'Divine sport'

Osman *(Sanskrit)* 'God's slave'
Usman

Osmar *(Anglo-Saxon)* 'Divinely glorious'

Osmond *(Anglo-Saxon)* 'Divine protector'

Osred *(Anglo-Saxon)* 'Divine counsellor'

Osric *(Scandinavian)* 'Divine ruler'

Ossie *see* Oscar

Oswald *(Anglo-Saxon)* 'Divinely powerful'

Oswin *(Old English)* 'Friend of God'

Otadan *(Native American)* 'Plenty'

Othman *(Teutonic)* 'The prosperous one'

Otho *see* Otto

Otis *(Greek)* 'Keen of sight and hearing'
Oates

Ottavio *(Italian from Latin)* 'Eighth'

Otte *(Teutonic)* 'Happy one'

Otto *(Teutonic)* 'Wealthy, prosperous man'
Otho

Ottokar *(German)* 'Happy warrior'

Ottway *see* Otway

Otway *(Teutonic)* 'Fortunate in battle'
Ottway

Ouray *(Native American)* 'Arrow'

Owain *see* Owen

Owen *(Celtic)* 'The young, well-born warrior'
Owain *see also* Evan

Oxford *(Anglo-Saxon)* 'From the ford where oxen crossed'

Oxton *(Anglo-Saxon)* 'From the town where the oxen graze'

Oz *see* Osbert or Oscar

Ozul *(Hebrew)* 'Shadow'

Ozzie *see* Osbert or Oscar

Pablo *see* Paul

Pace *see* Pascal

Pacian *(Latin)* 'Man of peace'

Paco *(Native American)* 'Brave eagle'

Padarn *(Welsh)* 'Fatherly'

Paddy *see* Patrick

Padget *see* Padgett

Padgett *(French)* 'The young attendant, a page'
Padget, Page, Paget, Paige

Padraic *see* Patrick

Padraig *see* Patrick

Padruig *see* Patrick

Page *see* Padgett

Paget *see* Padgett

Paige *see* Padgett

Paine *(Latin)* 'The country rustic, a pagan'
Payne

Paisley *(Latin)* 'From the country'

Pakavi *(Native American)* 'A reed from the river bank'

Paley *see* Paul

Palladin *(Native American)* 'Fighter'

Palm *see* Palmer

Palmer *(Latin)* 'The palm-bearing pilgrim'
Palm

Pancras *(Greek)* 'All strength'

Paolo *see* Paul

Parakram *(Sanskrit)* 'Strong one'

Pari *(French)* 'Fatherly'

Parish *see* Parrish

Park *(Anglo-Saxon)* 'From the park'
Parke

Parke *see* Park

Parker *(Anglo-Saxon)* 'The park-keeper'. One who guarded the park lands

Parkin *(Anglo-Saxon)* 'Little Peter'
Perkin, Peterkin

Parlan *see* Bartholomew

Parnell *see* Peter

Parr *(Anglo-Saxon)* 'One who lives by the cattle pen'

Parrish *(Anglo-Saxon)* 'From the church parish'
Parish

Parry *(French/Celtic)* 'Protector'

Parsefal *see* Percival

Parsifal *see* Percival

Pascal *(Italian)* 'Easter born'. The new-born pascal lamb
Pasquale

Pasquale *see* Pascal

Pat *see* Fitzpatrick, Patrick

Patera *(Sanskrit)* 'A bird'

Patin *see* Patton

Patric *see* Patrick

Patrice *see* Patrick

Patricio *see* Patrick

Patrick *(Latin)* 'The noble patrician'. One of noble birth and from a noble line
Paddy, Padraic, Padraig, Padruig, Pat, Patric, Patrice, Patricio, Patrizio, Patrizius, Patsy, Peyton, Rick *see also* Fitzpatrick

Patrizio *see* Patrick

Patrizius *see* Patrick

Patsy *see* Patrick

Patton *(Anglo-Saxon)* 'From the warrior's farm'
Patin

Patu *(Sanskrit)* 'Protector'

Paul *(Latin)* 'Little'
Pablo, Paley, Paolo, Pauley, Paulie, Pavel

Pauley *see* Paul

Paulie *see* Paul

Pavel *see* Paul

Pax *(Latin)* 'Peace'

Paxton *(Anglo-Saxon)* 'From the warrior's estate'

Payne *see* Paine

Payton *(Anglo-Saxon)* 'One who lives on the warrior's farm'
Peyton

Peadar *see* Peter

Pearce *see* Peter

Pedro *see* Peter

Pelex *(Greek)* 'Warrior's helmet'

Pell *(Anglo-Saxon)* 'Scarf'

Pelton *(Anglo-Saxon)* 'From the farm by the pool'

Pembroke *(Celtic)* 'From the headland'

Penley *(Anglo-Saxon)* 'From the enclosed meadow'

Penn *(Anglo-Saxon)* 'Enclosure'

Penrod *(Teutonic)* 'Famous commander'

Penrose *(Celtic)* 'Mountain promontory'

Penwyn *(Welsh)* 'Fair headed'

Pepi *see* Pepin

Pepin *(Teutonic)* 'The petitioner' or 'the persevered' Pepi, Peppi, Peppin

Peppi *see* Pepin

Peppin *see* Pepin

Perc *see* Percival

Perce *see* Percival

Perceval *see* Percival

Percival *(French)* 'Valley piercer' Parsefal, Parsifal, Perc, Perce, Perceval, Percy, Purcell

Percy *see* Percival

Peregrine *(Latin)* 'The wanderer' Perry

Pericles *(Greek)* 'Far famed'

Perkin *see* Parkin

Pernell *see* Peter

Perrin *see* Peter

Perry *(Anglo-Saxon)* 'From the pear tree' *see also* Peregrine

Perseus *(Greek)* 'Destroyer'

Perth *(Celtic)* 'Thorn bush thicket'

Pete *see* Peter

Peter *(Latin)* 'The stone, the rock'. The first pope Parnell, Peadar, Pearce, Pedro, Pernell, Perrin, Pete, Petrie, Pierce, Piero, Pierre, Pierro, Pierrot, Piers, Pietro

Peterkin *see* Parkin

Petrie *see* Peter

Petros *(Greek)* 'Made of stone'

Peveral *see* Peverall

Peverall *(French)* 'The piper'
Peveral, Peverel, Peverell, Peveril, Peverill

Peverel *see* Peverall

Peverell *see* Peverall

Peveril *see* Peverall

Peverill *see* Peverall

Peyton *see* Patrick or Payton

Phaon *(Greek)* 'Brilliant'

Pharamond *(German)* 'Journey protection'

Pharaol *(Egyptian)* 'The sun'

Pharos *(Greek)* 'Beacon of light'

Phelan *(Gaelic)* 'Brave as the wolf'

Phelips *see* Phillips

Phellipps *see* Phillips

Phellips *see* Phillips

Phelps *(Anglo-Saxon)* 'Son of Philip' *see also* Philip

Philander *(Greek)* 'The man who loves everyone'

Philaret *(Greek)* 'One who loves virtue'

Philbert *(Teutonic)* 'Brilliant'
Filbert

Philemon *(Greek)* 'Kiss'

Philetas *(Greek)* 'Beloved one'
Philetus

Philetus *see* Philetas

Philip *(Greek)* 'Lover of horses'
Filib, Filip, Filli, Phelps, Phill, Phillie, Philly, Philipp, Phillip, Phillopa, Pilib

Philipp *see* Philip

Philips *see* Phillips

Phill *see* Philip

Phillie *see* Philip

Phillip *see* Philip

Phillipps *see* Phillips

Phillips *(Anglo-Saxon)* 'Phillip's son'
Felips, Fellips, Phelips, Phellips, Phellipps, Philips, Phillipps

Phillopa *see* Philip

Philly *see* Philip

Philo *(Greek)* 'Friendly love'

Phineas *(Greek)* 'Mouth of brass'

Pickford *(Anglo-Saxon)* 'From the ford at the peak'

Pickworth *(Anglo-Saxon)* 'From the estate of the hewer'

Pierce *see* Peter

Piero *see* Peter

Pierre *see* Peter

Pierro *see* Peter

Pierrot *see* Melbourne or Peter

Piers *see* Pete

Pierson *(French)* 'Son of Pierre'

Pietro *see* Peter

Pilib *see* Philip

Pippin *(Dutch from Teutonic)* 'Father'

Pitney *(Dutch from Teutonic)* 'Preserving one's island'

Pitt *(Anglo-Saxon)* 'From the hollow'

Placide *see* Placido

Placido *(Spanish)* 'Serene' Placide

Plato *(Greek)* 'The broad-shouldered one'. The great philosopher

Platt *(French)* 'From the plateau'

Po Sin *(Chinese)* 'Grandfather elephant'

Poldo *(Teutonic)* 'Prince of the people'

Pollard *(Old German)* 'Cropped hair'

Pollock *(Anglo-Saxon)* 'Little Paul'

Pollux *(Greek)* 'Crown'

Pomeroy *(French)* 'From the apple orchard'

Porter *(French)* 'Gatekeeper'

Powa *(Native American)* 'Rich one'

Powell *(Celtic)* 'Alert' or 'son of Howell'

Prahlad *(Sanskrit)* 'Joy'

Pranjal *(Sanskrit)* 'Straight and simple'

Pravat *(Thai)* 'History'

Prentice *(Anglo-Saxon)* 'A learner or apprentice'
Prentiss

Prentiss *see* Prentice

Prescot *see* Prescott

Prescott *(Anglo-Saxon)* 'From the priest's house'
Prescot

Preston *(Anglo-Saxon)* 'From the priest's farm'

Preweet *see* Prewitt

Prewet *see* Prewitt

Prewett *see* Prewitt

Prewit *see* Prewitt

Prewitt *(French)* 'Little valiant warrior'
Prewet, Prewett, Prewit, Pruitt

Price *(Celtic)* 'Son of a loving man'

Primo *(Latin)* 'The first-born son'

Prince *(Latin)* 'Chief'

Prior *(Latin)* 'The Father Superior, the Head of the Monastery'
Pryor

Probus *(Latin)* 'Honest'

Proctor *(Latin)* 'The administrator'

Prosper *(Latin)* 'Fortunate'

Pruitt *see* Prewitt

Pryor *see* Prior

Purcell *see* Percival

Purdy *(Hindi)* 'Recluse'

Purvis *(English)* 'To provide food'

Putnam *(Anglo-Saxon)* 'From the pit estate'

Pwyll *(Welsh)* 'Prudence'

BOYS

Qabil *(Arabic)* 'Able'

Qadim *(Arabic)* 'Ancient'

Qadir *(Arabic)* 'Powerful'

Quemby *see* Quimby

Quenby *see* Quimby

Quennel *(French)* 'One who lives by the little oak'

Quent *see* Quentin

Quentin *(Latin)* 'The fifth born'
Quent, Quinton, Quintin, Quintus

Quigley *(Gaelic)* 'Distaff'

Quillan *(Gaelic)* 'Cub'

Quillon *(Latin)* 'Sword'

Quimby *(Norse)* 'From the woman's estate'
Quemby, Quenby, Quinby

Quinby *see* Quimby

Quincy *(French/Latin)* 'From the fifth son's estate'

Quinlan *(Gaelic)* 'The well formed one'. One with the body of an Adonis

Quinn *(Gaelic)* 'Wise and intelligent' *see also* Conan

Quintin *see* Quentin

Quinton *see* Quentin

Quintus *see* Quentin

Rab *see* Robert

Rabbi *see* Rabi

Rabbie *see* Robert

Rabby *see* Robert

Rabi *(Arabic)*
Rabbi

Race *see* Horace

Rachid *(Arabic)* 'Wise'

Rad *(Anglo-Saxon)*
'Counsellor, adviser' *see also* Radcliffe

Radbert *(Teutonic)*
'Brilliant counsellor'

Radborne *(Anglo-Saxon)*
'From the red stream'
Radbourn, Radbourne, Redbourn, Redbourne

Radbourn *see* Radborne

Radbourne *see* Radborne

Radcliff *see* Radcliffe

Radcliffe *(Anglo-Saxon)*
'From the red cliff'
Rad, Radcliff, Redcliff, Redcliffe

Radford *(Anglo-Saxon)*
'From the red ford'
Radvers, Redford, Redvers

Radi *(Arabic)* 'Content'

Radleigh *see* Radley

Radley *(Anglo-Saxon)*
'From the red meadow'
Radleigh, Redley, Ridley

Radman *(Slavic)* 'Joy'
Radmen

Radmen *see* Radman

Radmund *see* Redmond

Radnor *(Anglo-Saxon)*
'From the red shore'

Radolf *(Anglo-Saxon)* 'Wolf counsellor'. Wolf is used in the sense 'brave man'

Radvers *see* Radford

Rafael *see* Raphael

Rafaello *see* Raphael

Rafe *see* Raphael

Raff *see* Ralph or Raphael

Raffaello *see* Raphael

Rafferty *(Gaelic)*
'Prosperous and rich'

Raffi *(Arabic)* 'Exalting'
Raffin *see also* Raphael

Raffin *see* Raffi

Raghib *(Arabic)* 'Willing'

Raghnall *see* Reginald

Ragmar *(Teutonic)* 'Wise
warrior'

Ragnold *(Teutonic)*
'Powerful judge'

Raheem *(Arabic)* 'Kind'

Raimond *see* Raymond

Rainart *(German)* 'Strong
judgement'

Rainer *see* Raynor

Rainier *see* Raynor

Rajendra *(Sanskrit)* 'Royal
one'

Ralegh *see* Raleigh

Raleigh *(Anglo-Saxon)* 'One
who lives in the
meadow of the roe
deer'
Ralegh, Rawleigh,
Rawley

Ralf *see* Ralph

Ralph *(Anglo-Saxon)*
'Counsel wolf'
Raff, Ralf, Raoul, Raul,
Rolf, Rolph

Ralston *(Anglo-Saxon)* 'One
who lives on Ralph's
farm'

Rama *(Sanskrit)* 'One who
brings joy'

Rambert *(Teutonic)*
'Brilliant and mighty'

Ramiro *(Spanish)* 'Great
judge'

Ramon *see* Raymond

Ramsden *(Anglo-Saxon)*
'Ram's valley'

Ramsey *(Anglo-Saxon)*
'From Ram's island' or
'from the raven's island'

Rana *(Sanskrit)* 'Prince'

Rance *(African)* 'Borrowed
all'
Ransell

Rand *see* Randal

Randal *(Old English)*
'Shield wolf'
Rand, Randall, Randolf,
Randolph, Randy,
Ranulf, Rolf

Randall *see* Randal

Randolf *see* Randal

Randolph *see* Randal

Randy *see* Randal

Ranger *(French)* 'Keeper of the forest'. The gamekeeper who looked after the trees and the wildlife

Ranjit *(Sanskrit)* 'Victorious'

Rankin *(Anglo-Saxon)* 'Little shield'

Ransell *see* Rance

Ransford *(Anglo-Saxon)* 'From the raven's ford'

Ransley *(Anglo-Saxon)* 'From the raven's meadow'

Ransom *(Anglo-Saxon)* 'Shield warrior's son

Ranulf *see* Randal

Raoul *see* Ralph

Raphael *(Hebrew)* 'Healed by God' Rafael, Rafaello, Rafe, Raff, Raffaello, Rafi

Ras *see* Erasmus or Erastus

Rashid *(Arabic)* 'Director, pious'

Rasmus *see* Erasmus

Raul *see* Ralph

Ravi *(Sanskrit/Hindi)* 'The sun'

Rawleigh *see* Raleigh

Rawley *see* Raleigh

Rawlins *(French)* 'Son of the wolf counsellor'

Rawson *(Anglo-Saxon)* 'Son of the little wolf'

Ray *(French)* 'The sovereign' *see also* Raymond

Rayburn *(Old English)* 'From the deer brook'

Raymon *see* Raymond

Raymond *(Teutonic)* 'Wise protection' Raimond, Ramon, Ray, Raymon, Raymund, Reamonn

Raymund *see* Raymond

Raynard *see* Reynard

Raynold *see* Reginald

Raynor *(Scandinavian)* 'Mighty army' Rainer, Rainier

Read *see* Reade

Reade *(Anglo-Saxon)* 'The red-headed one' Read, Reed, Reede, Reid

Reading *(Anglo-Saxon)* 'Son of the red-haired one'
Redding

Reagan *see* Regan

Reagen *see* Regan

Reamonn *see* Raymond

Rearden *see* Riordan

Reardon *see* Riordan

Redbourn *see* Radborne

Redbourne *see* Radbourne

Redclife *see* Radcliffe

Redcliff *see* Radcliffe

Redding *see* Reading

Redford *see* Radford

Redley *see* Radley

Redman *(Anglo-Saxon)* 'Counsellor, advice-giver'

Redmond *(Anglo-Saxon)* 'Counsellor, protector, advisor'
Radmund, Redmund

Redmund *see* Redmond

Redpath *see* Ridpath

Redvers *see* Radford

Redwald *(Anglo-Saxon)* 'Mighty counsellor'

Reece *(Celtic)* 'The ardent one'. One who loves living
Rhett *see also* Rhys

Reed *see* Reade

Reede *see* Reade

Rees *see* Rhys

Reeve *(Anglo-Saxon)* 'The steward'. One who looked after a great lord's affairs

Reg *see* Reginald

Regan *(Gaelic)* 'Royalty, a king'
Reagan, Reagen, Regen

Regen *see* Regan

Reggie *see* Reginald

Reggy *see* Reginald

Reginald *(Teutonic)* 'Mighty and powerful ruler'
Naldo, Raghnall, Raynold, Reg, Reggie, Reggy, Reinhold, Renaldo, Renato, Renaud, Renault, Rene, Reynold, Rinaldo, Ron, Ronald, Ronnie, Ronny

Rehard *see* Reynard

Reid *see* Reade

Reilly *see* Riley

Reinhard *see* Reynard

Reinhart *(Teutonic)* 'Incorruptible'

Reinhold *see* Reginald

Remington *(Anglo-Saxon)* 'From the farm where the blackbirds sing'

Remus *(Latin)* 'Fast rower'. A speedy oarsman

Renaldo *see* Reginald

Renato *see* Reginald

Renaud *see* Reynard or Reginald

Renault *see* Reginald

Rene *see* Reginald

Renfred *(Anglo-Saxon)* 'Mighty and peaceful'. A peaceful warrior who could fight when necessary

Renfrew *(Celtic)* 'From the still river'

Rennard *see* Reynard

Renny *(Gaelic)* 'Little mighty and powerful' *see also* Reginald

Renshaw *(Anglo-Saxon)* 'From the forest of the ravens'

Renton *(Anglo-Saxon)* 'From the farm of the roe buck'

Renwick *(Teutonic)* 'Raven's nest'

Reuben *(Hebrew)* 'Behold a son' Rube, Ruben, Rubey, Ruby

Rex *(Latin)* 'The king'. The all-powerful monarch Rey, Roy

Rexford *(Anglo-Saxon)* 'From the king's ford'

Rey *see* Rex

Reyhan *(Arabic)* 'Favoured of God'

Reynard *(Teutonic)* 'Mighty courage' or 'the fox' Raynard, Rehard, Reinhard, Renaud, Rennard

Reynold *see* Reginald

Reza *(Arabic)* 'Resigned to life, accepting'

Rezon *(Hebrew)* 'Prince'

Rhain *(Welsh)* 'Lance'

Rhett *see* Reece

Rhodes *(Greek)* 'The place of roses'

Rhun *(Welsh)* 'Grand'

Rhydwyn *(Welsh)* 'One who lives by the white ford'

Rhys *(Celtic)* 'Hero' Reece, Rees

Ricard *see* Richard

Ricardo *see* Richard

Rich *see* Alaric or Richard

Richard *(Teutonic)* 'Wealthy, powerful one' Diccon, Dick, Dickie, Dickon, Dicky, Ricard, Ricardo, Rich, Richerd, Rick, Rickert, Rickie, Ricky, Riocard, Ritch, Ritchie

Richerd *see* Richard

Richie *see* Alaric

Richman *see* Richmond

Richmond *(Anglo-Saxon)* 'Powerful protector' Richman

Rick *see* Alaric, Aric, Cedric, Eric, Patrick, Richard or Roderick

Ricker *(Teutonic)* 'Powerful army'

Rickert *see* Richard

Rickie *see* Alaric, Aric, Cedric, Richard or Roderick

Rickward *(Anglo-Saxon)* 'Powerful guardian' Rickwood

Rickwood *see* Rickward

Ricky *see* Alaric, Aric, Cedric, Eric, Richard or Roderick

Ricy *see* Alaric

Riddock *(Gaelic)* 'From the barren field'

Rider *(Anglo-Saxon)* 'Knight, horse-rider' Ryder

Ridge *(Anglo-Saxon)* 'From the ridge'

Ridgeway *(Anglo-Saxon)* 'From the ridge road'

Ridgley *(Anglo-Saxon)* 'From the ridge meadow'

Ridley *see* Radley

Ridpath *(Anglo-Saxon)* 'From the red path' Redpath

Rigby *(Anglo-Saxon)* 'Valley of the ruler'

Rigg *(Anglo-Saxon)* 'From the ridge'

Rijul *(Sanskrit)* 'Innocent'

Riley *(Gaelic)* 'Valiant and war-like'
Reilly, Ryley

Rinaldo *see* Reginald

Ring *(Anglo-Saxon)* 'A ring'

Riocard *see* Richard

Riordan *(Gaelic)* 'Royal bard'
Rearden, Reardon

Rip *(Dutch)* 'Ripe, full-grown' *see also* Ripley or Robert

Ripley *(Anglo-Saxon)* 'From the valley of the echo'
Rip

Risley *(Anglo-Saxon)* 'From the brushwood meadow'

Riston *(Anglo-Saxon)* 'From the brushwood farm'

Ritch *see* Richard

Ritchie *see* Richard

Ritter *(Teutonic)* 'A knight'

Roald *(Teutonic)* 'Famous ruler'

Roan *(Anglo-Saxon)* 'From the rowan tree'
Rowan

Roarke *(Gaelic)* 'Famous ruler'
Rorke, Rourke, Ruark

Rob *see* Robert

Robbie *see* Robert

Robby *see* Robert

Robert *(Teutonic)* 'Bright, shining fame'. A man of brilliant reputation
Bob, Bobbie, Bobby, Rab, Rabbie, Rabby, Rip, Rob, Robbie, Robby, Roberto, Robin, Rupert, Ruprecht

Roberto *see* Robert

Robin *see* Robert

Robinson *(Anglo-Saxon)* 'Son of Robert'

Roc *see* Rock

Rochester *(Anglo-Saxon)* 'Camp on the rocks'

Rock *(Anglo-Saxon)* 'From the rock'
Roc, Rocky

Rockley *(Anglo-Saxon)* 'From the rocky meadow'
Rockly

Rockly *see* Rockley

Rockwell *(Anglo-Saxon)* 'From the rocky well'

Rocky *see* Rock

Rod *see* Roderick or Rodney

Rodd *see* Roderick

Roddie *see* Roderick or Rodney

Roddy *see* Roderick or Rodney

Roden *(Anglo-Saxon)* 'From the valley of the reeds'

Roderic *see* Roderick

Roderick *(Teutonic)* 'Famous wealthy ruler' Broderic, Broderick, Brodrick, Rick, Rickie, Ricky, Rod, Rodd, Roddie, Roddy, Roderic, Roderigo, Rodric, Rodrick, Rory, Rurik

Roderigo *see* Roderick

Rodge *see* Roger

Rodger *see* Roger

Rodhlann *see* Roland

Rodi *see* Rodney

Rodman *(Teutonic)* 'Famous hero' Rodmond, Rodmund

Rodmond *see* Rodman

Rodmund *see* Rodman

Rodney *(Teutonic)* 'Famous and renowned' Rod, Roddie, Roddy, Rodi

Rodolf *see* Rudolph

Rodolph *see* Rudolph

Rodric *see* Roderick

Rodrick *see* Roderick

Rodwell *(Anglo-Saxon)* 'From the Christian's well'

Roe *(Anglo-Saxon)* 'Roe deer'

Rog *see* Roger

Rogan *(Gaelic)* 'The red-haired one'

Roger *(Teutonic)* 'Famous spearman, renowned warrior' Rodge, Rodger, Rog, Rogerio

Rogerio *see* Roger

Roland *(Teutonic)* 'From the famed land' Lanny, Orlando, Rodhlann, Roley, Rollin, Rollo, Rowe, Rowland

Roley *see* Roland

Rolf *see* Ralph, Randal, Rudolph

Rolfe *see* Rudolph

Rollin *see* Roland

Rollo *see* Earl, Roland or Rudolph

Rolph see Ralph or Rudolph

Rolt (Teutonic) 'Power and fame'

Roma see Roman

Romain see Roman

Roman (Latin) 'From Rome'
Roma, Romain

Romaric (German)'Glorious king'

Rombaud (German) 'Bold glory'

Romeo (Latin) 'Man from Rome'

Romero (Latin) 'Wanderer'

Romford see Rumford

Romney (Celtic) 'Curving river'

Romolo (Latin/Spanish) 'Fame'

Romulus (Latin) 'Citizen of Rome'. According to mythology, Romulus and his twin brother Remus founded Rome

Ron see Aaron or Reginald

Ronald see Reginald

Ronan (Gaelic) 'Little seal'

Ronnie see Reginald

Ronny see Reginald

Ronson (Anglo-Saxon) 'Son of Ronald'

Rooney (Gaelic) 'The red one'. One with a ruddy complexion
Rowney, Ruan

Roosevelt (Old Dutch) 'From the rose field'. Sometimes used in compliment to two US presidents

Roper (Anglo-Saxon) 'Rope-maker'

Rorie see Rory

Rorke see Roarke

Rorry see Rory

Rory (Gaelic) 'Red king'
Rorie, Rorry, Ruaidhri
see also Roderick

Ros see Roscoe

Rosco see Roscoe

Roscoe (Scandinavian) 'From the deer forest'
Ros, Rosco, Roz

Roslin (French) 'Small red-haired one'
Roslyn, Rosselin, Rosslyn

Roslyn see Roslin

Ross *(Celtic)* 'From the peninsula' or *(Teutonic)* 'horse'

Rosselin *see* Roslin

Rosslyn *see* Roslin

Roswald *(Teutonic)* 'Mighty steed'
Roswall, Roswell

Roswall *see* Roswald

Roswell *see* Roswald

Roth *(Old German)* 'Red hair'

Rothwell *(Norse)* 'From the red well'

Rourke *see* Roarke

Routledge *see* Rutledge

Rover *(Anglo-Saxon)* 'A wanderer'

Rowan *(Gaelic)* 'Red haired'
Rowe, Rowen *see also* Roan

Rowe *see* Roland or Rowan

Rowell *(Anglo-Saxon)* 'From the deer well'

Rowen *see* Rowan

Rowland *see* Roland

Rowley *(Anglo-Saxon)* 'From the rough meadow'

Rowney *see* Rooney

Rowsan *(Anglo-Saxon)* 'Rowan's son'. Son of a red-haired man

Roxbury *(Anglo-Saxon)* 'From the fortress of the rock'

Roy *(Celtic)* 'Red haired' or 'the king' *see also* Conroy, Leroy or Rex

Royal *(French)* 'Regal one'

Royce *(Anglo-Saxon)* 'Son of the king'

Royd *(Norse)* 'From the forest clearing'

Roydon *(Norse)* 'One who lives on the rye hill'

Royston *(English)* Place in Yorkshire

Roz *see* Roscoe

Ruaidhri *see* Rory

Ruan *see* Rooney

Ruark *see* Roarke

Rube *see* Reuben

Ruben *see* Reuben

Rubey *see* Reuben

Ruby *see* Reuben

Ruck *(Anglo-Saxon)* 'The rock'. One with black hair

Rudd *(Anglo-Saxon)* 'Ruddy complexion'

Rudolf *see* Rudolph

Rudolph *(Teutonic)* 'Famous wolf' Dolf, Dolph, Rodolf, Rodolph, Rolf, Rolfe, Rollo, Rolph, Rudolf, Rudy

Rudy *see* Rudolph

Rudyard *(Anglo-Saxon)* 'From the red enclosure'

Ruelle *see* Rule

Rufe *see* Rufus

Ruff *(French)* 'The red-haired one' *see also* Rufus

Rufford *(Anglo-Saxon)* 'From the rough ford'

Ruford (Old English) 'From the red ford'

Rufus *(Latin)* 'Red haired' Griff, Griffin, Griffith, Rufe, Ruff *see also* Griffith

Rugby *(Anglo-Saxon)* 'From the rook estate'

Rule *(Latin)* 'The ruler' Ruelle

Rumford *(Anglo-Saxon)* 'From the wide ford' Romford

Rupert *see* Robert

Ruprecht *see* Robert

Rurik *see* Roderick

Rus *see* Russell

Rush *(French)* 'Red haired'

Rushford *(Anglo-Saxon)* 'From the rush ford'

Ruskin *(Teutonic)* 'Small red-haired one'

Russ *see* Cyrus or Russell

Russel *see* Russell

Russell *(Anglo-Saxon)* 'Red as a fox' Rus, Russ, Russel, Rusty

Russet *see* Rust

Rust *(Anglo-Saxon)* 'Red haired' Russet, Rusty

Rusty *see* Russell or Rust

Rutherford *(Anglo-Saxon)* 'From the cattle ford'

Rutland *(Norse)* 'From the stump land'

Rutledge *(Anglo-Saxon)* 'From the red pool' Routledge

Rutley *(Anglo-Saxon)* 'From the stump meadow'

Ryan *(Gaelic)* 'Small king'

Rycroft *(Anglo-Saxon)* 'From the rye field'

Ryder *see* Rider

Rye *(French)* 'From the riverbank'

Rylan *(Anglo-Saxon)* 'From the rye land'
Ryland

Ryland *see* Rylan

Ryle *(Anglo-Saxon)* 'From the rye hill'

Ryley *see* Riley

Ryman *(Anglo-Saxon)* 'The rye-seller'

Ryton *(Anglo-Saxon)* 'From the rye farm'

BOYS

Saadi *(Persian)* 'Wise one'

Sabas *(Hebrew)* 'Rest'

Sabeel *(Arabic)* 'The way'

Saber *(French)* 'A sword'

Sabin *(Latin)* 'Man from the Sabines'

Sadik *(Arabic)* 'Truthful'

Sadoc *(Hebrew)* 'Sacred'

Safford *(Anglo-Saxon)* 'From the willow ford'

Sahale *(Native American)* 'Above'

Sakima *(Native American)* 'King'

Saladin *(Arabic)* 'Goodness of the faith'

Salah *(Arabic)* 'Goodness'

Salim *(Arabic)* 'Safe, healthy, peace'

Salisbury *(Old English)* 'Fortified stronghold'

Salman *(Arabic)* 'Safe' or 'unharmed'

Salomon *(Hebrew)* 'Peaceful' *see also* Solomon

Salton *(Anglo-Saxon)* 'From the willow farm'

Salvador *(Latin)* 'The saviour' Salvadore, Salvator, Salvatore, Salvidor

Salvadore *see* Salvador

Salvator *see* Salvador

Salvatore *see* Salvador

Salvestro *(Italian)* 'Woody'

Salvidor *see* Salvador

Sam *see* Sampson or Samuel

Sama *(Sanskrit)* 'Tranquility'

Samborn *see* Sanborn

Samir *(Arabic)* 'Entertaining companion'

Sammy *see* Sampson or Samuel

345

Sampson *(Hebrew)* 'Sun's man'
Sam, Sammy, Samson, Sansom, Sim, Simpson, Simson

Samson *see* Sampson

Samuel *(Hebrew)* 'His name is God'
Sam, Sammie, Sammy

Samula *(Sanskrit)* 'Foundation'

Sanborn *(Anglo-Saxon)* 'From the sandy brook'
Samborn

Sanchia *(Spanish)* 'Holy'

Sancho *(Spanish)* 'Sincere and truthful'

Sander *see* Alexander

Sanders *(Anglo-Saxon)* 'Son of Alexander'
Sanderson, Sandie, Sandy, Saunders, Saunderson

Sanderson *see* Sanders

Sandford *(Anglo-Saxon)* 'Sandy ford'

Sandie *see* Alexander or Sanders

Sandy *see* Alexander, Lysander or Sanders

Sanford *(Anglo-Saxon)* 'From the sandy ford'

Sanjay *(Sanskrit)* 'Triumphant'

Sansom *see* Sampson

Santo *(Italian)* 'Saint-like'

Santon *(Anglo-Saxon)* 'From the sandy farm'

Sanuya *(Native American)* 'Cloud'

Sanzio *(Italian)* 'Holy'

Sardis *(Hebrew)* 'Prince of Joy'

Sarge *see* Sargent

Sargent *(Latin)* 'A military attendant'
Sarge, Sargie, Serge, Sergeant, Sergent, Sergio

Sargie *see* Sargent

Sarid *(Hebrew)* 'Survivor'

Sasha *see* Alexander

Saul *(Hebrew)* 'Called by God' Zollie, Zolly

Saunders *see* Alexander or Sanders

Saunderson *see* Sanders

Savero *(Arabic)* 'Bright one'

Savile *see* Saville

Saville *(French)* 'The willow estate'
Savile

Sawa *(Native American)* 'Rock'

Sawyer *(Anglo-Saxon)* 'A sawyer of wood'

Saxe *see* Saxon

Saxon *(Anglo-Saxon)* 'People of the swords' Saxe

Sayer *(Celtic)* 'Carpenter' Sayers, Sayre, Sayres

Sayers *see* Sayer

Sayre *see* Sayer

Sayres *see* Sayer

Scanlon *(Gaelic)* 'A snarer of hearts'

Schuyler *(Dutch)* 'A scholar, a wise man' or 'to shield'

Scipio *(Latin)* 'Walking stick'

Scot *see* Scott

Scott *(Celtic)* 'Tattooed warrior' or *(Latin)* 'from Scotland' Scot, Scottie, Scotty

Scottie *see* Scott

Scotty *see* Scott

Scoville *(French)* 'From the Scottish estate'

Scully *(Gaelic)* 'Town crier'. The bringer of news in the days before mass media

Seabert *(Anglo-Saxon)* 'Sea glorious' Seabright, Sebert

Seabright *see* Seabert

Seabrook *(Anglo-Saxon)* 'From a brook by the sea' Sebrook

Seadon *see* Seaton

Seager *see* Seger

Seain *see* John

Sealey *see* Seeley

Seamus *see* Jacob

Sean *see* John

Seann *see* John

Searle *(Teutonic)* 'Armed warrior' Searl

Seaton *(French)* 'From the Say's farm' Seadon, Seeton, Seetin, Seton

Seb *see* Sebastian

Sebald *(Old English)* 'Bold in victory'

Sebastian *(Latin)*
'Reverenced one'. An
august person
Seb, Sebastiano,
Sebastien

Sebastiano *see* Sebastian

Sebastien *see* Sebastian

Sebert *(Old English)*
'Famous for victory' *see
also* Seabert

Sebrook *see* Seabrook

Secundus *(Latin)* 'Second'

Sedgeley *see* Sedgley

Sedgley *(Anglo-Saxon)*
'From the swordsman's
meadow'
Sedgeley

Sedgwick *(Anglo-Saxon)*
'From the sword grass
place'

Seeley *(Anglo-Saxon)*
'Happy and blessed'
Sealey, Seely

Seely *see* Seeley

Seetin *see* Seaton

Segar *see* Seger

Seger *(Anglo-Saxon)* 'Sea
warrior'
Seager, Segar

Seigneur *see* Senior

Selby *(Teutonic)* 'From the
manor farm'

Selden *(Anglo-Saxon)* 'From
the valley of the willow
tree'
Seldon, Sheldon

Seldon *see* Selden

Selig *(Teutonic)* 'Blessed
happy one'

Selvac *(Celtic)* 'One who
has many cattle'

Selwin *see* Selwyn

Selwyn *(Teutonic)* 'Friend
at the manor house'
Selwin

Senior *(French)* 'Lord of
the manor'
Seigneur

Sennett *(French)* 'Old and
wise'. The all-knowing
seer

Seosaidh *see* Joseph

Septimus *(Latin)* 'Seventh-
born son'

Serge *see* Sargent

Sergeant *see* Sargent

Sergeant *see* Sargent

Sergent *see* Sargent

Sergio *see* Sargent

Serle *(Teutonic)* 'Bearer of
arms and weapons'

Seth *(Hebrew)* 'The appointed by God'

Seton *(Anglo-Saxon)* 'From the farm by the sea' *see also* Seaton

Seumas *see* Jacob

Severn *(Anglo-Saxon)* 'The boundary'

Sewald *see* Sewell

Sewall *see* Sewell

Seward *(Anglo-Saxon)* 'The sea defender'

Sewell *(Anglo-Saxon)* 'Sea powerful'
Sewald, Sewall, Siwald

Sexton *(Anglo-Saxon)* 'Sacristan'. A church official

Sextus *(Latin)* 'Sixth-born son'

Seyed *(Arabic)* 'Master'

Seymour *(Anglo-Saxon/ French)* 'From the moor by the sea'

Shadwell *(Anglo-Saxon)* 'From the well in the arbour'

Shafiq *(Arabic)* 'Kind, compassionate'

Shalom *(Hebrew)* 'Peace' Sholom

Shamus *(Irish)* Irish form of James *see also* James

Shanahan *(Gaelic)* 'The wise one'

Shanan *see* Shannon

Shandy *(Anglo-Saxon)* 'Little boisterous one'

Shane *(Celtic)* Celtic form of John *see also* John

Shanley *(Gaelic)* 'The venerable hero'

Shannon *(Gaelic)* 'Old wise one'
Shanan

Sharif *(Arabic)* 'Eminent' or 'honourable'

Shattuck *(Anglo-Saxon)* 'Little shad-fish'

Shaw *(Anglo-Saxon)* 'From the grove'

Shawn *see* John

Shay *see* Shea

Shea *(Gaelic)* 'Stately, courteous, and inventive person'. A man of many parts
Shay

Sheean *(Celtic)* 'Polite, courteous'

Sheehan *(Gaelic)* 'Peaceful one'

Sheffield *(Anglo-Saxon)* 'From the crooked field'

Shelby *(Anglo-Saxon)* 'From the estate on the cliff edge'

Sheldon *(Anglo-Saxon)* 'From the hill ledge' *see* also Selden

Shelley *(Anglo-Saxon)* 'From the meadow on the hill ledge'

Shelton *(Anglo-Saxon)* 'From the farm on the hill ledge'

Shem *(Hebrew)* 'Renown'

Shep *see* Shepard

Shepard *(Anglo-Saxon)* 'The sheep tender, the shepherd' Shep, Shepherd, Shepp, Sheppard, Shepperd, Sheppy

Shepherd *see* Shepard

Shepley *(Anglo-Saxon)* 'From the sheep meadow'

Shepp *see* Shepard

Sheppard *see* Shepard

Shepperd *see* Shepard

Sheppy *see* Shepard

Sherborne *(Anglo-Saxon)* 'From the clear stream' Sherbourn, Sherbourne, Sherburn, Sherburne

Sherbourn *see* Sherborne

Sherbourne *see* Sherborne

Sherburn *see* Sherborne

Sherburne *see* Sherborne

Sheridan *(Gaelic)* 'Wild savage'

Sherlock *(Anglo-Saxon)* 'White-haired man'

Sherman *(Anglo-Saxon)* 'Wool shearer, sheep shearer'

Sherwin *(Anglo-Saxon)* 'Loyal friend' or 'swift-footed' Sherwynd

Sherwood *(Anglo-Saxon)* 'Bright forest'

Sherwynd *see* Sherwin

Shing *(Chinese)* 'Victory'

Shipley *(Anglo-Saxon)* 'From the sheep meadow'

Shipton *(Anglo-Saxon)* 'From the sheep farm'

Sholom *see* Shalom

Sholto *(Gaelic)* 'The wild duck'

Si *see* Silas

Sian *see* John

Sid *see* Sidney

Siddell *(Anglo-Saxon)* 'From a wide valley'

Sidney *(French)* 'A follower of St Denis' or 'man from Sidon'
Sid, Syd, Sydney

Siegfrid *see* Sigfrid

Siegfried *see* Sigfrid

Sigerd *see* Sigurd

Sigfrid *(Teutonic)* 'Peace after victory'
Siegfried, Siegrid, Sigfried

Sigfried *see* Sigfrid

Sigismond *see* Sigmund

Sigismund *see* Sigmund

Sigmond *see* Sigmund

Sigmund *(Teutonic)* 'Victorious protector'
'Sigismond, Sigismund, Sigmond

Sigurd *(Scandinavian)* 'Victorious guardian'
Sigerd

Sigwald *(Teutonic)* 'Victorious ruler'

Silas *(Latin)* 'From the forest'
Si, Silvan, Silvano, Silvanus, Silvester, Sly, Sylvan, Sylvester

Silvan *see* Silas

Silvano *see* Silas

Silvanus *see* Silas

Silvester *see* Silas

Sim *see* Sampson or Simon

Simeon *see* Simon

Simon *(Hebrew)* 'One who hears'
Sim, Simeon, Siomonn, Ximenes

Simpson *see* Sampson

Simson *see* Sampson

Sinclair *(French)* 'From St Clair' or 'shining light'
St Clair

Siomonn *see* Simon

Siân *see* John

Sissil *see* Cecil

Siwald *see* Sewell

Siward *(Teutonic)* 'Conquering guardian'

Skeat *see* Skeets

Skeet *see* Skeets

Skeeter *see* Skeets

Skeets *(Anglo-Saxon)* 'The swift'
Skeat, Skeet, Skeeter

Skelly *(Gaelic)* 'Historian'

Skelton *(Anglo-Saxon)* 'From the farm on the hill ledge'

Skerry *(Scandinavian)* 'From the rocky island'

Skip *(Scandinavian)* 'Owner of the ship'
Skipp, Skippy

Skipp *see* Skip

Skippy *see* Skip

Skipton *(Anglo-Saxon)* 'From the sheep farm'

Slade *(Anglo-Saxon)* 'Valley dweller'

Slaven *see* Slevin

Slavin *see* Slevin

Sleven *see* Slevin

Slevin *(Gaelic)* 'The mountain climber'
Slaven, Slavin, Sleven

Sloan *(Gaelic)* 'Warrior'
Sloane

Sloane *see* Sloan

Sly *see* Silas

Smedley *(Anglo-Saxon)* 'From the flat meadow'
Smedly

Smedly *see* Smedley

Smith *(Anglo-Saxon)* 'The blacksmith'

Snowden *(Anglo-Saxon)* 'From the snowy hill'. Man from the snowcapped mountains

Socrates *(Greek)* 'Self-restrained'

Sol *(Latin)* 'The sun' *see also* Solomon

Solamon *see* Solomon

Sollie *see* Solomon

Solly *see* Solomon

Soloman *see* Solomon

Solomon *(Hebrew)* 'Wise and peaceful'
Salomon, Sol, Solamon, Sollie, Solly, Soloman, Zollie, Zolly

Solon *(Greek)* 'Wise man'. Greek form of Solomon

Somerled *(Teutonic)* 'Summer wanderer'

Somerset *(Anglo-Saxon)* 'From the summer place'. The place where wanderers rested for the summer

Somerton *(Anglo-Saxon)*
'From the summer
farm'

Somerville *(Anglo-Saxon)*
'From the summer
estate'
Sommerville

Sommerville *see*
Somerville

Sonny *see* Bronson or
Tyson

Sophocles *(Greek)* 'Glory of
wisdom'

Sorrel *(French)* 'With
brownish hair'

Southwell *(Anglo-Saxon)*
'From the south well'

Spalding *(Anglo-Saxon)*
'From the split
meadow'
Spaulding

Spangler *(Teutonic)* 'The
tinsmith

Spark *(Anglo-Saxon)* 'Gay
gallant'. The man about
town'

Spaulding *see* Spalding

Speed *(Anglo-Saxon)*
'Success, prosperity'

Spence *see* Spencer

Spencer *(French)*
'Shopkeeper, dispenser
of provisions'
Spence, Spenser

Spenser *see* Spencer

Spiro *(Greek)* 'Breath of the
gods'

Sprague *(Old French)*
'Lively'

Sproule *(Anglo-Saxon)*
'Energetic, active
person'
Sprowle

Sprowle *see* Sproule

Squire *(Anglo-Saxon)*
'Knight's shield-bearer'

St Clair *see* Sinclair

St John *(English)* A
contraction of Saint
John

Stacey *(Latin)* 'Prosperous
and stable'
Stacy

Stacy *see* Stacey

Staffard *see* Stafford

Stafford *(Anglo-Saxon)*
'From the ford by the
landing place'
Staffard

Stamford *(Anglo-Saxon)*
'From the stony
crossing'
Stanford

Stan *see* Stanislaus or
Stanley

Stanberry *see* Stanbury

Stanbury *(Anglo-Saxon)*
'From a stone fortress'
Stanberry

Stancliffe *(Anglo-Saxon)*
'From the rocky cliff'
Stancliff, Standcliff,
Standcliffe

Standcliff *see* Stancliffe

Standcliffe *see* Stancliffe

Standish *(Anglo-Saxon)*
'From the stony park'

Stanfield *(Anglo-Saxon)*
'From the stony field'

Stanford *see* Stamford

Stanhope *(Anglo-Saxon)*
'From the stony hollow'

Stanislas *see* Stanislaus

Stanislaus *(Slavic)* 'Stand
of glory'
Aineislis, Stan,
Stanislas, Stanislav,
Stanislaw

Stanislav *see* Stanislaus

Stanislaw *see* Stanislaus

Stanleigh *see* Stanley

Stanley *(Anglo-Saxon)*
'From the stony
meadow' or *(Slavic)*
'pride of the camp'
Stan, Stanleigh, Stanly

Stanly *see* Stanley

Stanton *(Anglo-Saxon)*
'From the rocky lake'
or 'from the stony farm'

Stanway *(Anglo-Saxon)*
'From the stony road'

Stanwick *(Anglo-Saxon)*
'From the stony village'

Stanwood *(Anglo-Saxon)*
'From the stony forest'

Starling *(Anglo-Saxon)* 'The
starling'

Starr *(Anglo-Saxon)* 'A star'

Staton *(Teutonic)* 'One who
lives in the stone
house'

Stavros *(Greek)* 'Cross'

Stearn *see* Sterne

Stearne *see* Sterne

Stedman *(Anglo-Saxon)*
'Farm owner'. One who
owns the land he tills

Stefan *see* Stephen

Steffen *see* Stephen

Stein *(Teutonic)* 'The stone'

Stephanus *see* Stephen

Stephen *(Greek)* 'The crowned one'. A man who wears the victor's laurel wreath
Etienne, Stefan, Steffen, Stephanus, Stephenson, Steve, Steven, Stevenson, Stevie

Stephenson *see* Stephen

Sterling *(Teutonic)* 'Good honest, worthy'
Stirling

Stern *see* Sterne

Sterne *(Anglo-Saxon)* 'The austere one, an ascetic'
Stearn, Stearne, Stern

Steve *see* Stephen

Steven *see* Stephen

Stevenson *see* Stephen

Stevie *see* Stephen

Stew *see* Stewart

Steward *see* Stewart

Stewart *(Anglo-Saxon)* 'The steward'. Name of the Royal House of Scotland
Stew, Steward, Stu, Stuart

Stiless *see* Styles

Stillman *(Anglo-Saxon)* 'Quiet and gentle man'
Stilman

Stilman *see* Stillman

Stinson *(Anglo-Saxon)* 'Son of stone'

Stirling *see* Sterling

Stockley *(Anglo-Saxon)* 'From the cleared meadow'

Stockton *(Anglo-Saxon)* 'From the farm in the clearing'

Stockwell *(Anglo-Saxon)* 'From the well in the clearing'

Stoddard *(Anglo-Saxon)* 'The horse-keeper'

Stoke *(Anglo-Saxon)* 'A village'

Storm *(Anglo-Saxon)* 'The tempest'

Storr *(Scandinavian)* 'Great man'

Stowe *(Anglo-Saxon)* 'From the place'

Strahan *(Gaelic)* 'The poet'

Stratford *(Anglo-Saxon)* 'The street crossing the ford'

Strephon (*Greek*) 'One who turns'
Strephonn, Strepphon

Strephonn *see* Strephon

Strepphon *see* Strephon

Strothers *see* Struthers

Stroud (*Anglo-Saxon*) 'From the thicket'

Struthers (*Gaelic*) 'From the rivulet'
Strothers

Stu *see* Stewart

Stuart *see* Stewart

Styles (*Anglo-Saxon*) 'From the dwelling by the stile'
Stiles

Suffield (*Anglo-Saxon*) 'From the south field'

Sujit (*Sanskrit*) 'Winner'

Sulien (*Welsh*) 'Sun-born'

Sullie *see* Sullivan

Sullivan (*Gaelic*) 'Man with black eyes'
Sullie, Sully

Sully (*Anglo-Saxon*) 'From the south meadow' *see also* Sullivan

Sulwyn (*Welsh*) 'Fair from the sun'

Sumitra (*Sanskrit*) 'Good friend'

Sumner (*Latin*) 'One who summons'. The church official who summoned the congregation to prayer

Sunil (*Sanskrit*) 'Very dark blue'

Sunny (*English*) 'Cheery'

Supriya (*Sanskrit*) 'Loved'

Surinder (*Hindi*) 'Mightiest of the gods'

Sushil (*Sanskrit*) 'Well behaved'

Sutcliff *see* Sutcliffe

Sutcliffe (*Anglo-Saxon*) 'From the south cliff'
Sutcliff

Sutherland (*Scandinavian*) 'From a southern land'

Sutton (*Anglo-Saxon*) 'From the south town'

Sven (*Scandinavian*) 'Youth'

Swain (*Anglo-Saxon*) 'Herdsman' or 'Knight's attendant'
Swayne, Sweyn

Swami (*Sanskrit*) 'Master'

Swayne *see* Swain

Sweeney *(Gaelic)* 'Little hero'

Sweyn *see* Swain

Swinton *(Anglo-Saxon)* 'From the pig farm'

Swithin *(Old English)* 'Strong' Swithun

Swithun *see* Swithin

Syd *see* Sidney

Sydney *see* Sidney

Syena *(Sanskrit)* 'Falcon'

Sylvan *see* Silas

Sylvester *see* Silas

Symington *(Anglo-Saxon)* 'From Simon's farm'

Tab *(Teutonic)* 'The drummer'
Tabb, Tabby, Taber

Tabb *see* Tab

Tabby *see* Tab

Taber *see* Tab

Tabib (Turkish) 'Physician'

Tabor *(Turkish)* 'The encampment'

Tad *see* Tadd or Thaddeus

Tadd *(Celtic)* 'Father'
Tad *see also* Thaddeus and Theodore

Taddeo *see* Thaddeus

Taddy *see* Thaddeus

Tadeas *see* Tadeo

Tadeo *(Spanish/Latin)* 'Praise'
Tadeas

Taffy *(Celtic)* Welsh form of David

Tafryn *(Welsh)* 'Brow of the hill'

Taggart *(Gaelic)* 'Son of the prelate'

Tahurer *(English)* 'Drummer'

Taiesin *(Welsh)* 'Radiant brow'

Taillefer *see* Telford

Tailor *see* Taylor

Tait *see* Tate

Tait *(Scandinavian)* 'Cheerful'

Tal *(English)* 'Tail'

Talbert *see* Talbot

Talbot *(French)* 'The looter'
Talbert

Talfryn *(Welsh)* 'Brow of the hill'

Taliesin *(Welsh)* 'Radiant brow'

Tallon *(English)* 'Tall'

Talmadge *(English)* 'Tall'

Talon *(English)* 'Claw'

Tam *see* Thomas

Tama *(Native American)* 'Thunderbolt'

Tamal *(Sanskrit)* 'Tree with the black bark'

Tamar *(Hebrew)* 'Palm tree'

Tamas *see* Thomas

Tammany *see* Thomas

Tammy *see* Thomas

Tamtun *(English)* 'From the quiet river farm'

Tancred *(Old German)* 'Thoughtful adviser'

Tangwyn *(Welsh)* 'Blessed peace'
Tanigwyn

Tanigwyn *see* Tangwyn

Tann *see* Tanner

Tanner *(Anglo-Saxon)* 'Leather worker'
Tann, Tannere

Tannere *see* Tanner

Tanton *(Anglo-Saxon)* 'From the quiet river farm'

Tarak *(Sanskrit)* 'Protector'

Tareesh *(Sanskrit)* 'An expert' or 'the ocean'

Tarik *(Sanskrit)* 'He who crosses the river of life'

Tariq *(Arabic)* 'Conqueror'

Tarleton *(Anglo-Saxon)* 'Thor's farm'

Taro *(Japanese)* 'First-born male'

Taron *see* Tarrin

Tarrance *(Latin)* Roman clan name

Tarrant *(Old Welsh)* 'Thunder'

Tarrin *(English)* 'Man of the earth'
Taron, Terran, Terron

Tarron *see* Tarrin

Taru *(Sanskrit)* 'Tree'

Tarun *(Sanskrit)* 'Young'

Tassa *(English)* 'Born at Christmas'

Tate *(Anglo-Saxon)* 'Cheerful'
Tait, Tayt, Tayte, Teyte

Tavey *see* Octavius

Tavis *(Celtic)* 'Son of David'. Scottish form of Thomas
Tavish, Tevis

Tavish *see* Tavis

Tay *(Welsh)* Form of David

Tayib *(Indian)* 'Good' or 'delicate'

Taylan *(English)* 'Tailor'
Taylon, Taylor, Tayson

Taylon *see* Taylan

Taylor *(Anglo-Saxon)* 'The Tailor'
Tailor *see also* Taylan

Tayson *see* Taylan

Tayt *see* Tate

Tayte *see* Tate

Teador *see* Theodore

Teague *(Celtic)* 'The poet'

Tearlach *see* Charles

Tearle *(Anglo-Saxon)* 'Stern, severe one'

Tecwyn *(Welsh)* 'Fair and white'

Ted *see* Edgar, Edward, Theodore or Theodoric

Teddie *see* Edgar, Edward, Theodore or Theodoric

Teddy *see* Edgar, Edward, Theodore or Theodoric

Tedman *(Teutonic)* 'Protector of the nation'

Tedmond *(Anglo-Saxon)* 'King's protector'

Tedric *see* Theodoric

Tejeshwar *(Sanskrit)* 'The sun'

Tejpal *(Sanskrit)* 'Glorious'

Telfer *see* Telford

Telfor *see* Telford

Telford *(French)* 'Iron hewer'
Taillefer, Telfer, Telfor, Telfour

Telfour *see* Telford

Templeton *(Anglo-Saxon)* 'Town of the temple'

Tenison *see* Tennyson

Tennison *see* Tennyson

Tennyson *(Anglo-Saxon)* 'Son of Dennis'
Tenison, Tennison

Teodorico *see* Theodoric

Terell *see* Terrill

Terence *(Latin)* 'Smooth, polished and tender'
Terencio, Terrene, Terry, Torrance

Terencio *see* Terence

Terrall *(English)* 'Powerful'

Terran *see* Tarrin

Terrel *see* Terrill

Terrell *see* Terrill or Thorald

Terrene *see* Terence

Terrill *(Teutonic)* 'Follower of Thor'
Terell, Terrel, Terrell, Tirell, Tirrel, Tirrell, Tyrell, Tyrrel, Tyrrell

Terry *see* Terence

Tevis *see* Tavis

Teyen *(Anglo-Saxon)* 'From the enclosure'

Teyte *see* Tate

Thacher *(English)* 'Roofer'
Thacker, Thackere

Thacker *see* Thacher

Thackere *see* Thacher

Thad *see* Thaddeus

Thaddeus *(Greek)*
'Courageous and stout
hearted' or *(Hebrew)*
'praise to God'
Tad, Thad, Taddy,
Taddeo

Thaine *(Anglo-Saxon)*
'Warrior attendant'
Thane, Thayne

Thane *see* Taine

Thatch *see* Thatcher

Thatcher *(Anglo-Saxon)* 'A
thatcher of roofs'
Thatch, Thaxter

Thaw *(Anglo-Saxon)* 'Ice-
breaker'

Thaxter *see* Thatcher

Thayer *(Greek)* 'The
nation's army'

Thayne *see* Taine

Themistocles *(Greek)* 'Law
and right'

Theo Diminutive of all
names beginning with
'Theo'

Theobald *(Teutonic)* 'Bold
leader of the people'
Thibaud, Thibaut,
Tibbald, Tioboid, Tybalt

Theodore *(Greek)* 'Gift of
God'
Dore, Feodor, Feodore,
Teador, Ted, Teddie,
Teddy, Tudor

Theodoric *(Teutonic)* 'Ruler
of the people'
Derek, Derk, Derrick,
Dietrich, Dirk, Ted,
Teddie, Teddy, Tedric,
Teodorico, Theodorick

Theodorick *see* Theodoric

Theodosius *(Greek)* 'God
given'

Theomund *(English)*
'National protector'

Theon *(Greek)* 'Godly man'

Theophilus *(Greek)*
'Divinely loved'

Theron *(Greek)* 'The
hunter'

Thibaud *(French)* 'People's
prince' *see also*
Theobald

Thibaut *see* Theobald

Thom *see* Thomas

Thomas *(Hebrew)* 'The twin'. The devoted brother
Massey, Tam, Tamas, Tammany, Tammy, Thom, Tom, Tomas, Tomaso, Tomkin, Tomlin, Tommy

Thor *(Scandinavian)* 'God of thunder'. The ancient Norse god
Thorin, Tor, Turpin, Tyrus

Thorald *(Scandinavian)* 'Thor's ruler'. One who ruled in the name of the thunder-god
Terrell, Torald, Tyrell
see also Thorold

Thorbert *(Scandinavian)* 'Brilliance of Thor'
Torbert

Thorburn *(Scandinavian)* 'Thor's bear'
Torburn

Thorfinn *see* Torin

Thorin *see* Thor

Thorley *(Anglo-Saxon)* 'From Thor's meadow'
Torley, Thurleah, Thurleigh

Thormond *see* Thormund

Thormund *(Anglo-Saxon)* 'Protected by Thor'
Thormond, Thurmond, Tormond, Tormund

Thorn *see* Thornton

Thorndyke *(Anglo-Saxon)* 'From the thorny ditch'

Thorne *(Anglo-Saxon)* 'From the thorn tree'

Thorneley *see* Thornley

Thornely *see* Thornley

Thornley *(Anglo-Saxon)* 'From the thorny meadow'
Thorneley, Thornely, Thornly

Thornly *see* Thornley

Thornton *(Anglo-Saxon)* 'From the thorny place'
Thorn

Thorold *(Old English)* 'Thor's strength'

Thorp *see* Thorpe

Thorpe *(Anglo-Saxon)* 'From the small village'
Thorp

Thorstein *see* Thurston

Thurleah *see* Thorley

Thurleigh *see* Thorley

Thurlow *(Anglo-Saxon)* 'From Thor's hill'

Thurmond *see* Thormund

Thurstan *see* Thurston

Thurston *(Anglo-Saxon)* 'Thor's jewel' Thorstein, Thurstan

Tibbald *see* Theobald

Tibor *(Slavonic)* 'Holy place'

Tierman *(Gaelic)* 'Lord and master' Tierney

Tiernan *(Celtic)* 'Kingly'

Tierney *see* Tierman

Tiffany *(French)* 'The divine appearance of God' Tiphani

Tilden *(Anglo-Saxon)* 'From the fertile valley'

Tiler *see* Tyler

Tilford *(Anglo-Saxon)* 'From the good man's farm'

Tim *see* Timothy

Timmie *see* Timothy

Timmy *see* Timothy

Timon *(Greek)* 'Honour, reward, value'

Timoteo *see* Timothy

Timotheus *see* Timothy

Timothy *(Greek)* 'Honouring God' Tim, Timmie, Timmy, Timoteo, Timotheus, Tiomoid, Tymon

Tioboid *see* Theobald or Tobias

Tiomoid *see* Timothy

Tirell *see* Terrill

Tirrel *see* Terrill

Tirrell *see* Terrill

Tirtha *(Sanskrit)* 'Holy place'

Tito *see* Titus

Titus *(Greek)* 'Of the giants' or *(Latin)* 'saved' Tito

Tobe *see* Tobias

Tobiah *see* Tobias

Tobias *(Hebrew)* 'God is good' Tioboid, Tobe, Tobiah, Tobit, Toby

Tobit *see* Tobias

Toby *see* Tobias

Todd *(Latin)* 'The fox'

Toft *(Anglo-Saxon)* 'A small farm'

Toland *see* Tolland

Tolland *(Anglo-Saxon)* 'One who owns taxed land' Toland

Tolman *(Old English)* 'Tax collector'

Tom *see* Thomas

Tomas *see* Thomas

Tomaso *see* Thomas

Tomkin *(Anglo-Saxon)* Diminutive of Thomas Tomlin *see* Thomas

Tomlin *see* Tomkin or Thomas

Tommy *see* Thomas

Tony *see* Anthony or Dalton

Toole *(Celtic)* 'Lordly, noble'

Tor *see* Thor

Torald *see* Thorald

Torbert *see* Thorbert

Torburn *see* Thorburn

Torey *(Anglo-Saxon)* 'From the craggy hills' Tory

Torin *(Gaelic)* 'Chief' Thorfinn

Torley *see* Thorley

Tormey *(Gaelic)* 'Thunder spirit' Tormy

Tormond *see* Thormund

Tormund *see* Thormund

Tormy *see* Tormey

Torquil *(Teutonic)* 'Thor's pledge'

Torr *(Anglo-Saxon)* 'From the tower'

Torrance *(Gaelic)* 'From the little hills' *see also* Terence

Torrey *(Celtic)* 'One who lives by the tower'

Tory *see* Torey

Tostig *(Welsh)* 'Sharp'

Towley *see* Townley

Townley *(Anglo-Saxon)* 'From the town meadow' Towley, Townley, Townly

Townly *see* Townley

Townsend *(Anglo-Saxon)* 'From the end of the town'

Tracy *(Latin)* 'Bold and courageous'

Trahearn *see* Trahern

Trahearne *see* Trahern

Trahern *(Celtic)* 'Iron strength'
Trahearn, Trahearne, Trehearn, Trehearne, Trehern

Travers *(Latin)* 'From the crossroads'
Travis, Travus

Travis *see* Travers

Travon *see* Trevelyan

Travus *see* Travers

Tredway *(Anglo-Saxon)* 'Mighty warrior'

Trefor *see* Trevor

Trehearn *see* Trahern

Trehearne *see* Trahern

Trehern *see* Trahern

Trelawney *see* Trelawny

Trelawny *(Cornish)* 'From the church town'
Trelawney

Tremaine *see* Tremayne

Tremayne *(Celtic)* 'From the house in the rock'
Tremaine

Trent *(Latin)* 'The torrent'

Trevan *see* Trevelyan

Trevelyan *(Celtic)* 'From Elian's farm'. An old Cornish name
Trevan, Treven, Trevian, Trevion, Trevyan, Trevyon

Treven *see* Trevelyan

Trevian *see* Trevelyan

Trevion *see* Trevelyan

Trevor *(Gaelic)* 'Prudent, wise and discreet'
Trefor

Trevyan *see* Trevelyan

Trevyon *see* Trevelyan

Trey *(Middle English)* 'The third'

Trigg *(Scandinavian)* 'True and faithful'

Trigun *(Sanskrit)* 'Three-dimensional'

Trip *see* Tripp

Tripp *(Anglo-Saxon)* 'The traveller'
Trip, Tripper

Tripper *see* Tripp

Tristan *(Celtic)* 'The noisy one'
Drostan, Tristen, Tristin

Tristen *see* Tristan

Tristin *see* Tristan

Tristram *(Celtic)* 'The sorrowful one'. Do not confuse with Tristan

Trowbridge *(Anglo-Saxon)* 'From the tree bridge'

Troy *(French)* 'From the land of the people with curly hair'

True *(Anglo-Saxon)* 'Faithful and loyal'

Trueman *see* Truman

Truesdale *(Anglo-Saxon)* 'The home of the beloved one' Trusdale

Truman *(Anglo-Saxon)* 'A faithful follower'. Trueman, Trumane

Trumane *see* Truman

Trumble *(Anglo-Saxon)* 'Bold and strong'

Trusdale *see* Truesdale

Tucker *(Anglo-Saxon)* 'Cloth thickener' *see also* Fuller

Tudor *see* Theodore

Tufan *(Sanskrit)* 'Storm'

Tuhin *(Sanskrit)* 'Snow'

Tulio *(Spanish)* 'Lively'

Tully *(Gaelic)* 'Obedient to the will of God'

Tung *(Chinese)* 'Everyone'

Tupper *(Anglo-Saxon)* One who reared and tended sheep

Turner *(Latin)* 'Lathe worker'

Turpin *(Scandinavian)* 'Thunder-like'. Finnish form of Thor *see also* Thor

Tushar *(Sanskrit)* 'Snow'

Tut *(Arabic)* 'Strong and courageous'. Used to honour the Ancient Egyptian king Tutankamen

Tuxford *(Scandinavian)* 'From the ford of the champion spear-thrower'

Twain *(Anglo-Saxon)* 'Divided in two'. A co-heir

Twitchell *(Anglo-Saxon)* 'From a narrow passageway'

Twyford *(Anglo-Saxon)* 'From the twin river'

Ty *see* Tyler or Tyson

Tybalt *see* Theobald

Tye *(Anglo-Saxon)* 'From the enclosure'

Tyler *(Anglo-Saxon)* 'Maker of tiles or bricks'
Tiler, Ty

Tymon *see* Timothy

Tynam *(Gaelic)* 'Dark, grey'
Tynan

Tynan *see* Tynam

Tyree *(Scottish)* Island dweller

Tyrell *see* Terrill or Thorald

Tyrone *(Greek)* 'The sovereign'

Tyrrel *see* Terrill

Tyrrell *see* Terrill

Tyrus *see* Thor

Tyson *(Teutonic)* 'Son of the German'
Sonny, Ty

Udale *see* Udell

Udall *see* Udell

Udell *(Anglo-Saxon)* 'From the yew tree valley' Udale, Udall

Udo *(Latin)* 'Hot and humid'

Udolf *(Anglo-Saxon)* 'Prosperous wolf'

Uilleam *see* William

Uilliam *see* William

Uillioc *see* Ulysses

Uland *(Teutonic)* 'Noble land'

Ulbrecht *(German)* 'Noble splendour'

Ulfred *(Anglo-Saxon)* 'Peace of the wolf'

Ulger *(Anglo-Saxon)* 'Courageous wolf' or 'spearman'

Ulick *see* Ulysses

Ulises *see* Ulysses

Ullock *(Anglo-Saxon)* 'Sport of the wolf'

Ulmar *see* Ulmer

Ulmer *(Anglo-Saxon)* 'Famous wolf' Ulmar

Ulric *(Teutonic)* 'Ruler of all' Alric, Ulrich *see also* Alaric

Ulrich *see* Alaric or Ulric

Ulrick *see* Alaric

Ultann *(Welsh)* 'Saintly'

Ulysses *(Greek)* 'The angry one' or 'the hater' Uillioc, Ulick, Ulises

Umberto *see* Humbert

Umed *(Sanskrit)* 'Hope'

Uno *(Latin)* 'The one'

Unwin *(Anglo-Saxon)* 'The enemy'

Upton *(Anglo-Saxon)* 'From the hill farm'

Upwood *(Anglo-Saxon)* 'From the hill forest'

Urban *(Latin)* 'From the city'. A townsman Urbano

Urbano *see* Urban

Uri *see* Uriah

Uriah *(Hebrew)* 'The Lord is my light' or 'the Lord's light'
Uri, Urias, Uriel, Yuri

Urias *see* Uriah

Uriel *see* Uriah

Urien *(Welsh)* 'Town-born'

Urlwin *(Teutonic)* 'Noble friend'

Urson *see* Orson

Ushakanta *(Sanskrit)* 'The sun'

Usman *(Sanskrit)* *see* Osman

Utsav *(Sanskrit)* 'Celebration'

Uttam *(Sanskrit)* 'The best'

Uziel (Hebrew) 'Strength' or 'a mighty force'

Uzziah *(Hebrew)* 'Might of the Lord'

Vachel *(French)* 'Little cow'

Vadim *see* Vladimir

Vail *(Anglo-Saxon)* 'From the valley'
Vale, Valle

Vailintin *see* Valentine

Val *(Teutonic)* 'Mighty power'. Also diminutive for any name beginning with 'Val'

Valarian *(Latin)* 'Healthy'
Valarius

Valarius *see* Valarian

Valdemar *(Teutonic)* 'Famous ruler'
Valdimar, Waldemar

Valdimar *see* Valdemar

Vale *see* Vail

Valente *see* Valentine

Valentin *see* Valentine

Valentine *(Latin)* 'Healthy, strong and valorous'
Vailintin, Valente, Valentin, Valentino, Valiant

Valentino *see* Valentine

Valerian *(Latin)* 'Strong and powerful' or 'belonging to Valentine'

Valiant *see* Valentine

Valle *see* Vail

Vallis *(French)* 'The Welshman'

Van *(Dutch)* 'From' or 'of'. More generally used as a prefix to a surname, but occasionally found on its own as a forename

Vance *(Anglo-Saxon)* 'From the grain barn'

Varden *(Anglo-Saxon)* 'From a green hill'
Vardon, Verden, Verdon

Vardon *see* Varden

Varian *(Latin)* 'Changeable'

Varick *(Teutonic)* 'Protecting ruler'

Vasileior *see* Vasilis

Vasilis *(Greek)* 'Knightly, magnificent'
Vasileior, Vasos

Vasos *see* Vasilis

Vassily *(Slavic)*
'Unwavering protector'
see also Basil

Vaughan *(Celtic)* 'The
small one'
Vaughn, Vawn

Vaughn *see* Vaughan

Vawn *see* Vaughan

Venn *(Old English)*
'Handsome'

Verden *see* Varden

Verdon *see* Varden

Vere *(Latin)* 'Faithful and
true'. The loyal one

Vergil *see* Virgil

Verill *see* Verrell

Vern *see* Vernon

Verne *see* Vernon

Verner *see* Vernon or
Warner

Verney *(French)* 'From the
alder grove'

Vernon *(Latin)* 'Growing,
flourishing'. Like trees
in spring
Vern, Verne, Verner

Verral *see* Verrell

Verrell *(French)* 'The
honest one'
Verill, Verrall, Verrill

Verrill *see* Verrell

Vic *see* Victor

Vick *see* Victor

Victoir *see* Victor

Victor *(Latin)* 'The
conqueror'
Vic, Vick, Victoir,
Vince, Vincent, Vinny,
Vittorio

Vidyut *(Sanskrit)*
'Lightning'

Vijay *(Sanskrit)* 'Victor,
victory'

Vince *see* Victor

Vincent *see* Victor

Vinny *see* Victor

Vinson *(Anglo-Saxon)* 'Son
of Vincent'

Viresh *(Sanskrit)* 'Brave
leader'

Virge *see* Virgil

Virgie *see* Virgil

Virgil *(Latin)* 'Staff-bearer'
or 'strong and
flourishing'
Vcrgil, Virge, Virgie,
Virgy

Virgy *see* Virgil

Vismay *(Sanskrit)* 'Surprise'

Vito *(Latin)* 'Alive, vital'

Vittorio *see* Victor

Vivian *see* Vivien

Vivien *(Latin)* 'Lively one' Ninian, Vivian

Vladimir *(Slavic)* 'Royally famous'. A renowned monarch Vadim

Vladislav *(Slavic)* 'Glorious ruler'

Volney *(Teutonic)* 'Of the people'

Vychan *(Welsh)* 'Little'

Vyvyan *(Latin)* 'Lively'

Wace (*Anglo-Saxon*) 'A vassal'

Wade (*Anglo-Saxon*) 'Mover, wanderer'

Wadley (*Anglo-Saxon*) 'From the wanderer's meadow'

Wadsworth (*Anglo-Saxon*) 'From the wanderer's estate'

Wagner (*Teutonic*) 'A waggoner'

Wahab (*Sanskrit*) 'Big-hearted'

Wain *see* Wayne

Waine *see* Waync

Wainwright (*Anglo-Saxon*) 'Waggon maker'

Waite (*Anglo-Saxon*) 'A guard, a watchman'

Wake (*Anglo-Saxon*) 'Alert and watchful' *see also* Wakefield

Wakefield (*Anglo-Saxon*) 'From the west field' Wake

Wakeley (*Anglo-Saxon*) 'From the wet meadow'

Wakeman (*Anglo-Saxon*) 'Watchman'

Walbert (*Old English*) 'Bright power'

Walby (*Anglo-Saxon*) 'From the ancient walls'

Walcott (*Anglo-Saxon*) 'Cottage dweller'

Waldemar *see* Valdemar

Walden (*Anglo-Saxon*) 'One who lives in the valley in the woods'

Waldo (*Teutonic*) 'The ruler'

Waldron (*Teutonic*) 'Strength of the raven'

Walford (*Old English*) 'Welshman's ford'

Walker (*Anglo-Saxon*) 'The walker'

Wallace *(Anglo-Saxon)* 'The Welshman' or 'the stranger'
Wallache, Wallie, Wallis, Wally, Walsh, Welch, Welsh

Wallache *see* Wallace

Wallie *see* Wallace

Wallis *see* Wallace

Wally *see* Wallace or Walter

Walmond *(Teutonic)* 'Mighty protector'
Walmund

Walmund *see* Walmond

Walsh *see* Wallace

Walstan *(Anglo-Saxon)* 'Cornerstone'

Walt *see* Walter

Walter *(Teutonic)* 'Mighty warrior'
Wally, Walt, Walters, Walther, Wat

Walters *see* Walter

Walther *see* Walter

Walton *(Anglo-Saxon)* 'From the forest town'

Walworth *(Anglo-Saxon)* 'From the stranger's farm'

Walwyn *(Anglo-Saxon)* 'Friendly stranger'

Warand *(Teutonic)* 'Protecting'

Warburton *(Anglo-Saxon)* 'From the castle town'

Ward *(Anglo-Saxon)* 'Watchman, guardian'
Warden *see also* Durward

Wardell *(Anglo-Saxon)* 'From the hill watch'

Warden *see* Ward

Wardley *(Anglo-Saxon)* 'From the watchman's meadow'

Ware *(Anglo-Saxon)* 'Prudent one'. A very astute person

Warfield *(Anglo-Saxon)* 'From the field by the weir'

Warford *(Anglo-Saxon)* 'From the ford by the weir'

Waring *see* Warren

Warley *(Anglo-Saxon)* 'From the meadow by the weir'

Warmond *see* Warmund

Warmund *(Teutonic)* 'Loyal protector'
Warmond

Warner *(Teutonic)*
'Protecting army'
Verner, Werner

Warren *(Teutonic)* 'The gamekeeper'. One who looked after the game preserves
Waring

Warrick *see* Warwick

Warton *(Anglo-Saxon)*
'From the farm by the weir'

Warwick *(Anglo-Saxon)*
'Strong fortress'
Warrick

Washburn *(Anglo-Saxon)*
'From the river in spate'

Washington *(Anglo-Saxon)*
'From the keen-eyed one's farm'

Wat *see* Walter

Watford *(Anglo-Saxon)*
'From the hurdle by the ford'

Watkins *(Anglo-Saxon)* 'Son of Walter'
Watson

Watson *see* Watkins

Waverley *(Anglo-Saxon)*
'The meadow by the aspen trees'
Waverly

Waverly *see* Waverley

Wayland *(Anglo-Saxon)*
'From the pathway near the highway'
Weylin

Wayne *(Teutonic)* 'Waggon maker'
Wain, Waine

Webb *(Anglo-Saxon)* 'A weaver'
Webber, Weber, Webster

Webber *see* Wcbb

Weber *see* Wcbb

Webley *(Anglo-Saxon)*
'From the weaver's meadow'

Webster *(Old English)*
'Weaver' *see also* Webb

Weddell *(Anglo-Saxon)*
'From the wanderer's hill'

Welborne *(Anglo-Saxon)*
'From the spring by the brook'
Welbourne

Welbourne *see* Welborne

Welby *(Anglo-Saxon)* 'From the farm by the spring'

Welch *see* Wallace

Weldon *(Anglo-Saxon)* 'From the well on the hill'

Welford *(Anglo-Saxon)* 'From the ford by the spring'

Wellington *(Anglo-Saxon)* 'From the rich man's farm'

Wells *(Anglo-Saxon)* 'From the spring'

Welsh *see* Wallace

Welton *(Anglo-Saxon)* 'From the farm by the spring'

Wenceslas *see* Wenceslaus

Wenceslaus *(Slavic)* 'Wreath of glory' Wenceslas

Wendall *see* Wendell

Wendell *(Teutonic)* 'The wanderer' Wendall

Wentworth *(Anglo-Saxon)* 'Estate belonging to the white-haired one'

Werner *see* Warner

Wes Diminutive of all names beginning with 'Wes'

Wesleigh *see* Wesley

Wesley *(Anglo-Saxon)* 'From the west meadow' Wesleigh, Westleigh

Westbrook *(Anglo-Saxon)* 'From the west brook'

Westby *(Anglo-Saxon)* 'From the homestead in the west'

Westcott *(Anglo-Saxon)* 'From the west cottage'

Westleigh *see* Wesley

Westley *(Anglo-Saxon)* 'From the west meadow'

Weston *(Anglo-Saxon)* 'From the west farm'

Wetherall *see* Wetherell

Wetherell *(Anglo-Saxon)* 'From the sheep hill' Wetherall, Wetherill

Wetherill *see* Wetherell

Wetherley *(Anglo-Saxon)* 'From the sheep meadow' Wetherly

Wetherly *see* Wetherley

Weylin *(Celtic)* 'Son of the wolf' *see also* Wayland

Wharton *(Anglo-Saxon)*
'Farm in the hollow'

Wheatley *(Anglo-Saxon)*
'From the wheat
meadow'

Wheeler *(Anglo-Saxon)*
'The wheel-maker'

Whistler *(Anglo-Saxon)*
'The whistler, the piper'

Whitaker *see* Whittaker

Whitby *(Anglo-Saxon)*
'From the white
farmstead'

Whitcomb *(Anglo-Saxon)*
'From the white hollow'
Whitcombe

Whitcombe *see* Whitcomb

Whitelaw *(Anglo-Saxon)*
'From the white hill'

Whitfield *(Anglo-Saxon)*
'From the white field'

Whitford *(Anglo-Saxon)*
'From the white ford'

Whitley *(Anglo-Saxon)*
'From the white meadow'

Whitlock *(Anglo-Saxon)*
'White-haired one'

Whitman *(Anglo-Saxon)*
'White-haired man'

Whitmore *(Anglo-Saxon)*
'From the white moor'

Whitney *(Anglo-Saxon)*
'From the white island'
Whitny, Witney, Witny

Whitny *see* Whitney

Whittaker *(Anglo-Saxon)*
'One who dwells in the
white field'
Whitaker

Wiatt *see* Guy

Wickham *(Anglo-Saxon)*
'From the enclosed
field by the village'
Wykeham

Wickley *(Anglo-Saxon)*
'From the village
meadow'

Wilbert *see* Wilbur

Wilbur *(Teutonic)* 'Resolute
and brilliant'. A
determined and clever
person
Wilbert

Wildon *(Old English)* 'From
the wooden hill'

Wiley *see* William

Wilford *(Anglo-Saxon)*
'From the willow ford'

Wilfred *(Teutonic)* 'Firm
peace-maker'. Peace,
but not at any price
Fred, Freddie, Freddy,
Wilfrid

Wilfrid *see* Wilfred

Wilhelm *see* William

Wilkes *see* William

Wilkie *see* William

Will *see* William

Willard *(Anglo-Saxon)*
'Resolute and brave'

Willet *see* William

William *(Teutonic)*
'Determined protector'.
The strong guardian
Bill, Billie, Billy,
Gwylim, Liam,
Uilleam, Uilliam,
Wiley, Wilhelm, Wilkes,
Wilkie, Will, Willet,
Williamson, Willie,
Willis, Willy, Wilson

Williamson *see* William

Willis *see* William

Willoughby *(Anglo-Saxon)*
'From the farmstead by
the willows'

Willy *see* William

Wilmer *(Teutonic)*
'Resolute and famous'.
One renowned for his
firmness
Wilmot

Wilmot *see* Wilmer

Wilson *(Anglo-Saxon)* 'Son
of William' *see also*
William

Wilton *(Anglo-Saxon)*
'From the farm by the
well'

Win Diminutive of all
names containing 'Win'

Winchell *(Anglo-Saxon)*
'The bend in the road'

Windham *see* Wyndham

Windsor *(Anglo-Saxon)*
'The boundary bank'

Winfield *(Anglo-Saxon)*
'From a friend's field'

Winfred *(Anglo-Saxon)*
'Peaceful friend'
Winifred

Wing *(Chinese)* 'Glory'

Wingate *(Anglo-Saxon)*
'From the winding lane'

Winifred *see* Winfred

Winslow *(Anglo-Saxon)*
'From a friend's hill'

Winston *(Anglo-Saxon)*
'From a friend's estate'

Winter *(Anglo-Saxon)* 'Born
during winter months'

Winthrop *(Teutonic)* 'From
a friendly village'

Winton *(Anglo-Saxon)*
'From a friend's farm'

Winwald *see* Winward

Winward *(Anglo-Saxon)*
'From the friendly
forest'
Winwald

Wirt *see* Wirth

Wirth *(Teutonic)* 'The
master'
Wirt

Witha *(Arabic)* 'Handsome'

Witney *see* Whitney

Witny *see* Whitney

Witram *(German)* 'Forest
river'

Witt *see* Witter

Witter *(Teutonic)* 'Wise
warrior'
Witt

Witton *(Teutonic)* 'From a
wise man's farm'

Wolcott *(Anglo-Saxon)*
'From the cottage of the
wolf'
Wulcott

Wolfe *(Teutonic)* 'A wolf. A
man of courage

Wolfgang *(Teutonic)* 'The
advancing wolf'. A
warrior in the vanguard
of the army

Wolfram *(Teutonic)*
'Respected and feared'

Wolseley *see* Woolsey

Wolsey see Woolsey

Woodley *(Anglo-Saxon)*
'From the forest
meadow'
Woodly

Woodly *see* Woodley

Woodrow *(Anglo-Saxon)*
'From the hedge in the
wood'

Woodruff *(Anglo-Saxon)*
'Forest bailiff'

Woodward *(Anglo-Saxon)*
'Forest guardian'

Woody Familiar form of all
names containing Wood

Woolsey *(Anglo-Saxon)*
'Victorious wolf'
Wolseley, Wolsey

Wooster *see* Worcester

Worcester *(Anglo-Saxon)*
'Camp in the forest of
the alder trees'
Wooster

Wordsworth *(Anglo-Saxon)* 'From the farm of the wolf'

Worrall *(Anglo-Saxon)* 'From the loyal man's manor'
Worrell, Worrill

Worrell *see* Worrall

Worrill *see* Worrall

Worth *(Anglo-Saxon)* 'The farmstead'

Worthington *(Anglo-Saxon)* 'Riverside'

Worton *(Anglo-Saxon)* 'From the vegetable farm'

Wray *(Scandinavian)* 'One who lives in the house on the corner'

Wren *(Celtic)* 'The chief'

Wright *(Anglo-Saxon)* 'Craftsman in woodwork, a carpenter'

Wulcott *see* Wolcott

Wulfstan *(Old English)* 'Wolf stone'

Wyatt *see* Guy

Wybert *(Old English)* 'Battle famous'

Wyborn *(Scandinavian)* 'Warrior bear'
Wyborne

Wyborne *see* Wyborn

Wycliff *(Anglo-Saxon)* 'From the white cliff'

Wykeham *see* Wickham

Wylie *(Anglo-Saxon)* 'The enchanter, the beguiler'

Wyman *(Anglo-Saxon)* 'The warrior'

Wymer *(Anglo-Saxon)* 'Renowned in battle'

Wyndham *(Anglo-Saxon)* 'From the village with the winding path'
Windham

Wynford *(Welsh)* 'White torrent'

Wynn *(Celtic)* 'The fair one'

Wystan *see* Wystand

Wystand *(Old English)* 'Battle stone'
Wystan

Wythe *(Anglo-Saxon)* 'From the dwelling by the willow tree'

BOYS

Xanthus *(Latin)* 'Golden haired'

Xavier *(Arabic/Spanish)* 'Bright'
Javier

Xenek *(Greek)* 'The stranger'

Xenophon *(Greek)* 'Strong sounding'

Xenos *(Greek)* 'The stranger'

Xerxes *(Persian)* 'The king'

Ximenes *see* Simon

Xylon *(Greek)* 'From the forest'

BOYS

Yahya *(Arabic)* 'Living'

Yale *(Teutonic/Anglo-Saxon)* 'The one who pays, the vanquished'

Yance *see* Yancy

Yancy *(Native American)* 'The Englishman'. Name given to settlers in New England which subsequently became Yankee
Yance

Yardan *(Arabic)* 'Merciful king'

Yardley *(Old English)* 'From the enclosed meadow'

Yarin *(Hebrew)* 'Understand'

Yasir *(Arabic)* 'Easy, soft'

Yates *(Anglo-Saxon)* 'One who lives at the gates'

Yehudi *(Hebrew)* 'Praise to the Lord'

Yemon *(Japanese)* 'The one who guards the gate'

Yeoman *(Anglo-Saxon)* 'The tenant farmer'

Yestin *(Welsh)* 'Just'

Ynyr *(Welsh)* 'Honour'

Yorick *see* George or York

York *(Anglo-Saxon/Celtic/ Latin)* 'Sacred yew tree'
Yorick, Yorke

Yul *(Mongolian)* 'Beyond the horizon'

Yule *see* Yules

Yules *(Anglo-Saxon)* 'Born at Christmas'
Yule

Yuma *(Native American)* 'Son of a chief'

Yuri *see* Uric

Yves *see* Ives

Yvon *(Teutonic)* 'The archer'

Ywain *(Celtic)* 'Young warrior'

Zabros *(Greek)* 'Glutton'

Zach *see* Zacharias

Zachaeus *(Aramaic)* 'Pure'

Zachariah *see* Zacharias

Zacharias *(Hebrew)* 'The Lord has remembered'
Zach, Zachariah, Zachary, Zack

Zachary *see* Zacharias

Zack *see* Zacharias

Zadok *(Hebrew)* 'The righteous one'
Zaloc

Zahid *(Sanskrit/Arabic)* 'Intelligent and pious'

Zahir *(Arabic)* 'Splendid'

Zaloc *see* Zadok

Zane *see* John

Zarab *(Arabic)* 'Protector against enemies'

Zared *(Hebrew)* 'The ambush'

Zeb *see* Zebulon

Zebedee *see* Zebediah

Zebediah *(Hebrew)* 'Gift of the Lord'
Zebedee

Zebulen *see* Zebulon

Zebulon *(Hebrew)* 'The dwelling place'
Lonny, Zeb, Zebulen

Zechariah *(Hebrew)* 'The Lord is renowned'

Zedekiah *(Hebrew)* 'The Lord's justice'

Zeeman *(Dutch)* 'The sailor'

Zeke *see* Ezekiel

Zel *(Persian)* 'Cymbal'

Zelig *(Teutonic)* 'Blessed one'

Zelos *(Greek)* 'Emulation'

Zelotes *(Greek)* 'The zealous one'

Zenas *(Greek)* 'Living being'

Zeno *(Greek)* 'Stranger'

Zenos *(Greek)* 'Gift from Jupiter'

Zephan *see* Zephaniah

Zephaniah *(Hebrew)* 'Treasured by the lord' Zephan

Zerah *(Hebrew)* 'Rising light'

Zeus *(Greek)* 'Father of the gods'

Zia *(Sanskrit)* 'Enlightened'

Zimraan *(Arabic)* 'Celebrated'

Zollie *see* Solomon

Zolly *see* Solomon

Zurial *see* Zuriel

Zuriel *(Hebrew)* 'The Lord is my rock and foundation' Zurial